C# 2005 For Dummies®

Cheat Sheet

Operators

Precedence	Operators	Cardinality	Associativity
High	() [] . new typeof	Unary	Left to right
	! ~ + - ++ -- (cast)	Unary	Left to right
	* / %	Binary	Left to right
	+ -	Binary	Left to right
	< <= > >= is as	Binary	Left to right
	== !=	Binary	Left to right
	&	Binary	Left to right
	^	Binary	Left to right
	|	Binary	Left to right
	&&	Binary	Left to right
	||	Binary	Left to right
	?:	Ternary	Right to left
Low	= *= /= %= += -= &= ^= |= <<= >>=	Binary	Right to left

Integer Variable Types

Type	Size (bytes)	Range	In Use
sbyte	1	−128 to 127	sbyte sb = -12;
byte	1	0 to 255	byte b = 12;
short	2	−32,768 to 32,767	short sn = -123;
ushort	2	0 to 65,535	ushort usn = 123;
int	4	−2,147,483,648 to 2,147,483,647	int n = 123;
uint	4	0 to 4,294,967,295	uint un = 123U;
long	8	−9,223,372,036,854,775,808 to 9,223,372,036,854,775,807 — "a whole lot"	long l = 123L;
ulong	8	0 to 18,446,744,073,709,551,615	long ul = 123UL;

Other Variable Types

Type	Range	In Use
decimal	Up to 28 digits	decimal d = 123M;
char	0 to 65,535 (codes in the Unicode character set)	
string	From empty ("") to a very large number of characters in the Unicode character set	
bool	True and false	

D1472672

For Dummies: Bestselling Book Series for Beginners

C# 2005 For Dummies®

Floating Point Variable Types

Type	Size (bytes)	Range	Accuracy	In Use
float	8	$1.5 * 10^{-45}$ to $3.4 * 10^{38}$	6–7 digits	float f = 1.2F;
double	16	$5.0 * 10^{-324}$ to $1.7*10^{308}$	15–16 digits	double d = 1.2;

Controlling Program Flow

```
if (i < 10)
{
    // go here if i is less than 10
}
else
{
    // go here otherwise
}

while(i < 10)
{
    // keep looping through here as long as i is less than 10
}

for(int i = 0; i < 10; i++)
{
    // loop 10 times
}

foreach(MyClass mc in myCollection)
{
    // ... execute once for each mc object in myCollection
}
```

Defining a Class

```
[access][<abstract | sealed>]class MyClassName [: [BaseClass] [, Interface, ...]]
{
  [static][access]type dataMember;
  [<static|virtual|abstract|new|override>][access]type method(... args ...)
}
for classes, access is public|protected|internal|private
  for class members, access can also be protected internal
```

Notes:

[feature]	feature is optional
<feature1 | feature2>	Either feature1 or else feature2
...	Unspecified number of statements or expressions

For Dummies: Bestselling Book Series for Beginners

C# 2005 FOR DUMMIES®

**by Stephen Randy Davis
and Chuck Sphar**

WILEY

Wiley Publishing, Inc.

C# 2005 For Dummies®

Published by
Wiley Publishing, Inc.
111 River Street
Hoboken, NJ 07030-5774

www.wiley.com

Copyright © 2006 by Wiley Publishing, Inc., Indianapolis, Indiana

Published by Wiley Publishing, Inc., Indianapolis, Indiana

Published simultaneously in Canada

For general information on our other products and services, please contact our Customer Care Department within the U.S. at 800-762-2974, outside the U.S. at 317-572-3993, or fax 317-572-4002.

For technical support, please visit www.wiley.com/techsupport.

Wiley also publishes its books in a variety of electronic formats. Some content that appears in print may not be available in electronic books.

Library of Congress Control Number: 2005927620

ISBN-13: 978-0-7645-9704-6

ISBN-10: 0-7645-9704-3

Manufactured in the United States of America

10 9 8 7 6 5 4 3

1B/TR/RQ/QW/IN

WILEY

About the Authors

Stephen R. Davis, who goes by the name of Randy, lives with his wife and son near Dallas, Texas. He and his family have written numerous books, including *C++ For Dummies* and *C++ Weekend Crash Course*. Stephen works for L-3 Communications.

Chuck Sphar escaped Microsoft's C++ documentation camps in 1997, after six years' hard labor as a senior technical writer. He's perpetrated two previous tomes, one on object-oriented programming for the Mac and one on Microsoft's MFC class library. He's currently finishing a novel about ancient Rome (againstrome.com) and gobbling mouthfuls of .NET programming. Chuck can be reached for praise and minor nits at csharp@chucksphar.com.

Dedication

For Pam and the Moms — Chuck Sphar

Acknowledgments

I would like to thank Claudette Moore and Debbie McKenna, who brought the book to me. I also want to thank Randy Davis for being willing to hand over his baby to a guy he didn't know. I'd have found that very hard, and I hope I've done justice in extending his excellent first edition.

Many thanks are due as well to the fine folks at Wiley, starting with Acquisitions Editor Katie Feltman and Project Editor Kim Darosett. Kim's astute shaping helped turn me into a *For Dummies* author, no mean feat. I'd also like to thank Chris Bower for his sharp technical eye and excellent C# knowledge, John Edwards for much of the book's consistency, and the art, media, and other production folks who turn my files into a real book.

The most heartfelt thanks are due to Pam for constant encouragement and much enabling. She's my partner in all things.
— Chuck Sphar

Publisher's Acknowledgments

We're proud of this book; please send us your comments through our online registration form located at www.dummies.com/register/.

Some of the people who helped bring this book to market include the following:

Acquisitions, Editorial, and Media Development

Project Editor: Kim Darosett

Acquisitions Editor: Katie Feltman

Copy Editor: John Edwards

Technical Editor: Chris Bower

Editorial Manager: Leah Cameron

Media Project Supervisor: Laura Moss

Media Development Specialists: Angie Denny, Travis Silvers, Kit Malone, Steve Kudirka

Media Development Manager: Laura VanWinkle

Media Development Supervisor: Richard Graves

Editorial Assistant: Amanda Foxworth

Cartoons: Rich Tennant (www.the5thwave.com)

Composition Services

Project Coordinator: Jennifer Theriot

Layout and Graphics: Carl Byers, Andrea Dahl, Joyce Haughey, Stephanie D. Jumper, Heather Ryan, Erin Zeltner

Proofreaders: Leeann Harney, Carl William Pierce, Dwight Ramsey, TECHBOOKS Production Services

Indexer: TECHBOOKS Production Services

Publishing and Editorial for Technology Dummies

Richard Swadley, Vice President and Executive Group Publisher

Andy Cummings, Vice President and Publisher

Mary Bednarek, Executive Acquisitions Director

Mary C. Corder, Editorial Director

Publishing for Consumer Dummies

Diane Graves Steele, Vice President and Publisher

Joyce Pepple, Acquisitions Director

Composition Services

Gerry Fahey, Vice President of Production Services

Debbie Stailey, Director of Composition Services

Contents at a Glance

Table of Contents

Part VI: The Part of Tens *365*

Introduction

. . . .

*T*he C# programming language is a powerful, relatively new descendant of the earlier C, C++, and Java languages. Programming with it is a lot of fun, as you're about to find out in this book.

Microsoft created C# as a major part of its .NET initiative. For what are probably political reasons, Microsoft turned the specifications for the C# language over to the ECMA (pronounced *ek-ma*) international standards committee in the summer of 2000, long before .NET was a reality. In theory, any company can come up with its own version of C# written to run on any operating system, on any machine larger than a calculator.

When the first edition of this book came out, Microsoft's C# compiler was the only game in town, and its Visual Studio .NET suite of tools offered the only way to program C# (other than at the Windows command line). Since then, however, Visual Studio has gone through two major revisions — Visual Studio 2003 and, very recently, Visual Studio 2005. And at least two other players have entered the C# game.

It's now possible to write and compile C# programs on a variety of Unix-based machines using either the Mono or Portable .NET implementations of .NET and C#:

- ✔ Mono (www.go-mono.com) is an open-source software project sponsored by Novell Corporation. Version 1.1.8 came out in June 2005. While Mono lags Microsoft's .NET, just now implementing the 1.1 version that Microsoft released a couple of years ago, it appears to be moving fast.

- ✔ Portable .NET, under the banner of Southern Storm Software and DotGNU (www.dotgnu.org/pnet.html), is also open-source. Portable .NET is at version 0.7.0 as of this writing.

Both Mono and Portable .NET claim to run C# programs on Windows and a variety of Unix flavors, including Linux and Apple's Macintosh operating system. At this writing, Portable .NET reaches the greater number of flavors, while Mono boasts a more complete .NET implementation. So choosing between them can be complicated, depending on your project, your platform, and your goals. (Books about programming for these platforms are becoming available already. Check www.amazon.com.)

Open-source software is written by collaborating groups of volunteer programmers and is usually free to the world.

Making C# and other .NET languages portable to other operating systems is far beyond the scope of this book. But you can expect that within a few years, the C# Windows programs you discover how to write in this book will run on all sorts of hardware under all sorts of operating systems — matching the claim of Sun Microsystems' Java language to run on any machine. That's undoubtedly a good thing, even for Microsoft. The road to that point is still under construction, so it's no doubt riddled with potholes and obstacles to true universal portability for C#. But it's no longer just Microsoft's road.

For the moment, however, Microsoft's Visual Studio has the most mature versions of C# and .NET and the most feature-filled toolset for programming with them.

If all you need is C#, I've included a bonus chapter called "C# on the Cheap" on the CD that accompanies this book. That chapter tells you how you can write C# code virtually for free. (You'll be missing lots of amenities, including the nice visual design tools that Visual Studio 2005 provides, but you *can* write Windows code without them, especially the kind of code in this book. Bonus Chapter 5 explains how.)

Note: Two authors wrote this book, but it seemed more economical to say "I" instead of "we," so that's what we (I?) do throughout.

What's New in C# 2.0

While C# version 2.0 does have a number of small changes here and there, most of C# 2.0 is still virtually the same as the previous version. The big new additions that this book covers include the following:

- ✔ **Iterator blocks:** An *iterator* is an object that lets you step through all the items in a *collection* of objects. That's always been possible, but C# 2.0 makes it far simpler to implement. Bonus Chapter 3 on the CD helps you take advantage of the simplicity and flexibility of iterator blocks. Chapter 15 covers collections.

- ✔ **Generics:** This is the big one! Generic features allow you to write highly general, more flexible code. It's a powerhouse — a programmer's dream. Chapter 15 shows you how to write far simpler and more *type-safe* code using generics.

Leaving aside a few of the more esoteric and advanced additions, we'll mention a few smaller items here and there as appropriate. (Don't worry if parts of this Introduction are Greek to you. You'll get there.)

About This Book

The goal of this book is to explain C# to you, but to write actual programs you need a specific coding environment. We're betting that most readers will be using Microsoft Visual Studio, although we do provide alternatives. In basing the book on Visual Studio, we've tried to keep the Visual Studio portions to a reasonable minimum. we could just tell you, "Run your program any way you want," but instead we may say, "Execute your C# program from Visual Studio by pressing F5." We want you to be able to focus on the C# language and not on the mechanics of getting simple things to work.

We realize that many, if not most, readers will want to use C# to write graphical Windows applications. C# is a powerful tool for programming graphical Windows applications, but that's only one area for using C#, and this book must focus on C# as a language. We touch briefly on graphical Windows programs in Chapter 1, but you should get a good grasp of C# before seeking another source to understand Windows programming in full. We also realize that some power users will be using C# to build Web-ready, distributed applications; however, publishing limitations require us to draw the line somewhere. *C# 2005 For Dummies* does not tackle the challenges of distributed programming. The book does explain quite a bit of .NET, though, for the simple reason that much of C#'s power comes from the .NET Framework class libraries that it uses.

What You Need to Use the Book

At a minimum, you need the Common Language Runtime (CLR) before you can even execute the programs generated by C#. Visual Studio 2005 copies the CLR onto your machine for you as part of the installation procedure. Alternatively, you can download the entire .NET package, including the C# compiler and many other nice tools, from Microsoft's Web site at http://msdn.microsoft.com. Look for the .NET Software Development Toolkit (SDK). Bonus Chapter 5 on the CD explains how to get these items.

You can still create most of the programs in this book with Visual Studio 2003, if you need to. The exceptions are those that cover the new features available only with C# 2.0, primarily generics and iterator blocks. A less-costly C# Express 2005 version of Visual Studio 2005 is also available, and don't overlook the cheap options covered in Bonus Chapter 5 on the CD.

How to Use This Book

We've made this book as easy to use as possible. Figuring out a new language is hard enough. Why make it any more complicated than it needs to be? The book is divided into six parts. Part I introduces you to C# programming with Visual Studio. This part guides you step by step in the creation of two different types of programs. We strongly encourage you to start here and read these two chapters in order before branching out into the other parts of the book. Even if you've programmed before, the basic program framework created in Part I is reused throughout the book.

The chapters in Parts II through V stand alone. We have written these chapters so that you can open the book to any one of them and start reading. If you're new to programming, however, you will have to read Part II before you can jump ahead. But when you return to refresh your memory on some particular topic, you should have no trouble flipping to a section without the need to restart 20 pages back.

Of course, the Part of Tens finishes out the lineup, and there's more on the CD that accompanies the book.

How This Book Is Organized

Here's a brief rundown on what you'll find in each part of the book.

Part I: Creating Your First C# Programs

This part shows you, step by step, how to write the smallest graphical Windows application possible using the Visual Studio 2005 interface. Part I also shows you how to create the basic nongraphical C# framework that's used in the other parts of this book.

Part II: Basic C# Programming

At the most basic level, Shakespeare's plays are just a series of words all strung together. By the same token, 90 percent of any C# program you ever write consists of creating variables, performing arithmetic operations, and controlling the execution path through a program. This part concentrates on these core operations.

Part III: Object-Based Programming

It's one thing to declare variables here or there and to add them and subtract them. It's quite another thing to write real programs for real people. Part III focuses on how to organize your data to make it easier to use in creating a program.

Part IV: Object-Oriented Programming

You can organize the parts of an airplane all you want, but until you make it do something, it's nothing more than a collection of parts. It's not until you fire up the engines and start the wings flapping that it's going anywhere.

In like fashion, Part IV explains how to turn a collection of data into a real object — an object that has internal members, sure, but an object that can mimic the properties of a real-world item. This part presents the essence of object-oriented programming.

Part V: Beyond Basic Classes

After the airplane gets off the ground, it has to go somewhere. Figuring out classes and the fundamentals of object-oriented programming is only a start. Part V takes the next step, introducing structures, interfaces, and generics, your gateway to more advanced object-oriented concepts — and the wild blue yonder.

Part VI: The Part of Tens

C# is great at finding errors in your programs — at times, it seems a little too good at pointing out my shortcomings. However, believe it or not, C# is trying to do you a favor. Every problem it finds is another problem that you would otherwise have to find on your own.

Unfortunately, the error messages can be confusing. One chapter in this part presents the ten most common C# build error messages, what they mean, and how the heck to get rid of them.

Many readers are coming to C# from another programming language. The second chapter in The Part of Tens describes the ten major differences between C# and its progenitor, C++.

About the CD-ROM

The enclosed CD-ROM contains a host of goodies. First, you find all the source code from this book. A set of utilities is also included. We don't recommend the SharpDevelop utility for full-scale development of commercial programs, but it's useful for writing small applications or making a quick change without waiting for Visual Studio to boot up. It's perfectly adequate for everything in this book. The TextPad editor is Notepad on steroids. It makes a fine cheap platform for programming C#. The NUnit testing tool, wildly popular among C# programmers, makes testing your code easy, whether from Visual Studio, SharpDevelop, or TextPad. Finally, the CD contains a bunch of bonus chapters covering features and techniques that wouldn't fit into the book. Don't ignore the CD.

Don't forget the ReadMe file, which has all the most up-to-date information.

Icons Used in This Book

Throughout the pages of this book, we use the following icons to highlight important information.

This icon flags technical stuff that you can skip on the first reading.

The Tip icon highlights a point that can save you a lot of time and effort.

Remember this. It's important.

Remember this, too. This one can sneak up on you when you least expect it and generate one of those really hard-to-find bugs.

This icon identifies code that you can find on the CD-ROM that comes with this book. This feature is designed to save you some typing when your fingers start to cramp, but don't abuse it. You'll gain a better understanding of C# by entering the programs yourself.

Conventions Used in This Book

Throughout this book, we use several conventions to help you out. Terms that are not "real words," such as the name of some program variable, appear in `this` font to minimize the confusion factor. Program listings are offset from text as follows:

```
use System;
namespace MyNameSpace
{
  public class MyClass
  {
  }
}
```

Each listing is followed by a clever, insightful explanation. Complete programs are included on the CD-ROM for your viewing pleasure. Small code segments are not.

Finally, you'll see command arrows, as in the phrase, "Choose File⇨Open With⇨Notepad." That means choose the File menu option. Then, from the pull-down menu that appears, choose Open With. Finally, from the resulting submenu, choose Notepad.

Where to Go from Here

Obviously, the first step is to figure out the C# language, ideally using *C# 2005 For Dummies,* of course. You may want to give yourself a few months of writing simple C# programs before taking on the next step of discovering how to create Windows applications. Give yourself many months of Windows application experience before you branch out into writing programs intended to be distributed over the Internet.

In the meantime, you can keep up with C# goings and comings in several locations. First, check out the official source: `http://msdn.microsoft.com/msdn`. In addition, various programmer Web sites have extensive material on C#, including lively discussions all the way from how to save a source file to the relative merits of deterministic versus nondeterministic garbage collection. Around my house, garbage collection is very deterministic: It's every Wednesday morning. Here are a few large C# sites:

- `www.gotdotnet.com`, the .NET team's official site

- `http://msdn.microsoft.com`, which gets you to related team sites, including C# and the .NET Framework

- ✔ `http://blogs.msdn.com/csharpfaq`, a C# Frequently Asked Questions blog

- ✔ `http://msdn.microsoft.com/vcsharp/team/blogs`, which is comprised of personal blogs of C# team members

- ✔ `www.cs2themax.com`

One of the authors maintains a Web site, `www.chucksphar.com`, containing a set of Frequently Asked Questions (FAQs). If you encounter something that you can't figure out, try going there — maybe the FAQs have already answered your question. In addition, the site includes a list of any mistakes that may have crept into the book. Finally, and we do mean finally, you can find a link to the authors' e-mail addresses, in case you can't find the answer to your question on the site.

Part I
Creating Your First C# Programs

The 5th Wave   By Rich Tennant

"We met on the Internet and I absolutely fell in looove with his syntax."

In this part . . .

You have a long way to go before you've mastered C#, so have a little fun just to get your feet wet. Part I gives you a taste of Windows graphics programming by taking you through the steps for creating the most basic Windows application possible using the Visual Studio 2005 interface. Part I also shows you how to create the basic C# framework for the example programs that appear throughout this book.

Chapter 1

Creating Your First C# Windows Program

In This Chapter

▶ What's a program? What is C#? Where am I?

▶ Creating a Windows program

▶ Making sure your Visual Studio 2005 C# is in tune

*I*n this chapter, I explain a little bit about computers, computer languages, C#, and Visual Studio 2005. Then, I take you through the steps for creating a very simple Windows program written in C#.

Getting a Handle on Computer Languages, C#, and .NET

A computer is an amazingly fast, but incredibly stupid servant. Computers will do anything you ask them to (within reason), and they do it extremely fast — and they're getting faster all the time. As of this writing, the common PC processing chip can handle well over a billion instructions per second. That's *billion,* with a "b."

Unfortunately, computers don't understand anything that resembles a human language. Oh, you may come back at me and say something like, "Hey, my telephone lets me dial my friend by just speaking his name. I know that a tiny computer runs my telephone. So that computer speaks English." But it's a computer program that understands English, not the computer itself.

The language that computers understand is often called *machine language.* It is possible, but extremely difficult and error prone, for humans to write machine language.

For historical reasons, machine language is also known as assembly language. In the old days, each manufacturer provided a program called an assembler that would convert special words into individual machine instructions. Thus, you might write something really cryptic like MOV AX, CX. (That's an actual Intel processor instruction, by the way.) The assembler would convert that instruction into a pattern of bits corresponding to a single machine instruction.

Humans and computers have decided to meet somewhere in the middle. Programmers create their programs in a language that is not nearly as free as human speech but a lot more flexible and easy to use than machine language. The languages that occupy this middle ground — C#, for example — are called *high-level* computer languages. (*High* is a relative term here.)

What's a program?

What is a program? In one sense, a Windows program is an executable file that you can run by double-clicking its icon. For example, the version of Microsoft Word that I'm using to write this book is a program. You call that an *executable program,* or *executable* for short. The names of executable program files generally end with the extension .exe.

But a program is something else, as well. An executable program consists of one or more *source files.* A C# program file is a text file that contains a sequence of C# commands, which fit together according to the laws of C# grammar. This file is known as a *source file,* probably because it's a source of frustration and anxiety.

What's C#?

The C# programming language is one of those intermediate languages that programmers use to create executable programs. C# fills the gap between the powerful-but-complicated C++ and the easy-to-use-but-limited Visual Basic — well, versions 6.0 and earlier, anyway. (Visual Basic's newer .NET incarnation is almost on par with C# in most respects. As the flagship language of .NET, C# tends to introduce most new features first.) A C# program file carries the extension .cs.

Some wags have pointed out that C-sharp and D-flat are the same note, but you should not refer to this new language as D-flat within earshot of Redmond, Washington.

C# is

- ✔ **Flexible:** C# programs can execute on the current machine, or they can be transmitted over the Web and executed on some distant computer.

- ✔ **Powerful:** C# has essentially the same command set as C++, but with the rough edges filed smooth.

- ✔ **Easier to use:** C# modifies the commands responsible for most C++ errors so you spend far less time chasing down those errors.

- ✔ **Visually oriented:** The .NET code library that C# uses for many of its capabilities provides the help needed to readily create complicated display frames with drop-down lists, tabbed windows, grouped buttons, scroll bars, and background images, to name just a few.

- ✔ **Internet friendly:** C# plays a pivotal role in the .NET Framework, Microsoft's current approach to programming for Windows, the Internet, and beyond. .NET is pronounced *dot net*.

- ✔ **Secure:** Any language intended for use on the Internet must include serious security to protect against malevolent hackers.

Finally, C# is an integral part of .NET.

What's .NET?

.NET began a few years ago as Microsoft's strategy to open up the Web to mere mortals like you and me. Today it's bigger than that, encompassing everything Microsoft does. In particular, it's the new way to program for Windows. It also gives a C-based language, C#, the simple, visual tools that made Visual Basic so popular. A little background will help you see the roots of C# and .NET.

Internet programming was traditionally very difficult in older languages like C and C++. Sun Microsystems responded to that problem by creating the Java programming language. To create Java, Sun took the grammar of C++, made it a lot more user friendly, and centered it around distributed development.

When programmers say "distributed," they're describing geographically dispersed computers running programs that talk to each other — in many cases, via the Internet.

When Microsoft licensed Java some years ago, it ran into legal difficulties with Sun over changes it wanted to make to the language. As a result, Microsoft more or less gave up on Java and started looking for ways to compete with it.

Being forced out of Java was just as well because Java has a serious problem: Although Java is a capable language, you pretty much have to write your entire program in Java to get its full benefit. Microsoft had too many developers and too many millions of lines of existing source code, so Microsoft had to come up with some way to support multiple languages. Enter .NET.

.NET is a framework, in many ways similar to Java's libraries, because the C# language is highly similar to the Java language. Just as *Java* is both the language itself and its extensive code library, *C#* is really much more than just the keywords and syntax of the C# language. It's those things empowered by a thoroughly object-oriented library containing thousands of code elements that simplify doing about any kind of programming you can imagine, from Web-based databases to cryptography to the humble Windows dialog box.

The previous generation platform was made up of a hodgepodge of tools with cryptic names. .NET updates all that with Visual Studio 2005, with more focused .NET versions of its Web and database technologies, newer versions of Windows, and .NET-enabled servers. .NET supports emerging communication standards such as XML and SOAP rather than Microsoft's proprietary formats. Finally, .NET supports the hottest buzzwords since *object-oriented*: Web Services.

Microsoft would claim that .NET is much superior to Sun's suite of Web tools based on Java, but that's not the point. Unlike Java, .NET does not require you to rewrite existing programs. A Visual Basic programmer can add just a few lines to make an existing program "Web knowledgeable" (meaning that it knows how to get data off the Internet). .NET supports all the common Microsoft languages and more than 40 other languages written by third-party vendors (see www.gotdotnet.com/team/lang for the latest list). However, C# is the flagship language of the .NET fleet. C# is always the first language to access every new feature of .NET.

What is Visual Studio 2005? What about Visual C#?

You sure ask lots of questions. The first "Visual" language from Microsoft was Visual Basic, code-named "Thunder." The first popular C-based programming language from Microsoft was Visual C++. Like Visual Basic, it was called "Visual" because it had a built-in graphical user interface (GUI — pronounced *gooey*). This GUI included everything you needed to develop nifty-gifty C++ programs.

Eventually, Microsoft rolled all its languages into a single environment — Visual Studio. As Visual Studio 6.0 started getting a little long in the tooth, developers anxiously awaited Version 7. Shortly before its release, however, Microsoft decided to rename it Visual Studio .NET to highlight this new environment's relationship to .NET.

That sounded like a marketing ploy to me until I started delving into it. Vi
Studio .NET differed quite a bit from its predecessors — enough so to warrant
a new name. Visual Studio 2005 is the successor to the original Visual Studio
.NET. (See Bonus Chapter 4 on the CD for a tour of some of Visual Studio's more
potent features.)

Microsoft calls its implementation of the language Visual C#. In reality, Visual
C# is nothing more than the C# component of Visual Studio. C# is C#, with or
without the Visual Studio.

Okay, that's it. No more questions.

Creating a Windows Application with C#

To help you get your feet wet with C# and Visual Studio, this section takes you
through the steps for creating a simple Windows program. Windows programs
are commonly called Windows applications, WinApps or WinForms apps for
short.

Because this book focuses on the C# language, it's not a Web-programming
book, a database book, or a Windows programming book per se. In particular,
this chapter constitutes the only coverage of Windows Forms visual programming. All I have room to do is give you this small taste.

In addition to introducing Windows Forms, this program serves as a test of
your Visual Studio environment. This is a test; this is only a test. Had it been
an actual Windows program . . . Wait, it *is* an actual Windows program. If you
can successfully create, build, and execute this program, your Visual Studio
environment is set up properly, and you're ready to rock.

Creating the template

Writing Windows applications from scratch is a notoriously difficult process.
With numerous session handles, descriptors, and contexts, creating even a
simple Windows program poses innumerable challenges.

Visual Studio 2005 in general and C# in particular greatly simplify the task of
creating your basic WinApp. To be honest, I'm a little disappointed that you
don't get to go through the thrill of doing it by hand. In fact, why not switch
over to Visual C++ and . . . okay, bad idea.

Because Visual C# is built specifically to execute under Windows, it can shield
you from many of the complexities of writing Windows programs from scratch.
In addition, Visual Studio 2005 includes an Applications Wizard that builds
template programs.

Typically, *template programs* don't actually do anything — at least, not anything useful (sounds like most of my programs). However, they do get you beyond that initial hurdle of getting started. Some template programs are reasonably sophisticated. In fact, you'll be amazed at how much capability the App Wizard can build on its own.

After you've completed the Visual Studio 2005 installation, follow these steps to create the template:

1. **To start Visual Studio, choose Start⇨All Programs⇨Microsoft Visual Studio 2005⇨Microsoft Visual Studio 2005, as shown in Figure 1-1.**

   After some gnashing of CPU teeth and thrashing of disk, the Visual Studio desktop appears. Now things are getting interesting.

2. **Choose File⇨New⇨Project, as shown in Figure 1-2.**

   Visual Studio responds by opening the New Project dialog box, as shown in Figure 1-3.

   A *project* is a collection of files that Visual Studio builds together to make a single program. You'll be creating C# source files, which carry the extension .CS. Project files use the extension .CSPROJ.

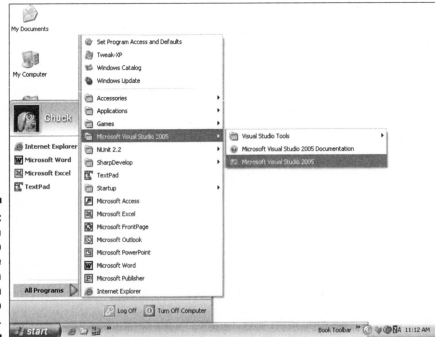

Figure 1-1: What a tangled web we weave when a C# program we do conceive.

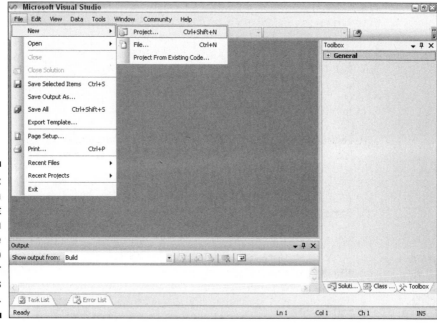

Figure 1-2:
Creating a
new project
starts you
down the
road to
a better
Windows
application.

Figure 1-3:
The Visual
Studio
Application
Wizard is
just waiting
to create
a new
Windows
program
for you.

3. Under Project Types, select Visual C#, and under that, click Windows. Under Templates, click Windows Application.

If you don't see the correct template icon right away, don't panic — you may need to scroll around in the Templates pane a bit.

Don't click OK, yet.

4. In the Name text box, enter a name for your project, or use the default name.

The Application Wizard will create a folder in which it stores various files, including the project's initial C# source file. The Application Wizard uses the name you enter in the Name text box as the name of that folder. The initial default name is WindowsApplication1. If you've been here before, the default name may be WindowsApplication2, WindowsApplication3, and so on.

For this example, you can use the default name and the default location for this new folder: My Documents\Visual Studio Projects\ WindowsApplication1. I put my real code there too, but for this book, I've changed the default location to a shorter file path. To change the default location, choose Tools⇨Options⇨Projects and Solutions⇨General. Select the new location — C:\C#Programs for this book — in the Visual Studio Projects Location box, and click OK. (You can create the new directory in the Project Location dialog box at the same time. Click the folder icon with a small sunburst at the top of the dialog box. The directory may already exist if you've installed the example programs from the CD.)

5. Click OK.

The Application Wizard makes the disk light blink for a few seconds before opening a blank *Form1* in the middle of the display.

Building and running your first Windows Forms program

After the Application Wizard loads the template program, Visual Studio opens the program in Design mode. You should convert this empty C# source program into a Windows Application, just to make sure that the template the Application Wizard generated doesn't have any errors.

The act of converting a C# source file into a living, breathing Windows Application is called *building* (or *compiling*). If your source file has any errors, Visual C# will find them during the build process.

To build and run your first Windows Forms program, follow these steps:

1. Choose Build⇨Build *projectname* (where *projectname* is a name like WindowsApplication1 or MyProject).

The Output window may open. If not, you can open it before you build if you like. Choose View⇨Other Windows⇨Output. Then Build. In the Output window, a set of messages scrolls by. The last message in the Output window should be Build: 1 succeeded, 0 failed, 0 skipped (or something very close to that). This is the computer equivalent of "No runs, no hits, no errors." If you don't bother with the Output window, you should see `Build succeeded` or `Build failed` in the status bar just above the Start menu.

Figure 1-4 shows what Visual Studio looks like after building the default Windows program, complete with Output window. Don't sweat the positions of the windows. You can move them around as needed. The important parts are the Forms Designer window and the Output window. The designer window's tab is labeled "Form1.cs [Design]."

Forms Designer   Forms
toolbar   Designer

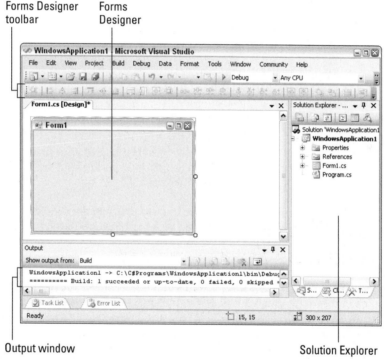

Figure 1-4:
The initial
Windows
template
program
isn't very
exciting.

Output window   Solution Explorer

2. **You can now execute this program by choosing Debug⇨Start Without Debugging.**

The program starts and opens a window that looks just like the one in the Forms Designer window, as shown in Figure 1-5.

In C# terms, this window is called a *form*. A form has a border and a title bar across the top with the little Minimize, Maximize, and Close buttons.

Figure 1-5:
The
template
Windows
application
works, but
it won't
convince
your spouse
that Visual
Studio 2005
is worth the
price.

3. **Click the little Close button in the upper-right corner of the frame to terminate the program.**

   See! C# programming isn't so hard.

As much as anything, this initial program is a test of your installation. If you've gotten this far, your Visual Studio is in good shape and ready for the programs throughout the rest of this book.

Go ahead and update your resume to note that you are officially a Windows applications programmer. Well, maybe an application (as in one) programmer, so far.

Painting pretty pictures

The default Windows program isn't very exciting, but you can jazz it up a little bit. Return to Visual Studio and select the window with the tab Form1.cs [Design] (refer to Figure 1-4). This is the Forms Designer window.

The Forms Designer is a powerful feature that enables you to "paint" your program into the form. When you're done, click Build, and the Forms Designer creates the C# code necessary to make a C# application with a pretty frame just like the one you painted.

In this section, I introduce several new Forms Designer features that simplify your Windows Forms programming. You find out how to build an application with two text boxes and a button. The user can type into one of the text boxes (the one labeled Source) but not in the other (which is labeled Target). When the user clicks a button labeled Copy, the program copies the text from the Source text box into the Target text box. That's it.

Putting some controls in place

The labeled windows that make up the Visual Studio user interface are called *document windows* and *control windows*. Document windows are for creating and editing documents, such as the C# source files that make up a C# program. Control windows like the Solution Explorer shown in Figure 1-4 are for managing things in Visual Studio while you program. For much more about Visual Studio's windows, menus, and other features, read the first half of Bonus Chapter 4 on the CD that accompanies this book.

All those little doodads like buttons and text boxes are known as *controls*. (You also may hear the term *widget*.) As a Windows programmer, you use these tools to build the graphical user interface (GUI), usually the most difficult part of a Windows program. In the Forms Designer, these tools live in a control window known as the Toolbox.

If your Toolbox isn't open, choose View➪Toolbox. Figure 1-6 shows Visual Studio with the Toolbox open on the right side of the screen.

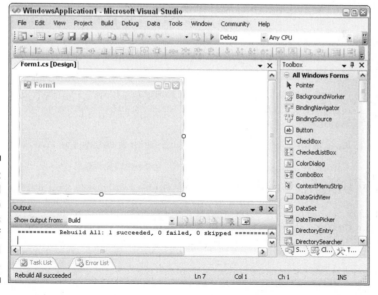

Figure 1-6:
The Visual Studio Toolbox is chock-full of interesting controls.

Don't worry if your windows are not in the same places as in Figure 1-6. For example, your Toolbox may be on the left side of the screen, on the right, or in the middle. You can move any of the views anywhere on the desktop, if you want. Bonus Chapter 4 on the CD explains how.

The Toolbox has various sections, including Data, Components, and Windows Forms. These sections, commonly known as tabs, simply organize the controls so you're not overwhelmed by them all. The Toolbox comes loaded with many controls, and you can make up your own.

Click the plus sign next to Common Controls (or the one labeled All Windows Forms) to reveal the options below it, as shown in Figure 1-6. You use these controls to jazz up a form. The scroll bar on the right enables you to scroll up and down within the controls listed in the Toolbox.

You add a control to a form by dragging the control and dropping it where you want. Follow these steps to use the Toolbox to create two text boxes and a button:

1. **Grab the Textbox control, drag it over to the form labeled Form1, and release the mouse button.**

   You might have to scroll the Toolbox. After you drag the control, a text box appears in the form. If the text box contains text (it may not), it says textBox1. This is the name the Forms Designer assigned to that particular control. (In addition to its Name property, a control has a Text property that needn't match the Name.) You can resize the text box by clicking and dragging its corners.

   You can only make the text box wider. You can't make it taller because by default these are single-line text boxes. The little right-pointing arrow on the text box — called a *smart tag* — lets you change that, but ignore it until you read Bonus Chapter 4 on the CD.

2. **Grab the Textbox control again and drop it underneath the first text box.**

   Notice that thin blue alignment guides — called *snaplines* — appear to help you align the second text box with other controls. That's a cool new feature.

3. **Now grab the Button control and drop it below the two text boxes.**

   A button now appears below the two text boxes.

4. **Resize the form and use the alignment guides as you move everything around until the form looks pretty.**

   Figure 1-7 shows the form. Yours may look a little different.

Figure 1-7:
The initial layout of the form looks like this.

Form1

textBox1

textBox2

button1

Controlling the properties

The most glaring problem with the application now is that button label.
button1 is not very descriptive. You need to fix that first.

Each control has a set of properties that determine the control's appearance
and the way it works. You access these properties through the Properties
window. Follow these steps to change the properties of different controls:

1. **Select the button by clicking it.**

2. **Enable the Properties window by choosing View⇨Properties Window.**

   The button control has several sets of properties: the appearance set
   listed at the top, the behavior properties down below, and several
   others. You need to change the Text property, which is under
   Appearance. (To see the properties listed alphabetically rather than in
   categories, click the icon at the top of the window with AZ on it.)

3. **In the Properties view, select the box in the right-hand column next to
   the Text property. Type in Copy and then press Enter.**

   Figure 1-8 shows these settings in the Properties view and the resulting
   form. The button is now labeled Copy.

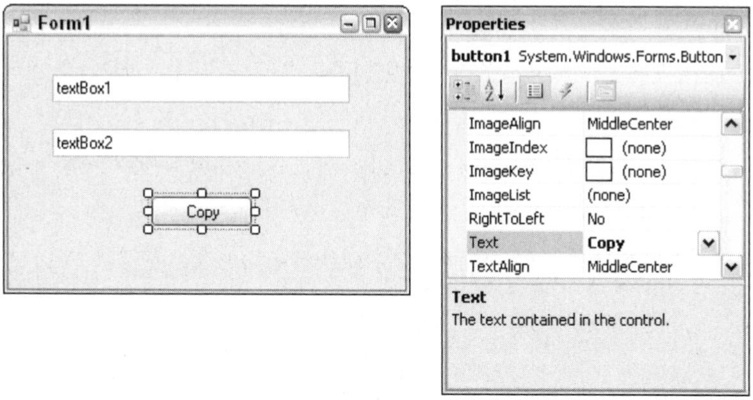

Figure 1-8:
The
Properties
view gives
you control
over your
controls.

4. **Change the initial contents of the Textbox controls. Select the upper
   text box and repeat Step 3, typing the text** User types in here. **Do
   the same for the lower text box, typing the text** Program copies text
   into here.

   Doing this lets the user know what to do when the program starts.
   Nothing baffles users more than a confusing dialog box.

5. **Similarly, changing the Text property of the Form changes the text in the title bar. Click somewhere in the Form, type in the new name in the Text property, and then press Enter.**

    I set the title bar to "Text Copy Application."

6. **While you're changing Form properties, click the AcceptButton property (under Misc in the Properties window). Click the space to the right of AcceptButton to specify which button responds when the user presses the Enter key. In this case, select button1.**

    "Copy" is the text on this button, but the name is still button1. You could change that too, if you like. It's the Form's Name property — a form property, not a button property.

7. **Select the lower text box and scroll through the Behavior properties until you get to one called ReadOnly. Set that to True by clicking it and selecting from the drop-down list, as shown in Figure 1-9.**

Figure 1-9:
Setting the
text box to
read only
keeps users
from editing
the field
when the
program is
executing.

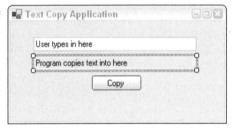

8. **Click the Save button in the Visual Studio toolbar to save your work.**

While you work, click the Save button every once in awhile just to make sure you don't lose too much if your dog trips over the computer's power cord. Unsaved files show an asterisk in the tab at the top of the Forms Designer window.

Building the application

Choose Build➪Build *WindowsApplication1* to rebuild the application. This step builds a new Windows Application with the Form you've just created. In the Output window you should see a 1 succeeded, 0 failed, 0 skipped message.

Now execute the program by choosing Debug➪Start Without Debugging. The resulting program opens a form that looks like the one you've been editing, as shown in Figure 1-10. You can type into the upper text box, but you can't type into the lower text box (unless you forgot to change the ReadOnly property).

Figure 1-10:
The
program
window
looks like
the Form
you just
built.

Make it do something, Daddy

The program looks right but it doesn't do anything. If you click the Copy button, nothing happens. So far, you've only set the Appearance properties — the properties that manage the appearance of the controls. Now, follow these steps to put the smarts into the Copy button to actually copy the text from the source text box to the target:

1. **In the Forms Designer, select the Copy button again.**

2. **In the Properties window, click the little lightning bolt icon above the list of properties to open a new set of properties.**

   These are called the control's *events*. They manage what a control does while the program executes.

   You need to set the Click event. This determines what the button does when the user clicks it. That makes sense.

3. **Double-click the Click event and watch all heck break loose.**

   The Design view is one of two different ways of looking at your application. The other is the Code view, which shows the C# source code that the Forms Designer has been building for you behind the scenes. Visual Studio knows that you need to enter some C# code to make the program transfer the text.

   Instead of the lightning bolt, you can simply double-click the button itself on the Forms Designer.

When you set the Click event, Visual Studio switches the display to the Code view and creates a new *method*. Visual Studio gives this method the descriptive name `button1_Click()`. When the user clicks the Copy button, this method will perform the actual transfer of text from `textBox1`, the source, to `textBox2`, the target.

TIP

Don't worry too much about what a method is. I describe methods in Chapter 8. Just go with the flow for now.

This method simply copies the Text property from `textBox1` to `textBox2`, right at the blinking insertion point.

4. **Because `button1` is now labeled "Copy," rename the method with the Refactor menu. Double-click the name `button1_Click` in the Code window. Choose Refactor⇨Rename. In the New Name box, type `CopyClick`. Press Enter twice (but take a look at the dialog boxes).**

It's good for a control's text to reflect its purpose clearly.

New in Visual Studio 2005, the Refactor menu is the safest way to make certain changes to the code. For instance, just manually changing the name `button1_Click` for the method would miss another reference to the method elsewhere in the code that the Forms Designer has generated on your behalf.

The second dialog box for the Rename refactoring shows things that will change: the method and any references to it in comments, text strings, or other places in the code. You can deselect items in the upper pane to prevent them from changing. The lower Preview Code Changes pane lets you see what will actually change. Use the Refactor menu to save yourself lots of error-prone work.

5. **Add the following line of code to the `CopyClick()` method:**

```
textBox2.Text = textBox1.Text;
```

TECHNICAL STUFF

Notice how C# tries to help you out as you type. Figure 1-11 shows the display as you type the last part of the preceding line. The drop-down list of the properties for a text box helps to jog your memory about which properties are available and how they're used. This auto-complete feature is a great help during programming. (If auto-complete doesn't pop up, press Ctrl-Space to display it.)

6. **Choose Build⇨Build *WindowsApplication1* to add the new click method into the program.**

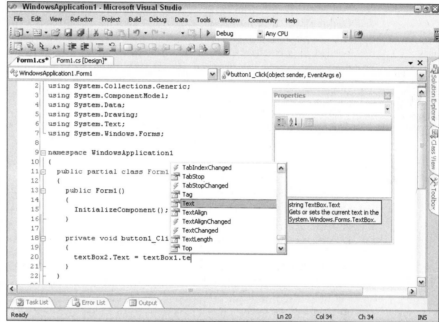

Figure 1-11:
The auto-complete feature displays the property names as you type.

Trying out the final product

Choose Debug⇨Start Without Debugging to execute the program one last time. Type some text in the source text box and then click the Copy button. The text is magically copied over to the target text box, as shown in Figure 1-12. Gleefully repeat the process, typing whatever you want and copying away until you get tired of it.

Figure 1-12:
It works!

Looking back on the creation process, you may be struck by how picture-oriented it all is. Grab controls, drop them around on the frame, set properties, and that's about it. You only had to write one line of C# code.

You could argue that the program doesn't do much, but I would disagree. Look back at some of the earlier Windows programming books in the days before App Wizards, and you'll see how many hours of coding even a simple application like this would have taken.

Visual Basic 6.0 programmers, beware!

To those Visual Basic 6.0 programmers among you, this probably seems mundane. In fact, the Forms Designer works a lot like the one in later versions of Visual Basic. However, the .NET Forms Designer, which Visual C# uses, is much more powerful than its Visual Basic 6.0 counterpart. .NET and C# (and Visual Basic .NET, for that matter) use the .NET library of routines, which is more powerful, extensive, and consistent than the old Visual Basic library. And .NET supports developing distributed programs for the network as well as programs using multiple languages, which Visual Basic did not. But the chief improvement in the Forms Designer used by C# and Visual Basic .NET over the Visual Basic 6.0 predecessor is that all the code it generates for you is just code, which you can easily modify. In Visual Basic 6.0, you were stuck with what the designer gave you.

Chapter 2

Creating Your First C# Console Application

*E*ven the most basic Windows programs can be daunting to the beginning C# programmer. Just check out Chapter 1 if you don't believe me. A so-called *console application* program — or console app (all of us in-the-know types drop off unnecessary syllables when poss) — generates significantly less C# code and is much easier to understand.

In this chapter, you use Visual Studio to create a template console app. Then, you manually simplify that template just a little more. You can use the result as a template for many of the programs I describe in this book.

The primary purpose of this book is to help you understand C#. You can't create the next Starship graphics game in C# until you know the C# language.

Creating a Console Application Template

The following instructions are for Visual Studio. If you use anything other than Visual Studio, you have to refer to the documentation that came with your environment. Alternatively, you can just type the source code directly into your C# environment. See Bonus Chapter 5 for some alternatives to Visual Studio.

Creating the source program

Complete these steps to create your C# console app template:

1. **Choose File⇨New⇨Project to create a new project.**

   Visual Studio presents you with a window of icons representing the different types of applications that you can create.

2. **From this New Project window, click the Console Application icon.**

   Make sure that you select Visual C# and under it, Windows, in the Project Types pane; otherwise, Visual Studio may create something awful like a Visual Basic or Visual C++ application. Then click the Console Application icon in the Templates pane.

   Visual Studio requires you to create a project before you can start to enter your C# program. A project is like a bucket in which you throw all the files that go into making your program. When you tell your compiler to build the program, it sorts through the project to find the files it needs to re-create the program.

   The default name for your first application is `ConsoleApplication1`, but change it this time to `ConsoleAppTemplate`. In future chapters, you can open the template, save it as a new name, and already have the essentials in place.

   The default place to store this file is somewhere deep in `My Documents`. Maybe because I'm difficult (or maybe because I'm writing a book), I like to put my programs where I want them, not necessarily where Visual Studio wants them. In Chapter 1, I show you how to change the default project location to `C:\C#Programs` (if you want to simplify working with this book).

3. **Click the OK button.**

   After a bit of disk whirring and chattering, Visual Studio generates a file called `Program.cs`. (If you look in the window labeled Solution Explorer, you see some other files; ignore them for now. If Solution Explorer isn't visible, choose View⇨Solution Explorer.) C# source files carry the extension `.cs`. The name `Program` is the default name assigned for the program file.

The contents of your first console app appear as follows:

```
using ...

namespace ConsoleAppTemplate
{
  class Program
  {
    static void Main(string[] args)
```

```
        {

        }
    }
}
```

Along the left edge of the code window, you see several small plus (+) and minus (–) signs in boxes. Click the + sign next to using.... This expands a *code region,* a handy Visual Studio feature that keeps down the clutter. Here are the directives when you expand the region in the default console app:

```
using System;
using System.Collections.Generic;
using System.Text;
```

Regions help you focus on the code you're working on by hiding code that you aren't. Certain blocks of code — such as the namespace block, class block, methods, and other code items — get a +/– automatically without a #region directive. You can add your own collapsible regions, if you like, by typing **#region** above a code section and **#endregion** after it. It helps to supply a name for the region, such as Public methods. Note that this name can include spaces. Also, you can nest one region inside another (an advantage over Visual Basic), but regions can't overlap.

For now, using System; is the only using directive you really need. You can delete the others; the compiler lets you know whether you're missing one.

Taking it out for a test drive

To convert your C# program into an executable program, choose Build⇨Build ConsoleAppTemplate. Visual Studio responds with the following message:

```
- Build started: Project: ConsoleAppTemplate, Configuration: Debug Any CPU -

Csc.exe /noconfig /nowarn ... (and much more)

Compile complete -- 0 errors, 0 warnings
ConsoleAppTemplate -> C:\C#Programs\ ... (and more)==Build: 1 succeeded or up-
            to-date, 0 failed, 0 skipped==
```

The key point here is the 1 succeeded part on the last line.

As a general rule of programming, "succeeded" is good; "failed" is bad.

To execute the program, choose Debug⇨Start Without Debugging. The program brings up a black console window and terminates immediately. The program has seemingly done nothing. In fact, this is the case. The template is nothing but an empty shell.

Creating Your First Real Console App

Edit the `Program.cs` template file until it appears as follows:

```
using System;

namespace ConsoleAppTemplate
{ // these are curly braces
  // class Program is the "object" containing our code
  public class Program
  {
    // This is where our program starts
    // Every program has a Main() method somewhere
    static void Main(string[] args)
    {
      // here's our code to make it do something
      // prompt user to enter a name
      Console.WriteLine("Enter your name, please:");

      // now read the name entered
      string sName = Console.ReadLine();

      // greet the user with the name that was entered
      Console.WriteLine("Hello, " + sName);

      // wait for user to acknowledge the results
      Console.WriteLine("Press Enter to terminate...");
      Console.Read();
      // our code in Main() ends here
    } // Main() ends here
  }   // class Program ends here
}     // namespace ConsoleAppTemplate ends here
```

Don't sweat the stuff following the double or triple slashes (`//` or `///`), and don't worry about whether to enter one or two spaces or one or two new lines. However, do pay attention to capitalization.

Choose Build⇨Build ConsoleAppTemplate to convert this new version of `Program.cs` into the `ConsoleAppTemplate.exe` program.

From within Visual Studio 2005, choose Debug⇨Start Without Debugging. The black console window appears and prompts you for your name. (You may need to activate the console window by clicking it.) Then the window shows `Hello`, followed by the name entered, and displays `Press Enter to terminate....` Pressing Enter closes the window.

You can also execute the program from the DOS command line. To do so, open a DOS window and enter the following:

```
CD \C#Programs\ConsoleAppTemplate\bin\Debug
```

Now enter **ConsoleAppTemplate** to execute the program. The output should be identical. You can also navigate to the `\C#Programs\ConsoleAppTemplate\bin\Debug` folder in Windows Explorer and then double-click the `ConsoleAppTemplate.exe` file.

To open a DOS window, try choosing Tools⇨Command Window. If that command isn't available on your Visual Studio Tools menu, choose Start⇨All Programs⇨Microsoft Visual Studio 2005⇨Visual Studio Tools⇨Visual Studio 2005 Command Prompt.

Reviewing the Console Application Template

In the following sections, you take this first C# console app apart one section at a time to understand how it works.

The program framework

The basic framework for all console applications starts with the following code:

```
using System;
using System.Collections.Generic;
using System.Text;

namespace ConsoleAppTemplate
{
  public class Program
  {
    // This is where our program starts
    public static void Main(string[] args)
    {
        // your code goes here
    }
  }
}
```

The program starts executing right after the statement containing `Main()` and ends at the closed brace following `Main()`. I explain the meaning of these statements in due course. More than that I cannot say for now.

The list of `using directives` can come immediately before or immediately after the phrase `namespace HelloWorld {`. The order doesn't matter. You can apply `using` to lots of things in .NET. The whole business of namespaces and `using` is explained in Bonus Chapter 2 on the CD.

Comments

The template already has lots of lines, and I've added several other lines, such as the following:

```
// This is where our program starts
public static void Main(string[] args)
```

C# ignores the first line in this example. This line is known as a *comment*.

Any line that begins with // or /// is free text and is ignored by C#. Consider // and /// to be equivalent for now.

Why include lines in your program if the computer ignores them? Because writing comments enables you to explain your C# statements. A program, even a C# program, isn't easy to understand. Remember that a programming language is a compromise between what computers understand and what humans understand. These comments can help you while you write the code, and they're especially helpful to the poor sap — possibly you — who has to come along a year later and try to re-create your logic. Adding extra explanatory text makes the job much easier.

Comment early and often. It helps you and other programmers to remember what you meant when you wrote all those C# statements.

The meat of the program

The real core of this program is embedded within the block of code marked with Main(), as follows:

```
// prompt user to enter a name
Console.WriteLine("Enter your name, please:");

// now read the name entered
string sName = Console.ReadLine();

// greet the user with the name that was entered
Console.WriteLine("Hello, " + sName);
```

Save a ton of routine typing with the new C# Code Snippets feature. Snippets are great for common statements like Console.WriteLine. Press Ctrl+K and then Ctrl+X to see a pop-up menu of snippets. Scroll down the menu to cw and press Enter. Visual Studio inserts the body of a Console.WriteLine() statement with the insertion point between the parentheses, ready to go.

When you have a few of the shortcuts like `cw`, `for`, and `if` memorized, use the even quicker technique: Type `cw` and press Tab. (Also try selecting some lines of code, pressing Ctrl+K, and then pressing Ctrl+S. Choose something like `if`. An `if` statement surrounds the selected code lines.) After you get going, you can even create your own custom snippets.

The program begins executing with the first C# statement: `Console.WriteLine`. This command writes the character string `Enter your name, please:` to the console.

The next statement reads in the user's answer and stores it in a variable, a kind of "workbox," called `sName`. (See Chapter 3 for more on these storage locations.) The last line combines the string `Hello,` and the user's name and outputs the result to the console.

The final three lines cause the computer to wait for the user to press Enter before proceeding. These lines ensure that the user has time to read the output before the program continues, as follows:

```
// wait for user to acknowledge the results
Console.WriteLine("Press Enter to terminate...");
Console.Read();
```

This step can be important depending on how you execute the program and depending on the environment. Within Visual Studio, you can execute a program in either of two ways. If you use the Debug⇨Start command, Visual Studio closes the output window as soon as the program terminates. The same thing happens when you execute the program by double-clicking the executable file's icon in Windows Explorer.

No matter how you execute the program, waiting for the user to press Enter before quitting solves any problems.

At this point, you can delete the lines from the first `Console.WriteLine` through the next-to-last one, if you want a clean, empty `Main()` method as a template for the next console app you write. Just don't delete the final `Console.WriteLine` and `Console.Read` statements. You'll want those in all of your console apps.

Part II
Basic C# Programming

The 5th Wave   By Rich Tennant

"Before I go on to explain more advanced procedures like the 'Zap-Rowdy-Students-who-Don't-Pay-Attention' function, we'll begin with some basics."

In this part . . .

The newest e-commerce, B2B, dot-com, whiz-bang program uses the same basic building blocks as the most simple temperature-conversion program. This part presents the basics of creating variables, performing arithmetic operations, and controlling the execution path through a program. This fundamental C# is essential training, especially if you're new to programming.

Chapter 3

Living with Variability — Declaring Value-Type Variables

*T*he most fundamental of all concepts in programming is that of the variable. A C# variable is like a small box in which you can store things, particularly numbers, for later use. The term *variable* is borrowed from the world of mathematics. For example, the mathematician may say the following:

```
n = 1
```

This statement means that from this point forward, the mathematician can use the term *n* to mean 1 — that is, until the mathematician changes it to something else (a number, an equation, a concept, and so on).

The meaning of the term *variable* doesn't differ much in the programming world. The C# programmer may say the following:

```
int n;
n = 1;
```

Those statements define a "thing" n and assign it the value 1. From that point forward in the program, the variable n has the value 1, until the programmer changes it to some other number.

Unfortunately for programmers, C# places several limitations on variables — limitations that mathematicians don't have to consider.

Declaring a Variable

When the mathematician says, "n is equal to 1," that means the term n is equivalent to 1 in some ethereal way. The mathematician is free to introduce variables in a willy-nilly fashion. For example, the mathematician may say the following:

```
x = y² + 2y + y
if k = y + 1 then
x = k²
```

Here, the mathematician has written a quadratic equation. Perhaps the variables x and y were previously defined somewhere. However, the mathematician then presents another variable k, sort of out of the blue. Here, k doesn't so much mean that k has the value of y plus 1 but that k takes the place of the concept of y plus one — a sort of shorthand. Skim through any mathematics book and you'll see what I mean.

Programmers must be precise in their terminology. For example, a C# programmer may write the following code:

```
int n;
n = 1;
```

The first line means, "Carve off a small amount of storage in the computer's memory and assign it the name n." This step is analogous to reserving one of those storage lockers at the train station and slapping the label n on the side. The second line says, "Store the value 1 in the variable n, thereby replacing whatever that storage location already contains." The train-locker equivalent is, "Open the train locker, rip out whatever happens to be there, and shove a 1 in its place."

The equals symbol (=) is called the *assignment operator*.

The mathematician says, "n equals 1." The C# programmer says in a more precise way, "Store the value 1 in the variable n." (Think about the train locker, and you see why that is preferable.) C# operators tell the computer what you want to do. In other words, operators are verbs and not descriptors. The assignment operator takes the value on its right and stores it in the variable on the left.

What's an int?

Mathematicians deal with concepts. They can make up variables any time they want, and a single variable may have different meanings throughout the same equation. At best, mathematicians look at a variable as some amorphous value — at worst, some vague concept.

The mathematician may write the following:

```
n = 1;
n = 1.1;
n = House
n = "Texas is a dump"
```

Those lines equate the variable *n* with all sorts of things, and the mathematician thinks nothing of it. I don't think about it much either except for that last line. As the bumper stickers down here say, "Don't mess with Texas."

C# is not nearly that flexible. In C#, each variable has a fixed type. When you allocate one of those train lockers, you have to pick the size you need. If you picked an "integer locker," you couldn't turn around and hope to stuff the entire state of Texas in it — maybe Rhode Island, but not Texas.

For the example in the preceding section of this chapter, you select a locker that's designed to handle an integer — C# calls it an `int`. Integers are the counting numbers 1, 2, 3, and so on, plus 0 and the negative numbers –1, –2, –3, and so on.

Before you can use a variable, you must declare it. After you declare a variable as `int`, it can hold and regurgitate integer values, as the following example demonstrates:

```
// declare a variable n
int n;
// declare an int variable m and initialize it
// with the value 2
int m = 2;
// assign the value stored in m to the variable n
n = m;
```

The first line after the comment is a *declaration* that creates a little storage area, n, designed to hold an integer value. The initial value of n is not specified until it is *assigned* a value. The second declaration not only declares an `int` variable m but also *initializes* it with a value of 2.

The term *initialize* means to assign an initial value. To initialize a variable is to assign it a value for the first time. You don't know for sure what the value of a variable is until it has been initialized.

The final statement in the program assigns the value stored in m, which is 2, to the variable n. The variable n continues to contain the value 2 until it is assigned a new value. (The variable n doesn't lose its value when you assign it to m.)

Rules for declaring variables

You can initialize a variable as part of the declaration, as follows:

```
// declare another int variable and give it
// the initial value of 1
int o = 1;
```

This is equivalent to sticking a 1 into that `int` storage locker when you first rent it, rather than opening the locker and stuffing in the value later.

Initialize a variable when you declare it. In most, but not all cases, C# initializes the variable for you, but don't rely on that fact.

You may declare variables anywhere (well, almost anywhere) within a program. However, you may not use a variable until you declare it and set it to some value. Thus, the following two assignments are not legal:

```
// the following is illegal because m is not assigned
// a value before it is used
int m;
n = m;
// the following is illegal because p has not been
// declared before it is used
p = 2;
int p;
```

Finally, you cannot declare the same variable twice.

Variations on a theme — different types of int

Most simple variables are of type `int`. However, C# provides a number of twists to the `int` variable type for special occasions.

All integer variable types are limited to whole numbers. The `int` type suffers from other limitations as well. For example, an `int` variable can only store values in the range from roughly –2 billion to 2 billion.

A distance of 2 billion inches is greater than the circumference of the Earth. In case 2 billion isn't quite large enough for you, C# provides an integer type called `long` (short for `long int`) that can represent numbers as large as you can imagine. The only problem with a `long` is that takes a larger train locker: A `long` consumes 8 bytes (64 bits) — twice as much as a garden-variety `int`.

C# provides several other integer variable types, as shown in Table 3-1.

Table 3-1		The Size and Range of C# Integer Types	
Type	*Size (bytes)*	*Range of Values*	*In Use*
sbyte	1	−128 to 127	sbyte sb = 12;
byte	1	0 to 255	byte b = 12;
short	2	−32,768 to 32,767	short sn = 12345;
ushort	2	0 to 65,535	ushort usn = 62345;
int	4	−2 billion to 2 billion	int n = 1234567890;
uint	4	0 to 4 billion (exact values in the Cheat Sheet inside the front cover of this book)	uint un = 3234567890U
long	8	-10^{20} to 10^{20} — "a whole lot"	long l = 123456789012L
ulong	8	0 to 2×10^{20}	long ul = 123456789012UL

As I explain in the section "Declaring Numeric Constants," later in this chapter, fixed values such as 1 also have a type. By default, a simple constant such as 1 is assumed to be an int. Constants other than an int must be marked with their variable type. For example, 123U is an unsigned integer, uint.

Most integer variables are called *signed,* which means they can represent negative values. Unsigned integers can only represent positive values, but you get twice the range in return. As you can see from Table 3-1, the names of most unsigned integer types start with a u, while the signed types generally don't have a prefix.

Representing Fractions

Integers are great for most calculations. I made it into the 6th grade before I ever found out that anything else existed. I still haven't forgiven my 6th-grade teacher for starting me down the slippery slope of fractions.

Many calculations involve fractions, which simple integers can't accurately represent. The common equation for converting from Fahrenheit to Celsius temperatures demonstrates the problem, as follows:

```
// convert the temperature 41 degrees Fahrenheit
int nFahr = 41;
int nCelsius = (nFahr - 32) * (5 / 9)
```

This equation works just fine for some values. For example, 41 degrees Fahrenheit is 5 degrees Celsius. "Correct, Mr. Davis," says my 6th-grade teacher.

Okay, try a different value: 100 degrees Fahrenheit. Working through the equation, 100 – 32 is 68; 68 times ⅝ is 37. "No," she says, "the answer is 37.78." Even that's wrong, because it's really 37.777 . . . with the 7s repeating forever, but I'm not going to push the point.

An int can only represent integer numbers. The integer equivalent of 37.78 is 37. This lopping off of the fractional part of a number to get it to fit into an integer variable is called integer *truncation*.

Truncation is not the same thing as *rounding*. Truncation lops off the fractional part. Rounding picks the closest integer value. Thus, truncating 1.9 results in 1. Rounding 1.9 results in 2.

For temperatures, 37 may be good enough. It's not like you wear short-sleeve shirts at 37.7 degrees but pull on a sweater at 37 degrees. But integer truncation is unacceptable for many, if not most, applications.

Actually, the problem is much worse than that. An int can't handle the ratio ⅝ either; it always yields the value 0. Consequently, the equation as written in this example calculates nCelsius as 0 for all values of nFahr. Even I admit that's unacceptable.

This book's CD includes an int-based temperature conversion program contained in the ConvertTemperatureWithRoundOff directory. At this point, you may not understand all the details, but you can see the conversion equations and execute the program ConvertTemperatureWithRoundOff.exe to see the results.

Handling Floating Point Variables

The limitations of an int variable are unacceptable for some applications. The range generally isn't a problem — the double-zillion range of a 64-bit-long integer should be enough for anyone. However, the fact that an int is limited to whole numbers is a bit harder to swallow.

In some cases, you need numbers that can have a nonzero fractional part. Mathematicians call these *real numbers*. Somehow that always seemed like a ridiculous name for a number. Are integer numbers somehow unreal?

Notice that I said a real number *can* have a nonzero fractional part — that is, 1.5 is a real number, but so is 1.0. For example, 1.0 + 0.1 is 1.1. Just keep that point in mind as you read the rest of this chapter.

Fortunately, C# understands real numbers. Real numbers come in two flavors: floating point and decimal. Floating point is the most common type. I describe the decimal type a little later in this chapter.

Declaring a floating point variable

A floating point variable carries the designation `float`, and you declare one as shown in the following example:

```
float f = 1.0;
```

After you declare it as `float`, the variable `f` is a `float` for the rest of its natural instructions.

Table 3-2 describes the set of floating point types. All floating point variables are signed (that is, there's no such thing as a floating point variable that can't represent a negative value).

Table 3-2		The Size and Range of the Floating Point Variable Types		
Type	*Size (bytes)*	*Range of Values*	*Accuracy (no. of digits)*	*In Use*
`float`	8	$1.5 * 10^{-45}$ to $3.4 * 10^{38}$	6–7	`float f = 1.2F;`
`double`	16	$5.0 * 10^{-324}$ to $1.7 * 10^{308}$	15–16	`double d = 1.2;`

You might think `float` is the default floating point variable type, but it's actually the `double`. If you don't specify the type for, say, 12.3, C# calls it a `double`.

The Accuracy column in Table 3-2 refers to the number of significant digits that such a variable type can represent. For example, ⅚ is actually 0.555 . . . with an unending sequence of 5s. However, a `float` variable is said to have six significant digits of accuracy, which means numbers after the sixth digit are ignored. Thus, ⅚ may appear as follows when expressed as a `float`:

```
0.5555551457382
```

You know that all the digits after the sixth 5 are untrustworthy.

A `float` actually has 6.5 significant digits. The extra half-digit of significance stems from the fact that floating point accuracy is related to $10^{\log \text{ to the base } 2}$. Probably more than you wanted to know.

The same number — ⅝ — may appear as follows when expressed as a `double`:

```
0.55555555555555557823
```

The `double` packs a whopping 15 to 16 significant digits.

C# floating point numbers default to double precision, so use `double` variable types unless you have a specific reason to do otherwise. However, programs that use either `double` or `float` are still said to be floating point programs.

Converting some more temperatures

Here's the formula for converting from Fahrenheit to Celsius temperatures using floating point variables:

```
double dCelsius = (dFahr - 32.0) * (5.0 / 9.0)
```

Your CD contains a floating point version of the temperature conversion program called `ConvertTemperatureWithFloat`.

The following example shows the result of executing the `double`-based `ConvertTemperatureWithFloat` program:

```
Enter temp in degrees Fahrenheit:100
Temperature in degrees Celsius = 37.7777777777778
Press Enter to terminate...
```

Examining some limitations of floating point variables

You may be tempted to use floating point variables all the time because they solve the truncation problem so nicely. Sure they use up a bit more memory, but memory is cheap these days, so why not? But floating point variables also have limitations.

Counting

You can't use floating point variables as counting numbers. Some C# structures need to count (as in 1, 2, 3, and so on). You and I know that 1.0, 2.0, and 3.0 are counting numbers just as well as 1, 2, and 3, but C# doesn't know that. For example, given the accuracy limitations of floating points, how does C# know that you aren't actually saying 1.000001?

Whether you find that argument convincing or not, you can't use a floating point variable when counting things.

Comparing numbers

You have to be careful when comparing floating point numbers. For example, 12.5 may be represented as 12.500001. Most people don't care about that little extra bit (no pun intended) on the end. However, the computer takes things extremely literally. To C#, 12.500000 and 12.500001 are not the same numbers.

So, if you add 1.1 to 1.1, you can't tell whether the result is 2.2 or 2.200001. And if you ask, "Is dDoubleVariable equal to 2.2?" you may not get the results you expect. Generally, you have to resort to some bogus comparison like this: "Is the absolute value of the difference between dDoubleVariable and 2.2 less than .000001?" In other words, "within an acceptable margin of error."

The Pentium processor plays a trick to make this problem less troublesome than it otherwise may be: It performs floating point arithmetic in an especially long `double` format — that is, rather than using 64 bits, it uses a whopping 80 bits. When rounding off an 80-bit `float` into a 64-bit `float`, you (almost) always get the expected result, even if the 80-bit number was off a bit or two.

Calculation speed

Processors such as the *x*86 varieties used in older Windows-based PCs could perform integer arithmetic much faster than arithmetic of the floating point persuasion. In those days, programmers would go out of their way to limit a program to integer arithmetic.

The ratio in additional speed on a Pentium III processor for a simple (perhaps too simple) test of about 300,000,000 additions and subtractions was about 3 to 1. That is, for every `double` add, you could have done three `int` adds. (Computations involving multiplication and division may show different results.)

I had to write my addition and subtraction operations to avoid cache effects. The program and the data were cached, but the compiler was not able to cache any intermediate results in CPU registers.

Not-so-limited range

In the past, a floating point variable could represent a considerably larger range of numbers than an integer type. It still can, but the range of the `long` is large enough to render the point moot.

Even though a simple `float` can represent a very large number, the number of significant digits is limited to about six. For example, 123,456,789F is the same as 123,456,000F. (For an explanation of the F notation at the end of these numbers, see "Declaring Numeric Constants" later in this chapter.)

Using the Decimal Type — A Combination of Integers and Floats

As I explain in previous sections of this chapter, both the integer and floating point types have their problems. Floating point variables have rounding problems associated with limits to their accuracy, while `int` variables just lop off the fractional part of a variable. In some cases, you need a variable type that offers the best of two worlds, as follows:

- ✔ Like a floating point variable, it can store fractions.
- ✔ Like an integer, numbers of this type offer exact values for use in computations — for example, 12.5 is really 12.5 and not 12.500001.

Fortunately, C# provides such a variable type, called `decimal`. A `decimal` variable can represent a number between 10^{-28} and 10^{28} — that's a lot of zeros! And it does so without rounding problems.

Declaring a decimal

Decimal variables are declared and used like any variable type, as follows:

```
decimal m1;          // good
decimal m2 = 100;    // better
decimal m3 = 100M;   // best
```

The declaration of `m1` allocates a variable `m1` without initializing it to anything. Until you assign it a value, the contents of `m1` are indeterminate. But that's okay, because C# doesn't let you use `m1` for anything until you assign it a value.

The second declaration creates a variable `m2` and initializes it to a value of 100. What isn't obvious is that 100 is actually of type `int`. Thus, C# must convert the `int` into a `decimal` type before performing the initialization. Fortunately, C# understands what you mean and performs the conversion for you.

The declaration of `m3` is the best. This clever declaration initializes `m3` with the `decimal` constant 100M. The letter *M* at the end of the number specifies that the constant is of type `decimal`. No conversion is required. (See the section "Declaring Numeric Constants," later in this chapter.)

Comparing decimals, integers, and floating point types

The `decimal` variable type seems to have all the advantages and none of the disadvantages of `int` or `double` types. Variables of this type have a very large range, they don't suffer from rounding problems, and 25.0 is 25.0 and not 25.00001.

The `decimal` variable type has two significant limitations, however. First, a `decimal` is not considered a counting number because it may contain a fractional value. Consequently, you can't use them in flow control loops, which I explain in Chapter 5.

The second problem with `decimal` variables is equally as serious or even more so. Computations involving `decimal` values are significantly slower than those involving either simple integer or floating point values — and I do mean significant. On a crude benchmark test of 300,000,000 adds and subtracts, the operations involving `decimal` variables were approximately 50 times slower than those involving simple `int` variables. The relative computational speed gets even worse for more complex operations. In addition, most computational functions, such as calculating sines or exponents, are not available for the `decimal` number type.

Clearly, the `decimal` variable type is most appropriate for applications such as banking, in which accuracy is extremely important but the number of calculations is relatively small.

Examining the bool Type — Is It Logical?

Finally, a logical variable type. Except in this case, I really mean a type logical. The Boolean type `bool` can have two values: `true` or `false`. I kid thee not — a whole variable type for just two values.

Former C and C++ programmers are accustomed to using the `int` value 0 (zero) to mean `false` and nonzero to mean `true`. That doesn't work in C#.

You declare a `bool` variable as follows:

```
bool thisIsABool = true;
```

No conversion path exists between `bool` variables and any other types. In other words, you can't convert a `bool` directly into something else. (Even if you could, you shouldn't because it doesn't make any sense.) In particular, you can't cast a `bool` into an `int` (such as `false` becomes 0) or a `string` (such as `false` becomes "false").

Checking Out Character Types

A program that can do nothing more than spit out numbers may be fine for mathematicians, accountants, insurance agents with their mortality figures, and folks calculating cannon-shell trajectories. (Don't laugh. The original computers were built to generate tables of cannon-shell trajectories to help artillery gunners.) However, for most applications, programs must deal with letters as well as numbers.

C# treats letters in two distinctly different ways: individual characters of type char (usually pronounced "char" as in singe or burn) and strings of characters called, cleverly enough, *string*.

Char variable type

The char variable is a box capable of holding a single character. Character constants appear as a character surrounded by a pair of single quotation marks, as in this example:

```
char c = 'a';
```

You can store any single character from the Roman, Hebrew, Arab, Cyrillic, and most other alphabets. You can also store Japanese katakana and hiragana characters and many Japanese and Chinese kanjis.

In addition, char is considered a counting type. That means you can use a char type to control the looping structures that I describe in Chapter 5. Character variables do not suffer from rounding problems.

The character variable includes no font information. So, you may store in a char variable what you think is a perfectly good kanji (and it may well be); however, when you view the character, it can look like garbage if you are not looking at it through the eyes of the proper font.

Special char types

Some characters within a given font are not printable in the sense that you don't see anything when you look at them on the computer screen or printer. The most obvious example of this is the space, which is represented by the character ' ' (single quote, space, single quote). Other characters have no letter equivalent — for example, the tab character. C# uses the backslash to flag these characters, as shown in Table 3-3.

Table 3-3	Special Characters
Character Constant	*Value*
'\n'	New line
'\t'	Tab
'\0'	Null character
'\r'	Carriage return
'\\'	Backslash

The string type

Another common variable type is the string. The following examples show how you declare and initialize string variables:

```
// declare now, initialize later
string someString1;
someString1 = "this is a string";
// or initialize when declared
string someString2 = "this is a string";
```

A string constant, often called a string literal, is a set of characters surrounded by double quotes. The characters in a string include the special characters shown in Table 3-3. A string cannot be written across a line in the C# source file, but it can contain the new-line character, as the following examples show:

```
// the following is not legal
string someString = "This is a line
and so is this";
// however, the following is legal
string someString = "This is a line\nand so is this";
```

When written out with Console.WriteLine, the last line in this example places the two phrases on separate lines, as follows:

```
This is a line
and so is this
```

A `string` is not a counting type. A `string` is also not a value-type — no "string" exists that's intrinsic to the processor. Only one of the common operators works on `string` objects: The + operator concatenates two strings into one. For example:

```
string s = "this is a phrase"
         + " and so is this";
```

This code sets the `string` variable s equal to the following character string:

```
"this is a phrase and so is this"
```

One other thing: The `string` with no characters, written `""` (two double quotes in a row), is a valid `string`, called an empty `string` (or sometimes a null `string`). A null `string` (`""`) is different from a null `char` (`'\0'`) and from a `string` containing any amount of space (`" "`).

By the way, all the other data types in this chapter are *value types*. The `string` type, however, is not a value type, as the next section explains.

What's a Value-Type?

All C# instructions have to be implemented in the machine instructions of the native CPU — an Intel-class processor in the case of PCs. These CPUs also have the concept of variables. For example, the Intel processor has eight internal locations known as *registers,* each of which can store a single `int`. Without getting into the details of the CPU, however, I'll just say that the types described in this chapter, with the exception of `decimal` and `string`, are intrinsic to the processor. Thus, a CPU instruction exists that says, "Add one `int` to another `int`." A similar instruction exists for adding a `double` to a `double`. Because these types of variables are built into the processor, they are known as *intrinsic* variable types.

In addition, the variable types that I describe in this chapter are of fixed length — again with the exception of `string`. A fixed-length variable type always occupies the same amount of memory. So, if you assign a = b, C# can transfer the value of b into a without taking extra measures designed to handle variable-length types. This characteristic gives these types of variables the name *value-types*.

The types `int`, `double`, and `bool`, and their close derivatives, like unsigned `int`, are intrinsic variable types. The intrinsic variable types plus `decimal` are also known as value-types. The `string` type is neither.

The programmer-defined types that I explain in Chapter 6, known as reference-types, are neither value-types nor intrinsic. The string type is a reference type, although the C# compiler does accord it some special treatment because strings are so widely used.

Comparing string and char

Although strings deal with characters, the string type is amazingly different from the char. Of course, certain trivial differences exist. You enclose a character with single quotes as in the following example:

```
'a'
```

On the other hand, you put double quotes around a string:

```
"this is a string"
```

The rules concerning strings are not the same as those concerning characters. For one thing, you know right up front that a char is a single character, and that's it. For example, the following code makes no sense, either as addition or as concatenation:

```
char c1 = 'a';
char c2 = 'b';
char c3 = c1 + c2
```

Actually, this code almost compiles, but with a completely different meaning than intended. These statements convert c1 into an int consisting of the numeric value of c1. C# also converts c2 into an int and then adds the two integers. The error occurs when trying to store the results back into c3 — numeric data may be lost storing an int into the smaller char. In any case, the operation makes no sense.

A string, on the other hand, can be any length. So, concatenating two strings, as follows, does make sense:

```
string s1 = "a";
string s2 = "b";
string s3 = s1 + s2;  // result is "ab"
```

As part of its library, C# defines an entire suite of string operations. I describe them in Chapter 9.

Naming conventions

Programming is hard enough without programmers making it harder. To make your C# source code easier to wade through, adopt a naming convention and stick to it. As much as possible, your naming convention should follow those adopted by other C# programmers:

✔ **The names of things other than variables start with a capital letter, and variables start with a lowercase letter.** Make these names as descriptive as possible, which often means that a name consists of multiple words. These words should be capitalized but butted up against each other with no underscore between them — for example, thisIsALongVariableName.

✔ **The first letter of the variable name indicates the type of the variable.** Most of these letters are straightforward: f for float, d for double, s for string, and so on. The only one that's even the slightest bit different

is n for int. One exception to this rule exists: For reasons that stretch way back into the Fortran programming language of the '60s, the single letters i, j, and k are also used as common names for an int.

Hungarian notation seems to have fallen out of favor, at least in .NET programming circles. I still prefer it, however, because it enables me to know in a flash the type of each variable in a program without referring back to the declaration. For the record, the non-Hungarians have a point. With recent Visual Studio versions, you can simply rest the cursor on a variable to have its data type revealed in a tooltip box. That makes the Hungarian prefix a bit less useful, though as a creature of habit, I've held out for Hungarian. Rather than jump into the religious wars about such things, you can just choose the naming convention you prefer.

Declaring Numeric Constants

There are very few absolutes in life; however, I'm about to give you a C# absolute: Every expression has a value and a type. In a declaration such as int n, you can easily see that the variable n is an int. Further, you can reasonably assume that the type of a calculation n + 1 is an int. However, what type is the constant 1?

The type of a constant depends on two things: its value and the presence of an optional descriptor letter at the end of the constant. Any integer type less than 2 billion is assumed to be an int. Numbers larger than 2 billion are assumed to be long. Any floating pointing number is assumed to be a double.

Table 3-4 demonstrates constants that have been declared to be of a particular type. The case of these descriptors is not important. Thus, 1U and 1u are equivalent.

Table 3-4	Common Constants Declared along with Their Type
Constant	**Type**
`1`	`int`
`1U`	`unsigned int`
`1L`	`long int` (avoid lowercase *l*; it's too much like the digit 1)
`1.0`	`double`
`1.0F`	`float`
`1M`	`decimal`
`true`	`bool`
`false`	`bool`
`'a'`	`char`
`'\n'`	`char` (the character newline)
`'\x123'`	`char` (the character whose numeric value is hex 123)[1]
`"a string"`	`string`
`""`	`string` (an empty string)

[1] *"hex" is short for hexadecimal (numbers in base 16 rather than base 10).*

Changing Types — The Cast

Humans don't treat different types of counting numbers differently. For example, a normal person (as distinguished from a C# programmer) doesn't think about the number 1 as being signed, unsigned, short, or long. Although C# considers these types to be different, even C# realizes that a relationship exists between them. For example, the following code converts an `int` into a `long`:

```
int nValue = 10;
long lValue;
lValue = nValue;  // this is OK
```

An `int` variable can be converted into a `long` because any value of an `int` can be stored in a `long` and because they are both counting numbers. C# makes the conversion for you automatically without comment.

A conversion in the opposite direction can cause problems, however. For example, the following is illegal:

```
long lValue = 10;
int nValue;
nValue = lValue;  // this is illegal
```

Some values that you can store in a `long` do not fit in an `int` (4 billion, for example). C# generates an error in this case because data may be lost during the conversion process. This type of bug is difficult to catch.

But what if you know that the conversion is okay? For example, even though `lValue` is a `long`, maybe you know that its value can't exceed 100 in this particular program. In that case, converting the `long` variable `lValue` into the `int` variable `nValue` would be okay.

You can tell C# that you know what you're doing by means of a *cast:*

```
long lValue = 10;
int nValue;
nValue = (int)lValue;  // this is now OK
```

In a cast, you place the name of the type you want in parentheses and put it immediately in front of the value you want to convert. This cast says, "Go ahead and convert the long `lValue` into an `int` — I know what I'm doing." In retrospect, the assertion that you know what you're doing may seem overly confident, but it's often valid.

A counting number can be converted into a floating point number automatically, but a cast from a floating point into a counting number requires a cast, as follows:

```
double dValue = 10.0;
long lValue = (long)dValue;
```

All conversions to and from a `decimal` require a cast. In fact, all numeric types can be converted into all other numeric types through the application of a cast. Neither `bool` nor `string` can be converted directly into any other type.

Built-in C# functions can convert a number, character, or boolean into its string "equivalent." For example, you can convert the `bool` value `true` into the `string` "true"; however, you cannot consider this a direct conversion. The `bool` `true` and `string` "true" are completely different things.

Chapter 4

Smooth Operators

- -

In This Chapter

▶ Performing a little arithmetic

▶ Doing some logical arithmetic

▶ Complicating matters with compound logical operators

- -

*M*athematicians create variables and manipulate them in various ways, adding them, multiplying them, and — here's a toughie — even integrating them. Chapter 3 describes how to declare and define variables. However, it says nothing about how to use variables to get anything done after you've declared them. This chapter looks at the operations you can perform on variables to actually get something done. Operations require *operators,* such as +, – , =, <, and &. I cover arithmetic, logical, and other operators in this chapter.

Writing programs that get things done is good. You'll never make it as a C# programmer if your programs don't actually do something — unless, of course, you're a consultant.

Performing Arithmetic

The set of arithmetic operators breaks down into several groups: the simple arithmetic operators, the assignment operators, and a set of special operators unique to programming. After you've digested these, you also need to digest a separate set of logical operators. *Bon appétit!*

Simple operators

You learned most of the simple operators in elementary school. Table 4-1 lists them. ***Note:*** Computers use an asterisk (*) for multiplication, not the multiplication sign (×).

Table 4-1	The Simple Operators
Operator	*What It Means*
– (unary)	Take the negative of
*	Multiply
/	Divide
+	Add
– (binary)	Subtract
%	Modulo

Most of these operators are called *binary operators* because they operate on two values: one on the left side of the operator and one on the right side. The one exception is the unary negative. However, this one is just as straightforward as the others, as I show in the following example:

```
int n1 = 5;
int n2 = -n1;   // n2 now has the value -5
```

The value of –n is the negative of the value of n.

The modulo operator may not be quite as familiar to you. Modulo is similar to the remainder after division. Thus, 5 % 3 is 2 (5 / 3 = 1, remainder 2), and 25 % 3 is 1 (25 / 3 = 8, remainder 1). Read it "five modulo three" or simply "five mod three."

The strict definition of % is "the operator such that: $x = (x / y) + x \% y$." Divide x by y. Add x modulo y (which equals the remainder after x / y). The result is x.

The arithmetic operators other than modulo are defined for all the numeric types. The modulo operator is not defined for floating point numbers because you have no remainder after division of floating point values.

Operating orders

The value of some expressions may not be clear. Consider, for example, the following expression:

```
int n = 5 * 3 + 2;
```

Does the programmer mean "multiply 5 times 3 and then add 2," which is 17, or does this line mean "multiply 5 times the sum of 3 and 2," which gives you 25?

C# generally executes common operators from left to right. So, the preceding example assigns the value 17 to the variable n.

C# determines the value of n in the following example by first dividing 24 by 6 and then dividing the result of that operation by 2 (as opposed to dividing 24 by the ratio 6 over 2):

```
int n = 24 / 6 / 2
```

However, the various operators have a hierarchy, or order of precedence. C# scans an expression and performs the operations of higher precedence before those of lower precedence. For example, multiplication has higher precedence than addition. Many books take great pains to explain the order of precedence, but frankly that's a complete waste of time (and brain cells).

Don't rely on yourself or someone else knowing the precedence order. Make your meaning (to human readers of the code as well as to the compiler) explicit with parentheses.

The value of the following expression is clear, regardless of the operators' order of precedence:

```
int n = (7 % 3) * (4 + (6 / 3));
```

Parentheses can override the order of precedence by stating exactly how the compiler is to interpret the expression. C# looks for the innermost parentheses for the first expression to evaluate, dividing 6 by 3 to yield 2. The result follows:

```
int n = (7 % 3) * (4 + 2);   // 2 = 6 / 3
```

Then C# works its way outward, evaluating each set of parentheses in turn, innermost to outermost, as follows:

```
int n = 1 * 6;   // 6 = (4 + 2)
```

And here's the final result:

```
int n = 6
```

The "always use parentheses" rule has perhaps one exception. I don't condone this behavior, but many programmers omit parentheses in examples like the following, because multiplication has higher precedence than addition. Consider the following example:

```
int n = 7 + 2 * 3;     // same as 7 + (2 * 3)
```

In this case, the value of the variable n is 13 (not 27).

The assignment operator

C# has inherited an interesting concept from C and C++: Assignment is itself a binary operator. The assignment operator has the value of the argument to the right. The assignment has the same type as both arguments, which must match.

This new view of the assignment operator has no effect on the expressions you've seen so far:

```
n = 5 * 3;
```

In this example, 5 * 3 is 15 and an int. The assignment operator stores the int on the right into the int on the left and returns the value 15. However, this new view of the assignment operator allows the following:

```
m = n = 5 * 3;
```

Assignments are evaluated in series from right to left. The right-hand assignment stores the value 15 into n and returns 15. The left-hand assignment stores 15 into m and returns 15, which is then dropped on the floor, leaving the value of each variable as 15.

This strange definition for assignment makes the following rather bizarre expressions legal (but I would avoid this):

```
int n;
int m;
n = m = 2;
```

I avoid chaining assignments that way because it's less clear to human readers. Anything that can confuse people reading your code (including you) is worth avoiding because confusion breeds errors. A huge proportion of computer programming, from language rules and constructs to naming conventions and recommended programmer practices, is devoted to fighting error. Join the fight.

C# extends the simple operators with a set of operators constructed from other binary operators. For example:

```
n += 1;
```

This expression is equivalent to the following:

```
n = n + 1;
```

An assignment operator exists for just about every binary operator. I'm really not sure how these various assignment operators came to be, but there they are. Table 4-2 shows the most common compound assignment operators.

Table 4-2	Common Compound Assignment Operators
Operator	*Meaning*
a += b	Assign a + b to a
a -= b	Assign a - b to a
a *= b	Assign a * b to a
a /= b	Assign a / b to a
a %= b	Assign a % b to a
a &= b	Assign a & b to a (& is a logical operator, discussed later)
a |= b	Assign a | b to a (| is a logical operator)
a ^= b	Assign a ^ b to a (^ is a logical operator)

Table 4-2 omits a couple of advanced compound assignment operators, <<= and >>=. I mention the "bit-shifting" operators later in the chapter.

The increment operator

Of all the additions that you may perform in programming, adding 1 to a variable is the most common, as follows:

```
n = n + 1;  // increment n by 1
```

Why have an increment operator?

The reason for the increment operator lies in the obscure fact that the PDP-8 computer of the 1970s had an increment instruction. This would be of little interest today were it not for the fact that the C language, the original precursor to C#, was originally written for the PDP-8. Because that machine had an increment instruction, n++ generated fewer machine instructions than n = n + 1. As slow as those machines were, saving a few machine instructions was a big deal.

Today, compilers are smarter and no difference exists in the execution time for n++ and n = n + 1, so the increment operator is no longer needed. However, programmers are creatures of habit, and the operator remains to this day. You almost never see a C++ programmer increment a value using the longer but more intuitive n = n + 1. Instead, you see the increment operator.

Further, when standing by itself (that is, not part of a larger expression), the postincrement operator almost always appears instead of the preincrement operator. There's no reason other than habit and the fact that it looks cooler, especially to C++ programmers: n++.

C# defines the assignment operator shorthand as follows:

```
n += 1;     // increment n by 1
```

Even that's not good enough. C# provides this even shorter version:

```
++n;        // increment n by 1
```

All three of the preceding statements are equivalent — they all increment n by 1.

The increment operator is strange enough, but believe it or not, C# has two increment operators: ++n and n++. The first one, ++n, is called the *preincrement operator,* while n++ is the *postincrement operator.* The difference is subtle but important.

Remember that every expression has a type and a value. In the following code, both ++n and n++ are of type int:

```
int n;
n = 1;
int p = ++n;
n = 1;
int m = n++;
```

But what are the resulting values of m and p? (Hint: The choices are 1 or 2.) The value of p is 2, and the value of m is 1. That is, the value of the expression ++n is the value of n *after* being incremented, while the value of the expression n++ is the value of n *before* it is incremented. Either way, the resulting value of n is 2.

Equivalent decrement operators — that is, n-- and --n — exist to replace n = n - 1. These work in exactly the same way as the increment operators.

Performing Logical Comparisons — Is That Logical?

C# also provides a set of logical comparison operators, as shown in Table 4-3. These operators are called *logical comparisons* because they return either a true or a false of type bool.

Table 4-3	The Logical Comparison Operators
Operator	*Operator Is True If . . .*
`a == b`	a has the same value as b
`a > b`	a is greater than b
`a >= b`	a is greater than or equal to b
`a < b`	a is less than b
`a <= b`	a is less than or equal to b
`a != b`	a is not equal to b

Here's an example that involves a logical comparison:

```
int m = 5;
int n = 6;
bool b = m > n;
```

This example assigns the value `false` to the variable `b` because 5 is not greater than 6.

The logical comparisons are defined for all numeric types, including `float`, `double`, `decimal`, and `char`. All the following statements are legal:

```
bool b;
b = 3 > 2;       // true
b = 3.0 > 2.0;   // true
b = 'a' > 'b';   // false - alphabetically later = greater
b = 'A' < 'a';   // true - upper A is less than lower a
b = 'A' < 'b';   // true - all upper are less than all lower
b = 10M > 12M;   // false
```

The comparison operators always produce results of type `bool`. The comparison operators other than `==` are not valid for variables of type `string`. (Not to worry; C# offers other ways to compare `string`s.)

Comparing floating point numbers: Is your float bigger than mine?

Comparing two floating values can get dicey, and you need to be careful with these comparisons. Consider the following comparison:

```
float f1;
float f2;
f1 = 10;
f2 = f1 / 3;
bool b1 = (3 * f2) == f1;
f1 = 9;
f2 = f1 / 3;
bool b2 = (3 * f2) == f1;
```

Notice that the fifth and eighth lines in the preceding example each contain first an assignment operator (=) and then a logical comparison (==). These are different animals. C# does the logical comparison and then assigns the result to the variable on the left.

The only difference between the calculations of b1 and b2 is the original value of f1. So, what are the values of b1 and b2? The value of b2 is clearly true: 9 / 3 is 3; 3 * 3 is 9; and 9 equals 9. Voilà!

The value of b1 is not so obvious: 10 / 3 is 3.333.... 3.333... * 3 is 9.999.... Is 9.999... equal to 10? That depends on how clever your processor and compiler are. On a Pentium or later processor, C# is not smart enough to realize that b1 should be true if the calculations are moved away from the comparison.

You can use the system absolute value function to compare f1 and f2 as follows:

```
Math.Abs(f1 - 3.0 * f2) < .00001; // use whatever level of accuracy
```

This function returns true for both cases. You can use the constant Double.Epsilon instead of .00001 to get the maximum level of accuracy. Epsilon is the smallest possible difference between two nonequal double variables.

For a self-guided tour of the System.Math class, where Abs and many other useful mathematical functions live, choose Help⇨Index and type **Math** in the Look For box.

Compounding the confusion with compound logical operations

The bool variables have another set of operators defined just for them, as shown in Table 4-4.

Table 4-4	The Compound Logical Operators
Operator	*Operator Is True If . . .*
`!a`	a is false.
`a & b`	a and b are true.
`a	b`	Either a or b or else both are true (also known as a and/or b).
`a ^ b`	a is true or b is true but not both (also known as a xor b).
`a && b`	a is true and b is true with short-circuit evaluation.
`a || b`	a is true or b is true with short-circuit evaluation. (I discuss short-circuit evaluation in the nearby text.)

The `!` operator is the logical equivalent of the minus sign. For example, `!a` (read "not a") is true if a is false and false if a is true. Can that be true?

The next two operators are straightforward enough. First, `a & b` is only true if both a and b are true. And `a | b` is true if either a or b is true (or both). The `^` (also known as *exclusive or — xor*) operator is sort of an odd beast. An exclusive or is true if either a or b is true but not if both a and b are true.

All three operators produce a logical `bool` value as their result.

The `&`, `|`, and `^` operators also have a *bitwise operator* version. When applied to `int` variables, these operators perform their magic on a bit-by-bit basis. Thus, 6 & 3 is 2 (0110_2 & 0011_2 is 0010_2), 6 | 3 is 7 (0110_2 | 0011_2 is 0111_2), and 6 ^ 3 is 5 (0110_2 ^ 0011_2 is 0101_2). Binary arithmetic is really cool but beyond the scope of this book.

The remaining two logical operators are similar to, but subtly different from, the first three. Consider the following example:

```
bool b = (boolExpression1) & (boolExpression2);
```

In this case, C# evaluates `boolExpression1` and `boolExpression2`. It then looks to see whether they are both true before deciding the value of b. However, this may be a wasted effort. If one expression is false, there's no reason to perform the other. Regardless of the value of the second expression, the result will be false.

The `&&` operator enables you to avoid evaluating both expressions unnecessarily, as shown in the following example:

```
bool b = (boolExpression1) && (boolExpression2);
```

In this case, C# evaluates `boolExpression1`. If it's false, `b` is set to false and the program continues on its merry way. On the other hand, if `boolExpression1` is true, C# evaluates `boolExpression2` and stores the result in `b`.

The `&&` operator uses *short-circuit evaluation* because it short-circuits around the second boolean expression, if necessary.

The `||` operator works the same way, as shown in the following expression:

```
bool b = (boolExpression1) || (boolExpression2);
```

If `boolExpression1` is true, there's no point in evaluating `boolExpression2` because the result is always true.

You can read these operators as "short-circuit and" and "short-circuit or."

Finding the Perfect Date — Matching Expression Types

In calculations, an expression's type is just as important as its value. Consider the following expression:

```
int n;
n = 5 * 5 + 7;
```

My calculator says the resulting value of `n` is 32. However, that expression also has a type.

Written in "type language," the preceding expression becomes the following:

```
int [=] int * int + int;
```

To evaluate the type of an expression, follow the same pattern you use to evaluate the expression's value. Multiplication takes precedence over addition. An `int` times an `int` is an `int`. Addition comes next. An `int` plus an `int` is an `int`. In this way, you can reduce the preceding expression as follows:

```
int * int + int
int + int
int
```

Calculating the type of an operation

The matching of types burrows down to the *subexpression*. Each expression has a type, and the type of the left- and right-hand sides of an operator must match what is expected of that operator, as follows:

```
type1 <op> type2 ⇨ type3
```

(The arrow means "produces.") Both `type1` and `type2` must be compatible with the operator `op`.

Most operators come in various flavors. For example, the multiplication operator comes in the following forms:

```
int     * int     ⇨ int
uint    * uint    ⇨ uint
long    * long    ⇨ long
float   * float   ⇨ float
decimal * decimal ⇨ decimal
double  * double  ⇨ double
```

Thus, 2 * 3 uses the `int` * `int` version of the * operator to produce the `int` 6.

Implicit type conversion

Okay, that's great for multiplying two `int`s or two `float`s. But what happens when the left- and right-hand arguments are not of the same type? For example, what happens in the following case?

```
int n1 = 10;
double d2 = 5.0;
double dResult = n1 * d2;
```

First, C# doesn't have an `int` * `double` operation. C# could just generate an error message and leave it at that; however, it tries to make sense out of what the programmer intended. C# does have `int` * `int` and `double` * `double` versions of multiplication. C# could convert d2 into its `int` equivalent, but that would involve losing any fractional part of the number (digits to the right of the decimal point). Instead, C# converts the `int` n1 into a `double` and uses the `double` * `double` operator. This is known as an *implicit promotion*.

An implicit promotion is *implicit* because C# does it automatically, and it's a *promotion* because it involves some natural concept of uphill and downhill. The list of multiplication operators is in promotion order from `int` to `double` or from `int` to `decimal` — from narrower type to wider type. No implicit conversion exists between the floating point types and `decimal`. Converting from the more capable type, such as `double`, to a less capable type, such as `int`, is known as a *demotion*.

A promotion is also known as an *up conversion,* and a demotion is also known as a *down conversion.*

Implicit demotions, or down conversions, are not allowed. C# generates an error message in such cases.

Explicit type conversion — the cast

What if C# was wrong? What if the programmer really did want to perform integer multiplication?

You can change the type of any value-type variable through the use of the cast operator. A *cast* consists of the desired type contained in parentheses and placed immediately in front of the variable or expression in question.

Thus, the following expression uses the `int * int` operator:

```
int n1 = 10;
double d2 = 5.0;
int nResult = n1 * (int)d2;
```

The cast of d2 to an `int` is known as an *explicit demotion* or *downcast.* The conversion is explicit because the programmer explicitly declared her intent — duh.

You can make an explicit conversion between any two value types, whether up or down the promotion ladder.

Avoid implicit type conversion. Make any changes in value-types explicit through the use of a cast.

Leave logical alone

C# offers no type conversion path to or from the `bool` type.

Assigning types

The same matching of types applies to the assignment operator.

Inadvertent type mismatches that generate compiler error messages usually occur in the assignment operator, not at the point of the actual mismatch.

Consider the following multiplication example:

```
int n1 = 10;
int n2 = 5.0 * n1;
```

The second line in this example generates an error message due to a type mismatch, but the error occurs at the assignment — not at the multiplication. Here's the horrible tale: To perform the multiplication, C# implicitly converts n1 to a double. C# can then perform double multiplication, the result of which is the all-powerful double.

The type of the right-hand and left-hand operators of the assignment operator must match, but the type of the left-hand operator cannot change. Because C# refuses to demote an expression implicitly, the compiler generates the following error message: Cannot implicitly convert type double to int.

C# allows this expression with an explicit cast, as follows:

```
int n1 = 10;
int n2 = (int)(5.0 * n1);
```

(The parentheses are necessary because the cast operator has very high precedence.) This works — *explicit* demotion is okay. The n1 is promoted to a double, the multiplication is performed, and the double result is demoted to an int. However, you have to worry about the sanity of the programmer because 5 * n1 is so much easier for both the programmer and the C# compiler.

The Ternary Operator — I Wish It Were a Bird and Would Fly Away

Most operators take two arguments — a few take one. Only one operator takes three arguments — the *ternary* operator. This operator is maligned — and for good reason. It has the following format:

```
bool expression ? expression1 : expression2
```

I'll confuse you even more with the following example:

```
int a = 1;
int b = 2;
int nMax = (a > b) ? a : b;
```

If a is greater than b (the condition in parentheses), the value of the expression is a. If a is not greater than b, the value of the expression is b.

Expressions 1 and 2 can be as complicated as you like, but they must be true expressions; they cannot contain declarations or other nonexpression-type statements.

The ternary operator is unpopular for the following reasons:

- ✔ **It isn't necessary.** Using the type of `if` statements described in Chapter 5 has the same effect and is easier to understand.

- ✔ **The ternary is a true expression no matter how much it may look like some type of cryptic `if` statement.** For example, expressions 1 and 2 must be of the same type. This leads to the following:

```
int a = 1;
double b = 0.0;
int nMax = (a > b) ? a : b;
```

This statement doesn't compile, even though nMax would have ended up with the value of a. Because a and b must be of the same type, a is promoted to a `double` to match b. The resulting type of `?:` is now `double`, which must be demoted to an `int` before the assignment is allowed, as follows:

```
int a = 1;
double b = 0.0;
int nMax;
// this works
nMax = (int)((a > b) ? a : b);
// so does this
nMax = (a > b) ? a : (int)b;
```

You rarely see the ternary operator in use.

Chapter 5

Controlling Program Flow

Consider the following simple program:

```csharp
using System;
namespace HelloWorld
{
  public class Program
  {
    // This is where the program starts
    static void Main(string[] args)
    {
      // prompt user to enter a name
      Console.WriteLine("Enter your name, please:");
      // now read the name entered
      string sName = Console.ReadLine();
      // greet the user with the entered name
      Console.WriteLine("Hello, " + sName);
      // wait for user to acknowledge the results
      Console.WriteLine("Press Enter to terminate...");
      Console.Read();
    }
  }
}
```

Besides introducing you to a few fundamentals of C# programming, this program is almost worthless. It simply spits back out whatever you typed in. You can imagine more complicated example programs that take in input, perform some type of calculations, generate some type of output (otherwise, why do the calculations?), and then exit at the bottom. However, even a program such as that can be of only limited use.

One of the key elements of any computer processor is its ability to make decisions. When I say "make decisions," I mean the processor sends the flow of execution down one path of instructions if a condition is true or down another path if the condition is not true. Any programming language must offer this fundamental capability to control the flow of execution.

The three basic types of flow control are the `if` statement, the loop, and the jump. I describe one of the looping controls, the `foreach`, in Chapter 6.

Controlling Program Flow

The basis of all C# decision-making capability is the `if` statement (the basis of all my decisions is the `maybe`), as follows:

```
if (bool-expression)
{
    // control passes here if the expression is true
}
// control passes to this statement whether the expression is true or not
```

A pair of parentheses immediately following the keyword `if` contains some conditional expression of type `bool`. (See Chapter 4 for a discussion of `bool` expressions.) Immediately following the expression is a block of code set off by a pair of braces. If the expression is true, the program executes the code within the braces. If the expression is not true, the program skips the code in the braces.

The `if` statement is easier to understand with a concrete example:

```
// make sure that a is not negative:
// if a is less than 0 . . .
if (a < 0)
{
    //  . . .then assign 0 to a
    a = 0;
}
```

This segment of code makes sure that the variable a is nonnegative — greater than or equal to 0. The `if` statement says, "If a is less than 0, assign 0 to a."

The braces are not required. C# treats `if(bool-expression) statement;` as if it had been written `if(bool-expression) {statement;}`. The general consensus (and my preference) is to always use braces for better clarity. In other words, don't ask — just do it.

Introducing the if statement

Consider a small program that calculates interest. The user enters the principal and the interest rate, and the program spits out the resulting value for each year. (This is not a sophisticated program.) The simplistic calculation appears as follows in C#:

```
// calculate the value of the principal plus interest
decimal mInterestPaid;
mInterestPaid = mPrincipal * (mInterest / 100);
// now calculate the total
decimal mTotal = mPrincipal + mInterestPaid;
```

The first equation multiplies the principal `mPrincipal` times the interest `mInterest` to get the interest to be paid, `mInterestPaid`. (You divide by 100 because interest is usually input in percent.) The interest to be paid is then added back into the principal, resulting in a new principal, which is stored in the variable `mTotal`.

The program must anticipate almost anything when dealing with human input. For example, you don't want to accept a negative principal or interest (even if you do end up paying negative interest). The following `CalculateInterest` program includes checks to make sure that neither of these things happen:

```
// CalculateInterest
//            calculate the interest amount
//            paid on a given principal. If either
//            the principal or the interest rate is
//            negative, then generate an error message.
using System;
namespace CalculateInterest
{
  public class Program
  {
    public static void Main(string[] args)
    {
      // prompt user to enter source principal
      Console.Write("Enter principal:");
      string sPrincipal = Console.ReadLine();
      decimal mPrincipal = Convert.ToDecimal(sPrincipal);
      // make sure that the principal is not negative
      if (mPrincipal < 0)
      {
        Console.WriteLine("Principal cannot be negative");
        mPrincipal = 0;
      }
      // enter the interest rate
      Console.Write("Enter interest:");
      string sInterest = Console.ReadLine();
      decimal mInterest = Convert.ToDecimal(sInterest);
```

```
    // make sure that the interest is not negative either
    if (mInterest < 0)
    {
      Console.WriteLine("Interest cannot be negative");
      mInterest = 0;
    }
    // calculate the value of the principal
    // plus interest
    decimal mInterestPaid;
    mInterestPaid = mPrincipal * (mInterest / 100);
    // now calculate the total
    decimal mTotal = mPrincipal + mInterestPaid;
    // output the result
    Console.WriteLine();  // skip a line
    Console.WriteLine("Principal    = " + mPrincipal);
    Console.WriteLine("Interest     = " + mInterest + "%");
    Console.WriteLine();
    Console.WriteLine("Interest paid = " + mInterestPaid);
    Console.WriteLine("Total        = " + mTotal);
    // wait for user to acknowledge the results
    Console.WriteLine("Press Enter to terminate...");
    Console.Read();

  }
 }
}
```

The `CalculateInterest` program begins by prompting the user for his name using `WriteLine()` to write a `string` to the console.

Tell the user exactly what you want. If possible, specify the format you want as well. Users don't respond well to uninformative prompts like >.

The example program uses the `ReadLine()` command to read in whatever the user types, until he presses Enter, in the form of a `string`. Because the program is looking for the principal in the form of a `decimal`, the input `string` must be converted using the `Convert.ToDecimal()` command. The result is stored in `mPrincipal`.

The `ReadLine()`, `WriteLine()`, and `ToDecimal()` commands are all examples of *function calls*. A function call delegates some work to another part of the program, called a function. I describe function calls in detail in Chapter 7; however, these function calls are straightforward. You should be able to get at least the gist of the meaning using my extraordinarily insightful explanatory narrative. If that doesn't work, ignore my narrative. If that still doesn't work, skim through the beginning of Chapter 7.

The next line checks `mPrincipal`. If it's negative, the program outputs a nasty-gram, indicating that the user has fouled up. The program does the same thing for the interest rate. That done, the program performs the simplistic interest calculation outlined earlier and spits out the result using a series of `WriteLine()` commands.

The program generates the following output with a legitimate principal and a usurious interest rate that is legal in most states:

```
Enter principal:1234
Enter interest:21

Principal    = 1234
Interest     = 21%

Interest paid = 259.14
Total         = 1493.14
Press Enter to terminate...
```

Executing the program with illegal input generates the following output:

```
Enter principal:1234
Enter interest:-12.5
Interest cannot be negative

Principal    = 1234
Interest     = 0%

Interest paid = 0
Total         = 1234
Press Enter to terminate...
```

Indent the lines within an `if` clause to enhance readability. C# ignores such indentation, but it helps us humans. Most programming editors support auto-indenting, whereby the editor automatically indents as soon as you enter the `if` command. To set auto-indenting in Visual Studio, choose Tools⇨Options. Then expand the Text Editor node. From there, expand C#. Finally, click Tabs. On this page, enable Smart Indenting and set the number of spaces per indent to your preference. I use two spaces per indent for this book. Set the Tab Size to the same value.

Examining the else statement

Some functions must check for mutually exclusive conditions. For example, the following code segment stores the maximum of two numbers, a and b, in the variable `max`:

```
// store the maximum of a and b into the variable max
int max;
// if a is greater than b . . .
if (a > b)
{
    //  . . .save off a as the maximum
    max = a;
}
// if a is less than or equal to b . . .
if (a <= b)
{
    //  . . .save off b as the maximum
    max = b;
}
```

The second `if` statement is needless processing because the two conditions are mutually exclusive. If `a` is greater than `b`, `a` can't possibly be less than or equal to `b`. C# defines an `else` clause for just this case. The `else` keyword defines a block of code that's executed if the `if` block is not.

The code segment to calculate the maximum now appears as follows:

```
// store the maximum of a and b into the variable max
int max;
// if a is greater than b . . .
if (a > b)
{
    //  . . .save off a as the maximum; otherwise . . .
    max = a;
}
else
{
    //  . . .save off b as the maximum
    max = b;
}
```

If `a` is greater than `b`, the first block is executed; otherwise, the second block is executed. In the end, `max` contains the greater of `a` or `b`.

Avoiding even the else

Sequences of `else` clauses can get confusing. Some programmers, myself included, like to avoid them when doing so doesn't cause even more confusion. You could write the maximum calculation like this:

```
// store the maximum of a and b into the variable max
int max;
// start by assuming that a is greater than b
max = a;
```

```
// if it is not . . .
if (b > a)
{
  // ...then you can change your mind
  max = b;
}
```

Some programmers avoid this style like the plague, and I can sympathize. That doesn't mean I'm going to change; it just means I sympathize. You see both this style and the "else style" in common use.

Embedded if statements

The `CalculateInterest` program warns the user of illegal input; however, continuing with the interest calculation, even if one of the values is illogical, doesn't seem quite right. It causes no real harm here because the interest calculation takes little or no time and the user can ignore the results, but some calculations aren't nearly so quick. In addition, why ask the user for an interest rate after she has already entered an invalid value for the principal? The user knows that the results of the calculation will be invalid no matter what she enters next.

The program should only ask the user for an interest rate if the principal is reasonable and only perform the interest calculation if both values are valid. To accomplish this, you need two `if` statements, one within the other.

An `if` statement found within the body of another `if` statement is called an *embedded* or *nested* statement.

The following program, `CalculateInterestWithEmbeddedTest`, uses embedded `if` statements to avoid stupid questions if a problem with the input is detected:

```
// CalculateInterestWithEmbeddedTest
//              calculate the interest amount
//              paid on a given principal. If either
//              the principal or the interest rate is
//              negative, then generate an error message
//              and don't proceed with the calculation.
using System;
namespace CalculateInterestWithEmbeddedTest
{
  public class Program
  {
    public static void Main(string[] args)
    {
      // define a maximum interest rate
      int nMaximumInterest = 50;
```

```
      // prompt user to enter source principal
      Console.Write("Enter principal:");
      string sPrincipal = Console.ReadLine();
      decimal mPrincipal = Convert.ToDecimal(sPrincipal);
      // if the principal is negative . . .
      if (mPrincipal < 0)
      {
        // . . .generate an error message . . .
        Console.WriteLine("Principal cannot be negative");
      }
      else
      {
        // . . .otherwise, enter the interest rate
        Console.Write("Enter interest:");
        string sInterest = Console.ReadLine();
        decimal mInterest = Convert.ToDecimal(sInterest);
        // if the interest is negative or too large . . .
        if (mInterest < 0 || mInterest > nMaximumInterest)
        {
          // . . .generate an error message as well
          Console.WriteLine("Interest cannot be negative " +
                            "or greater than " + nMaximumInterest);
          mInterest = 0;
        }
        else
        {
          // both the principal and the interest appear to be
          // legal; calculate the value of the principal
          // plus interest
          decimal mInterestPaid;
          mInterestPaid = mPrincipal * (mInterest / 100);
          // now calculate the total
          decimal mTotal = mPrincipal + mInterestPaid;
          // output the result
          Console.WriteLine();  // skip a line
          Console.WriteLine("Principal     = " + mPrincipal);
          Console.WriteLine("Interest      = " + mInterest + "%");
          Console.WriteLine();
          Console.WriteLine("Interest paid = " + mInterestPaid);
          Console.WriteLine("Total         = " + mTotal);
        }
      }
      // wait for user to acknowledge the results
      Console.WriteLine("Press Enter to terminate...");
      Console.Read();
    }
  }
}
```

The program first reads the principal from the user. If the principal is negative, the program outputs an error message and quits. If the principal is not negative, control passes to the else clause, where the program continues executing.

The interest-rate test has been improved in this sample. Here, the program requires an interest rate that's nonnegative (a mathematical law) and less than some maximum (a judiciary law — we can only wish that credit cards had an interest rate limit). This `if` statement uses the following compound test:

```
if (mInterest < 0 || mInterest > nMaximumInterest)
```

This statement is true if `mInterest` is less than 0 or `mInterest` is greater than `nMaximumInterest`. Notice that I declare `nMaximumInterest` at the top of the program rather than *hard code* it as a constant here.

Define important constants at the top of your program.

Encoding constants in variables at the top of your program serves the following purposes:

- ✔ **It gives each constant an explanatory name.** `nMaximumInterest` is much more descriptive than 50.
- ✔ **It makes the constant easy to find in the event that you need to change it.**
- ✔ **It makes the constant easier to change.** Notice that the same `nMaximumInterest` appears in the error message. Changing `nMaximumInterest` to 60, for example, changes not only the test but also the error message.

Chapter 6 has more to say about using constants.

Entering a correct principal but a negative interest rate generates the following output:

```
Enter principal:1234
Enter interest:-12.5
Interest cannot be negative or greater than 50.
Press Enter to terminate...
```

Only by entering both a legal principal and a legal interest rate does the program generate the desired calculation, as follows:

```
Enter principal:1234
Enter interest:12.5

Principal     = 1234
Interest      = 12.5%

Interest paid = 154.250
Total         = 1388.250
Press Enter to terminate...
```

Looping Commands

The `if` statement enables a program to take a different path through the code being executed depending on the results of a `bool` expression. This statement allows drastically more interesting programs than a program without decision-making capability. Adding the ability to execute a set of instructions in an iterative manner adds another quantum jump in capability.

Consider the `CalculateInterest` program from the section "Introducing the if statement," earlier in this chapter. Performing this simple interest calculation with a calculator or by hand with a piece of paper would be much easier than writing and executing a program.

What if you could calculate the amount of principal for each of several succeeding years? That would be a lot more useful. A simple macro in a Microsoft Excel spreadsheet would still be easier, but at least you're getting closer.

What you need is a way for the computer to execute the same short sequence of instructions multiple times. This is known as a *loop*.

Introducing the while loop

The C# keyword `while` introduces the most basic form of execution loop, as follows:

```
while(bool-expression)
{
    // . . . .repeatedly executed as long as the expression is true
}
```

When the `while` loop is first encountered, the `bool` expression is evaluated. If the expression is true, the code within the block is executed. When the block of code reaches the closed brace, control returns to the top, and the whole process starts over again. (It's kind of the way I feel when I'm walking the dog. He and I loop around and around the yard until he . . . well, until we're finished.) Control passes beyond the closed brace the first time the `bool` expression is evaluated and turns out to be false.

If the condition is not true the first time the `while` loop is encountered, the set of commands within the braces is never executed.

Programmers often get sloppy in their speech. (Programmers are sloppy most of the time.) A programmer may say that a loop is executed until some condition is false. To me, that implies that control passes outside the loop no matter where the program happens to be executing as soon as the condition becomes false. This is definitely not the case. The program does not check whether the condition is still true until control specifically passes back to the top of the loop.

You can use the `while` loop to create the `CalculateInterestTable` program, a looping version of the `CalculateInterest` program. `CalculateInterestTable`, as follows, calculates a table of principals showing accumulated annual payments:

```
// CalculateInterestTable - calculate the interest
//              paid on a given principle over a period
//              of years
using System;
namespace CalculateInterestTable
{
  using System;
  public class Program
    {
    public static void Main(string[] args)
    {
      // prompt user to enter source principal
      Console.Write("Enter principal:");
      string sPrincipal = Console.ReadLine();
      decimal mPrincipal = Convert.ToDecimal(sPrincipal);
      // if the principal is negative . . .
      if (mPrincipal < 0)
      {
        // . . .generate an error message . . .
        Console.WriteLine("Principal cannot be negative");
      }
      else
      {
        // . . .otherwise, enter the interest rate
        Console.Write("Enter interest:");
        string sInterest = Console.ReadLine();
        decimal mInterest = Convert.ToDecimal(sInterest);
        // if the interest is negative . . .
        if (mInterest < 0)
        {
          // . . .generate an error message as well
          Console.WriteLine("Interest cannot be negative");
          mInterest = 0;
        }
        else
        {
          // both the principal and the interest appear to be
          // legal; finally, input the number of years
          Console.Write("Enter number of years:");
          string sDuration = Console.ReadLine();
          int nDuration = Convert.ToInt32(sDuration);
          // verify the input
          Console.WriteLine();  // skip a line
```

```
             Console.WriteLine("Principal     = " + mPrincipal);
             Console.WriteLine("Interest      = " + mInterest + "%");
             Console.WriteLine("Duration      = " + nDuration + "years");
             Console.WriteLine();
             // now loop through the specified number of years
             int nYear = 1;
             while(nYear <= nDuration)
             {
                 // calculate the value of the principal
                 // plus interest
                 decimal mInterestPaid;
                 mInterestPaid = mPrincipal * (mInterest / 100);
                 // now calculate the new principal by adding
                 // the interest to the previous principal
                 mPrincipal = mPrincipal + mInterestPaid;
                 // round off the principal to the nearest cent
                 mPrincipal = decimal.Round(mPrincipal, 2);
                 // output the result
                 Console.WriteLine(nYear + "-" + mPrincipal);
                 // skip over to next year
                 nYear = nYear + 1;
             }
         }
     }
     // wait for user to acknowledge the results
     Console.WriteLine("Press Enter to terminate...");
     Console.Read();
   }
 }
}
```

The output from a trial run of `CalculateInterestTable` appears as follows:

```
Enter principal:1234
Enter interest:12.5
Enter number of years:10

Principal     = 1234
Interest      = 12.5%
Duration      = 10years

1-1388.25
2-1561.78
3-1757.00
4-1976.62
5-2223.70
6-2501.66
7-2814.37
8-3166.17
9-3561.94
10-4007.18
Press Enter to terminate...
```

Each value represents the total principal after the number of years elapsed, assuming simple interest compounded annually. For example, the value of $1,234 at 12.5 percent is $3,561.94 after 9 years.

Most of the values show two decimal places for the cents in the amount. Because trailing zeros are not displayed in some versions of C#, some values may show only a single or even no digit after the decimal point. Thus, $12.70 may be displayed as 12.7. If so, you can fix this by using the special formatting characters described in Chapter 9. (C# 2.0 appears to show trailing zeros by default.)

The `CalculateInterestTable` program begins by reading the principal and interest values from the user and checking to make sure that they're valid. `CalculateInterestTable` then reads the number of years over which to iterate and stores this value in the variable `nDuration`.

Before entering the `while` loop, the program declares a variable `nYear`, which it initializes to 1. This will be the "current year" — that is, this number changes "each year" as the program loops. If the year number contained in `nYear` is less than the total duration contained in `nDuration`, the principal for "this year" is recalculated by calculating the interest based on the "previous year." The calculated principal is output along with the current-year offset.

The statement `decimal.Round()` rounds the calculated value to the nearest fraction of a cent.

The key to the program lies in the last line within the block. The statement `nYear = nYear + 1;` increments `nYear` by 1. If `nYear` begins with the value 3, its value will be 4 after this expression. This incrementing moves the calculations along from one year to the next.

After the year has been incremented, control returns to the top of the loop, where the value `nYear` is compared to the requested duration. In the example run, if the current year is less than 10, the calculation continues. After being incremented 10 times, the value of `nYear` becomes 11, which is greater than 10, and program control passes to the first statement after the `while` loop. That is to say, the program stops looping.

Most looping commands follow this same basic principle of incrementing a counter until it exceeds a previously defined value.

The counting variable `nYear` in `CalculateInterestTable` must be declared and initialized before the `while` loop in which it is used. In addition, the `nYear` variable must be incremented, usually as the last statement within the loop. As this example demonstrates, you have to look ahead to see what variables you will need. This pattern is easier after you've written a few thousand `while` loops, like I have.

When writing `while` loops, don't forget to increment the counting variable, as I have in this example:

```
int nYear = 1;
while (nYear < 10)
{
    // . . .whatever . . .
}
```

(I left off the `nYear = nYear + 1;`.) Without the increment, `nYear` is always 1, and the program loops forever. This is called an *infinite loop*. The only way to exit an infinite loop is to terminate the program (or reboot). (I guess nothing is truly infinite, with the possible exception of a particle passing through the event window of a black hole.)

Make sure that the terminating condition can be satisfied. Usually, this means your counting variable is being incremented properly. Otherwise, you're looking at an infinite loop, an angry user, bad press, and 50 years of poor harvest.

Infinite loops are a common mistake, so don't get embarrassed when you get caught in one.

Using the do...while loop

A variation of the `while` loop is the `do. . .while` loop. In this case, shown as follows, the condition is not checked until the end of the loop:

```
int nYear = 1;
do
{
    // . . .some calculation . . .
    nYear = nYear + 1;
} while (nYear < nDuration);
```

In contrast to the `while` loop, the `do. . .while` loop is executed at least once, regardless of the value of `nDuration`. The `do. . .while` loop is fairly uncommon in practice.

Breaking up is easy to do

You can use two special controls to bail out of a loop: `break` and `continue`. Executing the `break` command causes control to pass to the first expression immediately following the loop. The similar `continue` command passes control straight back up to the conditional expression at the top of the loop to start over and get it right this time.

I have rarely used `continue` in my programming career, and I doubt that many programmers even remember that it exists. Don't forget about it completely because it may be a trick question in an interview or crossword puzzle.

For example, suppose you want to take your money out of the bank as soon as the principal exceeds a certain number of times the original amount, irrespective of how many years' duration. (After all, how much money do you really need?) You could easily accommodate this by adding the following code within the loop:

```
if (mPrincipal > (maxPower * mOriginalPrincipal))
{
  break;
}
```

Anyone who watches *The Simpsons* as much as I do knows who `maxPower` is. (Hint: Doh!)

The `break` clause is not executed until the condition within the `if` comparison is true — in this case, until the calculated principal is `maxPower` times the original principal or more. Executing the `break` statement passes control outside of the `while(nYear <= nDuration)` statement, and the program continues on to resume execution immediately after the loop.

For a version of the interest table program with this addition, see the `CalculateInterestTableWithBreak` program on the CD. (I don't include the listing here, for brevity's sake.)

An example output from this program appears as follows:

```
Enter principal:100
Enter interest:25
Enter number of years:100

Principal    = 100
Interest     = 25%
Duration     = 100 years
Quit if a multiplier of 10 is reached

1-125.00
2-156.25
3-195.31
4-244.14
5-305.18
6-381.48
7-476.85
8-596.06
9-745.08
10-931.35
11-1164.19
Press Enter to terminate...
```

The program terminates as soon as the calculated principal exceeds $1,000 — thank goodness, you didn't have to wait 100 years!

Looping until you get it right

The CalculateInterestTable program is smart enough to terminate in the event that the user enters an invalid balance or interest amount. However, jumping immediately out of the program just because the user mistypes seems to be a little harsh. Even my user-unfriendly accounting program gives me three chances to get my password right before it gives up.

A combination of while and break enables the program to be a little more flexible. The CalculateInterestTableMoreForgiving program demonstrates the principle as follows:

```
// CalculateInterestTableMoreForgiving - calculate the interest
//          paid on a given principal over a period
//          of years. This version lets the user try again
//          to input the legal principal and interest.
using System;
namespace CalculateInterestTableMoreForgiving
{
  using System;
  public class Program
  {
    public static void Main(string[] args)
    {
      // define a maximum interest rate
      int nMaximumInterest = 50;
      // prompt user to enter source principal; keep prompting
      // until you get the correct value
      decimal mPrincipal;
      while(true)
      {
        Console.Write("Enter principal:");
        string sPrincipal = Console.ReadLine();
        mPrincipal = Convert.ToDecimal(sPrincipal);
        // exit if the value entered is correct
        if (mPrincipal >= 0)
        {
          break;
        }
        // generate an error on incorrect input
        Console.WriteLine("Principal cannot be negative");
        Console.WriteLine("Try again");
        Console.WriteLine();
      }
      // now enter the interest rate
      decimal mInterest;
      while(true)
```

```csharp
    {
      Console.Write("Enter interest:");
      string sInterest = Console.ReadLine();
      mInterest = Convert.ToDecimal(sInterest);
      // don't accept interest that is negative or too large . . .
      if (mInterest >= 0 && mInterest <= nMaximumInterest)
      {
        break;
      }
      //  . . .generate an error message as well
      Console.WriteLine("Interest cannot be negative " +
                        "or greater than " + nMaximumInterest);
      Console.WriteLine("Try again");
      Console.WriteLine();
    }
    // both the principal and the interest appear to be
    // legal; finally, input the number of years
    Console.Write("Enter number of years:");
    string sDuration = Console.ReadLine();
    int nDuration = Convert.ToInt32(sDuration);
    // verify the input
    Console.WriteLine();  // skip a line
    Console.WriteLine("Principal    = " + mPrincipal);
    Console.WriteLine("Interest     = " + mInterest + "%");
    Console.WriteLine("Duration     = " + nDuration + " years");
    Console.WriteLine();
    // now loop through the specified number of years
    int nYear = 1;
    while(nYear <= nDuration)
    {
      // calculate the value of the principal
      // plus interest
      decimal mInterestPaid;
      mInterestPaid = mPrincipal * (mInterest / 100);
      // now calculate the new principal by adding
      // the interest to the previous principal
      mPrincipal = mPrincipal + mInterestPaid;
      // round off the principal to the nearest cent
      mPrincipal = decimal.Round(mPrincipal, 2);
      // output the result
      Console.WriteLine(nYear + "-" + mPrincipal);
      // skip over to next year
      nYear = nYear + 1;
    }
    // wait for user to acknowledge the results
    Console.WriteLine("Press Enter to terminate...");
    Console.Read();
  }
 }
}
```

This program works largely the same way as do the previous examples, except in the area of the user input. This time, a `while` loop replaces the `if` statement used in previous examples to detect invalid input:

```
decimal mPrincipal;
while(true)
{
  Console.Write("Enter principal:");
  string sPrincipal = Console.ReadLine();
  mPrincipal = Convert.ToDecimal(sPrincipal);
  // exit if the value entered is correct
  if (mPrincipal >= 0)
  {
    break;
  }
  // generate an error on incorrect input
  Console.WriteLine("Principal cannot be negative");
  Console.WriteLine("Try again");
  Console.WriteLine();
}
```

This section of code inputs a value from the user within a loop. If the value of the text is okay, the program exits the loop and continues. However, if the input has an error, the user is presented with an error message, and control passes back to start over.

Think about it this way: The program continues to loop until the user gets it right.

Notice that the conditionals have been reversed because the question is no longer whether illegal input should generate an error message, but whether the correct input should exit the loop. In the interest section, for example, consider the following test:

```
mPrincipal < 0 || mPrincipal > nMaximumInterest
```

This test changes to the following:

```
mInterest >= 0 && mInterest <= nMaximumInterest
```

Clearly, `mInterest >= 0` is the opposite of `mInterest < 0`. What may not be so obvious is that the OR (`||`) operator is replaced with an AND (`&&`) operator. This says, "Exit the loop if the interest is greater than zero AND less than the maximum amount (in other words, is correct)."

By the way, how could you revise `CalculateInterestTableMoreForgiving` to let the user run calculation after calculation, entering new principal and interest figures each time until she wanted to quit? Hint: Use another `while(true)` loop with its own exit condition.

One last point to note: The mPrincipal variable must be declared outside of the loop due to scope rules, which I explain in the next section of this chapter.

It may sound obvious, but the expression true evaluates to true. Therefore, while(true) is your archetypical infinite loop. It is the embedded break command that exits the loop. Therefore, if you use the while(true) loop, make sure that your break condition can occur.

The output from an example execution of this program showing my ignorance appears as follows:

```
Enter principal:-1000
Principal cannot be negative
Try again

Enter principal:1000
Enter interest:-10
Interest cannot be negative or greater than 50
Try again

Enter interest:10
Enter number of years:5

Principal    = 1000
Interest     = 10%
Duration     = 5 years

1-1100.0
2-1210.00
3-1331.00
4-1464.10
5-1610.51
Press Enter to terminate...
```

The program refuses to accept a negative principal or interest, patiently explaining the mistake on each loop.

Explain exactly what the user did wrong before looping back for further input. Showing an example may also help, especially for formatting problems. A little diplomacy can't hurt, either.

Focusing on scope rules

A variable declared within the body of a loop is only defined within that loop. Consider the following code snippet:

```
int nDays = 1;
while(nDays < nDuration)
{
    int nAverage = nValue / nDays;
    //  . . .some series of commands . . .
    nDays = nDays + 1;
}
```

The variable nAverage is not defined outside the while loop. Various reasons for this exist, but consider this one: The first time the loop executes, the program encounters the declaration int nAverage and the variable is defined. On the second loop, the program again encounters the declaration for nAverage, and were it not for the scope rules, this would be an error because the variable is already defined.

I could provide other, more convincing reasons than this one, but this should do for now.

Suffice it to say that the variable nAverage goes away, as far as C# is concerned, as soon as the program reaches the closed brace and gets redefined each time through the loop.

Experienced programmers say that the *scope* of the variable nAverage is limited to the while loop.

Understanding the Most Common Control: the for Loop

The while loop is the simplest and second most commonly used looping structure in C#. However, the while loop is used about as often as metric tools in an American machine shop compared to the for loop.

The for loop has the following structure:

```
for(initExpression; condition; incrementExpression)
{
    // . . .body of code . . .
}
```

When the for loop is encountered, the program first executes the initExpression expression. It then executes the condition. If the condition expression is true, the program executes the body of the loop, which is surrounded by the braces immediately following the for command. Upon reaching the closed brace, control passes to incrementExpression and then back to condition, where the loop starts over again.

In fact, the definition of a `for` loop can be converted into the following `while` loop:

```
initExpression;
while(condition)
{
    //  . . .body of code . . .
    incrementExpression;
}
```

An example

You can better see how the `for` loop works with the following example:

```
// here is some C# expression or other
a = 1;
// now loop for awhile
for(int nYear = 1; nYear < nDuration; nYear = nYear + 1)
{
    //  . . .body of code . . .
}
// the program continues here
a = 2;
```

Assume that the program has just executed the `a = 1;` expression. Next, the program declares the variable `nYear` and initializes it to 1. That done, the program compares `nYear` to `nDuration`. If `nYear` is less than `nDuration`, the body of code within the braces is executed. Upon encountering the closed brace, the program jumps back to the top and executes the `nYear = nYear + 1` clause before sliding back over to the `nYear < nDuration` comparison.

The `nYear` variable is undefined outside the scope of the `for` loop, which includes the loop's heading as well as its body.

Why do you need another loop?

Why do you need the `for` loop if C# has an equivalent `while` loop? The short answer is that you don't — the `for` loop doesn't bring anything to the table that the `while` loop can't already do.

However, the sections of the `for` loop exist for convenience and to clearly establish the three parts that every loop should have: the setup, exit criteria, and increment. Not only is this easier to read, but it's also easier to get right. (Remember that the most common mistakes in a `while` loop are forgetting to increment the counting variable and failing to provide the proper exit criteria.)

Beyond any sort of song-and-dance justification that I may make, the most important reason to understand the `for` loop is that it's the loop that every-one uses and it's the one that you'll see 90 percent of the time when reading other people's code.

The `for` loop is designed so that the first expression initializes a counting vari-able and the last section increments it; however, the C# language does not enforce any such rule. You can do anything you want in these two sections — however, you would be ill-advised to do anything but initialize and increment the counting variable.

The increment operator is particularly popular when writing `for` loops. (I describe the increment operator along with other operators in Chapter 4.) The previous `for` loop is usually written as follows:

```
for(int nYear = 1; nYear < nDuration; nYear++)
{
    //  . . .body of code . . .
}
```

You almost always see the postincrement operator used in a `for` loop instead of the preincrement operator, although the effect in this case is the same. There's no reason other than habit and the fact that it looks cooler. (Next time you want to break the ice, just haul out your C# listing full of postincre-ment operators to show how cool you really are. It almost never works, but it's worth a try.)

The `for` loop has one variation that I really can't claim to understand. If the logical condition expression is missing, it is assumed to be `true`. Thus, `for(;;)` is an infinite loop.

You will see `for(;;)` used as an infinite loop more often than `while(true)`. I have no idea why that's the case.

Nested Loops

One loop can appear within an outer loop, as follows:

```
for( . . .some condition . . .)
{
  for( . . .some other condition . . .)
  {
    //  . . .do whatever . . .
  }
}
```

The inner loop is executed to completion upon each pass through the outer loop. The loop variable (such as `nYear`) used in the inner `for` loop is not defined outside the inner loop's scope.

A loop contained within another loop is called a *nested* loop. Nested loops cannot "cross." For example, the following is not possible:

```
do                   // start a do loop
{
  for( . . .)        // start some for loop
  {
  } while( . . .)    // end do..while loop
}                    // end for loop
```

I'm not even sure what that would mean, but that doesn't matter because the compiler will tell you it's not legal anyway.

A break statement within a nested loop breaks out of the inner loop only. In the following example, the break statement exits loop B and goes back into loop A:

```
// for loop A
for( . . .some condition . . .)
{
  // for loop B
  for( . . .some other condition . . .)
  {
    //  . . .do whatever . . .
    if (something is true)
    {
      break;          // breaks out of loop B and not A
    }
  }
}
```

C# doesn't have a `break` command that exits both loops simultaneously.

That's not as big a limitation as it sounds. In practice, the often-complex logic contained within such nested loops is better encapsulated in a function. Executing a `return` from within any of the loops exits the function, thereby bailing out of all loops, no matter how nested they may be. I describe functions and the `return` statement in Chapter 7.

The following whimsical `DisplayXWithNestedLoops` program uses a pair of nested loops to display a large *X* down the application console:

```
// DisplayXWithNestedLoops - use a pair of nested loops to
//                           create an X pattern
using System;
namespace DisplayXWithNestedLoops
```

```
{
  public class Program
  {
    public static void Main(string[] args)
    {
      int nConsoleWidth = 40;
      // iterate through the rows of the "box"
      for(int nRowNum = 0;
          nRowNum < nConsoleWidth;
          nRowNum += 2)
      {
        // now iterate through the columns
        for (int nColumnNum = 0;
             nColumnNum < nConsoleWidth;
             nColumnNum++)
        {
          // the default character is a space
          char c = ' ';
          // if the column number and row number are the same . . .
          if (nColumnNum == nRowNum)
          {
            //  . . .replace the space with a backslash
            c = '\\';
          }
          // if the column is on the opposite side of the row . . .
          int nMirrorColumn = nConsoleWidth - nRowNum;
          if (nColumnNum == nMirrorColumn)
          {
            //  . . .replace the space with a slash
            c = '/';
          }
          // output whatever character at the current
          // row and column
          Console.Write(c);
        }
        Console.WriteLine();
      }
      // wait for user to acknowledge the results
      Console.WriteLine("Press Enter to terminate...");
      Console.Read();
    }
  }
}
```

The `DisplayXWithNestedLoops` program begins by defining an arbitrary number of rows and columns representing the size of the *X* to be drawn. Make this number larger, and the *X* stretches off the bottom of the application window.

The program uses a `for` loop to iterate through the rows of the *X*. The program then enters a second `for` loop, which iterates across the columns of the display. This draws a matrix on the display. The only problem left is to decide which cells within the matrix get spaces, thereby making them invisible, and which cells get characters. Fill in the proper cells, and you get an *X*.

The program first defines a `char c`, which it initializes to the default value of space. The program then compares the row and column number. If they're equal, the program replaces the space with a backward slash.

Remember that a backslash is used to mark special characters. For example, `'\n'` is a newline. The special character `'\\'` is the backslash. This is called *escaping* a character, specifically the character after the backslash. Escaping a character tells the compiler to treat it in a special way.

By itself, replacing the space when the rows and columns are equal would draw a line from the upper left of the matrix to the bottom right. To get a mirrored slash, the program places a forward slash (`'/'`) when the number of the column on the opposite side is equal to the row number.

The result from this program is as follows:

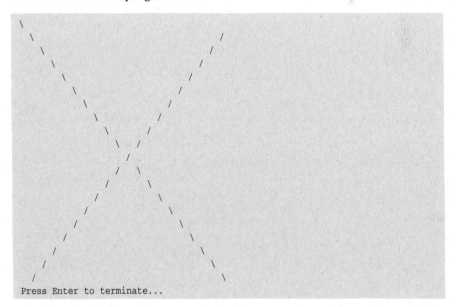

Not much to it, but I thought it was cute.

If you want to get serious, check out the `DisplaySin` program on the CD, which uses the same type of logic to display a sine wave vertically down the application display. I may be a nerd (actually there's no doubt about it), but I think that program is really cool. I cut my programming teeth on programs like that.

The switch Control

You often want to test a variable for numerous different values. For example, nMaritalStatus may be 0 for unmarried, 1 for married, 2 for divorced, 3 for widowed (I think I got them all — oh, wait), or 4 for none of your business. To differentiate among these values, you could use the following series of if statements:

```
if (nMaritalStatus == 0)
{
  // must be unmarried
  // . . .do something . . .
}
else
{
  if (nMaritalStatus == 1)
  {
    // must be married
    // . . .do something else . . .
```

And so on.

You can see that these repetitive if statements get old quickly. Testing for multiple cases is such a common occurrence that C# provides a special construct to decide between a set of mutually exclusive conditions. This control is called the switch, and it works as follows:

```
switch(nMaritalStatus)
{
  case 0:
          // . . .do the unmarried stuff . . .
          break;
  case 1:
          // . . .do the married stuff . . .
          break;
  case 2:
          // . . .do the divorced stuff . . .
          break;
  case 3:
          // . . .do the widowed stuff . . .
          break;
  case 4:
          // . . .get out of my face . . .
          break;
  default:
          // goes here if doesn't pass any of the cases;
          // this is probably an error condition
          break;
}
```

The expression at the top of the switch statement is evaluated. In this case, the expression is simply the variable nMaritalStatus. The value of that expression is then compared against the value of each of the cases. Control passes to the default clause if no match is found.

The argument to the switch statement can also be a string, as follows:

```
string s = "Davis";
switch(s)
{
  case "Davis":
          // . . .control will actually pass here . . .
          break;
  case "Smith":
          // . . .do the married stuff . . .
          break;
  case "Jones":
          // . . .do the divorced stuff . . .
          break;
  case "Hvidsten":
          // . . .do the widowed stuff . . .
          break;
  default:
          // goes here if doesn't pass any of the cases
          break;
}
```

Using the switch statement involves the following severe restrictions:

✔ The argument to the switch() must be one of the counting types or a string.

✔ Floating point values are excluded.

✔ The various case values must refer to values of the same type as the switch expression.

✔ The case values must be constant in the sense that their value must be known at compile time. (A statement such as case x is not legal unless x is some type of constant.)

✔ Each clause must end in a break statement (or some other exit command that you haven't seen yet, like return). The break statement passes control out of the switch.

This rule has one exception: A single case clause may have more than one case label, as in the following example:

```
string s = "Davis";
switch(s)
{
  case "Davis":
  case "Hvidsten":
```

```
          // do the same thing whether s is Davis or Hvidsten
          // since they're related
             break;
  case "Smith":
          //  . . .do the married stuff . . .
             break;
  default:
          // goes here if doesn't pass any of the cases
             break;
}
```

This approach enables the program to perform the same operation, whether the input is Davis or Hvidsten.

The Lowly goto Statement

You can transfer control in an unstructured fashion by using the goto statement. The goto statement is followed by one of these items:

- ✔ A label
- ✔ A case in a switch statement
- ✔ The keyword default, meaning the default clause of a switch statement

The idea of the latter two items is to jump from one case to another.

The following snippet demonstrates how the goto statement is used:

```
// if the condition is true . . .
if (a > b)
{
  //  . . .control passes unconditionally from the goto to the label
  goto exitLabel;
}
//  . . .whatever other code goes here . . .
exitLabel:
  // control continues here
```

The goto statement is unpopular for the very reason that makes it such a powerful control: It is almost completely unstructured. Tracking the flow of control through anything larger than a trivial piece of code can be difficult if you use goto. Can you say, "spaghetti code"?

Religious wars have sprung up over the use of the goto statement. In fact, the C# language itself has been criticized for the very inclusion of the control. Actually, goto is neither all that horrible nor necessary. Because you can almost always avoid using goto, I recommend staying away from it.

Part III

Object-Based Programming

The 5th Wave
By Rich Tennant

In this part . . .

It's one thing to declare a variable here or there and to add them and subtract them. It's quite another thing to write real programs that people can use — simple people, but people nonetheless. In this part, you discover how to group data and how to operate on that data. You begin to think about programs as collections of collaborating *objects* and start designing your own custom objects. These skills form the basis of all programming jobs you'll find in the classifieds.

Chapter 6

Collecting Data — The Class and the Array

*Y*ou can freely declare and use all the intrinsic data types — such as `int`, `double`, and `bool` — to store the information necessary to make your program the best that it can be. For some programs, these simple variables are enough. However, most programs need a means to bundle related data in a neat package.

Some programs need to bundle pieces of data that logically belong together but aren't of the same type. For example, a college enrollment application handles students, each with his or her own name, rank (grade point average), and serial number. Logically, the student's name may be a `string`, the grade point average could be a `double`, and the serial number a `long`. That type of program needs some way to bundle these three different types of variables into a single structure called `Student`. Fortunately, C# provides a structure known as the *class* for accommodating groupings of unlike-typed variables.

In other cases, programs need to collect a series of like-typed objects. Take, for example, a program designed to average grades. A `double` does a good job of representing an individual grade. However, you need some type of collection of `double` variables to contain all the many grades that students collect during their careers. C# provides the *array* for just this purpose.

Finally, a real program to process student records would need to graduate groups of students before they can set out on a life of riches and fame. This type of program needs both the class and the array concept rolled into one: arrays of students. Through the magic of C# programming, you can do this as well.

Showing Some Class

A *class* is a bundling of unlike data and functions that logically belong together into one tidy package. C# gives you the freedom to foul up your classes any way you want, but good classes are designed to represent *concepts*.

Analysts say that "a class maps concepts from the problem into the program." For example, suppose your problem is to build a traffic simulator. This traffic simulator is to model traffic patterns for the purpose of building streets, intersections, and highways. (I would really like you to build a traffic simulator that could fix the intersection in front of my house.)

Any description of a problem concerning traffic would include the term *vehicle* in its solution. Vehicles have a top speed that must be figured into the equation. They also have a weight, and some of them are clunkers. In addition, vehicles stop and vehicles go. Thus, as a concept, *vehicle* is part of the problem domain.

A good C# traffic simulator program would necessarily include the class `Vehicle`, which describes the relevant properties of a vehicle. The C# `Vehicle` class would have properties like `dTopSpeed`, `nWeight`, and `bClunker`. I address the `stop` and `go` parts in Chapters 7 and 8.

Because the class is so central to C# programming, the chapters in Part IV of this book spelunk the ins and outs of classes in much more detail. This chapter gets you started.

Defining a class

An example of the class `Vehicle` may appear as follows:

```
public class Vehicle
{
  public string sModel;         // name of the model
  public string sManufacturer;  // ditto
  public int nNumOfDoors;       // the number of doors on the vehicle
  public int nNumOfWheels;      // you get the idea
}
```

A class definition begins with the words `public class`, followed by the name of the class — in this case, `Vehicle`.

Like all names in C#, the name of the class is case sensitive. C# doesn't enforce any rules concerning class names, but an unofficial rule holds that the name of a class starts with a capital letter.

The class name is followed by a pair of open and closed braces. Within the braces, you have zero or more *members*. The members of a class are variables that make up the parts of the class. In this example, class `Vehicle` starts with the member `string sModel`, which contains the name of the model of the vehicle. Were this a car, the model name could be Trouper II. Hmm, have you ever seen or heard of a Trouper I? The second member of this example `Vehicle` class is the `string sManufacturer`. The final two properties are the number of doors and the number of wheels on the vehicle.

As with any variable, make the names of the members as descriptive as possible. Although I've added comments to the data members, that really isn't necessary. The name of each variable says it all.

The `public` modifier in front of the class name makes the class universally accessible throughout the program. Similarly, the `public` modifier in front of the member names makes them accessible to everything else in the program. Other modifiers are possible. Chapter 11 covers the topic of accessibility in more detail.

The class definition should describe the properties of the object that are salient to the problem at hand. That's a little hard to do right now because you don't know what the problem is, but you can see where I'm headed here.

What's the object?

Defining a `Vehicle` design is not the same thing as building a car. Someone has to cut some sheet metal and turn some bolts before anyone can drive an actual vehicle. A class object is declared in a similar but not identical fashion to an intrinsic object.

The term *object* is used universally to mean a "thing." Okay, that isn't too helpful. An `int` variable is an `int` object. A vehicle is a `Vehicle` object. You are a reader object. I am an author . . . Okay, forget that last one.

The following code segment creates a car of class `Vehicle`:

```
Vehicle myCar;
myCar = new Vehicle();
```

The first line declares a variable `myCar` of type `Vehicle`, just like you can declare a nSomethingOrOther of class `int`. (Yes, a class is a type, and all C# objects are defined as classes.) The `new Vehicle()` command creates a specific object of type `Vehicle` and stores the location into the variable `myCar`. The `new` has nothing to do with the age of `myCar`. My car could qualify for an antique license plate if it weren't so ugly. The `new` operator creates a new block of memory in which your program can store the properties of `myCar`.

In C# terms, you say that `myCar` is an object of class `Vehicle`. You also say that `myCar` is an instance of `Vehicle`. In this context, *instance* means "an example of" or "one of." You can also use the word *instance* as a verb, as in instantiating a `Vehicle`. That's what *new* does.

Compare the declaration of `myCar` with that of an `int` variable called `num`:

```
int num;
num = 1;
```

The first line declares the variable `num`, and the second line assigns an already-created constant of type `int` into the location of the variable `num`.

The intrinsic `num` and the object `myCar` are stored differently in memory. The constant 1 does not occupy memory because both the CPU and the C# compiler already know what a 1 is. Your CPU doesn't have the concept of a `Vehicle`. The `new Vehicle` expression allocates the memory necessary to describe a vehicle to the CPU, to C#, to the world, and yes, to the universe!

Accessing the members of an object

Each object of class `Vehicle` has its own set of members. The following expression stores the number 1 into the `nNumberOfDoors` member of the object referenced by `myCar`:

```
myCar.nNumberOfDoors = 1;
```

Every C# operation must be evaluated by type as well as by value. The object `myCar` is an object of type `Vehicle`. The variable `Vehicle.nNumberOfDoors` is of type `int` (look again at the definition of the `Vehicle` class). The constant 5 is also of type `int`, so the type of the variable on the right side of the assignment operator matches the type of the variable on the left.

Similarly, the following code stores a reference to the `string`s describing the model and manufacturer name of `myCar`:

```
myCar.sManufacturer = "BMW";      // don't get your hopes up
myCar.sModel = "Isetta";          // the Urkle-mobile
```

(The Isetta was a small car built during the 1950s with a single door that opened the entire front of the car.)

An example object-based program

The simple `VehicleDataOnly` program does the following:

- Defines the class `Vehicle`
- Creates an object `myCar`
- Assigns properties to `myCar`
- Retrieves those values out of the object for display

The code for the `VehicleDataOnly` program is as follows:

```csharp
// VehicleDataOnly - create a Vehicle object, populate its
//                   members from the keyboard and then write it
//                   back out
using System;
namespace VehicleDataOnly
{
  public class Vehicle
  {
    public string sModel;        // name of the model
    public string sManufacturer; // ditto
    public int nNumOfDoors;      // the number of doors on the vehicle
    public int nNumOfWheels;     // you get the idea
  }
  public class Program
  {
    // This is where the program starts
    static void Main(string[] args)
    {
      // prompt user to enter her name
      Console.WriteLine("Enter the properties of your vehicle");
      // create an instance of Vehicle
      Vehicle myCar = new Vehicle();
      // populate a data member via a temporary variable
      Console.Write("Model name = ");
      string s = Console.ReadLine();
      myCar.sModel = s;
      // or you can populate the data member directly
      Console.Write("Manufacturer name = ");
      myCar.sManufacturer = Console.ReadLine();
      // enter the remainder of the data
      // a temp is useful for reading ints
      Console.Write("Number of doors = ");
      s = Console.ReadLine();
      myCar.nNumOfDoors = Convert.ToInt32(s);
      Console.Write("Number of wheels = ");
      s = Console.ReadLine();
      myCar.nNumOfWheels = Convert.ToInt32(s);
      // now display the results
      Console.WriteLine("\nYour vehicle is a ");
      Console.WriteLine(myCar.sManufacturer + " " + myCar.sModel);
      Console.WriteLine("with " + myCar.nNumOfDoors + " doors, "
                        + "riding on " + myCar.nNumOfWheels
                        + " wheels");
      // wait for user to acknowledge the results
      Console.WriteLine("Press Enter to terminate...");
      Console.Read();
    }
  }
}
```

The program listing begins with a definition of the `Vehicle` class.

The definition of a class can appear either before or after class `Program` — it doesn't matter. However, you should adopt a style and stick with it. Bonus Chapter 2 on the CD shows the more conventional technique of creating a separate `.cs` file to contain each class, but just put the extra class in your `Program.cs` file for now.

The program creates an object `myCar` of class `Vehicle` and then populates each of the fields by reading the appropriate data from the keyboard. The input data isn't checked for legality. The program then spits out the information just entered in a slightly different format.

The output from executing this program appears as follows:

```
Enter the properties of your vehicle
Model name = Metropolitan
Manufacturer name = Nash
Number of doors = 2
Number of wheels = 4

Your vehicle is a
Nash Metropolitan
with 2 doors, riding on 4 wheels
Press Enter to terminate...
```

The calls to `Read()` as opposed to `ReadLine()` leave the cursor right after the output string. This makes the user's input appear on the same line as the prompt. In addition, adding the newline character `'\n'` generates a blank line without the need to execute `WriteLine()`.

Discriminating between objects

Detroit car manufacturers can track each car that they make without getting the cars confused. Similarly, a program can create numerous objects of the same class, as follows:

```
Vehicle car1 = new Vehicle();
car1.sManufacturer = "Studebaker";
car1.sModel = "Avanti";
// the following has no effect on car1
Vehicle car2 = new Vehicle();
car2.sManufacturer = "Hudson";
car2.sModel = "Hornet";
```

Creating an object `car2` and assigning it the manufacturer name Hudson has no effect on the `car1` Studebaker.

In part, the ability to discriminate between objects is the real power of the class construct. The object associated with the Hudson Hornet can be created, manipulated, and dispensed with as a single entity, separate from other objects, including the Avanti. (These are both classic automobiles, especially the latter.)

Can you give me references?

The dot operator and the assignment operator are the only two operators defined on reference types, as follows:

```
// create a null reference
Vehicle yourCar;
// assign the reference a value
yourCar = new Vehicle();
// use dot to access a member
yourCar.sManufacturer = "Rambler";
// create a new reference and point it to the same object
Vehicle yourSpousalCar = yourCar;
```

The first line creates an object yourCar without assigning it a value. A reference that has not been initialized is said to point to the *null object*. Any attempt to use an uninitialized reference generates an immediate error that terminates the program.

The C# compiler can catch most attempts to use an uninitialized reference and generate a warning at build time. If you somehow slip one past the compiler, accessing an uninitialized reference terminates the program immediately.

The second statement creates a new Vehicle object and assigns it to yourCar. The last statement in this code snippet assigns the reference yourSpousalCar to the reference yourCar. As shown in Figure 6-1, this has the effect of causing yourSpousalCar to refer to the same object as yourCar.

Figure 6-1:
The relationship between two references to the same object.

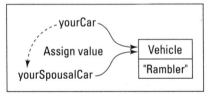

The following two calls have the same effect:

```
// build your car
Vehicle yourCar = new Vehicle();
yourCar.sModel = "Kaiser";
// it also belongs to your spouse
Vehicle yourSpousalCar = yourCar;
// changing one changes the other
yourSpousalCar.sModel = "Henry J";
Console.WriteLine("your car is a " + yourCar.sModel);
```

Executing this program would output `Henry J` and not `Kaiser`. Notice that `yourSpousalCar` does not point to `yourCar`; rather, both `yourCar` and `yourSpousalCar` refer to the same vehicle.

In addition, the reference `yourSpousalCar` would still be valid, even if the variable `yourCar` were somehow "lost" (went out of scope, for example), as shown in the following code:

```
// build your car
Vehicle yourCar = new Vehicle();
yourCar.sModel = "Kaiser";
// it also belongs to your spouse
Vehicle yourSpousalCar = yourCar;
// when she takes your car away . . .
yourCar = null;              // yourCar now references the "null object"
//  . . .yourSpousalCar still references the same vehicle
Console.WriteLine("your car was a " + yourSpousalCar.sModel);
```

Executing this program generates the output `your car was a Kaiser`, even though the reference `yourCar` is no longer valid.

The object is no longer *reachable* from the reference `yourCar`. The object does not become completely unreachable until both `yourCar` and `yourSpousalCar` are "lost" or nulled out.

At that point — well, at some unpredictable later point, anyway — C#'s *garbage collector* steps in and returns the space formerly used by that particular `Vehicle` object to the pool of space available for allocating more `Vehicles` (or `Students`, for that matter). I say a little more about garbage collection at the end of Chapter 12.

Classes that contain classes are the happiest classes in the world

The members of a class can themselves be references to other classes. For example, vehicles have motors, which have power and efficiency factors, including displacement. (I suppose a bicycle doesn't have a displacement.) You could throw these factors directly into the class as follows:

```
public class Vehicle
{
  public string sModel;        // name of the model
  public string sManufacturer; // ditto
  public int nNumOfDoors;      // the number of doors on the vehicle
  public int nNumOfWheels;     // you get the idea
  public int nPower;           // power of the motor [horsepower]
  public double displacement;  // engine displacement [liter]
}
```

However, power and engine displacement are not properties of the car. For example, my son's Jeep comes with two different motor options with drastically different horsepower. The 2.4-liter Jeep is a snail while the same car outfitted with the 4.0-liter engine is quite peppy.

The motor is a concept of its own and deserves its own class, as follows:

```
public class Motor
{
    public int nPower;              // power [horsepower]
    public double displacement;     // engine displacement [liter]
}
```

You can combine this class into the Vehicle as follows:

```
public class Vehicle
{
    public string sModel;           // name of the model
    public string sManufacturer;    // ditto
    public int nNumOfDoors;         // the number of doors on the vehicle
    public int nNumOfWheels;        // you get the idea
    public Motor motor;
}
```

Creating myCar now appears as follows:

```
// first create a Motor
Motor largerMotor = new Motor();
largerMotor.nPower = 230;
largerMotor.displacement = 4.0;
// now create the car
Vehicle sonsCar = new Vehicle();
sonsCar.sModel = "Cherokee Sport";
sonsCar.sManfacturer = "Jeep";
sonsCar.nNumOfDoors = 2;
sonsCar.nNumOfWheels = 4;
// attach the motor to the car
sonsCar.motor = largerMotor;
```

From the Vehicle, you can access the motor displacement in two stages. You can take one step at a time, as this code shows:

```
Motor m = sonsCar.motor;
Console.WriteLine("The motor displacement is " + m.displacement);
```

Or, you can access it directly, as shown here:

```
Console.Writeline("The motor displacement is " + sonsCar.motor.displacement);
```

Either way, you can only access the displacement through the Motor.

This example is bundled in the simple program `VehicleAndMotor` on the enclosed CD, not shown in full here.

Generating static in class members

Most data members of a class describe each object. Consider the `Car` class, as follows:

```
public class Car
{
  public string sLicensePlate;     // the license plate ID
}
```

The license plate ID is an *object property,* meaning that it describes each object of class `Car` uniquely. For example, thank goodness that my car has a different license plate from yours; otherwise, you may not make it out of your driveway, as shown in the following code:

```
Car cousinsCar = new Car();
cousinsCar.sLicensePlate = "XYZ123";

Car yourCar = new Car();
yourCar.sLicensePlate = "ABC789";
```

However, some properties exist that all cars share. For example, the number of cars built is a property of the class `Car` but not of any one object. These are called *class properties* and are flagged in C# with the keyword `static`, as follows:

```
public class Car
{
  public static int nNumberOfCars; // the number of cars built
  public string sLicensePlate;     // the license plate ID
}
```

Static members are not accessed through the object. Instead, you access them via the class itself, as the following code snippet demonstrates:

```
// create a new object of class Car
Car newCar = new Car();
newCar.sLicensePlate = "ABC123";
// now increment the count of cars to reflect the new one
Car.nNumberOfCars++;
```

The object member `newCar.sLicensePlate` is accessed through the object `newCar`, while the class (static) member `Car.nNumberOfCars` is accessed through the class `Car`. All `Car`s share the same `nNumberOfCars` member.

Defining const data members

One special type of static is the `const` data member, which represents a constant. You must establish the value of a `const` variable in the declaration, and you may not change it anywhere within the program, as shown in the following code:

```
class Program
{
  // number of days in the year (including leap day)
  public const int nDaysInYear = 366;
  public static void Main(string[] args)
  {
    // this is an array, covered later in this chapter
    int[] nMaxTemperatures = new int[nDaysInYear];
    for(int index = 0; index < nDaysInYear; index++)
    {
      //  . . .accumulate the maximum temperature for each
      // day of the year . . .
    }
  }
}
```

You can use the constant `nDaysInYear` in place of the value 366 anywhere within your program. The `const` variable is useful because it can replace a mysterious constant such as 366 with the descriptive name `nDaysInYear` to enhance the readability of your program.

Actually, C# provides a second way to declare constants. You can preface a variable declaration with the `readonly` modifier, like so:

```
public readonly int nDaysInYear = 366;  // this could also be static
```

As with `const`, after you assign the initial value, it can't be changed. Although the reasons are too technical for this book, the `readonly` approach to declaring constants is preferable to `const`.

An alternative convention also exists for naming constants. Instead of naming them like variables (as in `nDaysInYear`), many programmers prefer to use uppercase letters separated by underscores, as in `DAYS_IN_YEAR`. This convention separates constants clearly from ordinary read-write variables.

The C# Array

Variables that contain single values are all well and good. Even class structures that can describe compound objects like a vehicle are critical. But you also need a construct for holding a set of objects, such as Bill Gates's extensive collection of vintage cars. The built-in class `Array` is a structure that can contain a series of elements of the same type (all `int` values, all `double` values, and so on, or all `Vehicle` objects, `Motor` objects, and so on).

The argument for the array

Consider the problem of averaging a set of 10 floating point numbers. Each of the 10 numbers requires its own `double` storage (averaging `int` variables could result in rounding errors, as described in Chapter 3), as follows:

```
double d0 = 5;
double d1 = 2;
double d2 = 7;
double d3 = 3.5;
double d4 = 6.5;
double d5 = 8;
double d6 = 1;
double d7 = 9;
double d8 = 1;
double d9 = 3;
```

Now, you need to accumulate each of these values into a common sum, which you then divide by 10 (the number of values):

```
double dSum = d0 + d1 + d2 + d3 + d4 + d5 + d6 + d7 + d8 + d9;
double dAverage = dSum / 10;
```

Listing each element by name is tedious. Okay, maybe it's not so tedious when you have only 10 numbers to average, but imagine averaging 100 or even 1,000 floating point values.

The fixed-value array

Fortunately, you don't need to name each element separately. C# provides the array structure that can store a sequence of values. Using an array, you can rewrite the preceding code segment as follows:

```
double[] dArray = {5, 2, 7, 3.5, 6.5, 8, 1, 9, 1, 3};
```

The `Array` class provides a special syntax that makes it more convenient to use. The double brackets [] refer to the way you access individual elements in the array, as follows:

```
dArray[0] corresponds to d0
dArray[1] corresponds to d1
. . .
```

Array bounds checking

The `FixedArrayAverage` program (see the section "The fixed-value array" in this chapter) loops through an array of 10 elements. Fortunately, the loop iterates through all 10 elements. But what if you had made a mistake and didn't iterate through the loop properly? You have the following two cases to consider:

What if you had only iterated through 9 elements? C# would not have considered this an error. If you want to read 9 elements of a 10-element array, who is C# to say any differently? Of course, the average would be incorrect, but the program wouldn't know that.

What if you had iterated through 11 (or more) elements? Now, C# cares a lot. C# does not allow you to index beyond the end of an array, for fear that you will overwrite some important value in memory. To test this, change the comparison in the `for` loop to the following, replacing the value 10 with 11 in the comparison:

```
for(int i = 0; i < 11; i++)
```

When you execute the program, you get a dialog box with the following error message:

```
IndexOutOfRangeException was unhandled
Index was outside the bounds of the array.
```

At first glance, this error message seems imposing. However, you can get the gist rather quickly: An `IndexOutOfRangeException` was reported. Clearly, C# is telling you that the program tried to access an array beyond the end of its range — accessing element 11 in a 10-element array. (Buried in the message details — under `StackTrace` — is information about the exact line from which the access was made, but you haven't progressed far enough in the book to understand the entire message completely.)

The 0th element of the array corresponds to d0, the 1th element to d1, and so on. It's common to refer to the 0th element as "dArray sub-0," the 1st element as "dArray sub-1," and so on.

The array's element numbers — 0, 1, 2, . . . — are known as the *index*.

In C#, the array index starts at 0 and not at 1. Therefore, you typically don't refer to the element at index 1 as the first element but the "oneth element" or the "element at index 1." The first element is the zeroth element. If you insist on using normal speech, just be aware that the first element is at index 0 and the second element is at index 1.

dArray wouldn't be much of an improvement were it not for the fact that the index of the array can be a variable. Using a `for` loop is easier than writing each element out by hand, as the following program demonstrates:

```
// FixedArrayAverage - average a fixed array of
//                      numbers using a loop
namespace FixedArrayAverage
{
  using System;
  public class Program
  {
    public static void Main(string[] args)
    {
      double[] dArray = {5, 2, 7, 3.5, 6.5, 8, 1, 9, 1, 3};
      // accumulate the values in the array
      // into the variable dSum
      double dSum = 0;
      for (int i = 0; i < 10; i++)
      {
        dSum = dSum + dArray[i];
      }
      // now calculate the average
      double dAverage = dSum / 10;
      Console.WriteLine(dAverage);
      // wait for user to acknowledge the results
      Console.WriteLine("Press Enter to terminate...");
      Console.Read();
    }
  }
}
```

The program begins by initializing a variable dSum to 0. The program then loops through the values stored in dArray, adding each one to dSum. By the end of the loop, dSum has accumulated the sum of all the values in the array. The resulting sum is divided by the number of elements to create the average. The output from executing this program is the expected 4.6. (You can check it with your calculator.)

The variable-length array

The array used in the example program FixedArrayAverage suffers from the following two serious problems:

- ✔ The size of the array is fixed at 10 elements.

- ✔ Worse yet, the value of those 10 elements is specified directly in the program.

A program that could read in a variable number of values, perhaps determined by the user during execution, would be much more flexible. It would work not only for the 10 values specified in FixedArrayAverage but also for any other set of values.

The format for declaring a variable-sized array differs slightly from that of a fixed-size, fixed-value array as follows:

```
double[] dArray = new double[N];
```

Here, N represents the number of elements to allocate.

The updated program VariableArrayAverage enables the user to specify the number of values to enter. Because the program retains the values entered, not only does it calculate the average, but it also displays the results in a pleasant format, as shown here:

```
// VariableArrayAverage - average an array whose size is
//                        determined by the user at run time.
//                        Accumulating the values in an array
//                        allows them to be referenced as often
//                        as desired. In this case, the array
//                        creates an attractive output.
namespace VariableArrayAverage
{
  using System;
  public class Program
  {
    public static void Main(string[] args)
    {
      // first read in the number of doubles
      // the user intends to enter
      Console.Write("Enter the number of values to average:");
      string sNumElements = Console.ReadLine();
      int numElements = Convert.ToInt32(sNumElements);
      Console.WriteLine();
      // now declare an array of that size
      double[] dArray = new double[numElements];
      // accumulate the values into an array
      for (int i = 0; i < numElements; i++)
      {
        // prompt the user for another double
        Console.Write("enter double #" + (i + 1) + ": ");
        string sVal = Console.ReadLine();
        double dValue = Convert.ToDouble(sVal);
        // add this to the array
        dArray[i] = dValue;
      }
      // accumulate 'numElements' values from
      // the array in the variable dSum
      double dSum = 0;
      for (int i = 0; i < numElements; i++)
      {
        dSum = dSum + dArray[i];
      }
      // now calculate the average
      double dAverage = dSum / numElements;
```

```
        // output the results in an attractive format
        Console.WriteLine();
        Console.Write(dAverage
                    + " is the average of ("
                    + dArray[0]);
        for (int i = 1; i < numElements; i++)
        {
          Console.Write(" + " + dArray[i]);
        }
        Console.WriteLine(") / " + numElements);
        // wait for user to acknowledge the results
        Console.WriteLine("Press Enter to terminate...");
        Console.Read();
      }
    }
  }
```

Look at the following output of a sample run in which you enter five sequential values, 1 through 5, and the program calculates the average to be 3:

```
Enter the number of values to average:5

enter double #1: 1
enter double #2: 2
enter double #3: 3
enter double #4: 4
enter double #5: 5


3 is the average of (1 + 2 + 3 + 4 + 5) / 5
Press Enter to terminate...
```

The VariableArrayAverage program begins by prompting the user for the number of values she intends to average. The result is stored in the int variable numElements. In the example, the number entered is 5.

The program continues by allocating an array dArray with the specified number of elements. In this case, the program allocates an array with five elements. The program loops the number of times specified by numElements, reading a new value from the user each time.

After the user enters the values, the program applies the same algorithm used in the FixedArrayAverage program to calculate the average of the sequence.

The final section generates the output of the average along with the numbers entered in an attractive format (attractive to me — beauty is in the eye of the beholder).

Getting console output just right is a little tricky. Follow each statement in the FixedArrayAverage carefully as the program outputs open parentheses, equal signs, plus signs, and each of the numbers in the sequence, and compare this with the output.

The `VariableArrayAverage` program probably doesn't completely satisfy your thirst for flexibility. You don't want to have to tell the program how many numbers you want to average. What you'd really like is to enter numbers to average as long as you want — and then tell the program to average what you've entered. In addition to the array, C# provides other types of *collections,* some of which can grow and shrink as necessary; Chapter 15 describes these collections, which give you a powerful, flexible alternative to arrays. Getting input directly from the user isn't the only way to fill up your array or other collection, either. Bonus Chapter 2 on the CD describes how to read an arbitrary number of data items from a file.

The Length property

The `for` loop used to populate the array in the `VariableArrayAverage` program begins as follows:

```
// now declare an array of that size
double[] dArray = new double[numElements];
// accumulate the values into an array
for (int i = 0; i < numElements; i++)
{
  // prompt the user for another double
  Console.Write("enter double #" + (i + 1) + ": ");
  string sVal = Console.ReadLine();
  double dValue = Convert.ToDouble(sVal);
  // add this to the array
  dArray[i] = dValue;
}
```

The `dArray` is declared to be `numElements` in length. Thus, the clever programmer (me) used a `for` loop to iterate through `numElements` of the array.

It would be a shame and a crime to have to schlep the variable `numElements` around with `dArray` everywhere it goes just so you know how long it is. Fortunately, that isn't necessary. An array has a property called `Length` that contains its length. `dArray.Length` has the same value as `numElements`.

The following `for` loop would have been preferable:

```
// accumulate the values into an array
for (int i = 0; i < dArray.Length; i++) ...
```

Why do the formats of fixed- and variable-length arrays differ so much?

On the surface, the syntax of fixed- and variable-length arrays look quite a bit different, as follows:

```
double[] dFixedLengthArray = {5, 2, 7, 3.5, 6.5, 8, 1, 9, 1, 3};
double[] dVariableLengthArray = new double[10];
```

The difference is that C# is trying to save you some work. C# allocates the memory for you in the case of the fixed-length array `dFixedLengthArray`. You could have done it yourself using the following code:

```
double[] dFixedLengthArray = new double[10] {5, 2, 7, 3.5, 6.5, 8, 1, 9, 1, 3};
```

Here, you have specifically allocated the memory using `new` and then followed that declaration with the initial values for the members of the array.

Lining Up Arrays of Objects

Programmers often must deal with sets of user-defined objects (classes). For example, a university needs some type of structure to describe the students who are attending the fine institution of higher learning. Pfft!

A bare-bones `Student` class appears as follows:

```
public class Student
{
  public string sName;
  public double dGPA;          // grade point average
}
```

This overly simple class contains nothing more than the student's name and grade point average.

The following line declares an array of `num` references to `Student` objects:

```
Student[] students = new Student[num];
```

`new Student[num]` does *not* declare an array of `Student` objects. This line declares an array of *references* to `Student` objects.

So far, each element `students[i]` references the `null` object because C# initializes new, undefined objects with `null`. You can also say that none of the elements in the array point to a `Student` object yet. First, you must populate the array as follows:

```
for (int i = 0; i < students.Length; i++)
{
    students[i] = new Student();
}
```

Now the program can enter the properties of the individual students as follows:

```
students[i] = new Student();
students[i].sName = "My Name";
students[i].dGPA = dMyGPA;
```

You can see this wonder in the following `AverageStudentGPA` program, which inputs information on a number of students and spits out the average of their GPAs:

```
// AverageStudentGPA - calculate the average GPAs (grade point
//                     averages) of a number of students.
using System;
namespace AverageStudentGPA
{
  public class Student
  {
    public string sName;
    public double dGPA;            // grade point average
  }
  public class Program
  {
    public static void Main(string[] args)
    {
      // find out how many students
      Console.WriteLine("Enter the number of students");
      string s = Console.ReadLine();
      int nNumberOfStudents = Convert.ToInt32(s);
      // allocate an array of Student objects
      Student[] students = new Student[nNumberOfStudents];
      // now populate the array
      for (int i = 0; i < students.Length; i++)
      {
        // prompt the user for the name - add one to
        // the index because people are 1-oriented while
        // C# arrays are 0-oriented
        Console.Write("Enter the name of student " + (i + 1) + ": ");
        string sName = Console.ReadLine();
        Console.Write("Enter grade point average: ");
        string sAvg = Console.ReadLine();
        double dGPA = Convert.ToDouble(sAvg);
        // create a Student from that data
        Student thisStudent = new Student();
        thisStudent.sName = sName;
        thisStudent.dGPA  = dGPA;
        // add the student object to the array
        students[i] = thisStudent;
      }
      // now average the students that you have
      double dSum = 0.0;
      for (int i = 0; i < students.Length; i++)
      {
        dSum += students[i].dGPA;
      }
      double dAvg = dSum / students.Length;
      // output the average
      Console.WriteLine();
      Console.WriteLine("The average of the " + students.Length
                        + " students is " + dAvg);
```

```
        // wait for user to acknowledge
        Console.WriteLine("Press Enter to terminate...");
        Console.Read();
      }
    }
  }
```

The program prompts the user for the number of students to consider. It then creates the properly sized array of references to Student objects.

The program now enters an initial for loop in which it populates the array. The user is prompted for the name and GPA of each student in turn. This data is used to create a Student object, which is promptly stuffed into the next element in the array.

After all the Student references are snuggled fast in their beds, the program enters a second loop. In this loop, the GPA of each student is read using the statement students[i].GPA. The GPAs are rounded up, summed, and averaged. The average is then output to the user.

Here's the output from a typical run from this program:

```
Enter the number of students
3
Enter the name of student 1: Randy
Enter grade point average: 3.0
Enter the name of student 2: Jeff
Enter grade point average: 3.5
Enter the name of student 3: Carrie
Enter grade point average: 4.0

The average of the 3 students is 3.5
Press Enter to terminate...
```

The name of an object reference variable should always be singular, as in student. The name of the variable should somehow include the name of the class, as in badStudent or goodStudent or sexyCoedStudent. The name of an array (or any other collection, for that matter) should be plural, as in students or phoneNumbers or phoneNumbersInMyPalmPilot. As always, this tip reflects the opinion of the authors and not this book's publisher nor any of its shareholders — C# doesn't care how you name your variables.

A Flow Control Made foreach Array

Given an array of objects of class Student, the following loop averages their grade point averages:

```
public class Student
{
```

```
    public string sName;
    public double dGPA;          // grade point average
}
public class Program
{
    public static void Main(string[] args)
    {
        //  . . .create the array . . .
        // now average the students that you have
        double dSum = 0.0;
        for (int i = 0; i < students.Length; i++)
        {
            dSum += students[i].dGPA;
        }
        double dAvg = dSum / students.Length;
        //  . . .do something with that array . . .
    }
}
```

The `for` loop iterates through the members of the array.

`students.Length` contains the number of elements in the array.

C# provides yet another control, called the `foreach` statement, that is designed specifically for iterating through containers such as the array. It works as follows:

```
// now average the students that you have
double dSum = 0.0;
foreach (Student stud in students)
{
    dSum += stud.dGPA;
}
double dAvg = dSum / students.Length;
```

The first time through the loop, the `foreach` fetches the first `Student` object in the array and stores it in the variable `stud`. On each subsequent pass, the `foreach` retrieves the next element. Control passes out of the `foreach` when all the elements in the array have been processed.

Notice that no index appears in the `foreach` statement. This greatly reduces the chance of error and is simpler to write.

Former C, C++, and Java programmers find the `foreach` a little uncomfortable at first because it is unique to C# (well, .NET); however, the `foreach` sort of grows on you. It is the easiest of all the looping commands for accessing arrays.

The `foreach` is actually more powerful than it would seem from this example. This statement works on other collection types in addition to arrays. (Chapter 15 and Bonus Chapter 3 discuss collections.) In addition, the example `foreach` handles multidimensional arrays (arrays of arrays, in effect), a topic beyond the scope of this book.

Sorting through Arrays of Objects

A common programming challenge is the need to sort the elements within an array. Just because an array cannot grow or shrink in size does not mean that the elements within the array cannot be moved, removed, or added. For example, the following code snippet swaps the location of two Student elements within the array students:

```
Student temp = students[i]; // save off the i'th student
students[i] = students[j];
students[j] = temp;
```

Here, the object reference in the *i*th location in the students array is saved off so that it is not lost when the second statement replaces it with another element. Finally, the temp variable is saved back into the *j*th location. Pictorially, this looks like Figure 6-2.

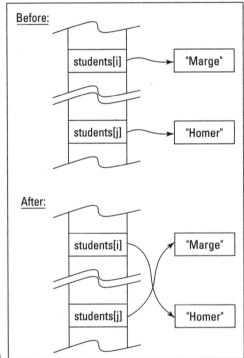

Figure 6-2: "Swapping two objects" actually means "swapping references to two objects."

Some data collections are more versatile than the array when it comes to adding and removing elements. Chapter 15 gets you started with collections.

The following program demonstrates how to use the ability to manipulate elements within an array as part of a sort. This particular sorting algorithm is called the *bubble sort.* It's not so great on large arrays with thousands of entries, but it's simple and effective on small arrays:

```
// SortStudents - this program demonstrates how to sort
//                an array of objects
using System;
namespace SortStudents
{
  class Program
  {
    public static void Main(string[] args)
    {
      // create an array of students
      Student[] students = new Student[5];
      students[0] = Student.NewStudent("Homer", 0);
      students[1] = Student.NewStudent("Lisa", 4.0);
      students[2] = Student.NewStudent("Bart", 2.0);
      students[3] = Student.NewStudent("Marge", 3.0);
      students[4] = Student.NewStudent("Maggie", 3.5);
      // output the list as is:
      Console.WriteLine("Before sorting:");
      OutputStudentArray(students);
      // now sort the list of students by grade (best
      // grade first)
      Console.WriteLine("\nSorting the list\n");
      Student.Sort(students);
      // display the resulting list
      Console.WriteLine("The students sorted by grade:");
      OutputStudentArray(students);
      // wait for user to acknowledge the results
      Console.WriteLine("Press Enter to terminate...");
      Console.Read();
    }
    // OutputStudentArray - display all the students in the array
    public static void OutputStudentArray(Student[] students)
    {
      foreach(Student s in students)
      {
        Console.WriteLine(s.GetString());
      }
    }
  }
  // Student - description of a student with name and grade
  class Student
  {
    public string sName;
    public double dGrade = 0.0;
    // NewStudent - return a new and initialized student object
    public static Student NewStudent(string sName, double dGrade)
    {
      Student student = new Student();
```

```
            student.sName = sName;
            student.dGrade = dGrade;
            return student;
        }
        // GetString - convert the current Student object into
        //             a string
        public string GetString()
        {
            string s = "";
            s += dGrade;
            s += " - ";
            s += sName;
            return s;
        }
        // Sort - sort an array of students in decreasing order
        //        of grade - use the bubble sort algorithm
        public static void Sort(Student[] students)
        {
            bool bRepeatLoop;
            // keep looping until the list is sorted
            do
            {
                // this flag is reset to true if an object is found
                // out of order
                bRepeatLoop = false;
                // loop through the list of students
                for(int index = 0; index < (students.Length - 1); index++)
                {
                    // if two of the students are in the wrong order . . .
                    if (students[index].dGrade <
                                      students[index + 1].dGrade)
                    {
                        // . . .then swap them . . .
                        Student to = students[index];
                        Student from = students[index + 1];
                        students[index]     = from;
                        students[index + 1] = to;
                        // . . .and flag the fact that you'll need to make
                        // another pass through the list of students
                        // (keep iterating through the loop checking
                        // until all the objects are in order)
                        bRepeatLoop = true;
                    }
                }
            } while (bRepeatLoop);
        }
    }
}
```

I start by examining the output of the program, just to convince myself that it works:

```
Before sorting:
0 - Homer
4 - Lisa
2 - Bart
3 - Marge
3.5 - Maggie

Sorting the list

The students sorted by grade:
4 - Lisa
3.5 - Maggie
3 - Marge
2 - Bart
0 - Homer
Press Enter to terminate...
```

In the interest of saving time, both yours and mine, I hard-coded the program to create five students. The NewStudent() method allocates a new Student object, initializes its name and grade, and returns the result. Homer gets his usual failing grade, while Lisa makes her A+. The program uses the OutputStudentArray() function to display the elements in the student array before it is sorted.

The program then invokes the Sort() function. After sorting, the program repeats the output process just to amaze you with the now-sorted result.

Of course, the key novelty to the SortStudents program is the Sort() method. This algorithm works by continuously looping through the list of students until the list is sorted. On each pass through the students array, the program compares each student to its neighbor. If the two are found to be out of order, the function swaps them and then flags the fact that the list was not found to be completely sorted. Figures 6-3 through 6-6 show the student list after each pass.

Figure 6-3:
Before
starting the
bubble sort.

Homer	0
Lisa	4
Bart	2
Marge	3
Maggie	3.5

Figure 6-4:
After pass 1 of the bubble sort.

Lisa	4
Bart	2
Marge	3
Maggie	3.5
Homer	0	←——— Homer works his way to the bottom.

Figure 6-5:
After pass 2 of the bubble sort.

Lisa	4	←——— Lisa stays at the top.
Marge	3	
Maggie	3.5	
Bart	2	←——— Bart drops down, too, but not below Homer.
Homer	0	

Figure 6-6:
The next-to-last pass results in a sorted list. The final pass terminates the sort because nothing changes.

Lisa	4
Maggie	3.5 ↰
Marge	3 ↲	} Swapping Maggie and Marge
Bart	2
Homer	0

Eventually, the best students, such as Lisa and Maggie, "bubble" their way to the top, while the worst students, like Homer, fall to the bottom as usual. Hence the name *bubble sort*.

The key to this or any other sort function is that the elements within the array can be reordered by assigning the reference value of one element in the array to that of another. Note that this assignment of references does not make a copy of the object and is, hence, a very quick operation.

Chapter 7

Putting on Some High-Class Functions

*P*rogrammers need the ability to break large programs into smaller chunks that are easier to handle. For example, the programs contained in previous chapters are reaching the limit of what a person can digest at one time.

C# lets you divide your code into chunks known as *functions*. Properly designed and implemented functions can greatly simplify the job of writing complex programs.

Defining and Using a Function

Consider the following example:

```
class Example
{
  public int nInt;                // non-static
  public static int nStaticInt    // static
  public void MemberFunction()    // non-static
  {
    Console.WriteLine("this is a member function");
  }
  public static void ClassFunction() // static
  {
    Console.WriteLine("this is a class function");
  }
}
```

The element `nInt` is a data member, just like those shown in Chapter 6. However, the element `MemberFunction()` is new. `MemberFunction()` is known as a *member function,* which is a set of C# code that you can execute by referencing the function's name. This is best explained by example — even I'm confused right now. (Actually, you've been seeing functions all along, starting with `Main()`.)

Note: The distinction between static and non-static class members is important. I cover part of that story in this chapter and continue in more detail in Chapter 8, where I also introduce the term *method,* which is commonly used in object-oriented languages like C# for non-static class functions.

The following code snippet assigns a value to the object data member `nInt` and the class, or static, member `nStaticInt`:

```
Example example = new Example(); // create an object
example.nInt = 1;                // initialize the data member through object
Example.nStaticInt = 2;          // initialize class member through class
```

The following snippet defines and accesses `MemberFunction()` and `ClassFunction()` in almost the same way:

```
Example example = new Example(); // create an object
example.MemberFunction();        // invoke the member function
                                 // with that object
Example.ClassFunction();         // invoke the class function with the class
// the following lines won't compile
example.ClassFunction();         // can't access class functions via an object
Example.MemberFunction();        // can't access member functions via class
```

The distinction between a class (static) function and a member (nonstatic) function, or method, mirrors the distinction between a class (static) variable and a member (nonstatic) variable that I describe in Chapter 6.

The expression `example.MemberFunction()` passes control to the code contained within the function. C# follows an almost identical process for `Example.ClassFunction()`. Executing this simple code snippet generates the output from the `WriteLine()` contained within each function, as follows:

```
this is a member function
this is a class function
```

After a function completes execution, it returns control to the point where it was called.

I include the parentheses when describing functions in text — as in `Main()` — to make them a little easier to recognize. Otherwise, I get confused trying to understand what I'm saying.

The bit of C# code within the two example functions does nothing more than write a silly `string` to the console, but functions generally perform useful and sometimes complex operations like calculating the sine of something, concatenating two `strings`, sorting an array of students, or surreptitiously e-mailing your URL to Microsoft. A function can be as large and complex as you want it to be, but it's best to strive for shorter functions, using the approach described in the next section.

An Example Function for Your Files

In this section, I take the monolithic `CalculateInterestTable` programs from Chapter 5 and divide them into several reasonable functions as a demonstration of how the proper definition of functions can help make the program easier to write and understand. The process of dividing up working code this way is known as *refactoring*, and Visual Studio 2005 provides a handy Refactor menu that automates the most common refactorings.

I explain the exact details of the function definitions and function calls in later sections of this chapter. This example simply gives an overview.

By reading the comments with the actual C# code removed, you should be able to get a good idea of a program's intention. If you cannot, you aren't commenting properly. (Conversely, if you can't strip out most comments and still understand the intention from the function names, you aren't naming your functions clearly enough and/or making them small enough.)

In outline form, the `CalculateInterestTable` program appears as follows:

```
public static void Main(string[] args)
{
  // prompt user to enter source principal
  // if the principal is negative, generate an error message

  // prompt user to enter the interest rate
  // if the interest is negative, generate an error message
  // finally, prompt user to input the number of years
  // display the input back to the user
  // now loop through the specified number of years
  while(nYear <= nDuration)
  {
    // calculate the value of the principal plus interest

    // output the result
  }
}
```

This illustrates a good technique for planning a function. If you stand back and study the program from a distance, you can see that it is divided into the following three sections:

- ✔ An initial input section in which the user inputs the principal, interest, and duration information
- ✔ A section that mirrors the input data so that the user can verify that the correct data was entered
- ✔ A final section that creates and outputs the table

These are good places to start looking for ways to refactor the program. In fact, if you further examine the input section of that program, you can see that the same basic code is used to input the following:

- ✔ The principal
- ✔ The interest
- ✔ The duration

That observation gives you another good place to look.

I have used this information to create the following `CalculateInterestTableWithFunctions` program:

```
// CalculateInterestTableWithFunctions - generate an interest table
//                                much like the other interest table
//                                programs, but this time using a
//                                reasonable division of labor among
//                                several functions.
using System;
namespace CalculateInterestTableWithFunctions
{
  public class Program
  {
    public static void Main(string[] args)
    {
        // Section 1 - input the data you will need to create the table
        decimal mPrincipal = 0;
        decimal mInterest = 0;
        decimal mDuration = 0;
        InputInterestData(ref mPrincipal,
                          ref mInterest,
                          ref mDuration);
        // Section 2 - verify the data by mirroring it back to the user
        Console.WriteLine();  // skip a line
        Console.WriteLine("Principal    = " + mPrincipal);
        Console.WriteLine("Interest     = " + mInterest + "%");
        Console.WriteLine("Duration     = " + mDuration + " years");
        Console.WriteLine();
        // Section 3 - finally, output the interest table
```

```
  OutputInterestTable(mPrincipal, mInterest, mDuration);
  // wait for user to acknowledge the results
  Console.WriteLine("Press Enter to terminate...");
  Console.Read();
}
// InputInterestData - retrieve from the keyboard the
//                     principal, interest, and duration
//                     information needed to create the
//                     future value table
// (This function implements Section 1 by breaking it down into
// its three components)
public static void InputInterestData(ref decimal mPrincipal,
                                     ref decimal mInterest,
                                     ref decimal mDuration)
{
  // 1a - retrieve the principal
  mPrincipal = InputPositiveDecimal("principal");
  // 1b - now enter the interest rate
  mInterest = InputPositiveDecimal("interest");
  // 1c - finally, the duration
  mDuration = InputPositiveDecimal("duration");
}
// InputPositiveDecimal - return a positive decimal number from
//                        the keyboard.
// (Inputting any one of principal, interest rate, or duration
// is just a matter of inputting a decimal number and making
// sure that it's positive)
public static decimal InputPositiveDecimal(string sPrompt)
{
  // keep trying until the user gets it right
  while(true)
  {
    // prompt the user for input
    Console.Write("Enter " + sPrompt + ":");
    // retrieve a decimal value from the keyboard
    string sInput = Console.ReadLine();
    decimal mValue = Convert.ToDecimal(sInput);
    // exit the loop if the value entered is correct
    if (mValue >= 0)
    {
      // return the valid decimal value entered by the user
      return mValue;
    }
    // otherwise, generate an error on incorrect input
    Console.WriteLine(sPrompt + " cannot be negative");
    Console.WriteLine("Try again");
    Console.WriteLine();
  }
}
// OutputInterestTable - given the principal and interest
//                       generate a future value table for
//                       the number of periods indicated in
//                       mDuration.
```

```
// (this implements section 3 of the program)
public static void OutputInterestTable(decimal mPrincipal,
                                       decimal mInterest,
                                       decimal mDuration)
{
  for (int nYear = 1; nYear <= mDuration; nYear++)
  {
    // calculate the value of the principal
    // plus interest
    decimal mInterestPaid;
    mInterestPaid = mPrincipal * (mInterest / 100);
    // now calculate the new principal by adding
    // the interest to the previous principal
    mPrincipal = mPrincipal + mInterestPaid;
    // round off the principal to the nearest cent
    mPrincipal = decimal.Round(mPrincipal, 2);
    // output the result
    Console.WriteLine(nYear + "-" + mPrincipal);
  }
}
```

I have divided the `Main()` section into three clearly distinguishable parts, each marked with bolded comments. I further divide the first section into 1a, 1b, and 1c.

Normally, you wouldn't include the bolded comments. The listings would get rather complicated with all the numbers and letters if you did. In practice, those types of comments aren't necessary if the functions are well thought out and their names clearly express the intent of each.

Part 1 calls the function `InputInterestData()` to input the three variables the program needs to create the table: `mPrincipal`, `mInterest`, and `mDuration`. Part 2 displays these three values just as the earlier versions of the program do. The final part outputs the table via the function `OutputInterestTable()`.

Starting at the bottom and working up, the `OutputInterestTable()` function contains an output loop with the interest rate calculations. This is the same loop used in the in-line, nonfunction `CalculateInterestTable` program in Chapter 5. The advantage of this version, however, is that when writing this section of code, you don't need to concern yourself with any of the details of inputting or verifying the data. In writing this function, you need to think, "Given the three numbers — principal, interest, and duration — output an interest table," and that's it. After you're done, you can return to the line that called the `OutputInterestTable()` function and continue from there.

OutputInterestTable() offers a good try-out of Visual Studio 2005's new Refactor menu. Take these steps to give it a whirl:

1. **Using the `CalculateInterestTableMoreForgiving` example from Chapter 5 as a starting point, select the code from the declaration of the `nYear` variable through the end of the `while` loop:**

```
int nYear = 0;            // you grab the loop variable
while(nYear <= nDuration)  // and the entire while loop
{
  //...
}
```

2. **Choose Refactor⇨Extract Method.**

3. **In the Extract Method dialog box, type** OutputInterestTable. **Examine the Preview Method Signature box and then click OK.**

   Notice that the proposed "signature" for the new "method" begins with the `private static` keywords and includes `mPrincipal`, `mInterest`, and `nDuration` in the parentheses. I introduce `private`, an alternative to `public`, in Chapter 11. For now, you can make the function `public` if you like. The rest is coming up.

The result of this refactoring consists of the following two pieces:

✔ A new `private static` function below `Main()`, called `OutputInterestTable()`

✔ The following line of code within `Main()` where the extracted code was:

```
mPrincipal = OutputInterestTable(mPrincipal, mInterest, nDuration);
```

Pretty cool! The same divide-and-conquer logic holds for `InputInterestData()`. However, the refactoring is more complex, so I do it by hand and don't show the steps. The full art of refactoring is beyond the scope of this book.

For `InputInterestData()`, you can focus solely on inputting the three decimal values. However, in this case, you realize that inputting each decimal involves identical operations on three different input variables. The `InputPositiveDecimal()` function bundles these operations into a set of general code that you can apply to principal, interest, and duration alike. Notice that the three `while` loops that take input in the original program get collapsed into one `while` loop inside `InputPositiveDecimal()`. This reduces code duplication, always a bad thing.

Making these kinds of changes to a program — making it clearer without changing its observable behavior — is called *refactoring*. Check out www.refactoring.com for tons of information about this technique.

This `InputPositiveDecimal()` function displays the prompt it was given and awaits input from the user. The function returns the value to the caller if it is not negative. If the value is negative, the function outputs an error message and loops back to try again.

From the user's standpoint, the modified program acts exactly the same as the in-line version in Chapter 5, which is just the point:

```
Enter principal:100
Enter interest:-10
interest cannot be negative
Try again

Enter interest:10
Enter duration:10

Principal    = 100
Interest     = 10%
Duration     = 10 years

1-110.0
2-121.00
3-133.10
4-146.41
5-161.05
6-177.16
7-194.88
8-214.37
9-235.81
10-259.39
Press Enter to terminate...
```

I have taken a lengthy, somewhat difficult program and refactored it into smaller, more understandable pieces while reducing some duplication. As we say in Texas, "You can't beat that with a stick."

Why bother with functions?

When Fortran introduced the function concept during the 1950s, the sole purpose was to avoid duplication of code by combining similar sections into a common element. Suppose you were to write a program that needed to calculate and display ratios in multiple places. Your program could call the `DisplayRatio()` function when needed, more or less for the sole purpose of avoiding duplicating code. The savings may not seem so important for a function as small as `DisplayRatio()`, but functions can grow to be much larger. Besides, a common function like `WriteLine()` may be invoked in hundreds of different places.

Quickly, a second advantage became obvious: It is easier to code a single function correctly — and doubly easier if the function is small. The `DisplayRatio()` function includes a check to make sure that the denominator is not zero. If you repeat the calculation code throughout your program, you could easily remember this test in some cases, and in other places forget.

Not so obvious is a third advantage: A carefully crafted function reduces the complexity of the program. A well-defined function should stand for some concept. You should be able to describe the purpose of the function without using the words *and* or *or*. The function should do one thing.

A function like `calculateSin()` is an ideal example. The programmer who has been tasked with this assignment can implement this complex operation without worrying about how it may be used. The applications programmer can use `calculateSin()` without worrying about how this operation is performed internally. This greatly reduces the number of things that the applications programmer has to worry about. By reducing the number of "variables," a large job gets accomplished by implementing two smaller, easier jobs.

Large programs such as a word processor are built up from many layers of functions at ever-increasing levels of abstraction. For example, a `RedisplayDocument()` function would undoubtedly call a `Reparagraph()` function to redisplay the paragraphs within the document. `Reparagraph()` would need to invoke a `CalculateWordWrap()` function to decide where to wrap the lines that make up the paragraph. `CalculateWordWrap()` would have to call a `LookUpWordBreak()` function to decide where to break a word at the end of the line, to make the sentences wrap more naturally. Each of these functions was described in a single, simple sentence. (Notice, also, how well-named these functions are.)

Without the ability to *abstract* complex concepts, writing programs of even moderate complexity would become almost impossible, much less creating an operating system such as Windows XP, a utility such as WinZip, a word processor like WordPerfect, or a game such as Halo, to name a few examples.

Having Arguments with Functions

A method such as the following example is about as useful as my hairbrush because no data passes into or out of the function:

```
public static void Output()
{
    Console.WriteLine("this is a function");
}
```

Compare this example to real-world functions that actually do something. For example, the sine operation requires some type of input — after all, you have to take the sine of something. Similarly, to concatenate two `string`s into one, you need two `string`s. So, the `Concatenate()` function requires at least two `string`s as input. "Gee, Wally, that sounds logical." You need some way to get data into and out of a function.

Passing an argument to a function

The values input to a function are called the *function arguments.* (Another name for argument is *parameter.*) Most functions require some type of arguments if they're going to do something. In this way, functions remind me of my son: We need to have an argument before he'll do anything. You pass arguments to a function by listing them in the parentheses that follow the function name. Consider the following small addition to the earlier Example class:

```
public class Example
{
  public static void Output(string funcString)
  {
    Console.WriteLine("Output() was passed the argument: "
                      + funcString);
  }
}
```

I could invoke this function from within the same class as follows:

```
Output("Hello");
```

I would get the following not-too-exciting output:

```
Output() was passed the argument: Hello
```

The program passes a reference to the string "Hello" to the function Output(). The function receives the reference and assigns it the name funcString. The Output() function can use funcString within the function just as it would any other string variable.

I can change the example in one minor way:

```
string myString = "Hello";
Output(myString);
```

This code snippet assigns the variable myString to reference the string "Hello". The call Output(myString) passes the object referenced by myString, which is your good old friend "Hello". Figure 7-1 depicts this process. From there, the effect is the same as before.

Passing multiple arguments to functions

When I ask my daughter to wash the car, she usually gives me more than just a single argument. Because she has lots of time on the couch to think about it, she can keep several at the ready.

Figure 7-1:
The call
`Output`
`(my`
`String)`
copies the
value of
`myString`
to `func`
`String`.

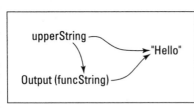

You can define a function with multiple arguments of varying types. Consider the following example function `AverageAndDisplay()`:

```
// AverageAndDisplay
using System;
namespace Example
{
  public class Program
  {
    public static void Main(string[] args)
    {
      // access the member function
      AverageAndDisplay("grade 1", 3.5, "grade 2", 4.0);
      // wait for user to acknowledge
      Console.WriteLine("Press Enter to terminate...");
      Console.Read();
    }
    // AverageAndDisplay - average two numbers with their
    //                     labels and display the results
    public static void AverageAndDisplay(string s1, double d1,
                                         string s2, double d2)
    {
      double dAverage = (d1 + d2) / 2;
      Console.WriteLine("The average of "  + s1
                      + " whose value is " + d1
                      + " and "            + s2
                      + " whose value is " + d2
                      + " is " + dAverage);
    }
  }
}
```

Executing this simple program generates the following output:

```
The average of grade 1 whose value is 3.5 and grade 2 whose value is 4 is 3.75
Press Enter to terminate...
```

The function `AverageAndDisplay()` is declared with several arguments in the order in which they are to be passed.

As usual, execution of the example program begins with the first statement after `Main()`. The first noncomment line in `Main()` invokes the function `AverageAndDisplay()`, passing the two `string`s `"grade 1"` and `"grade 2"` and the two `double` values 3.5 and 4.0.

The function `AverageAndDisplay()` calculates the average of the two `double` values, d1 and d2, passed to it along with their names contained in s1 and s2, and the calculated average is stored in `dAverage`.

Changing the value of an argument inside the function can lead to errors. It's wiser to assign the argument to a temporary variable and modify that.

Matching argument definitions with usage

Each argument in a function call must match the function definition in both type *and order.* The following is illegal and generates a build-time error:

```
// AverageWithCompilerError - this version does not compile!
using System;
namespace AverageWithCompilerError
{
  public class Program
  {
    public static void Main(string[] args)
    {
      Console.WriteLine("This program will not compile as-is.");
      // access the member function
      AverageAndDisplay("grade 1", "grade 2", 3.5, 4.0);
      // wait for user to acknowledge
      Console.WriteLine("Press Enter to terminate...");
      Console.Read();
    }
    // AverageAndDisplay - average two numbers with their
    //                     labels and display the results
    public static void AverageAndDisplay(string s1, double d1,
                                         string s2, double d2)
    {
      double dAverage = (d1 + d2) / 2;
      Console.WriteLine("The average of " + s1
                    + " whose value is " + d1
                    + " and "            + s2
                    + " whose value is " + d2
                    + " is " + dAverage);
    }
  }
}
```

C# can't match the type of each argument in the call to AverageAndDisplay() with the corresponding argument in the function definition. The string "grade 1" matches the first string in the function definition; however, the function definition calls for a double as its second argument rather than the string that's passed.

You can easily see that I simply transposed the second and third arguments. That's what I hate about computers — they take me too literally. I know what I said, but it's obvious what I meant!

To fix the problem, swap the second and third arguments.

Overloading a function does not mean giving it too much to do

You can give two functions within a given class the same name *as long as* their arguments differ. This is called *overloading* the function name.

The following example demonstrates overloading:

```
// AverageAndDisplayOverloaded - this version demonstrates that
//                               the average and display function
//                               can be overloaded
using System;
namespace AverageAndDisplayOverloaded
{
  public class Program
  {
    public static void Main(string[] args)
    {
      // access the first member function
      AverageAndDisplay("my GPA", 3.5, "your GPA", 4.0);
      Console.WriteLine();
      // access the second member function
      AverageAndDisplay(3.5, 4.0);
      // wait for user to acknowledge
      Console.WriteLine("Press Enter to terminate...");
      Console.Read();
    }
    // AverageAndDisplay - average two numbers with their
    //                     labels and display the results
    public static void AverageAndDisplay(string s1, double d1,
                                         string s2, double d2)
    {
      double dAverage = (d1 + d2) / 2;
      Console.WriteLine("The average of " + s1
                        + " whose value is " + d1);
      Console.WriteLine("and "             + s2
                        + " whose value is " + d2
```

```
                                      + " is " + dAverage);
        }
        public static void AverageAndDisplay(double d1, double d2)
        {
            double dAverage = (d1 + d2) / 2;
            Console.WriteLine("The average of " + d1
                            + " and "            + d2
                            + " is " + dAverage);
        }
    }
}
```

This program defines two versions of `AverageAndDisplay()`. The program invokes one and then the other by passing the proper arguments. C# can tell which function the program wants by comparing the call with the definition. The program compiles properly and generates the following output when executed:

```
The average of my GPA whose value is 3.5
and your GPA whose value is 4 is 3.75

The average of 3.5 and 4 is 3.75
Press Enter to terminate..
```

In general, C# does not allow two functions in the same program to have the same name. After all, how could C# tell which function you intended to call? However, C# includes the number and type of the function's arguments as part of its name. Normally, you may call a function `AverageAndDisplay()`. However, C# differentiates between the two functions `AverageAndDisplay(string, double, string, double)` and `AverageAndDisplay(double, double)`. When you say it that way, it's clear that the two functions are different.

Implementing default arguments

Often, you want to supply two (or more) versions of a function, as follows:

- ✔ One version would be the complicated version that provides complete flexibility but requires numerous arguments from the calling routine, several of which the user may not even understand.

    In practice, references to the "user" of a function often mean the programmer who is making use of the function. *User* does not always refer to the ultimate user of the program. Another term for this kind of user is client. (Often the client is you.)

- ✔ A second version of the function would provide acceptable, if somewhat bland, performance by assuming default values for some of the arguments.

You can easily implement default arguments using function overloading.

Consider the following pair of `DisplayRoundedDecimal()` functions:

```
// FunctionsWithDefaultArguments - provide variations of the same
//                      function, some with default arguments, by
//                      overloading the function name
using System;
namespace FunctionsWithDefaultArguments
{
  public class Program
  {
    public static void Main(string[] args)
    {
      // access the member function
      Console.WriteLine("{0}", DisplayRoundedDecimal(12.345678M, 3));
      // wait for user to acknowledge
      Console.WriteLine("Press Enter to terminate...");
      Console.Read();
    }
    // DisplayRoundedDecimal - convert a decimal value into a string
    //                      with the specified number of significant
    //                      digits
    public static string DisplayRoundedDecimal(decimal mValue,
                                    int nNumberOfSignificantDigits)
    {
      // first round the number off to the specified number
      // of significant digits
      decimal mRoundedValue =
                decimal.Round(mValue,
                                nNumberOfSignificantDigits);
      // convert that to a string
      string s = Convert.ToString(mRoundedValue);
      return s;
    }
    public static string DisplayRoundedDecimal(decimal mValue)
    {
      // invoke DisplayRoundedDecimal(decimal, int) specifying
      // the default number of digits
      string s = DisplayRoundedDecimal(mValue, 2);
      return s;
    }
  }
}
```

The `DisplayRoundedDecimal(decimal, int)` function converts the
`decimal` value provided into a `string` with the specified number of digits
after the decimal point. Because decimals are often used to display monetary
values, the most common choice is two digits after the decimal point. Therefore,
the `DisplayRoundedDecimal(decimal)` function provides the same conversion service but defaults the number of significant digits to two, thereby saving
the user from even worrying about the meaning of the second argument.

Notice that the generic (decimal) version of the function actually calls the more specific (decimal, int) version to perform its magic. This is more common than not, because it reduces duplication. The generic functions simply provide arguments that the programmer doesn't have the inclination to look up in the documentation.

Providing default arguments is more than just saving a lazy programmer a tiny bit of effort. Programming requires lots of concentration. Unnecessary trips to the reference documentation to look up the meaning of normally defaulted arguments distract the programmer from the main job at hand, thereby making the job more difficult, wasting time, and increasing the likelihood of mistakes. The author of the function understands the relationship between the arguments and therefore bears the onus of providing friendlier, overloaded versions of functions.

Visual Basic and C/C++ programmers take note: In C#, overloaded functions are the only way to implement default arguments. C# also doesn't allow optional arguments.

Passing value-type arguments

The basic variable types such as int, double, and decimal are known as *value-type* variables. You can pass value-type variables to a function in one of two ways. The default form is to *pass by value*. An alternate form is the *pass by reference*.

Programmers can get sloppy in their speech. In referring to value-types, when a programmer says "passing a variable to a function," that usually means "pass the value of a variable to a function."

Passing value-type arguments by value

Unlike object references, value-type variables like an int or a double are normally *passed by value*, which means that the value contained within the variable is passed to the function and not the variable itself.

Pass by value has the effect that changing the value of a value-type variable within a function does not change the value of that variable in the calling program. This is demonstrated in the following code:

```
// PassByValue - demonstrate pass by value semantics
using System;
namespace PassByValue
{
  public class Program
  {
    // Update - try to modify the values of the arguments
    //          passed to it; note that you can declare
```

```
//            functions in any order in a class
public static void Update(int i, double d)
{
  i = 10;
  d = 20.0;
}
public static void Main(string[] args)
{
  // declare two variables and initialize them
  int i = 1;
  double d = 2.0;
  Console.WriteLine("Before the call to Update(int, double):");
  Console.WriteLine("i = " + i + ", d = " + d);
  // invoke the function
  Update(i, d);
  // notice that the values 1 and 2.0 have not changed
  Console.WriteLine("After the call to Update(int, double):");
  Console.WriteLine("i = " + i + ", d = " + d);
  // wait for user to acknowledge
  Console.WriteLine("Press Enter to terminate...");
  Console.Read();
  }
 }
}
```

Executing this program generates the following output:

```
Before the call to Update(int, double):
i = 1, d = 2
After the call to Update(int, double):
i = 1, d = 2
Press Enter to terminate...
```

The call to Update() passes the *values* 1 and 2.0 and not a reference to the variables i and d. Thus, changing their value within the function has no more effect on the value of the variables back in the calling routine than asking for water with ice at an English pub.

Passing value-type arguments by reference

Passing a value-type argument to a function by reference is advantageous — in particular, when the caller wants to give the function the ability to change the value of the variable. The following PassByReference program demonstrates this capability.

C# gives the programmer the pass by reference capability via the ref and out keywords. The following slight modification to the example PassByValue program snippet from the previous section demonstrates the point:

```
// PassByReference - demonstrate pass by reference semantics
using System;
namespace PassByReference
{
  public class Program
  {
    // Update - try to modify the values of the arguments
    //          passed to it; note ref and out arguments
    public static void Update(ref int i, out double d)
    {
      i = 10;
      d = 20.0;
    }
    public static void Main(string[] args)
    {
      // declare two variables and initialize them
      int i = 1;
      double d;
      Console.WriteLine("Before the call to Update(ref int, out double):");
      Console.WriteLine("i = " + i + ", d is not initialized");
      // invoke the function
      Update(ref i, out d);
      // notice that i now equals 10 and d equals 20
      Console.WriteLine("After the call to Update(ref int, out double):");
      Console.WriteLine("i = " + i + ", d = " + d);
      // wait for user to acknowledge
      Console.WriteLine("Press Enter to terminate...");
      Console.Read();
    }
  }
}
```

The `ref` keyword indicates that C# should pass a reference to `i` and not just the value contained within this variable. Consequently, changes made within the function are exported back out of the calling routine.

In a similar vein, the `out` keyword says, "Pass back by reference, but I don't care what the initial value is because I'm going to overwrite it anyway." (That's a lot to pack into three words!) The `out` keyword is applicable when the function is only returning a value to the caller.

Executing the program generates the following output:

```
Before the call to Update(ref int, out double):
i = 1, d is not initialized
After the call to Update(ref int, out double):
i = 10, d = 20
Press Enter to terminate...
```

An out argument is always ref, though you don't say ref out. Also, you must pass *variables* to both ref and out. Passing literal values, such as 2, generates compiler errors.

Notice that the initial values of i and d are overwritten in the function Update(). After they are back in Main(), these variables retain their modified values. Compare this to the PassByValue() function in which the variables do not retain their modified values.

Don't pass a variable to a function by reference twice simultaneously

Do not, under any but the most dire circumstance, pass the same variable by reference twice in the same function call. This is more difficult to describe than it is to demonstrate. Consider the following Update() function:

```
// PassByReferenceError - demonstrate a potential error situation
//                        when calling a function using reference
//                        arguments
using System;
namespace PassByReferenceError
{
  public class Program
  {
    // Update - try to modify the values of the arguments
    //          passed to it
    public static void DisplayAndUpdate(ref int nVar1, ref int nVar2)
    {
      Console.WriteLine("The initial value of nVar1 is " + nVar1);
      nVar1 = 10;
      Console.WriteLine("The initial value of nVar2 is " + nVar2);
      nVar2 = 20;
    }
    public static void Main(string[] args)
    {
      // declare two variables and initialize them
      int n = 1;
      Console.WriteLine("Before the call to Update(ref n, ref n):");
      Console.WriteLine("n = " + n);
      Console.WriteLine();
      // invoke the function
      DisplayAndUpdate(ref n, ref n);
      // notice that n changes in an unexpected way
      Console.WriteLine();
      Console.WriteLine("After the call to Update(ref n, ref n):");
      Console.WriteLine("n = " + n);
      // wait for user to acknowledge
      Console.WriteLine("Press Enter to terminate...");
      Console.Read();
    }
  }
}
```

Update(ref int, ref int) is now declared to accept two int arguments by reference, which, in and of itself, is not a problem. The problem arises when the Main() function invokes Update() passing the same *variable* in both arguments. Within the function, Update() modifies nVar1, which references back to n from its initial value of 1 to the new value of 10. By the time Update() gets around to modifying nVar2, the value of n to which it refers has already been modified from its initial value of 1 to the new value of 10.

Why do some arguments come out but they don't go in?

C# is careful about keeping the programmer from doing something stupid. One of the stupid things that programmers do is forget to initialize a variable before they use it for the first time. (This is particularly true of counting variables.) C# generates an error when you try to use a variable that you've declared but not initialized:

```
int nVariable;
Console.WriteLine("this is an error " + nVariable);
nVariable = 1;
Console.WriteLine("but this is not " + nVariable);
```

However, C# cannot keep track of variables from within a function:

```
void SomeFunction(ref int nVariable)
{
    Console.WriteLine("is this an error or not? " + nVariable);
}
```

How can SomeFunction() know whether nVariable was initialized before being passed in the call? It can't. Instead, C# tracks the variable in the call — for example, the following call generates a compiler error:

```
int nUninitializedVariable;
SomeFunction(ref nUninitializedVariable);
```

If C# were to allow this call, SomeFunction() would have been passed a reference to an uninitialized (that is, *garbage*) variable. The out keyword lets both sides agree that the variable has not yet been assigned a value. The following example compiles just fine:

```
int nUninitializedVariable;
SomeFunction(out nUninitializedVariable);
```

By the way, passing an initialized variable as an out argument is legal:

```
int nInitializedVariable = 1;
SomeFunction(out nInitializedVariable);
```

The value in nInitializedVariable gets blown away within SomeFunction(), but there's no danger of garbage being passed about.

This is shown in the following example:

```
Before the call to Update(ref n, ref n):
n = 1

The initial value of nVar1 is 1
The initial value of nVar2 is 10

After the call to Update(ref n, ref n):
n = 20
Press Enter to terminate...
```

Exactly what's going on in this interplay between n, nVar1, and nVar2 is about as obvious as an exotic bird's mating dance. Neither the user programmer nor the Update() function author can anticipate this bizarre result. In other words, don't do it.

You can pass a single value as more than one argument in a single function call if all variables are passed by value.

Returning Values after Christmas

Many real-world operations create values to return to the caller. For example, sin() accepts an argument and returns the trigonometric sine. A function can return a value to the caller in two ways. The most common is via the return statement; however, a second method uses the *call by reference* feature.

Returning a value via return postage

The following code snippet demonstrates a small function that returns the average of its input arguments:

```
public class Example
{
  public static double Average(double d1, double d2)
  {
    double dAverage = (d1 + d2) / 2;
    return dAverage;
  }
  public static void Test()
  {
    double v1 = 1.0;
    double v2 = 3.0;
    double dAverageValue = Average(v1, v2);
    Console.WriteLine("The average of " + v1
                    + " and " + v2 + " is "
                    + dAverageValue);
```

```
    // this also works
    Console.WriteLine("The average of " + v1
                    + " and " + v2 + " is "
                    + Average(v1, v2));
  }
}
```

Notice first that I declare the function as `public static double Average()` — the `double` in front of the name refers to the fact that the `Average()` function returns a double-precision value to the caller.

The `Average()` function applies the names d1 and d2 to the double-precision values passed to it. It creates a variable dAverage to which it assigns the average of d1 and d2. It then returns the value contained in dAverage to the caller.

People sometimes say that "the function returns dAverage." This is a careless but common shorthand. Saying that dAverage or any other variable is passed or returned anywhere is imprecise. In this case, the value contained within dAverage is returned to the caller.

The call to `Average()` from the `Test()` function appears the same as any other function call; however, the `double` value returned by `Average()` is stored into the variable dAverageValue.

A function that returns a value, such as `Average()`, cannot return to the caller by encountering the closed brace of the function. If it did, how would C# know what value to return? You need a `return` statement.

Returning a value using pass by reference

A function can also return one or more values to the calling routine via the `ref` and `out` keywords. Consider the `Update()` example described in the section "Passing value-type arguments by reference," earlier in this chapter:

```
// Update - try to modify the values of the arguments
//          passed to it
public static void Update(ref int i, out double d)
{
  i = 10;
  d = 20.0;
}
```

The function is declared `void` because it does not return a value to the caller; however, because the variable i is declared `ref` and the variable d is declared `out`, any changes made to those variables within `Update()` retain their values in the calling function. In other words, they're passed back to the caller.

When do I return and when do I out?

You may be thinking, "A function can return a value to the caller, or it can use out (or ref, for that matter) to return a value to the caller. When do I use return and when do I use out?" After all, you could have written the Average() function as follows:

```
public class Example
{
  // Note: prefer putting 'out' parameters last
  public static void Average(double 1, double d2, out double dResults)
  {
    dResults = (d1 + d2) / 2;
  }
  public static void Test()
  {
    double v1 = 1.0;
    double v2 = 3.0;
    double dAverageValue;
    Average(dAverageValue, v1, v2);
    Console.WriteLine("The average of " + v1
                  + " and " + v2 + " is "
                  + dAverageValue;
  }
}
```

Typically, you return a value to the caller via the return statement rather than via the out directive, even though it's hard to argue with the results.

Outing a value-type variable like a double requires a somewhat inefficient extra process known as *boxing,* which I describe in Chapter 14. However, efficiency should not usually be a driving factor in your decision.

Typically, you use the out directive when a function returns more than one value to the caller — for example:

```
public class Example
{
  public static void AverageAndProduct(double d1, double d2, out double
                                    dAverage, out double dProduct)
  {
    dAverage = (d1 + d2) / 2;
    dProduct = d1 * d2;
  }
}
```

Returning multiple values from a single function doesn't happen as often as you may think. A function that returns multiple values usually does so by returning a single class object that encapsulates multiple values or by returning an array of values. Both approaches result in clearer code.

Null and zero references

A reference variable, as opposed to a value-type variable, is assigned the default value `null` when created. However, a null reference is not the same thing as a reference to zero. For example, the following two references are completely different:

```
class Example
{
  int nValue;
}


// create a null reference ref1
Example ref1;


// now create a reference to a zero object
Example ref2 = new Example();
ref2.nValue = 0;
```

The variable `ref1` is about as empty as my wallet. That variable points to the null object — that is, it points to no object. By comparison, `ref2` points to an object whose value is zero.

This difference is much less clear in the following example:

```
string s1;
string s2 = "";
```

This is essentially the same case: `s1` points to the null *object,* while `s2` points to an *empty string* (in programmer slang, an empty string is sometimes called a *null string* — a bit confusing). The difference is significant, as the following code shows:

```
// Test - test modules to utilize the TestLibrary
namespace Test
{
  using System;
  public class Program
  {
    public static void Main(string[] strings)
    {
      Console.WriteLine("This program exercises the function TestString()");
      Console.WriteLine();
      Example exampleObject = new Example();

      Console.WriteLine("Pass a null object:");
      string s = null;
      exampleObject.TestString(s);
      Console.WriteLine();

      // now pass the function a "null (empty) string"
      Console.WriteLine("Pass an empty string:");
      exampleObject.TestString("");
      Console.WriteLine();

      // finally, pass a real string
```

```
      Console.WriteLine("Pass a real string:");
      exampleObject.TestString("test string");
      Console.WriteLine();

      // wait for user to acknowledge the results
      Console.WriteLine("Press Enter to terminate...");
      Console.Read();
    }
  }

  class Example
  {
    public void TestString(string sTest)
    {
      // first test for a null string object (do this test first!)
      if (sTest == null)
      {
        Console.WriteLine("sTest is null");
        return;
      }
      // at this point, you know sTest doesn't point to the null object
      // but it could still point to an empty string
      // check to see if sTest points to a "null (empty) string"
      if (String.Compare(sTest, "") == 0)
      {
        Console.WriteLine("sTest references an empty string");
        return;
      }

      // Okay, output the string
      Console.WriteLine("sTest refers to: '" + sTest + "'");
    }
  }
}
```

The function `TestString()` uses the comparison `sTest == null` to test for a null string object. `TestString()` can use the `Compare()` function to test for an empty string. (`Compare()` returns a 0 if the two `string`s passed to it are equal.) Chapter 9 explains `string` comparison in detail.

The output from this program is as follows:

```
This program exercises the function TestString()
Pass a null object:
sTest is null
Pass an empty string:
sTest references an empty string
Pass a real string:
sTest refers to: 'test string'
Press Enter to terminate...
```

Defining a function with no value

The declaration `public static double Average(double, double)` declares a function `Average()` that returns the average of its arguments as a `double`. The number returned better be the average of the input values or someone has some serious explaining to do.

Some functions don't return a value to the caller. An earlier example function `AverageAndDisplay()` displays the average of its input arguments but doesn't return that average to the caller. That may not be such a good idea, but mine is not to question. Rather than leave the return type blank, a function like `AverageAndDisplay()` is declared as follows:

```
public void AverageAndDisplay(double, double)
```

The keyword `void`, where the return type would normally go, means the *non-type*. That is, the declaration `void` indicates that the `AverageAndDisplay()` function returns no value to the caller. (Regardless, every function declaration specifies a return type, even if it's `void`.)

A function that returns no value is referred to as a *void function*. That doesn't mean the function is empty or that it's used for some medical purposes. It simply refers to the initial keyword. By comparison, a function that returns some value is known as a *nonvoid function*.

A nonvoid function must pass control back to the caller by executing a `return` followed by the value to return to the caller. A `void` function has no value to return. A `void` function returns when it encounters a `return` with no value attached. Or, by default (if no `return` exists), a `void` function exits automatically when control reaches the closing brace of the function.

Consider the following `DisplayRatio()` function:

```
public class Example
{
  public static void DisplayRatio(double dNumerator,
                                  double dDenominator)
  {
    // if the denominator is zero . . .
    if (dDenominator == 0.0)
    {
      // . . .output an error message and . . .
      Console.WriteLine("The denominator of a ratio cannot be 0");
      // . . .return to the caller
      return;
    }
    // this is only executed if dDenominator is non-zero
    double dRatio = dNumerator / dDenominator;
    Console.WriteLine("The ratio of " + dNumerator
                + " over " + dDenominator
```

```
                           + " is " + dRatio);
    } // if the denominator isn't zero, the function exits here
}
```

The `DisplayRatio()` function first checks whether the `dDenominator` value is zero, as follows:

- ✔ If it is zero, the program displays an error message and returns to the caller without attempting to calculate a ratio. Doing so would divide the numerator value by zero and cause a CPU processor fault, also known by the more descriptive name *processor upchuck*.

- ✔ If `dDenominator` is nonzero, the program displays the ratio. The closed brace immediately following the `WriteLine()` is the closed brace of the `DisplayRatio()` function and, therefore, acts as the return point for the program.

The Main () Deal — Passing Arguments to a Program

Look at any console application in this book. In every case, execution begins with `Main()`. Consider the arguments in the following declaration of `Main()`:

```
public static void Main(string[] args)
{
   //  . . .your program goes here . . .
}
```

`Main()` is a static or class function of the class `Program` defined by the Visual Studio AppWizard. `Main()` returns no value and accepts as its arguments an array of `string` objects. What are these `string`s?

To execute a console application, the user enters the name of the program at the command line. The user has the option of adding arguments after the program name. You see this all the time in commands like `copy myfile C:\myDirectory`, which copies the file `myfile` into the `mydirectory` folder in the root directory of the `C:` drive.

As demonstrated in the following `DisplayArguments` example, the array of `string` values passed to `Main()` are the arguments to the current program:

```
// DisplayArguments - display the arguments passed to the
//                    program
using System;
namespace DisplayArguments
{
   public class Test  // the class containing Main() doesn't
```

```
                        // have to be called Program
  {
    public static int Main(string[] args)
    {
      // count the number of arguments
      Console.WriteLine("There are {0} program arguments",
                        args.Length);
      // the arguments are:
      int nCount = 0;
      foreach(string arg in args)
      {
        Console.WriteLine("Argument {0} is {1}",
                          nCount++, arg);
      }
      // wait for user to acknowledge the results
      Console.WriteLine("Press Enter to terminate...");
      Console.Read();
      return 0;  // other programs that run in the console window
                 // may check this return value; non-zero usually means failure
    }
  }
}
```

Notice first that `Main()` can also return a value rather than being declared `void`, as it is elsewhere in this book. But it must be `static`.

This program begins by displaying the length of the `args` array. This value corresponds to the number of arguments passed to the function. The program then loops through the elements of `args`, outputting each element to the console.

An example execution of this program (as described next, in which the first line is what you type at the command prompt) generates the following results:

```
DisplayArguments /c arg1 arg2
There are 3 program arguments
Argument 0 is /c
Argument 1 is arg1
Argument 2 is arg2
Press Enter to terminate...
```

You can see that the name of the program itself does not appear in the argument list. (Another function exists by which the program can find out its own name dynamically.) The user has typed three arguments, all strings. The first, /c, is a *switch*. Notice that the switch /c is not handled differently from other arguments — the program itself must handle the parsing of arguments to the program. Only the program knows what /c means to it.

Most console applications allow switches (codes) that control some details of the way the program operates. Bonus Chapter 5 has more to say about command-line switches.

Passing arguments from a DOS prompt

Execute the following steps to run the `DisplayArguments` program from a DOS prompt:

1. **Choose Start➪Programs➪Accessories➪Command Prompt.**

   You should be looking at a black window with a blinking cursor next to a silly `C:\>` prompt. (It may include some directories, too.)

2. **Navigate to the directory containing the** `DisplayArguments` **project by entering the following:**

   ```
   cd \C#Programs\DisplayArguments\bin\Debug
   ```

   (The default root folder for the example programs in this book is `C#Programs`. Use the root folder that you chose if it differs from the default.)

   The prompt changes to `C:\C#Programs\DisplayArguments\bin\ Debug>`.

   If all else fails, just use Windows to search for the folder. From Windows Explorer, right-click the folder `C:\C#Programs` and then choose Search, as shown in Figure 7-2.

Figure 7-2:
The Search facility is great for tracking down files, but narrow the search to a particular folder if your hard drive is large.

In the dialog box that's displayed, enter **DisplayArguments.exe,** and then click the Search button. The filename appears in the right pane of the Search Results window, as shown in Figure 7-3. Ignore the `DisplayArguments.exe` file in the `obj\Debug` directory — and the man behind the curtain, while you're at it. You want the one in `bin\Debug`. You may have to fiddle with Windows Explorer's right pane to find the full path name, depending on how deep in the folder hierarchy you find it. This is especially true if you store things in the `My Documents` folder. After you find the file, return to the console window and navigate to the file's location.

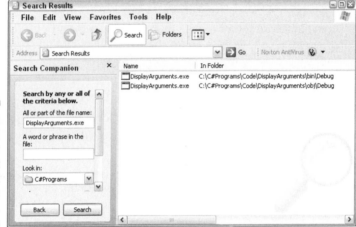

Figure 7-3:
There it is!
The folder
name is just
to the right
of the
filename.

Visual Studio 2005 normally places the executables it generates in a `bin\Debug` subdirectory; however, it could be `bin\release` or another directory, if you've changed the configuration in Visual Studio.

Windows has no problem with naming a file or directory with spaces included; however, DOS can get confused. For versions of Windows prior to Windows XP, you may need to put quotes around a filename or directory name with spaces. For example, I would navigate to a file in the `My Stuff` folder by using a command like this one:

```
cd \"My Stuff"
```

3. **With the command prompt showing** `C:\C#Programs\Display Arguments\bin\Debug>`, **execute the** `DisplayArguments.exe` **file found there by entering the following:**

```
displayarguments /c arg1 arg2
```

The program should respond with the output shown in Figure 7-4. Notice that the console window doesn't care whether you capitalize `DisplayArguments`, and you don't have to add the `.exe` extension.

Figure 7-4:
Executing
`Display`
`Arguments`
from the
DOS prompt
displays
arguments
of the
program
right back
at you.

```
C# Command Prompt - displayarguments /c arg1 arg2                    _ □ x
C:\C#Programs\DisplayArguments\bin\Debug>displayarguments /c arg1 arg2
There are 3 program arguments
Argument 0 is /c
Argument 1 is arg1
Argument 2 is arg2
Press Enter to terminate...
```

Passing arguments from a window

You can execute a program like `DisplayArguments` by typing its name on the command line of the Command Prompt window. You also can execute it from the Windows interface by double-clicking the name of the program either within a window or from Windows Explorer.

As shown in Figure 7-5, double-clicking `DisplayArguments` executes the program as if you had entered the program name on the command line with no arguments:

```
There are 0 program arguments
Press Enter to terminate...
```

Press Enter to terminate the program and close the window.

Dragging and dropping one or more files onto `DisplayArguments.exe` in Windows Explorer executes the program as if you had entered `Display Arguments` *filenames* on the command line. Simultaneously dragging and dropping the files `arg1.txt` and `arg2.txt` onto `DisplayArguments` executes the program with multiple arguments, as shown in Figure 7-6.

To drag and drop more than one file, select `file1.txt` in the list, hold down Ctrl, and then select the files you want, as shown in Figure 7-6. Now click and drag the set of files and drop them on `DisplayArguments`.

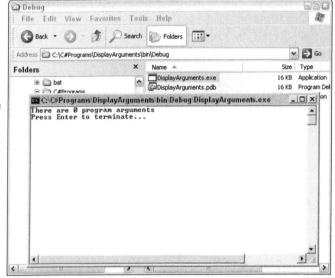

Figure 7-5:
In Windows
Explorer,
you can
execute the
console
program by
double-
clicking its
name.

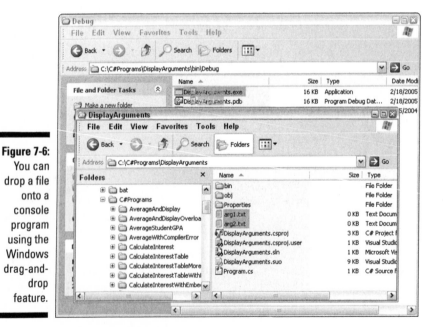

Figure 7-6:
You can
drop a file
onto a
console
program
using the
Windows
drag-and-
drop
feature.

The output from dropping the files `arg1.txt` and `arg2.txt` in Windows Explorer is shown in Figure 7-7.

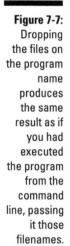

Figure 7-7:
Dropping
the files on
the program
name
produces
the same
result as if
you had
executed
the program
from the
command
line, passing
it those
filenames.

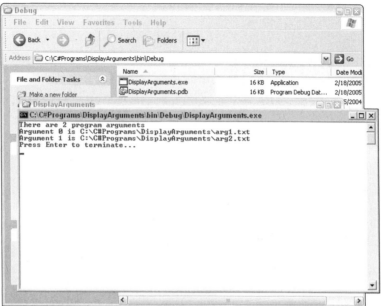

Notice that Windows passes the files to DisplayArguments in no particular order.

Passing arguments from Visual Studio 2005

To execute a program from Visual Studio 2005, make sure that the program builds without errors. Choose Build➪Build *programname* and check the Output window that appears for errors. The proper response is Build: 1 succeeded, 0 failed, 0 skipped. If you see anything else, your program will not start.

Executing your program without passing it any arguments is but a click away. After you have a successful build, choose Debug➪Start Debugging (or press F5) or Debug➪Start Without Debugging (press Ctrl+F5), and you're off to the races.

The `WriteLine()` function

You may have noticed that the `WriteLine()` construct that you've been using in the programs so far is nothing more than a function call that's invoked with something called a `Console` class, as follows:

```
Console.WriteLine("this is a function
    call");
```

`WriteLine()` is one of many predefined functions provided by the .NET framework library. `Console` is a predefined class that refers to the application console (also known as the Command Prompt or Command Window).

The argument to the `WriteLine()` that you've been using in previous examples is a single `string`. The + operator enables the programmer to combine `string`s, or to combine a `string` and an intrinsic variable before the sum is passed to `WriteLine()`, as follows:

```
string s = "Sarah"
Console.WriteLine("My name is " + s + "
    and my age is " + 3);
```

All that `WriteLine()` sees in this case is "My name is Sarah and my age is 3."

A second form of `WriteLine()` provides a more flexible set of arguments, as follows:

```
Console.WriteLine("My name is {0} and my
    age is {1}.",
              "Sarah", 3);
```

The first argument is called a format string. Here, the `string` `"Sarah"` is inserted where the symbol {0} appears — zero refers to the first argument after the format string. The integer 3 is inserted at the position marked by {1}. This form is more efficient than the previous example because concatenating `string`s is not as easy as it sounds. It's a time-consuming business, but someone has to do it.

It wouldn't be much to write home about if that were the only difference. However, this second form of `WriteLine()` also provides a number of controls on the output format. I describe these format controls in Chapter 9.

By default, Visual Studio executes a program without any arguments. If that's not what you want, you have to tell Visual Studio what arguments to use. Follow these steps to do so:

1. **Open the Solution Explorer by choosing View⇨Solution Explorer.**

   The Solution Explorer window provides a description of your *solution*. The solution consists of one or more projects. Each project describes a program. For example, the `DisplayArguments` project says that `Program.cs` is one of the files in your program and that your program is a Console application. The project also contains other properties, such as the arguments to use when executing `DisplayArguments` with Visual Studio.

2. **Right-click `DisplayArguments` in the Solution Explorer and choose Properties from the pop-up menu, as shown in Figure 7-8.**

   A window like that shown in Figure 7-9 appears, showing a lot of project variables that you can meddle with — please don't.

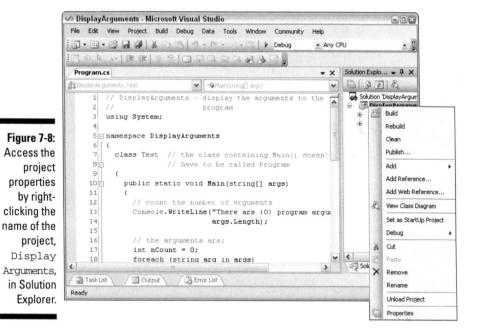

Figure 7-8:
Access the
project
properties
by right-
clicking the
name of the
project,
`Display`
`Arguments`,
in Solution
Explorer.

Figure 7-9:
Enter the
program
arguments
into the
Command
Line
Arguments
field of the
Debug tab
on the
`Display`
`Arguments`
tab.

3. **In the `DisplayArguments` tab, select Debug in the column of tabs down the left side.**

4. **In the `Command Line Arguments` field under Start Options, type in the arguments that you want to pass to your program when Visual Studio starts it.**

   Figure 7-9 shows the arguments `/c arg1.txt arg2.txt` being entered.

5. **Save, close the Properties window, and then execute the program normally by choosing Debug⇔Start.**

   As shown in Figure 7-10, Visual Studio opens a DOS window with the expected results:

   ```
   There are 3 program arguments
   Argument 0 is /c
   Argument 1 is arg1
   Argument 2 is arg2
   Press Enter to terminate...
   ```

The only difference between the output from executing the program from Visual Studio 2005 and from the command line is the absence of the program name in the display.

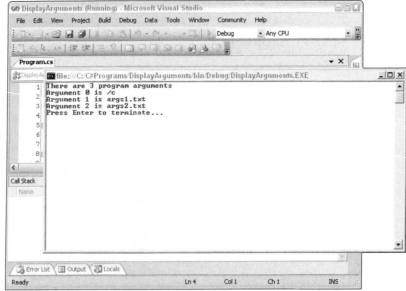

Figure 7-10:
Visual
Studio can
pass
arguments
to its
Console
Application
programs.

Chapter 8

Class Methods

*T*his chapter moves from the static functions discussed in Chapter 7 to nonstatic *methods* of a class. Static functions belong to the whole class, while methods belong to each instance created from the class. By the way, many programmers choose to call everything a method or everything a function rather than making the distinction as I have. But there are important differences between static and nonstatic class members.

Passing an Object to a Function

You pass object references as arguments to functions in the same way that you pass value-type variables, with one difference: You always pass objects by reference.

The following small program demonstrates how you pass objects — to functions, that is:

```
// PassObject - demonstrate how to pass an object

//                  to a function
using System;
namespace PassObject
{
  public class Student
  {
    public string sName;
  }
  public class Program
  {
```

```
public static void Main(string[] args)
{
  Student student = new Student();
  // set the name by accessing it directly
  Console.WriteLine("The first time:");
  student.sName = "Madeleine";
  OutputName(student);
  // change the name using a function
  Console.WriteLine("After being modified:");
  SetName(student, "Willa");
  OutputName(student);
  // wait for user to acknowledge
  Console.WriteLine("Press Enter to terminate...");
  Console.Read();
}
// OutputName - output the student's name
public static void OutputName(Student student)
{
  // output current student's name
  Console.WriteLine("Student's name is {0}", student.sName);
}
// SetName - modify the student object's name
public static void SetName(Student student, string sName)
{
  student.sName = sName;
}
}
}
```

The program creates a `student` object consisting of nothing but a name. (We like to keep 'em simple down here.) The program first sets the name of the `student` directly and passes it to the output function `OutputName()`. `OutputName()` displays the name of any `Student` object it receives.

The program then updates the name of the `student` by calling `SetName()`. Because all reference-type objects are passed by reference in C#, the changes made to `student` are retained back in the calling function. When `Main()` outputs the `student` object again, the name has changed, as shown in the following code:

```
The first time:
Student's name is Madeleine
After being modified:
Student's name is Willa
Press Enter to terminate...
```

The `SetName()` function can change the name within the `Student` object and make it stick.

Notice that you don't use the `ref` keyword when passing a *reference-type* object. Yet the effect is that the object's *contents* can be modified through the reference. However, if `OutputName()` tried to assign a whole new `Student` object to its `Student` parameter, this wouldn't affect the original `Student` object outside the function, as the following code shows:

```
Student student = new Student();
student.Name = "Madeleine";
OutputName(student);
Console.WriteLine(student.Name);  // still "Madeleine"
...
// a revised OutputName():
public static void OutputName(Student student)
{
  student = new Student(); // doesn't replace student outside OutputName()
  student.Name = "Pam";
}
```

Defining Object Functions and Methods

A class is supposed to collect the elements that describe a real-world object or concept. For example, a `Vehicle` class may contain data elements for maximum velocity, weight, carrying capacity, and so on. However, a `Vehicle` has active properties as well: the ability to start, to stop, and the like. These are described by the functions that go with that vehicular data. These functions are just as much a part of the `Vehicle` class as the data elements.

Defining a static member function

For example, you could rewrite the program from the previous section in a slightly better way as follows:

```
// PassObjectToMemberFunction - rely upon static member functions

//                               to manipulate fields within the object
using System;
namespace PassObjectToMemberFunction
{
  public class Student
  {
    public string sName;
    // OutputName - output the student's name
    public static void OutputName(Student student)
```

```
        {
            // output current student's name
            Console.WriteLine("Student's name is {0}", student.sName);
        }
        // SetName - modify the student object's name
        public static void SetName(Student student, string sName)
        {
            student.sName = sName;
        }
    }
    public class Program
    {
        public static void Main(string[] args)
        {
            Student student = new Student();
            // set the name by accessing it directly
            Console.WriteLine("The first time:");
            student.sName = "Madeleine";
            Student.OutputName(student);
            // change the name using a function
            Console.WriteLine("After being modified:");
            Student.SetName(student, "Willa");
            Student.OutputName(student);
            // wait for user to acknowledge
            Console.WriteLine("Press Enter to terminate...");
            Console.Read();
        }
    }
}
```

This program has only one significant change from the PassObject program in the previous section: I put the OutputName() and SetName() functions in the Student class.

Because of that change, Main() must reference the Student class in the calls to SetName() and OutputName(). The functions are now members of the class Student and not Program, the class in which Main() resides.

This is a small but significant step. Placing OutputName() within the class leads to a higher level of reuse: Outside functions that need to display the object can find OutputName(), along with other output functions, right there as part of the class. It doesn't have to be written separately by each program using the Student class.

This is also a better solution on a philosophical level. Class Program shouldn't need to worry about how to initialize the name of a Student object nor about how to output important material. The Student class should contain that information. Objects are responsible for themselves.

In fact, Main() should not initialize the name to Madeleine in the first place. It should call SetName() instead.

From within `Student`, one member function can invoke another without explicitly applying the class name. `SetName()` could invoke `OutputName()` without needing to reference the class name. If you leave off the class name, C# assumes that the function being accessed is in the same class.

Defining a method

The data members of an object — an *instance* of a class — are accessed with the object and not with the class. Thus, you may say the following:

```
Student student = new Student(); // create an instance of Student
student.sName = "Madeleine";     // access the member via the instance
```

C# enables you to invoke *nonstatic* member functions in the same way:

```
student.SetName("Madeleine");
```

The following example demonstrates this technique:

```
// InvokeMethod - invoke a member function through the object

using System;
namespace InvokeMethod
{
  class Student
  {
    // the name information to describe a student
    public string sFirstName;
    public string sLastName;
    // SetName - save off name information (no longer static)
    public void SetName(string sFName, string sLName)
    {
      sFirstName = sFName;
      sLastName  = sLName;
    }
    // ToNameString - convert the student object into a
    //                string for display (not static)
    public string ToNameString()
    {
      string s = sFirstName + " " + sLastName;
      return s;
    }
  }
  public class Program
  {
    public static void Main()
    {
      Student student = new Student();
      student.SetName("Stephen", "Davis");
      Console.WriteLine("Student's name is "
```

```
                      + student.ToNameString());
    // wait for user to acknowledge
    Console.WriteLine("Press Enter to terminate...");
    Console.Read();
  }
 }
}
```

The output from this program is this simple line:

```
Student's name is Stephen Davis
```

Other than having a much shorter name, this program is very similar to the earlier `PassObjectToMemberFunction` program. This version uses *nonstatic* functions to manipulate both a first and a last name.

The program begins by creating a new `Student` object, `student`. The program then invokes the `SetName()` function, which stores the two `strings` `"Stephen"` and `"Davis"` into the data members `sFirstName` and `sLastName`. Finally, the program calls the member function `ToNameString()`, which returns the name of the `student` by concatenating the two `strings`.

For historical reasons that have nothing to do with C#, a nonstatic member function is commonly known as a *method*. I use the term *method* for nonstatic member functions, and I use *function* for all other types. Some programmers use the terms *instance method* (nonstatic) and *class method* (static).

Look again at the `SetName()` method that updates the first and last name fields in the `Student` object. Which object does `SetName()` modify? Consider the following example to see how it works:

```
Student christa = new Student();   // here's one student
Student sarah = new Student();     // and here's a completely different one
christa.SetName("Christa", "Smith");
sarah.SetName("Sarah", "Jones");
```

The first call to `SetName()` updates the first and last name of the `christa` object. The second call updates the `sarah` object.

Thus, C# programmers say that a method operates on the *current* object. In the first call, the current object is `christa`; in the second, it's `sarah`.

Expanding a method's full name

A subtle but important problem exists with my description of method names. To see the problem, consider the following example code snippet:

```
public class Person
{
  public void Address()
  {
    Console.WriteLine("Hi");
  }
}
public class Letter
{
  string sAddress;
  // save off the address
  public void Address(string sNewAddress)
  {
    sAddress = sNewAddress;
  }
}
```

Any subsequent discussion of the Address() method is now ambiguous. The Address() method within Person has nothing to do with the Address() method in Letter. If my programmer friend tells me to access the Address() method, which Address() does he mean?

The problem lies not with the methods themselves, but with my description. In fact, no Address() method exists as an independent entity — only a Person.Address() and a Letter.Address() method. Attaching the class name to the beginning of the method name clearly indicates which method is intended.

This description is very similar to people's names. Within my family, I am known as Stephen. (Actually, within my family, I am known by my middle name, but you get the point.) There are no other Stephens within my family (at least not within my close family). However, there are two other Stephens where I work.

If I'm at lunch with some coworkers and the other two Stephens aren't present, the name *Stephen* clearly refers to me. Back in the trenches (or cubicles), yelling out "Stephen" is ambiguous because it could refer to any one of us. In that context, you need to yell out "Stephen Davis" as opposed to "Stephen Williams" or "Stephen Leija."

Thus, you can consider Address() to be the first name or nickname of a method, with its class as the family name.

Accessing the Current Object

Consider the following Student.SetName() method:

```
class Student
{
  // the name information to describe a student
  public string sFirstName;
  public string sLastName;
  // SetName - save off name information
  public void SetName(string sFName, string sLName)
  {
    sFirstName = sFName;
    sLastName  = sLName;
  }
}
public class Program
{
  public static void Main()
  {
    Student student1 = new Student();
    student1.SetName("Joseph", "Smith");
    Student student2 = new Student();
    student2.SetName("John", "Davis");
  }
}
```

The function `Main()` uses the `SetName()` method to update first `student1` and then `student2`. But you don't see a reference to either `Student` object within `SetName()` itself. In fact, no reference to a `Student` object exists. A method is said to operate on "the current object." How does a method know which one is the current object? Will the real current object please stand up?

The answer is simple. The current object is passed as an implicit argument in the call to a method — for example:

```
student1.SetName("Joseph", "Smith");
```

This call is equivalent to the following:

```
Student.SetName(student1, "Joseph", "Smith"); // equivalent call
                                  // (but this won't build properly)
```

I'm not saying you can invoke `SetName()` in two different ways, just that the two calls are semantically equivalent. The object identifying the current object — the hidden first argument — is passed to the function, just like other arguments. Leave that up to the compiler.

Passing an object implicitly is pretty easy to swallow, but what about a reference from one method to another? The following code illustrates calling one method from another:

```
public class Student
{
  public string sFirstName;
  public string sLastName;
  public void SetName(string sFirstName, string sLastName)
  {
    SetFirstName(sFirstName);
    SetLastName(sLastName);
  }
  public void SetFirstName(string sName)
  {
    sFirstName = sName;
  }
  public void SetLastName(string sName)
  {
    sLastName = sName;
  }
}
```

No object appears in the call to `SetFirstName()`. The current object continues to be passed along silently from one method call to the next. An access to any member from within an object method is assumed to be with respect to the current object. The upshot is that a method "knows" which object it belongs to.

What is the this keyword?

Unlike most arguments, the current object does not appear in the function argument list, so it is not assigned a name by the programmer. Instead, C# assigns this object the not-very-imaginative name `this`, useful in the few situations where you need to refer directly to the current object.

`this` is a C# keyword, and it may not be used for any other purpose, at least not without the express written permission of the National Football League.

Thus, you could write the previous example as follows:

```
public class Student
{
  public string sFirstName;
  public string sLastName;
  public void SetName(string sFirstName, string sLastName)
  {
    // explicitly reference the "current object" referenced by this
    this.SetFirstName(sFirstName);
    this.SetLastName(sLastName);
```

```
    }
    public void SetFirstName(string sName)
    {
      this.sFirstName = sName;
    }
    public void SetLastName(string sName)
    {
      this.sLastName = sName;
    }
}
```

Notice the explicit addition of the keyword `this`. Adding `this` to the member references doesn't add anything because `this` is assumed. However, when `Main()` makes the following call, `this` references `student1` throughout `SetName()` and any other method that it may call:

```
student1.SetName("John", "Smith");
```

When is this explicit?

You don't normally need to refer to `this` explicitly because it is understood where necessary by the compiler. However, two common cases require `this`. You may need it when initializing data members, as follows:

```
class Person
{
  public string sName;
  public int nID;
  public void Init(string sName, int nID)
  {
    this.sName = sName;  // argument names same as data member names
    this.nID = nID;
  }
}
```

The arguments to the `Init()` method are named `sName` and `nID`, which match the names of the corresponding data members. This makes the function easy to read because you know immediately which argument is stored where. The only problem is that the name `sName` in the argument list obscures the name of the data member. The compiler will complain about it.

The addition of `this` clarifies which `sName` is intended. Within `Init()`, the name `sName` refers to the function argument, but `this.sName` refers to the data member.

You also need `this` when storing off the current object for use later or by some other function. Consider the following example program `ReferencingThisExplicitly`:

```
// ReferencingThisExplicitly - this program demonstrates
//           how to explicitly use the reference to this
using System;
namespace ReferencingThisExplicitly
{
  public class Program
  {
    public static void Main(string[] strings)
    {
      // create a student
      Student student = new Student();
      student.Init("Stephen Davis", 1234);
      // now enroll the student in a course
      Console.WriteLine
            ("Enrolling Stephen Davis in Biology 101");
      student.Enroll("Biology 101");
      // display student course
      Console.WriteLine("Resulting student record:");
      student.DisplayCourse();
      // wait for user to acknowledge the results
      Console.WriteLine("Press Enter to terminate...");
      Console.Read();
    }
  }
  // Student - our university student class
  public class Student
  {
    // all students have a name and id
    public string sName;
    public int    nID;
    // the course in which the student is enrolled
    CourseInstance courseInstance;
    // Init - initialize the student object
    public void Init(string sName, int nID)
    {
      this.sName = sName;
      this.nID = nID;
      courseInstance = null;
    }
    // Enroll - enroll the current student in a course
    public void Enroll(string sCourseID)
    {
      courseInstance = new CourseInstance();
      courseInstance.Init(this, sCourseID);
    }
    // Display the name of the student
    // and the course
    public void DisplayCourse()
    {
      Console.WriteLine(sName);
      courseInstance.Display();
    }
  }
```

```
// CourseInstance - a combination of a student with
//                  university course
public class CourseInstance
{
  public Student student;
  public string sCourseID;
  // Init - tie the student to the course
  public void Init(Student student, string sCourseID)
  {
    this.student = student;
    this.sCourseID = sCourseID;
  }
  // Display - output the name of the course
  public void Display()
  {
    Console.WriteLine(sCourseID);
  }
}
}
```

This program is fairly mundane. The `Student` object has room for a name, an ID, and a single instance of a university course (not a very industrious student). `Main()` creates the `student` instance and then invokes `Init()` to initialize the instance. At this point, the `courseInstance` reference is set to `null` because the student is not yet enrolled in a class.

The `Enroll()` method enrolls the student by initializing `courseInstance` with a new object. However, the `CourseInstance.Init()` method takes an instance of `Student` as its first argument along with the course ID as the second argument. Which `Student` should you pass? Clearly, you need to pass the current `Student` — the `Student` referred to by `this`. (Thus, you can say that `Enroll()` enrolls `this` student in the `CourseInstance`.)

What happens when I don't have this?

Mixing class (static) functions and (nonstatic) object methods is like mixing cowboys and ranchers. Fortunately, C# gives you some ways around the problems between the two. Sort of reminds me of the song from *Oklahoma!* — "Oh, the function and the method can be friends . . ."

To see the problem, consider the following program snippet `MixingFunctionsAndMethods`:

```
// MixingFunctionsAndMethods - mixing class functions and object
//                             methods can cause problems
using System;
namespace MixingFunctionsAndMethods
{
  public class Student
```

```
  {
    public string sFirstName;
    public string sLastName;
    // InitStudent - initialize the student object
    public void InitStudent(string sFirstName, string sLastName)
    {
      this.sFirstName = sFirstName;
      this.sLastName = sLastName;
    }
    // OutputBanner - output the introduction
    public static void OutputBanner()
    {
      Console.WriteLine("Aren't we clever:");
      // Console.WriteLine(? what student do we use ?);
    }
    public void OutputBannerAndName()
    {
      // the class Student is implied but no this
      // object is passed to the static function
      OutputBanner();  // a static function
      // here, the current
Student object is passed explicitly
      OutputName(this);
    }
    // OutputName - output the student's name
    public static void OutputName(Student student)
    {
      // here the Student object is referenced explicitly
      Console.WriteLine("Student's name is {0}",
                        student.ToNameString());
    }
    // ToNameString - fetch the student's name
    public string ToNameString()
    {
      // here the current object is implicit -
      // this could have been written:
      // return this.sFirstName + " " + this.sLastName;
      return sFirstName + " " + sLastName;
    }
  }
  public class Program
  {
    public static void Main(string[] args)
    {
      Student student = new Student();
      student.InitStudent("Madeleine", "Cather");
      // output the banner and name
      Student.OutputBanner();
      Student.OutputName(student);
      Console.WriteLine();
      // output the banner and name again
      student.OutputBannerAndName();
```

```
        // wait for user to acknowledge
        Console.WriteLine("Press Enter to terminate...");
        Console.Read();
    }
  }
}
```

Start at the bottom of the program with `Main()` so that you can better see the problems. The program begins by creating a `Student` object and initializing its name. The simpleton program now wants to do nothing more than output the name preceded by a short message and banner.

`Main()` first outputs the banner and message using the class or static function approach. The program invokes the `OutputBanner()` function for the banner line and the `OutputName()` function to output the message and the student name. The function `OutputBanner()` outputs a simple message to the console. `Main()` passes the `student` object as an argument to `OutputName()` so that it can display the student's name.

Next, `Main()` uses the object function or method approach to outputting the banner and message by calling `student.OutputBannerAndName()`.

`OutputBannerAndName()` first invokes the static function `OutputBanner()`. The class `Student` is assumed. No object is passed because the static function does not need one. Next, `OutputBannerAndName()` calls the `OutputName()` function. `OutputName()` is also a static function, but it takes a `Student` object as its argument. `OutputBannerAndName()` passes `this` for that argument.

A more interesting case is the call to `ToNameString()` from within `OutputName()`. The latter function is declared `static` and therefore has no `this`. It does have an explicit `Student` object, which it uses to make the call.

The `OutputBanner()` function would probably like to call `ToNameString()` as well; however, it has no `Student` object to use. It has no `this` pointer because it is a static function and it was not passed an object explicitly.

 A static function cannot call a nonstatic method without explicitly providing an object. No object, no call. In general, static functions cannot access any nonstatic items in the class. But nonstatic (instance) methods can access static as well as instance items: static data members and static methods.

Getting Help from Visual Studio — Auto-Complete

Visual Studio has a powerful programming feature known as auto-complete. When you're typing in the name of a class or object in your source code,

Visual Studio tries to anticipate the name of the class or method that you're trying to enter.

Describing the Visual Studio auto-complete help is easiest by example. To show you how it works, I use the following section of code from the program `MixingFunctionsAndMethods`:

```
// output the banner and name
Student.OutputBanner();
Student.OutputName(student);
Console.WriteLine();
// output the banner and name again
student.OutputBannerAndName();
```

Auto-complete is great, but when you need more detail, choose Help⇨Index to browse online help. You can filter what the index shows, such as limiting it to C# or .NET. Start with the Index, using it like a book index. If necessary, also try Search (for a full-text search of topics) or Contents (to overview Help categories). You can also save favorite topics so that they're easy to find again. For much more on using Help, see Bonus Chapter 4 on the CD.

Getting help on built-in functions from the System Library

Using `MixingFunctionsAndMethods` as an example, as you begin typing `Console.`, Visual Studio responds with a list of all the methods of `Console`. When I enter **W**, Visual Studio moves the display down to the first method that begins with a *W*, which is `Write()`. Moving the selection down one by pressing the down-arrow key highlights `WriteLine()`. Immediately off to the right appears an explanation of the `WriteLine()` method, as shown in Figure 8-1. It also notes the 19 overloaded versions of the `WriteLine()` method — each with a different argument set, of course.

Figure 8-1:
The Visual Studio auto-complete feature is a great help in picking the proper method to use.

You complete the name of the function `WriteLine`. As soon as you enter the open parenthesis, Visual Studio changes the window to show the possible arguments, as shown in Figure 8-2.

Figure 8-2:
The Visual
Studio auto-
complete
feature also
displays a
list of the
possible
arguments
for `Write`
`Line()`.

```
42      Console.WriteLine (
43    )  ▲ 1 of 19 ▼  void Console.WriteLine ()
44           Writes the current line terminator to the standard output stream.
45      // ToNameString - fetch the student's name
46      public string ToNameString()
47      {
48          // here the current object is implicit -
49          // this could have been written:
50          // return this.sFirstName + " " + this.sLastName;
51          return sFirstName + " " + sLastName;
52      }
53    }
54
55    public class Program
56    {
57        public static void Main(string[] args)
```

Task List   Output   Error List

Ready   Ln 42   Col 25   Ch 25   INS

You don't actually have to type the name of the function. Suppose you had entered **WriteL**, enough to uniquely identify the method you want. Without completing `WriteLine`, enter the open parenthesis (or whatever the next character happens to be), and Visual Studio completes the name for you. Or press Ctrl-Spacebar to pop up the auto-complete menu.

Click the small arrows on the left side of the pop-up box to find the overloaded version of `WriteLine()` that you're looking for. Below the description of the function, you see the description of the first argument, if any. `WriteLine` has 19 overloaded versions for various data types. The first one you see in auto-complete (number 1 of 19) takes no arguments. Use the ↓ and ↑ keys to scroll through the overloads. For example, the second takes a `bool` argument. Number 14 of 19 first wants a *format string*, in which you can embed place-holders ({0}, {1}, . . .) for pieces of data that you list following the format string. And so on.

Using the WriteLine overload that takes a format string, as soon as you enter the `string` **"some string {0}"** (what do you want? it's late) followed by a comma, Visual Studio responds with a description of the second argument, as shown in Figure 8-3.

Visual Studio provides help with each subsequent argument as you move down the line. Of course, this help is available for every built-in method your program uses from the standard C# library.

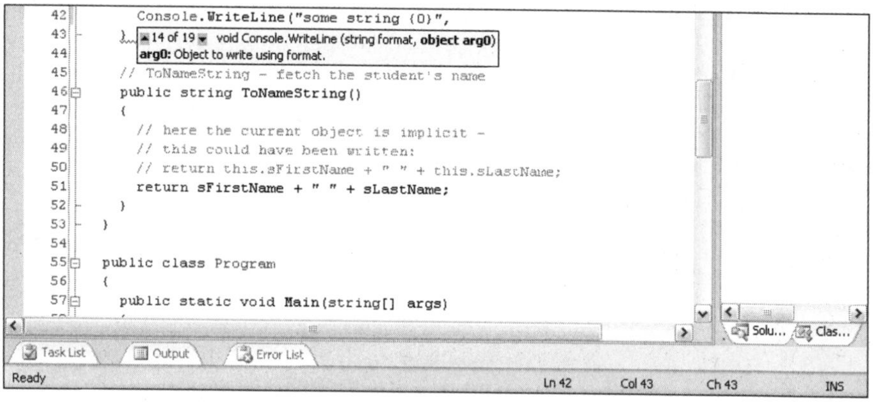

Figure 8-3:
The Visual
Studio auto-
complete
feature also
provides
help with
the different
arguments.

Getting help with your own functions and methods

Some help is available for your own functions, as well. (You can have just as much trouble remembering the arguments for your own as for .NET's.)

Continuing the example from the preceding section, say that you delete the very original `"some string {0}"` and replace it with the intended empty string: `Console.WriteLine()`. On the very next line, you enter **student.** As soon as you type the period, Visual Studio opens a list of the members of the `Student` object. If you continue typing the first letters of the member name, Visual Studio highlights the first item in the list that matches what you've typed so far, as shown in Figure 8-4. It also shows the highlighted method's declaration so you know how to use it.

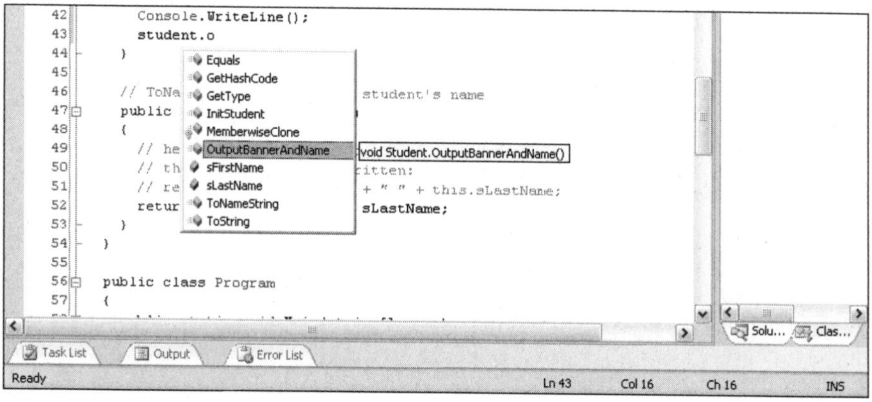

Figure 8-4:
Auto-
complete
works for
your own
methods,
as well.

The objects in the auto-complete list with the little boxes that slant from the lower left to the upper right denote data members. The little bricks that slant from upper left to lower right denote methods.

They're easier to discriminate in practice. The data member bricks are sort of an aqua color, and the method bricks are pink.

You may not recognize some of the methods. These are basic methods, such as `Equals` and `GetHashCode,` that all objects get for free. Mixed in with this standard group of methods is your very own `OutputBannerAndName()`.

Once again, entering an open parenthesis at this point allows the auto-complete feature to complete the name of the method.

The same feature works for functions, as well. As you enter the class name **Student** followed by the period, Visual Studio opens a list of the members of `Student`. As soon as you type **OutputN**, Visual Studio responds with a list of the arguments for the `OutputName()` method, as shown in Figure 8-5.

Figure 8-5:
The Visual Studio auto-complete feature gives you as much information as it can, whether for object methods or class functions.

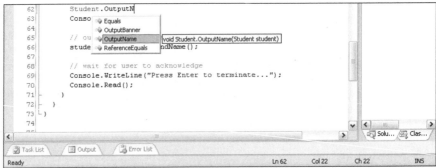

Adding to the help

The Visual Studio auto-complete feature gives you considerable help by anticipating the members you may want to access as soon you enter the class or object name.

Visual Studio can provide only limited help for user-created functions and classes. For example, Visual Studio doesn't know what the method `OutputName()` does, so there's no descriptive text below the basic method declaration you get in auto-complete. You would have to be dreaming about how nice it will be when you can finish this book and make megabucks as a

C# programmer to not get some idea because the name is reasonably descriptive. Fortunately, Visual Studio gives you a sneaky way to tell the auto-complete feature what the function does — and more. A lot more, if you want. Here's how.

You mark a normal comment line with two slashes: //. However, Visual Studio understands a special comment of three slashes in a row: ///. This type of *documentation comment* can provide Visual Studio with extra information to be used by the auto-complete feature.

To be fair, the Java language first introduced this concept. Java provides an extra program that can pull these three-slash comments out into a separate documentation file. C# adds an improvement by using such comments in its dynamic, edit-time help.

The documentation comment can contain any combination of the elements shown in Table 8-1.

Table 8-1	The Common Documentation Comment Instructions
Instruction	*What It Means*
`<summary></summary>`	Describes the function itself. Displays when you enter the name of the function during editing.
`<param></param>`	Describes an argument to the function. Displays after you type in the function name and the open parenthesis, prompting you about what you should enter next. Use one set of `<param>` tags per argument.
`<returns></returns>`	Describes the value returned by the function.

Documentation comments follow XML/HTML rules: A command starts with a `<command>` tag and ends with a `</command>` tag. In fact, they are normally known as *XML tags* due to their relationship to XML.

Numerous other XML tags are available for documentation comments. For more information, choose Help➪Index and then look under "XML documentation features [C#]."

The following example is a commented version of the `MixingFunctionsAnd-Methods` program:

```
// MixingFunctionsAndMethodsWithXMLTags - mixing class functions
//                       and object methods can cause problems
using System;
namespace MixingFunctionsAndMethods
{
    /// <summary>
```

```
/// Simple description of a student
/// </summary>
public class Student
{
  /// <summary>
  /// Student's given name
  /// </summary>
  public string sFirstName;
  /// <summary>
  /// Student's family name
  /// </summary>
  public string sLastName;

  // InitStudent
  /// <summary>
  /// Initializes the student object before it can be used.
  /// </summary>
  /// <param name="sFirstName">Student's given name</param>
  /// <param name="sLastName">Student's family name</param>
  public void InitStudent(string sFirstName, string sLastName)
  {
    this.sFirstName = sFirstName;
    this.sLastName = sLastName;
  }
  // OutputBanner
  /// <summary>
  /// Output a banner before displaying student names
  /// </summary>
  public static void OutputBanner()
  {
    Console.WriteLine("Aren't we clever:");
    // Console.WriteLine(? what student do we use ?);
  }

  // OutputBannerAndName
  /// <summary>
  /// Output a banner followed by the current student's name
  /// </summary>
  public void OutputBannerAndName()
  {
    // the class Student is implied but no this
    // object is passed to the static method
    OutputBanner();

    // no this object is passed, but the current
    // Student object is passed explicitly
    OutputName(this, 5);
  }

  // OutputName
  /// <summary>
  /// Outputs the student's name to the console
  /// </summary>
```

```
/// <param name="student">The student whose name you
///                        want to display</param>
/// <param name="nIndent">Number of spaces to indent</param>
/// <returns>The string that was output</returns>
public static string OutputName(Student student,
                                int nIndent)
{
  // here the Student object is referenced explicitly
  string s = new String(' ', nIndent);
  s += String.Format("Student's name is {0}",
                     student.ToNameString());
  Console.WriteLine(s);
  return s;
}

// ToNameString
/// <summary>
/// Convert the student's name into a string for display
/// </summary>
/// <returns>The stringified student name</returns>
public string ToNameString()
{
  // here the current object is implicit -
  // this could have been written:
  // return this.sFirstName + " " + this.sLastName;
  return sFirstName + " " + sLastName;
}
}

/// <summary>
/// Class to exercise the Student class
/// </summary>
public class Program
{
  /// <summary>
  /// The program starts here.
  /// </summary>
  /// <param name="args">Command-line arguments</param>
  public static void Main(string[] args)
  {
    Student student = new Student();
    student.InitStudent("Madeleine", "Cather");

    // output the banner and name
    Student.OutputBanner();
    string s = Student.OutputName(student, 5);
    Console.WriteLine();

    // output the banner and name again
    student.OutputBannerAndName();

    // wait for user to acknowledge
    Console.WriteLine("Press Enter to terminate...");
```

```
        Console.Read();
    }
  }
}
```

The comments go just above the function they describe. They explain the purpose of the function, the purpose of each argument, the type of data returned, and a reference to a related function. In practice, these steps describe the display as you add the function call `Student.OutputName()` to `Main()`:

1. Visual Studio offers you a list of functions. After you select the one you're looking for, `OutputName()`, Visual Studio gives you the short description from the `<summary></summary>`, as shown in Figure 8-6. The text you provided appears just below the function declaration in the yellow auto-complete box.

2. After you select or type the name of the function, Visual Studio displays a description of the first parameter taken from the `<param></param>` field along with its type. This appears in the same place, replacing the overall summary information.

3. Visual Studio repeats the process for the second argument, `nIndent`.

Figure 8-6:
Visual Studio can do a better job of describing the function and its arguments when armed with the extra XML documentation.

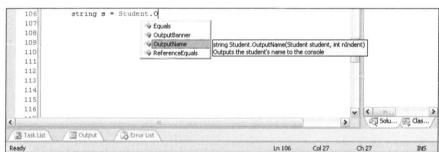

Although they're a little tedious to enter, documentation comments make methods considerably easier to use.

In Visual Studio, the XML comment blocks are collapsible regions, so you can hide the clutter while you work.

Generating XML documentation

You can easily persuade Visual Studio to output all the documentation you have provided in the form of an XML file.

This entire section is very technical stuff. If you don't know what an XML file is, this material won't mean much to you. However, if you do understand XML files, you'll want to know about this feature.

To generate XML documentation, follow these steps:

1. **Choose Project⇨*projectname* Properties.**

2. **In the Build section, scroll down to the Output section and find the property called** `XML Documentation File`. **Select the check box and fill in a name.**

   I chose the name `xmloutput.xml` just because I didn't know any better. (You can also prefix a path to where you want the documentation to go.)

3. **Save and close the Properties tab.**

   You can also access the project properties by right-clicking the project name in the Solution Explorer.

4. **Now choose Build⇨Rebuild Solution to make sure that you get everything rebuilt, regardless of whether it needs rebuilding.**

5. **Look in the** `bin\Debug` **subdirectory for the** `MixingFunctionsAnd-MethodsWithXMLTags` **project (or wherever you specified for the XML documentation file to go).**

   The new file `xmloutput.xml` describes all the functions that are documented with XML tags.

Chapter 9

Stringing in the Key of C#

*F*or many applications, you can treat a `string` like one of the built-in value-type variable types such as `int` or `char`. Certain operations that are otherwise reserved for these intrinsic types are available to strings, as follows:

```
int i = 1;          // declare and initialize an int
string s = "abc";   // declare and initialize a string
```

In other respects, shown as follows, a `string` is treated like a user-defined class:

```
string s1 = new String();
string s2 = "abcd";
int nLengthOfString = s2.Length;
```

Which is it — a value-type or a class? In fact, `String` is a class for which C# offers special treatment because strings are so widely used in programs. For example, the keyword `string` is synonymous with the class name `String`, as shown in the following code:

```
String s1 = "abcd"; // assign a string literal to a String obj
string s2 = s1;     // assign a String obj to a string variable
```

In this example, s1 is declared to be an object of class `String` (spelled with an uppercase *S*), while s2 is declared as a simple `string` (spelled with a lowercase *s*). However, the two assignments demonstrate that `string` and `String` are of the same (or compatible) types.

In fact, this same property is true of the other intrinsic variable types, to a more limited extent. Even the lowly `int` type has a corresponding class `Int32`, `double` has the class `Double`, and so on. The distinction here is that `string` and `String` really are the same thing.

Performing Common Operations on a String

C# programmers perform more operations on strings than Beverly Hills plastic surgeons do on Hollywood hopefuls. Virtually every program uses the "addition" operator that's used on `strings`, as shown in the following example:

```
string sName = "Randy";
Console.WriteLine("His name is " + sName); // means concatenate
```

The `String` class provides this special operator. However, the `String` class also provides other, more direct methods for manipulating strings. You can see the complete list by looking up `"String class"` in the Help Index.

The union is indivisible, and so are strings

You need to know at least one thing that you didn't learn before the 6th grade: You can't change a `string` object itself after it has been created. Even though I may speak of modifying a string, C# doesn't have an operation that modifies the actual `string` object. Plenty of operations appear to modify the `string` that you're working with, but they always return the modified `string` as a new object, instead.

For example, the operation `"His name is " + "Randy"` changes neither of the two strings, but generates a third string, `"His name is Randy"`. One side effect of this behavior is that you don't have to worry about someone modifying a `string` "out from under you."

Consider the following simplistic example program:

```
// ModifyString - the methods provided by the class String do not
//                modify the object itself (s.ToUpper() does not
//                modify s; rather, it returns a new string that
//                has been converted)using System;
namespace ModifyString
{
  class Program
  {
    public static void Main(string[] args)
    {
      // create a student object
      Student s1 = new Student();
      s1.sName = "Jenny";
      // now make a new object with the same name
      Student s2 = new Student();
      s2.sName = s1.sName;
      // "changing" the name in the s1 object does not
```

```
        // change the object itself because ToUpper() returns
        // a new string without modifying the original
        s2.sName = s1.sName.ToUpper();
        Console.WriteLine("s1 - {0}, s2 - {1}", s1.sName, s2.sName);
        // wait for user to acknowledge the results
        Console.WriteLine("Press Enter to terminate...");
        Console.Read();
    }
}
// Student - we just need a class with a string in it
class Student
{
    public string sName;
}
}
```

The Student objects s1 and s2 are set up so that their sName data member points to the same string data. The call to the ToUpper() method converts the string s1.sName to all uppercase characters. Normally, this would be a problem because both s1 and s2 point to the same object. However, ToUpper() does not change sName — it creates a new, independent uppercase string.

The following output of the program is simple:

```
s1 - Jenny, s2 - JENNY
Press Enter to terminate...
```

This property of strings is called *immutability* (meaning, unchangeability).

The immutability of strings is also important for string constants. A string such as "this is a string" is a form of a string constant, just like 1 is an int constant. In the same way that I reuse my shirts to reduce the size of my wardrobe, a compiler may choose to combine all accesses to the single constant "this is a string". Reusing string constants can reduce the footprint of the resulting program but would be impossible if a string could be modified.

Equality for all strings: The Compare () method

Numerous operations treat a string as a single object — for example, the Compare() method. Compare(), with the following properties, compares two strings as if they were numbers:

- If the left-hand string is *greater than* the right string, Compare() returns a 1.
- If the left-hand string is *less than* the right string, it returns a –1.
- If the two strings are equal, it returns a 0.

The algorithm works as follows when written in "notational C#" (that is, C# without all the details, also known as pseudocode):

```
compare(string s1, string s2)
{
  // loop through each character of the strings until
  // a character in one string is greater than the
  // corresponding character in the other string
  foreach character in the shorter string
    if (s1's character > s2's character when treated as a number)
      return 1
    if (s2's character < s1's character)
      return -1
  // Okay, every letter matches, but if the string s1 is longer
  // then it's greater
  if s1 has more characters left
    return 1
  // if s2 is longer, it's greater
  if s2 has more characters left
    return -1
  // if every character matches and the two strings are the same
  // length, then they are "equal"
  return 0
}
```

Thus, `"abcd"` is greater than `"abbd"`, and `"abcde"` is greater than `"abcd"`. More often than not, you don't care whether one string is greater than the other, but only whether the two strings are equal.

You do want to know which string is "bigger" when performing a sort.

The `Compare()` operation returns a 0 when two strings are identical. The following test program uses the equality feature of `Compare()` to perform a certain operation when the program encounters a particular string or strings.

`BuildASentence` prompts the user to enter lines of text. Each line is concatenated to the previous line to build a single sentence. This program exits if the user enters the word *EXIT*, *exit*, *QUIT*, or *quit*:

```
// BuildASentence - the following program constructs sentences
//                  by concatenating user input until the user
//                  enters one of the termination characters -
//
//                  this program shows when you need to look for
//                  string equality
using System;
namespace BuildASentence
{
  public class Program
  {
    public static void Main(string[] args)
    {
```

```
   Console.WriteLine("Each line you enter will be "
                 + "added to a sentence until you "
                 + "enter EXIT or QUIT");
   // ask the user for input; continue concatenating
   // the phrases input until the user enters exit or
   // quit (start with a null sentence)
   string sSentence = "";
   for(;;)
   {
     // get the next line
     Console.WriteLine("Enter a string ");
     string sLine = Console.ReadLine();
     // exit the loop if it's a terminator
     if (IsTerminateString(sLine))
     {
       break;
     }
     // otherwise, add it to the sentence
     sSentence = String.Concat(sSentence, sLine);
     // let the user know how she's doing
     Console.WriteLine("\nYou've entered: {0}", sSentence);
   }
   Console.WriteLine("\nTotal sentence:\n{0}", sSentence);
   // wait for user to acknowledge the results
   Console.WriteLine("Press Enter to terminate...");
   Console.Read();
 }
 // IsTerminateString - return a true if the source
 // string is equal to any of the termination strings
 public static bool IsTerminateString(string source)
 {
   string[] sTerms = {"EXIT", "exit", "QUIT", "quit" };
   // compare the string entered to each of the
   // legal exit commands
   foreach(string sTerm in sTerms)
   {
     // return a true if you have a match
     if (String.Compare(source, sTerm) == 0)
     {
       return true;
     }
   }
   return false;
 }
}
}
```

After prompting the user for what the program expects, the program creates an empty initial sentence string sSentence. From there, the program enters an "infinite" loop.

The controls `while(true)` and `for(;;)` loop forever, or at least long enough for some internal `break` or `return` to break you out. The two loops are equivalent, and in practice, you'll see them both. Looping is covered in Chapter 5.

`BuildASentence` prompts the user to enter a line of text, which the program reads using the `ReadLine()` method. Having read the line, the program checks to see whether it is a terminator by using the `IsTerminateString()` function, which I wrote for the job. This function returns `true` if `sLine` is one of the terminator phrases and `false` otherwise.

By convention, the name of a function that checks a property and returns a `true` or `false` starts with `Is`, `Has`, `Can`, or some similar word. In this case, the name of the function `IsTerminateString()` implies the question, "Is `sLine` a terminate string?" Of course, this is a human convention only — C# doesn't care.

If `sLine` is not one of the terminate strings, it is concatenated to the end of the sentence using the `String.Concat()` function. The program outputs the immediate result just so the user can see what's going on.

The `IsTerminateString()` method defines an array of strings `sTerms`. Each member of this array is one of the strings you're looking for. Any of these strings causes the program to return a `true`, which causes the program to quit faster than a programmer forced to write COBOL.

The program must include both `"EXIT"` and `"exit"` because `Compare()` considers the two strings different by default. (The way the program is written, these are the only two ways to spell *exit*. Strings such as `"Exit"` and `"eXit"` would not be recognized as terminators.)

The `IsTerminateString()` function loops through each of the strings in the array of target strings. If `Compare()` reports a match to any of the terminate phrases, the function returns a `true`. If the function reaches the end of the loop without a match, the function returns a `false`.

Iterating through an array is a great way to look for one of various possible values.

Here's an example run of the `BuildASentence` program:

```
Each line you entered will be added to a
sentence until you enter EXIT or QUIT
Enter a string
Programming with

You've entered: Programming with
Enter a string
 C# is fun

You've entered: Programming with C# is fun
```

```
Enter a string
(more or less)

You've entered: Programming with C# is fun (more or less)
Enter a string
EXIT

Total sentence:
Programming with C# is fun (more or less)
Press Enter to terminate...
```

I have flagged my input in bold to make the output easier to read.

Would you like your compares with or without case?

The Compare() method used within IsTerminateString() considers "EXIT" and "exit" to be different strings. However, the Compare() function is overloaded with a second version that includes a third argument. This argument indicates whether the comparison should ignore the letter case. A true indicates "ignore." (Chapter 7 discusses function overloading.)

The following version of IsTerminateString() returns a true whether the string passed is uppercase, lowercase, or a combination of the two:

```
// IsTerminateString - return a true if the source string is equal
// to any of the termination characters
public static bool IsTerminateString(string source)
{
  // indicate true if passed either exit or quit,
  // irrespective of case
  return (String.Compare("exit", source, true) == 0) ||
         (String.Compare("quit", source, true) == 0);
}
```

This version of IsTerminateString() is simpler than the previous looping version. The function doesn't need to worry about case, and it can use a single conditional expression because it now has only two options to consider.

This IsTerminateString() doesn't even use an if statement. The bool expression returns the calculated value directly to the user — it gets the if out.

What if I want to switch case?

I almost hate to bring it up, but you can use the switch() control to look for a particular string. Usually, you use the switch() control to compare a counting number to some set of possible values; however, the `switch()` does work on `string` objects, as well. The following version of `IsTerminate String()` uses the `switch()` control:

```
// IsTerminateString - return a true if the source
// string is equal to any of the termination strings
public static bool IsTerminateString(string source)
{
  switch(source)
  {
    case "EXIT":
    case "exit":
    case "QUIT":
    case "quit":
          return true;
  }
  return false;
}
```

This approach works because you're comparing only a limited number of strings. The `for()` loop offers a much more flexible approach for searching for string values. Using the case-less `Compare()` gives the program greater flexibility in understanding the user.

Reading character input

A program can read from the keyboard one character at a time, but you have to worry about newlines and so on. An easier approach reads a string and then parses the characters out of the string.

Parsing characters out of a string is another topic I don't like to mention for fear that programmers will abuse this technique. In some cases, programmers are too quick to jump down into the middle of a string and start pulling out what they find there. This is particularly true of C++ programmers because that's the only way they could deal with strings, until the addition of a string class.

Your programs can read strings as if they were arrays of characters using either the `foreach` control or the index operator `[ ]`. The following `StringToCharAccess` program demonstrates this technique:

```
// StringToCharAccess - access the characters in a string
//                      as if the string were an array
using System;
namespace StringToCharAccess
{
  public class Program
  {
    public static void Main(string[] args)
    {
```

```
    // read a string in from the keyboard
    Console.WriteLine("Input some random character string."
                    + "Make sure it's completely random");
    string sRandom = Console.ReadLine();
    // first output as a string
    Console.WriteLine("When output as a string: " + sRandom);
    Console.WriteLine();
    // now output as a series of characters
    Console.Write("When output using the foreach: ");
    foreach(char c in sRandom)
    {
      Console.Write(c);
    }
    Console.WriteLine(); // terminate the line
    // put a blank line divider
    Console.WriteLine();
    // now output as a series of characters
    Console.Write("When output using the for: ");
    for(int i = 0; i < sRandom.Length; i++)
    {
      Console.Write(sRandom[i]);
    }
    Console.WriteLine(); // terminate the line
    // wait for user to acknowledge the results
    Console.WriteLine("Press Enter to terminate...");
    Console.Read();
  }
 }
}
```

This program first outputs some string picked totally at random. In fact, I may have read it somewhere or done a tap dance on the keyboard. The program first outputs the string using the conventional `WriteLine(string)` method. It follows this by using the `foreach` to fetch each character in the string, one at a time. Finally, it uses a `for` loop with the array brackets `[]` to do the same thing. The results are as follows:

```
Input some random character string. Make sure it's completely random
Stephen Davis is one handsome individual

When output as a string: Stephen Davis is one handsome individual

When output using the foreach: Stephen Davis is one handsome individual

When output using the for: Stephen Davis is one handsome individual
Press Enter to terminate...
```

In some cases, you don't want to mess with any white space on either end of the string. The term *white space* refers to the characters that don't normally display on the screen, for example, space, newline (or \n),and tab (\t).

You can use the `Trim()` method to trim off the edges of the string as follows:

```
// get rid of any extra spaces on either end of the string
sRandom = sRandom.Trim();
```

`String.Trim()` returns a new string. The previous version of the string with the extra white space is lost and no longer usable.

Parsing numeric input

The `ReadLine()` function used for reading from the console returns a `string` object. A program that expects numeric input must convert this `string`. C# provides just the conversion tool you need in the `Convert` class. This class provides a conversion method from `string` to each built-in variable type. Thus, the following code segment reads a number from the keyboard and stores it into an `int` variable:

```
string s = Console.ReadLine();  // keyboard input is string data
int n = Convert.Int32(s);       // but you know it's meant to be a number
```

The other conversion methods are a bit more obvious: `ToDouble()`, `ToFloat()`, and `ToBoolean()`.

`ToInt32()` refers to a 32-bit, signed integer (32 bits is the size of a normal `int`), so this is the conversion function for `int`s. `ToInt64()` is the size of a `long`.

When `Convert()` encounters an unexpected character type, it can generate unexpected results. Thus, you must know for sure what type of data you're processing. (Bonus Chapter 1 on the CD covers dealing with unexpected occurrences, called *exceptions*.)

The following function returns a `true` if the string passed to it consists of only digits. You can call this function prior to converting into a type of integer, assuming that a sequence of nothing but digits is probably a legal number.

You would need to include the decimal point for floating point variables and include a leading minus sign for negative numbers — but hey, you get the idea.

Here's the function:

```
// IsAllDigits - return a true if all the characters
//               in the string are digits
public static bool IsAllDigits(string sRaw)
{
  // first get rid of any benign characters
  // at either end; if there's nothing left
  // then we don't have a number
  string s = sRaw.Trim();  // ignore whitespace on either side
```

```
  if (s.Length == 0)
  {
    return false;
  }
  // loop through the string
  for(int index = 0; index < s.Length; index++)
  {
    // a non-digit indicates that the string
    // probably is not a number
    if (Char.IsDigit(s[index]) == false)
    {
      return false;
    }
  }
  // no non-digits found; it's probably OK
  return true;
}
```

The function `IsAllDigits()` first removes any harmless white space at either end of the string. If nothing is left, the string was blank and could not be an integer. The function then loops through each character in the string. If any of these characters turns out to be a nondigit, the function returns a `false`, indicating that the string is probably not a number. If this function returns a `true`, the probability is high that the string can be converted into an integer successfully.

The following code sample inputs a number from the keyboard and prints it back out to the console. (I omitted the `IsAllDigits()` function from the listing to save space.)

```
// IsAllDigits - demonstrate the IsAllDigits method
using System;
namespace IsAllDigits
{
  class Program
  {
    public static void Main(string[] args)
    {
      // input a string from the keyboard
      Console.WriteLine("Enter an integer number");
      string s = Console.ReadLine();
      // first check to see if this could be a number
      if (!IsAllDigits(s))
      {
        Console.WriteLine("Hey! That isn't a number");
      }
      else
      {
        // convert the string into an integer
        int n = Int32.Parse(s);
        // now write out the number times 2
```

```
        Console.WriteLine("2 * {0} = {1}", n, 2 * n);
      }
      // wait for user to acknowledge the results
      Console.WriteLine("Press Enter to terminate...");
      Console.Read();
    }
  }
}
```

The program reads a line of input from the console keyboard. If `IsAllDigits()` returns a `false`, the program alerts the user. If not, the program converts the string into a number using an alternative to `Convert.ToInt32()` — the `Int32.Parse(s)` call. Finally, the program outputs both the number and two times the number (the latter to prove that the program did, in fact, convert the string as advertised).

The output from a sample run of the program appears as follows:

```
Enter an integer number
1A3
Hey! That isn't a number
Press Enter to terminate...
```

You could let `Convert` try to convert garbage and handle any exception it may decide to throw. However, a better-than-even chance exists that it won't throw an exception, but just return incorrect results — for example, returning 1 when presented with 1A3. It's best to validate input data yourself.

Handling a series of numbers

Often, a program receives a series of numbers in a single line from the keyboard. Using the `String.Split()` method, you can easily break the string into a number of substrings, one for each number, and parse them separately.

The `Split()` function chops up a single string into an array of smaller strings using some delimiter. For example, if you tell `Split()` to divide a string using a comma (`,`) as the delimiter, `"1,2,3"` becomes three strings, `"1"`, `"2"`, and `"3"`.

The following program uses the `Split()` method to input a sequence of numbers to be summed:

```
// ParseSequenceWithSplit - input a series of numbers
//                  separated by commas, parse them into
//                  integers, and output the sum
namespace ParseSequenceWithSplit
{
  using System;
  class Program
  {
```

```csharp
public static void Main(string[] args)
{
    // prompt the user to input a sequence of numbers
    Console.WriteLine(
        "Input a series of numbers separated by commas:");
    // read a line of text
    string input = Console.ReadLine();
    Console.WriteLine();
    // now convert the line into individual segments
    // based upon either commas or spaces
    char[] cDividers = {',', ' '};
    string[] segments = input.Split(cDividers);
    // convert each segment into a number
    int nSum = 0;
    foreach(string s in segments)
    {
        // (skip any empty segments)
        if (s.Length > 0)
        {
            // skip strings that aren't numbers
            if (IsAllDigits(s))
            {
                // convert the string into a 32-bit int
                int num = Int32.Parse(s);
                Console.WriteLine("Next number = {0}", num);
                // add this number into the sum
                nSum += num;
            }
        }
    }
    // output the sum
    Console.WriteLine("Sum = {0}", nSum);
    // wait for user to acknowledge the results
    Console.WriteLine("Press Enter to terminate...");
    Console.Read();
}
// IsAllDigits - return a true if all of the characters
//               in the string are digits
public static bool IsAllDigits(string sRaw)
{
    // first get rid of any benign characters
    // at either end; if there's nothing left
    // then we don't have a number
    string s = sRaw.Trim();
    if (s.Length == 0)
    {
        return false;
    }
    // loop through the string
    for(int index = 0; index < s.Length; index++)
    {
        // a non-digit indicates that the string
        // probably is not a number
```

```
        if (Char.IsDigit(s[index]) == false)
        {
          return false;
        }
      }
      // no non-digit found; it's probably OK
      return true;
    }
  }
}
```

The `ParseSequenceWithSplit` program begins by reading a string from the keyboard. The program passes the `cDividers` array of `char` to the `Split()` method to indicate that the comma and the space are the characters used to separate individual numbers.

The program iterates through each of the smaller "subarrays" created by `Split()` using the `foreach` control. The program skips any zero-length subarrays (this would result from two dividers in a row). The program next uses the `IsAllDigits()` method to make sure that the string contains a number. Valid numbers are converted into integers and then added to an accumulator, `nSum`. Invalid numbers are ignored. (I chose not to generate an error message.)

Here's the output of a typical run:

```
Input a series of numbers separated by commas:
1,2, a, 3 4

Next number = 1
Next number = 2
Next number = 3
Next number = 4
Sum = 10
Press Enter to terminate...
```

The program skips through the list, accepting either commas, spaces, or both as separators. It successfully skips over the *a* to generate the result of 10. In a real-world program, however, you probably don't want to skip over incorrect input without comment. You almost always want to draw the user's attention to garbage in the input stream.

Controlling Output Manually

Controlling the output from programs is an important aspect of string manipulation. Face it: The output from the program is what the user sees. No matter how elegant the internal logic of the program may be, the user probably won't be impressed if the output looks shabby.

The `String` class provides help in directly formatting string data for output. The following sections examine the `Trim()`, `Pad()`, `PadRight()`, `PadLeft()`, `Substring()`, and `Concat()` methods.

Using the Trim() and Pad() methods

You can use the `Trim()` method to remove unwanted characters from either end of a string. Typically, you use this method to remove spaces so that output strings line up correctly.

Another common method for formatting output is to use the `Pad` functions, which add characters to either end of a string to expand the string to some predetermined length. For example, you may add spaces to the left or right of a string to left- or right-justify it, or you can add `"*"` characters to the left of a currency number.

The following small `AlignOutput` program uses both of these functions to trim up and justify a series of names:

```
// AlignOutput - left justify and align a set of strings
//                to improve the appearance of program output
namespace AlignOutput
{
  using System;
  class Program
  {
    public static void Main(string[] args)
    {
      string[] names = {"Christa   ",
                        "  Sarah",
                        "Jonathan",
                        "Sam",
                        "  Schmekowitz "};
      // first output the names as they start out
      Console.WriteLine("The following names are of "
                        + "different lengths");

      foreach(string s in names)
      {
        Console.WriteLine("This is the name '{0}' before", s);
      }
      Console.WriteLine();

      // this time, fix the strings so they are
      // left justified and all the same length
      string[] sAlignedNames = TrimAndPad(names);
      // finally output the resulting padded, justified strings
      Console.WriteLine("The following are the same names "
                        + "normalized to the same length");
```

```
      foreach(string s in sAlignedNames)
      {
        Console.WriteLine("This is the name '{0}' afterwards", s);
      }
      // wait for user to acknowledge
      Console.WriteLine("Press Enter to terminate...");
      Console.Read();
    }
    // TrimAndPad - given an array of strings, trim whitespace from
    //              both ends and then repad the strings to align
    //              them with the longest member
    public static string[] TrimAndPad(string[] strings)
    {
      // copy the source array into an array that you can manipulate
      string[] stringsToAlign = new String[strings.Length];
      // first remove any unnecessary spaces from either
      // end of the names
      for(int i = 0; i < stringsToAlign.Length; i++)
      {
        stringsToAlign[i] = strings[i].Trim();
      }
      // now find the length of the longest string so that
      // all other strings line up with that string
      int nMaxLength = 0;
      foreach(string s in stringsToAlign)
      {
        if (s.Length > nMaxLength)
        {
          nMaxLength = s.Length;
        }
      }
      // finally justify all the strings to the length
      // of the maximum string
      for(int i = 0; i < stringsToAlign.Length; i++)
      {
        stringsToAlign[i] = stringsToAlign[i].PadRight(nMaxLength + 1);
      }
      // return the result to the caller
      return stringsToAlign;
    }
  }
}
```

AlignOutput defines an array of names of uneven alignment and length.
(You could just as easily write the program to read these names from the console or from a file.) The Main() function first displays the names as is.
Main() then aligns the names using the TrimAndPad() method before redis-
playing the resulting trimmed up strings, as follows:

```
The following names are of different lengths
This is the name 'Christa  ' before
This is the name '  Sarah' before
This is the name 'Jonathan' before
```

```
This is the name 'Sam' before
This is the name ' Schmekowitz ' before

The following are the same names rationalized to the same length
This is the name 'Christa    ' afterwards
This is the name 'Sarah     ' afterwards
This is the name 'Jonathan   ' afterwards
This is the name 'Sam       ' afterwards
This is the name 'Schmekowitz ' afterwards
```

The `TrimAndPad()` method begins by making a copy of the input `strings` array. In general, a function that operates on parameters passed to it should return a new modified value rather than modify the value passed. This is sort of like when I borrow my brother-in-law's pickup: He expects to get it back looking the same as when it left.

`TrimAndPad()` first loops through the array, calling `Trim()` on each element to remove unneeded white space on either end. The function loops again through the array to find the longest member. The function loops one final time, calling `PadRight()` to expand each array to match the length of the longest member in the array.

`PadRight(10)` expands a string to be at least 10 characters long. For example, `PadRight(10)` would add four spaces to the right of a six-character string.

`TrimAndPad()` returns the array of trimmed and padded strings for output. `Main()` iterates through this list, displaying each of the now-gussied-up strings that you see. Voilà.

Using the Concatenate function

You often face the problem of breaking up a string or inserting some substring into the middle of another. Replacing one character with another is most easily handled with the `Replace()` method, as follows:

```
string s = "Danger NoSmoking";
a.Replace(s, ' ', '!')
```

This example converts the string into `"Danger!NoSmoking"`.

Replacing all appearances of one character (in this case, a space) with another (an exclamation mark) is especially useful when generating comma-separated strings for easier parsing. However, the more common and more difficult case involves breaking a single string into substrings, manipulating them separately, and then recombining them into a single, modified string.

For example, consider the following `RemoveSpecialChars()` function, which removes all instances of a set of special characters from a given string. This example `RemoveWhiteSpace` program uses the `Replace()` function to remove white space (spaces, tabs, and newlines) from a string:

```
// RemoveWhiteSpace - define a RemoveSpecialChars() function
//                    which can remove any of a set of chars
//                    from a given string. Use this function
//                    to remove white space from a sample string.
/
namespace RemoveWhiteSpace
{
 using System;
  public class Program
  {
    public static void Main(string[] args)
    {
      // define the whitespace characters
      char[] cWhiteSpace = {' ', '\n', '\t'};
      // start with a string embedded with whitespace
      string s = " this is a\nstring"; // contains spaces & newline
      Console.WriteLine("before:" + s);
      // output the string with the whitespace missing
      Console.WriteLine("after:" + RemoveSpecialChars(s, cWhiteSpace));
      // wait for user to acknowledge the results
      Console.WriteLine("Press Enter to terminate...");
      Console.Read();
    }
    // RemoveSpecialChars - remove every occurrence of the specified
    //                      characters from the string
    public static string RemoveSpecialChars(string sInput, char[] cTargets)
    {
      string sOutput = sInput;
      for(;;)
      {
        // find the offset of the character; exit the loop
        // if there are no more
        int nOffset = sOutput.IndexOfAny(cTargets);
        if (nOffset == -1)
        {
          break;
        }
        // break the string into the part prior to the
        // character and the part after the character
        string sBefore = sOutput.Substring(0, nOffset);
        string sAfter  = sOutput.Substring(nOffset + 1);
        // now put the two substrings back together with the
        // character in the middle missing
        sOutput = String.Concat(sBefore, sAfter);
      }
      return sOutput;
    }
  }
}
```

The key to this program is the RemoveSpecialChars() function. This function returns a string consisting of the input string, sInput, with every one of a set of characters contained in the array cTargets removed. To better understand this function, assume that the string was "ab,cd,e" and that the array of special characters was the single character ','.

The RemoveSpecialChars() function enters a loop from which it does not return until every comma has been removed. The IndexOfAny() function returns the index within the array of the first comma that it can find. A return value of –1 indicates that no comma was found.

After the first call, IndexOfAny() returns a 2 ('a' is at index 0, 'b' is 1, and ',' is 2). The next two functions break the string apart at the index. Substring(0, 2) creates a substring consisting of two characters starting with index 0: "ab". The second call to Substring(3) creates a string consisting of the characters starting at index 3 and continuing to the end of the string: "cd,e". (It's the "+ 1" that skips the comma.) The Concat() function puts the two substrings back together to create "abcd,e".

Control passes back up to the top of the loop. The next iteration finds the comma at index 4. The concatenated string is "abcde". Because no comma is left, the index returned on the final pass is –1.

The RemoveWhiteSpace program prints out a string containing several forms of white space. The program then uses the RemoveSpecialChars() function to strip out white space characters. The output from this program appears as follows:

```
before: this is a
string
after:thisisastring
Press Enter to terminate...
```

Let's Split() that concatenate program

The RemoveWhiteSpace program demonstrates the use of the Concat() and IndexOf() methods; however, it doesn't use the most efficient approach. As usual, a little examination reveals a more efficient approach using our old friend Split(). You can find this program on the enclosed CD-ROM under RemoveWhiteSpaceWithSplit. The code is as follows:

```
// RemoveWhiteSpaceWithSplit - replaces RemoveSpecialChars() function
//                             from RemoveWhiteSpace program
// RemoveSpecialChars - remove every occurrence of the
//                      specified characters from the string
public static string RemoveSpecialChars(string sInput, char[] cTargets)
{
    // split the input string up using the target
```

```
    // characters as the delimiters
    string[] sSubStrings = sInput.Split(cTargets);
    // sOutput will contain the eventual output information
    string sOutput = "";
    // loop through the substrings originating from the split
    foreach(string subString in sSubStrings)
    {
      sOutput = String.Concat(sOutput, subString);
    }
    return sOutput;
  }
```

This version uses the `Split()` function to break the input string into a set of substrings using the characters to be removed as delimiters. The delimiter is not included in the substrings created, which has the effect of removing the character(s). The logic is much simpler and less error-prone.

The `foreach` loop in the second half of the program puts the pieces back together again. The output from the program is unchanged.

Controlling String.Format()

The `String` class also provides the `Format()` method for formatting output, especially the output of numbers. In its simplest form, `Format()` allows the insertion of string, numeric, or boolean input in the middle of a format string. For example, consider the following call:

```
string myString = String.Format("{0} times {1} equals {2}", 2, 3, 2*3);
```

The first argument to `Format()` is known as the *format string* — the quoted string you see. The `{n}` items in the middle of the format string indicate that the *n*th argument following the format string is to be inserted at that point. `{0}` refers to the first argument (in this case, the value 2), `{1}` refers to the next (3), and so on.

This returns a string, `myString`. The resulting string is as follows:

```
"2 times 3 equals 6"
```

Unless otherwise directed, `Format()` uses a default output format for each argument type. `Format()` enables you to affect the output format by including modifiers in the placeholders. See Table 9-1 for a listing of some of these controls. For example, `{0:E6}` says, "Output the number in exponential form, using six spaces for the fractional part."

Table 9-1	**Format Controls Using `string.Format()`**		
Control	*Example*	*Result*	*Notes*
C — currency	`{0:C}` of 123.456	$123.45	The currency sign depends on the localization setting.
	`{0:C}` of -123.456	($123.45)	
D — decimal	`{0:D5}` of 123	00123	Integers only.
E — exponential	`{0:E}` of 123.45	1.2345E+002	Also known as scientific notation.
F — fixed	`{0:F2}` of 123.4567	123.45	The number after the *F* indicates the number of digits after the decimal point.
N — number	`{0:N}` of 123456.789	123,456.79	Adds commas and rounds off to nearest 100th.
	`{0:N1}` of 123456.789	123,456.8	Controls the number of digits after the decimal point.
	`{0:N0}` of 123456.789	123,457	
X — hexadecimal	`{0:X}` of 123	0x7B	7B hex = 123 decimal (integers only).
`{0:0...}`	`{0:000.00}` of 12.3	012.30	Forces a 0 if a digit is not already present.
`{0:#...}`	`{0:###.##}` of 12.3	12.3	Forces the space to be left blank; no other field can encroach on the three digits to the left and two digits after the decimal point (useful for maintaining decimal point alignment).
	`{0:##0.0#}` of 0	0.0	Combining the # and zeros forces space to be allocated by the #s and forces at least one digit to appear, even if the number is 0.

(continued)

Table 9-1 *(continued)*

Control	Example	Result	Notes
`{0:# or 0%}`	`{0:#00.#%}` of .1234	12.3%	The % displays the number as a percentage (multiplies by 100 and adds the % sign).
	`{0:#00.#%}` of .0234	02.3%	

These format controls can seem a bit bewildering. (I didn't even mention the detailed currency and date controls.) Explore the topic "format specifiers, C#" in the Help index for more information. To help you wade through these options, the following OutputFormatControls program enables you to enter a floating point number followed by a control sequence. The program then displays the number using the specified Format() control:

```
// OutputFormatControls - allow the user to reformat input
//                        numbers using a variety of format
//                        controls input at run time
namespace OutputFormatControls
{
  using System;
  public class Program
  {
    public static void Main(string[] args)
    {
      // keep looping - inputting numbers until the user
      // enters a blank line rather than a number
      for(;;)
      {
        // first input a number - terminate when the user
        // inputs nothing but a blank line
        Console.WriteLine("Enter a double number");
        string sNumber = Console.ReadLine();
        if (sNumber.Length == 0)
        {
          break;
        }
        double dNumber = Double.Parse(sNumber);
        // now input the control codes; split them
        // using spaces as dividers
        Console.WriteLine("Enter the control codes"
                        + " separated by a blank");
        char[] separator = {' '};
        string sFormatString = Console.ReadLine();
        string[] sFormats = sFormatString.Split(separator);
        // loop through the individual format controls
        foreach(string s in sFormats)
        {
```

```
            if (s.Length != 0)
            {
                // create a complete format control
                // from the control letters entered earlier
                string sFormatCommand = "{0:" + s + "}";
                // output the number entered using the
                // reconstructed format control
                Console.Write(
                        "The format control {0} results in ", sFormatCommand);
                try
                {
                    Console.WriteLine(sFormatCommand, dNumber);
                }
                catch(Exception)
                {
                    Console.WriteLine("<illegal control>");
                }
                Console.WriteLine();
            }
        }
    }
    // wait for user to acknowledge
    Console.WriteLine("Press Enter to terminate...");
    Console.Read();
    }
  }
}
```

The OutputFormatControls program continues to read floating point numbers into a variable dNumber until the user enters a blank line. Notice that the program does not include any tests to determine whether the input is a legal floating point number. Just assume that the user is smart enough to know what a number looks like (a dangerous assumption!).

The program then reads a series of control strings separated by spaces. Each control is then combined with a "{0}" string (the number before the colon, which corresponds to the placeholder in the format string) into the variable sFormatCommand. For example, if you entered **N4**, the program would store the control "{0:N4}". The following statement writes the number dNumber using the newly constructed sFormatCommand:

```
Console.WriteLine(sFormatCommand, dNumber);
```

In the case of our lowly N4, the command would be rendered as follows:

```
Console.WriteLine("{0:N4}", dNumber);
```

Typical output from the program appears as follows (I boldfaced my input):

```
Enter a double number
12345.6789
Enter the control codes separated by a blank
C E F1 N0 0000000.00000
The format control {0:C} results in $12,345.68

The format control {0:E} results in 1.234568E+004

The format control {0:F1} results in 12345.7

The format control {0:N0} results in 12,346

The format control {0:0000000.00000} results in 0012345.67890

Enter a double number
.12345
Enter the control codes separated by a blank
00.0%
The format control {0:00.0%} results in 12.3%
Enter a double number

Press Enter to terminate...
```

When applied to the number 12345.6789, the control N0 adds commas in the proper place (the N part) and lops off everything after the decimal point (the 0 portion) to render 12,346 (the last digit was rounded off, not truncated).

Similarly, when applied to 0.12345, the control 00.0% outputs 12.3%. The percent sign multiplies the number by 100 and adds %. The 00.0 indicates that the output should include at least two digits to the left of the decimal point and only one digit after the decimal point. The number 0.01 is displayed as 01.0% using the same 00.0% control.

The mysterious try...catch catches any errors that spew forth in the event you enter an illegal format command such as a D, which stands for decimal. I cover exceptions in Bonus Chapter 1 on the CD.

Part IV
Object-Oriented Programming

The 5th Wave   By Rich Tennant

MARKETING MIS-STEPS:
The Magic-Eye GUI

I don't see it.

It looks like Explorer to me.

I see the opening screen for "DOOM"

I'm getting a headache.

In this part . . .

Object-oriented programming is the most hyped term in the programming world — dot-com and business-to-business e-commerce eclipsed it for a year or two, but their high-flying fortunes have 'er, subsided, since the dot-com crash of 2001.

C++ claims to be object-oriented — that's what differentiated it from good ol' C. Java is definitely object-oriented, as are a hundred or so other languages that were invented during the last ten years. But what is *object-oriented?* Do I have it? Can I get it? Do I want it?

Part IV demonstrates the features of C# that make it object-oriented to the core. Not only will you be programming objects, but you'll also take possession of the keys to powerful, flexible program designs — all right here in Part IV!

Chapter 10

Object-Oriented Programming — What's It All About?

This chapter answers the musical question, "What are the concepts behind object-oriented programming and how do they differ from the functional concepts covered in Part II of this book?"

Object-Oriented Concept #1 — Abstraction

Sometimes when my son and I are watching football, I whip up a terribly unhealthy batch of nachos. I dump some chips on a plate; throw on some beans, cheese, and lots of jalapeños; and nuke the whole mess in the microwave oven for a few minutes.

To use my microwave, I open the door, throw the stuff in, and punch a few buttons on the front. After a few minutes, the nachos are done. (I try not to stand in front of the microwave while it's working lest my eyes start glowing in the dark.)

Now think for a minute about all the things I don't do to use my microwave:

- ✔ I don't rewire or change anything inside the microwave to get it to work. The microwave has an interface — the front panel with all the buttons and the little time display — that lets me do everything I need.

- ✔ I don't have to reprogram the software used to drive the little processor inside my microwave, even if I cooked a different dish the last time I used the microwave.

- ✔ I don't look inside my microwave's case.

- ✔ Even if I were a microwave designer and knew all about the inner workings of a microwave, including its software, I still wouldn't think about all that stuff while I was using it to heat my nachos.

These are not profound observations. You can deal with only so much stress in your life. To reduce the number of things that you deal with, you work at a certain level of detail. In object-oriented (OO) computerese, the level of detail at which you are working is called the *level of abstraction*. To introduce another OO term while I have the chance, I *abstract away* the details of the microwave's innards.

Happily, computer scientists — and thousands of geeks — have invented object orientation and numerous other concepts that reduce the level of complexity at which programmers have to work. Using powerful abstractions makes the job simpler and far less error-prone than it used to be. In a sense, that's what the past half century or so of computing progress has been about: managing ever more complex concepts and structures with ever less errors.

When I'm working on nachos, I view my microwave oven as a box. (As I'm trying to knock out a snack, I can't worry about the innards of the microwave oven and still follow the Cowboys on the tube.) As long as I use the microwave only through its interface (the keypad), nothing I can do should cause the microwave to enter an inconsistent state and crash or, worse, turn my nachos — or my house — into a blackened, flaming mass.

Preparing functional nachos

Suppose I were to ask my son to write an algorithm for how Dad makes nachos. After he understood what I wanted, he would probably write, "Open a can of beans, grate some cheese, cut the jalapeños," and so on. When he came to the part about microwaving the concoction, he would write something like, "Cook in the microwave for five minutes" (on a good day).

That description is straightforward and complete. But it's not the way a functional programmer would code a program to make nachos. Functional programmers live in a world devoid of objects such as microwave ovens and other appliances. They tend to worry about flow charts with their myriad functional paths. In a functional solution to the nachos problem, the flow of control would pass through my finger to the front panel and then to the internals of the microwave. Pretty soon, flow would be wiggling around through complex logic paths about how long to turn on the microwave tube and whether to sound the "come and get it" tone.

In that world of functional programming, you can't easily think in terms of levels of abstraction. There are no objects and no abstractions behind which to hide inherent complexity.

Preparing object-oriented nachos

In an object-oriented approach to making nachos, I would first identify the types of objects in the problem: chips, beans, cheese, jalapeños, and an oven. Then, I would begin the task of modeling those objects in software, without regard for the details of how they will be used in the final program. For example, I can model cheese as an object pretty much in isolation from the other objects, and then combine it with the beans, the chips, the jalapeños, and the oven and make them interact.

While I do that, I'm said to be working (and thinking) at the level of the basic objects. I need to think about making a useful oven, but I don't have to think about the logical process of making nachos — yet. After all, the microwave designers didn't think about the specific problem of my making a snack. Rather, they set about solving the problem of designing and building a useful microwave.

After I have successfully coded and tested the objects I need, I can ratchet up to the next level of abstraction. I can start thinking at the nacho-making level, rather than the microwave-making level.

At this point, I can pretty much translate my son's instructions directly into C# code.

Object-Oriented Concept #2 — Classification

Critical to the concept of abstraction is that of classification. If I were to ask my son, "What's a microwave?" he would probably say, "It's an oven that. . . ." If I then asked, "What's an oven?" he might reply, "It's a kitchen appliance that. . . ." If I then asked "What's a kitchen appliance?" he would probably say, "Why are you asking so many stupid questions?"

The answers my son gave in my example questioning stem from his understanding of our particular microwave as an example of the type of things called microwave ovens. In addition, my son sees microwave ovens as just a special type of oven, which itself is just a special type of kitchen appliance.

In object-oriented computerese, my microwave is an *instance* of the class `microwave`. The class `microwave` is a *subclass* of the class `oven`, and the class `oven` is a subclass of the class `kitchen appliance`.

Humans classify. Everything about our world is ordered into taxonomies. We do this to reduce the number of things we have to remember. Take, for example, the first time you saw an SUV. The advertisement probably called the SUV "revolutionary, the likes of which have never been seen." But you and I know that just isn't so. I like the looks of some SUVs (others need to go back to take another crack at it), but hey, an SUV is a car. As such, it shares all (or at least most of) the properties of other cars. It has a steering wheel, seats, a motor, brakes, and so on. I bet I could even drive one without reading the user's manual first.

I don't have to clutter my limited storage with all the things that an SUV has in common with other cars. All I have to remember is "an SUV is a car that . . ." and tack on those few things that are unique to an SUV (like the price tag). I can go further. Cars are a subclass of wheeled vehicles along with other members, such as trucks and pickups. Maybe wheeled vehicles are a subclass of vehicles, which include boats and planes — and so on.

Why Classify?

Why should you classify? It sounds like a lot of trouble. Besides, people have been using the functional approach for so long, so why change now?

Designing and building a microwave oven specifically for this one problem may seem easier than building a separate, more generic oven object. Suppose, for example, that I want to build a microwave to cook nachos and nachos only. I would not need to put a front panel on it, other than a START button. I always cook nachos the same amount of time. I could dispense with all that DEFROST and TEMP COOK nonsense. The oven only needs to hold one flat little plate. Three cubic feet of space would be wasted on nachos.

For that matter, I can dispense with the concept of "microwave oven" altogether. All I really need is the guts of the oven. Then, in the recipe, I put the instructions to make it work: "Put nachos in the box. Connect the red wire to the black wire. Bring the radar tube up to about 3,000 volts. Notice a slight hum. Try not to stand too close if you intend to have children." Stuff like that.

But the functional approach has the following problems:

✔ **It's too complex.** I don't want the details of oven building mixed into the details of nacho building. If I can't define the objects and pull them out of the morass of details to deal with separately, I must deal with all the complexities of the problem at the same time.

✔ **It's not flexible.** Someday, I may need to replace the microwave oven with some other type of oven. I should be able to do so as long as the two ovens have the same interface. Without being clearly delineated and developed separately, one object type can't be cleanly removed and replaced with another.

✔ **It's not reusable.** Ovens are used to make lots of different dishes. I don't want to create a new oven every time I encounter a new recipe. Having solved a problem once, I'd like to be able to reuse the solution in other places within my program. If I'm really lucky, I may be able to reuse it in future programs as well.

Object-Oriented Concept #3 — Usable Interfaces

An object must be able to project an external interface that is sufficient but as simple as possible. This is sort of the reverse of Concept #4 (described in the next section). If the device interface is insufficient, users may start ripping the top off the device, in direct violation of the laws of God and Society — or at least the liability laws of the Great State of Texas. And believe me, you do not want to violate the laws of the Great State of Texas. On the flip side, if the device interface is too complex, no one will buy the device — or at least, no one will use all its features.

People complain constantly that their VCRs are too complex (this is less of a problem with today's on-screen controls). These devices have too many buttons with too many different functions. Often, the same button has different functions, depending on the state of the machine. In addition, no two VCRs seem to have the same interface. For whatever reason, the VCR projects an interface that is too difficult and too nonstandard for most people to use.

Compare this with an automobile. It would be difficult to argue that a car is less complicated than a VCR. However, people don't seem to have much trouble driving them.

All automobiles offer more or less the same controls in more or less the same place. For example (this is a true story), my sister once had a car — need I say, a French car — with the headlight control on the left-hand side of the steering wheel, where the turn signal handle normally would be. You pushed down on the light lever to turn off the lights, and you raised the lever to turn them on. This may seem like a small difference, but I never did learn to turn left in that car at night without turning off the lights.

Well-designed autos do not use the same control to perform more than one operation, depending on the state of the car. I can think of only one exception to this rule: Some buttons on most cruise controls are overloaded with multiple functions.

Object-Oriented Concept #4 — Access Control

A microwave oven must be built so that no combination of keystrokes that you can enter on the front keypad can cause the oven to hurt you. Certainly, some combinations don't do anything. However, no sequence of keystrokes should do the following:

- **Break the device:** You may be able to put the device into some sort of strange state in which it won't do anything until you reset it, like throwing an internal breaker. However, you shouldn't be able to break the device by using the front panel — unless, of course, you throw it to the ground in frustration. The manufacturer of such a device would probably have to send out some type of fix for a device like that.

- **Cause the device to catch fire and burn down the house:** Now, as bad as it may be for the device to break itself, catching fire is much worse. We live in a litigious society. The manufacturer's corporate officers would likely end up in jail, especially if I have anything to say about it.

However, to enforce these two rules, you have to take some responsibility. You can't make modifications to the inside of the device.

Almost all kitchen devices of any complexity, including microwave ovens, have a small seal to keep consumers from reaching inside the device. If that seal is broken, indicating that the cover of the device has been removed, the manufacturer no longer bears responsibility. If you modify the internals of an oven, you are responsible if it subsequently catches fire and burns down the house.

Similarly, a class must be able to control access to its data members. No sequence of calls to class members should cause your program to crash. The class cannot possibly ensure this if external elements have access to the internal state of the class. The class must be able to keep critical data members inaccessible to the outside world.

How Does C# Support Object-Oriented Concepts?

Okay, how does C# implement object-oriented programming? In a sense, this is the wrong question. C# is an object-oriented language; however, it doesn't implement object-oriented programming — the programmer does. You can certainly write a non-object-oriented program in C# or any other language (by, for instance, writing all of Microsoft Word in Main()). Something like "you can lead a horse to water" comes to mind. But you can easily write an object-oriented program in C#.

C# provides the following features necessary for writing object-oriented programs:

- ✔ **Controlled access:** C# controls the way in which members can be accessed. C# keywords enable you to declare some members wide open to the public while internal members are protected from view and some secrets are kept private. Notice the little hints. Access control secrets are revealed in Chapter 11.

- ✔ **Specialization:** C# supports specialization through a mechanism known as *class inheritance*. One class inherits the members of another class. For example, you can create a Car class as a particular type of Vehicle. Chapter 12 specializes in specialization.

- ✔ **Polymorphism:** This feature enables an object to perform an operation the way it wants to. The Rocket type of Vehicle may implement the Start operation much differently from the way the Car type of Vehicle does. At least, I hope it does every time I turn the key in my car — with my car you never know. Chapters 13 and 14 find their own way of describing polymorphism.

Chapter 11

Holding a Class Responsible

. . . .

In This Chapter

▶ Letting the class protect itself through access control

▶ Allowing an object to initialize itself via the constructor

▶ Defining multiple constructors for the same class

▶ Constructing static or class members

. . . .

A class must be held responsible for its actions. Just as a microwave oven shouldn't burst into flames if you press the wrong key, a class shouldn't allow itself to roll over and die when presented with incorrect data.

To be held responsible for its actions, a class must ensure that its initial state is correct, and control its subsequent state so that it remains valid. C# provides both of these capabilities.

Restricting Access to Class Members

Simple classes define all their members as `public`. Consider a `BankAccount` program that maintains a `balance` data member to retain the balance in each account. Making that data member `public` puts everyone on the honor system.

I don't know about your bank, but my bank is not nearly so forthcoming as to leave a pile of money and a register for me to mark down every time I add money to or take money away from the pile. After all, I may forget to mark my withdrawals in the register. I'm not as young as I used to be — my memory is beginning to fade.

Controlling access avoids little mistakes like forgetting to mark a withdrawal here or there. It also manages to avoid some really big mistakes with withdrawals.

I know exactly what you functional types out there are thinking: "Just make a rule that other classes can't access the `balance` data member directly, and that's that." That approach may work in theory, but in practice it never does. People start out with good intentions (like my intentions to work out every day), but those good intentions get crushed under the weight of schedule pressures to get the product out the door. Speaking of weight. . . .

A public example of public BankAccount

The following example `BankAccount` class declares all its methods `public` but declares its data members, including `nAccountNumber` and `dBalance`, to be `private`. Note that I've left it in an incorrect state to make a point. The following code won't compile correctly yet.

```
// BankAccount - create a bank account using a double variable
//                to store the account balance (keep the balance
//                in a private variable to hide its implementation
//                from the outside world)
// Note: Until you correct it, this program fails to compile
// because Main() refers to a private member of class BankAccount.
using System;
namespace BankAccount
{
  public class Program
  {
    public static void Main(string[] args)
    {
      Console.WriteLine("This program doesn't compile in its present state.");
      // open a bank account
      Console.WriteLine("Create a bank account object");
      BankAccount ba = new BankAccount();
      ba.InitBankAccount();
      // accessing the balance via the Deposit() method is OK -
      // Deposit() has access to all the data members
      ba.Deposit(10);
      // accessing the data member directly is a compile time error
      Console.WriteLine("Just in case you get this far"
                        + "\nThe following is supposed to "
                        + "generate a compile error");
      ba.dBalance += 10;
      // wait for user to acknowledge the results
      Console.WriteLine("Press Enter to terminate...");
      Console.Read();
    }
  }
  // BankAccount - define a class that represents a simple account
  public class BankAccount
  {
    private static int nNextAccountNumber = 1000;
    private int nAccountNumber;
```

```
// maintain the balance as a double variable
private double dBalance;
// Init - initialize a bank account with the next
//        account id and a balance of 0
public void InitBankAccount()
{
  nAccountNumber = ++nNextAccountNumber;
  dBalance = 0.0;
}
// GetBalance - return the current balance
public double GetBalance()
{
  return dBalance;
}
// AccountNumber
public int GetAccountNumber()
{
  return nAccountNumber;
}
public void SetAccountNumber(int nAccountNumber)
{
  this.nAccountNumber = nAccountNumber;
}
// Deposit - any positive deposit is allowed
public void Deposit(double dAmount)
{
  if (dAmount > 0.0)
  {
    dBalance += dAmount;
  }
}
// Withdraw - you can withdraw any amount up to the
//            balance; return the amount withdrawn
public double Withdraw(double dWithdrawal)
{
  if (dBalance <= dWithdrawal)
  {
    dWithdrawal = dBalance;
  }
  dBalance -= dWithdrawal;
  return dWithdrawal;
}
// GetString - return the account data as a string
public string GetString()
{
  string s = String.Format("#{0} = {1:C}",
                           GetAccountNumber(),
                           GetBalance());
  return s;
}
}
}
```

In this code, dBalance -= dWithdrawal is the same as dBalance = dBalance - dWithdrawal. C# programmers tend to use the shortest notation available.

Marking a member public makes that member available to any other code within your program.

The BankAccount class provides an InitBankAccount() method to initialize the members of the class, a Deposit() method to handle deposits, and a Withdraw() method to perform withdrawals. The Deposit() and Withdraw() methods even provide some rudimentary rules like "you can't deposit a negative number" and "you can't withdraw more than you have in your account" — both good rules for a bank, I'm sure you'll agree. However, everyone's on the honor system as long as dBalance is accessible to external methods. (In this context, *external* means "external to the class but within the same program.") That can be a problem on big programs written by teams of programmers. It can even be a problem for you (and me), given general human fallibility. Well-written code with rules that the compiler can enforce saves us all from the occasional bullet to the big toe.

Before you get too excited, however, notice that the program doesn't build. Attempts to do so generate the following error message:

```
'DoubleBankAccount.BankAccount.dBalance' is inaccessible due to its protection
        level.
```

I don't know why it doesn't just come out and say, "Hey, this is private so keep your mitts off," but that's essentially what it means. The statement ba.dBalance += 10; is illegal because dBalance is not accessible to Main(), a function outside the BankAccount class. Replacing this line with ba.Deposit(10) solves the problem. The BankAccount.Deposit() method is public and therefore accessible to Main().

The default access type is private. Forgetting to declare a member specifically is the same as declaring it private. However, you should include the private keyword to remove any doubt. Good programmers make their intentions explicit, which is another way to reduce errors.

Jumping ahead — other levels of security

This section depends on some knowledge of inheritance (Chapter 12) and namespaces (Bonus Chapter 2 on the CD). You can skip it for now if you want but just know that it's here when you need it.

C# provides the following levels of security:

✔ A `public` member is accessible to any class in the program.

✔ A `private` member is accessible only from the current class.

✔ A `protected` member is accessible from the current class and any of its subclasses. See Chapter 12.

✔ An `internal` member is accessible from any class within the same program module or assembly.

 A C# *module* or "assembly" is a separately compiled piece of code, either an executable program in an `.EXE` file or a supporting library module in a `.DLL` file. A single namespace can extend across multiple modules. Bonus Chapter 5 on the CD explains C# assemblies. Bonus Chapter 2 explains namespaces.

✔ An `internal protected` member is accessible from the current class and any subclass and from classes within the same module.

Keeping a member hidden by declaring it `private` offers the maximum amount of security. However, in many cases, you don't need that level of security. After all, the members of a subclass already depend on the members of the base class, so `protected` offers a nice, comfortable level of security.

Why Worry about Access Control?

Declaring the internal members of a class `public` is a bad idea for at least these reasons:

✔ **With all data members `public`, you can't easily determine when and how data members are getting modified.** Why bother building safety checks into the `Deposit()` and `Withdraw()` methods? In fact, why bother with these methods at all? Any method of any class can modify these elements at any time. If other functions can access these data members, they almost certainly will. (Bang! You just shot yourself in the foot.)

Your `BankAccount` program may execute for an hour or so before you notice that one of the accounts has a negative balance. The `Withdraw()` method would have made sure this didn't happen. Obviously, some other function accessed the balance without going through `Withdraw()`. Figuring out which function is responsible and under what conditions is a difficult problem.

✔ **Exposing all the data members of the class makes the interface too complicated.** As a programmer using the `BankAccount` class, you don't want to know about the internals of the class. You just need to know that you can deposit and withdraw funds. It's like a candy machine with fifty buttons versus one with just a few buttons.

✔ **Exposing internal elements leads to a distribution of the class rules.** For example, my `BankAccount` class does not allow the balance to go negative under any circumstances. That's a business rule that should be isolated within the `Withdraw()` method. Otherwise, you have to add this check everywhere the balance is updated.

What happens when the bank decides to change the rules so that "valued customers" are allowed to carry a slightly negative balance for a short period to avoid unintended overdrafts? You now have to search through the program to update every section of code that accesses the balance to make sure that the safety checks — not the bank checks — are changed.

Don't make your classes and methods any more accessible than necessary. This isn't so much paranoia about snoopy hackers as a prudent step that helps reduce errors as you code. Use `private` if possible, and then escalate to `protected`, `internal`, `internal protected`, or `public` as necessary.

Accessor methods

If you look more carefully at the `BankAccount` class, you see a few other methods. One, `GetString()`, returns a `string` version of the account fit for presentation to any `Console.WriteLine()` for display. However, displaying the contents of a `BankAccount` object may be difficult if the contents are inaccessible. In addition, using the "Render unto Caesar" policy, the class should have the right to decide how it gets displayed.

In addition, you see one "getting" method, `GetBalance()`, and a set of "setting" methods, `GetAccountNumber()` and `SetAccountNumber()`. You may wonder why I would bother to declare a data member like `dBalance` `private` but provide a `GetBalance()` method to return its value. I actually have two reasons, as follows:

✔ **`GetBalance()` does not provide a way to modify `dBalance` — it merely returns its value.** This makes the balance read-only. To use the analogy of an actual bank, you can look at your balance any time you want; you just can't take money out of your account without going through the bank's withdrawal mechanism.

✔ **`GetBalance()` hides the internal format of the class from external methods.** `GetBalance()` may go through an extensive calculation, reading receipts, adding account charges, and accounting for anything else your bank may want to subtract from your balance. External functions don't know and don't care. Of course, you care what fees are being charged. You just can't do anything about them, short of changing banks.

Finally, `GetBalance()` provides a mechanism for making internal changes to the class without the need to change the users of `BankAccount`. If the FDIC mandates that your bank store deposits differently, that shouldn't change the way you access your account.

Access control to the rescue — an example

The following `DoubleBankAccount` program demonstrates a potential flaw in the `BankAccount` program. The entire program is on your CD; however, the following listing shows just `Main()` — the only portion of the program that differs from the earlier `BankAccount` program:

```
// DoubleBankAccount - create a bank account using a double variable
//                     to store the account balance (keep the balance
//                     in a private variable to hide its implementation
//                     from the outside world)
namespace DoubleBankAccount
{
  using System;
  public class Program
  {
    public static void Main(string[] args)
    {
      // open a bank account
      Console.WriteLine("Create a bank account object");
      BankAccount ba = new BankAccount();
      ba.InitBankAccount();
      // make a deposit
      double dDeposit = 123.454;
      Console.WriteLine("Depositing {0:C}", dDeposit);
      ba.Deposit(dDeposit);
      // account balance
      Console.WriteLine("Account = {0}", ba.GetString());
      // here's the problem
      double dAddition = 0.002;
      Console.WriteLine("Adding {0:C}", dAddition);
      ba.Deposit(dAddition);
      // resulting balance
      Console.WriteLine("Resulting account = {0}", ba.GetString());
      // wait for user to acknowledge the results
      Console.WriteLine("Press Enter to terminate...");
      Console.Read();
    }
  }
```

The `Main()` function creates a bank account and then deposits $123.454, an amount that contains a fractional number of cents. `Main()` then deposits a small fraction of a cent to the balance and displays the resulting balance.

The output from this program appears as follows:

```
Create a bank account object
Depositing $123.45
Account = #1001 = $123.45
Adding $0.00
Resulting account = #1001 = $123.46
Press Enter to terminate...
```

Users start to complain. "I just can't reconcile my checkbook with my bank statement." Personally, I'm happy if I can get to the nearest $100, but some people insist that their account match to the penny. Apparently, the program has a bug.

The problem, of course, is that $123.454 shows up as $123.45. To avoid the problem, the bank decides to round deposits and withdrawals to the nearest cent. Deposit $123.454, and the bank takes that extra 0.4 cent. On the other side, the bank gives up enough 0.4 cents that everything balances out in the long run.

The easiest way to do this is by converting the bank accounts to `decimal` and using the `Decimal.Round()` method, as shown in the following `DecimalBankAccount` program:

```
// DecimalBankAccount - create a bank account using a decimal
//                      variable to store the account balance
using System;
namespace DecimalBankAccount
{
  public class Program
  {
    public static void Main(string[] args)
    {
      // open a bank account
      Console.WriteLine("Create a bank account object");
      BankAccount ba = new BankAccount();
      ba.InitBankAccount();
      // make a deposit
      double dDeposit = 123.454;
      Console.WriteLine("Depositing {0:C}", dDeposit);
      ba.Deposit(dDeposit);
      // account balance
      Console.WriteLine("Account = {0}", ba.GetString());
      // now add in a very small amount
      double dAddition = 0.002;
      Console.WriteLine("Adding {0:C}", dAddition);
      ba.Deposit(dAddition);
```

```
      // resulting balance
      Console.WriteLine("Resulting account = {0}", ba.GetString());
      // wait for user to acknowledge the results
      Console.WriteLine("Press Enter to terminate...");
      Console.Read();
   }
}
// BankAccount - define a class that represents a simple account
public class BankAccount
{
   private static int nNextAccountNumber = 1000;
   private int nAccountNumber;
   // maintain the balance as a single decimal variable
   private decimal mBalance;
   // Init - initialize a bank account with the next
   //        account id and a balance of 0
   public void InitBankAccount()
   {
      nAccountNumber = ++nNextAccountNumber;
      mBalance = 0;
   }

   // GetBalance - return the current balance
   public double GetBalance()
   {
      return (double)mBalance;
   }
   // AccountNumber
   public int GetAccountNumber()
   {
      return nAccountNumber;
   }
   public void SetAccountNumber(int nAccountNumber)
   {
      this.nAccountNumber = nAccountNumber;
   }
   // Deposit - any positive deposit is allowed
   public void Deposit(double dAmount)
   {
      if (dAmount > 0.0)
      {
         // round off the double to the nearest cent before depositing
         decimal mTemp = (decimal)dAmount;
         mTemp = Decimal.Round(mTemp, 2);
         mBalance += mTemp;
      }
   }
   // Withdraw - you can withdraw any amount up to the
   //            balance; return the amount withdrawn
   public decimal Withdraw(decimal dWithdrawal)
   {
      if (mBalance <= dWithdrawal)
      {
         dWithdrawal = mBalance;
      }
```

```
    mBalance -= dWithdrawal;
    return dWithdrawal;
  }
  // GetString - return the account data as a string
  public string GetString()
  {
    string s = String.Format("#{0} = {1:C}",
                            GetAccountNumber(),
                            GetBalance());
    return s;
  }
 }
}
```

I've converted all the internal representations to decimal values, a type better adapted to handling bank account balances than double in any case. The Deposit() method now uses the Decimal.Round() function to round the deposit amount to the nearest cent before making the deposit. The output from the program is now as expected:

```
Create a bank account object
Depositing $123.45
Account = #1001 = $123.45
Adding $0.00
Resulting account = #1001 = $123.45
Press Enter to terminate...
```

So what?

You could argue that I should have written the BankAccount program using decimal input arguments to begin with, and I would probably agree. But the point is that I didn't. Other applications were written using double as the form of storage. A problem arose. The BankAccount class was able to fix the problem internally with no changes to the application software. (Notice that the class's public interface didn't change: Balance() still returns a double.)

I repeat: Applications using class BankAccount didn't have to change.

In this case, the only function potentially affected was Main(), but the effects could have extended to dozens of functions that accessed bank accounts, and those functions could have been spread over hundreds of modules. None of those functions would have to change because the fix was within the confines of the BankAccount class. This would not have been possible if the internal members of the class had been exposed to external functions.

Internal changes to a class still require some retesting of other code, even though you didn't have to modify that code.

Defining class properties

The GetX() and SetX() methods demonstrated in the BankAccount programs are called *access functions,* or simply *accessors.* Although they signify good programming habits in theory, access functions can get clumsy in practice. For example, the following code is necessary to increment nAccountNumber by 1:

```
SetAccountNumber(GetAccountNumber() + 1);
```

C# defines a construct called a *property,* which makes using access functions much easier. The following code snippet defines a read-write property, AccountNumber:

```
public int AccountNumber       // no parentheses here
{
  get{return nAccountNumber;}  // curly braces & semicolon
  set{nAccountNumber = value;} // value is a keyword
}
```

The get section is implemented whenever the property is read, while the set section is invoked on the write. The following Balance property is read-only because only the get section is defined:

```
public double Balance
{
  get
  {
    return (double)mBalance;
  }
}
```

In use, these properties appear as follows:

```
BankAccount ba = new BankAccount();
// set the account number property
ba.AccountNumber = 1001;
// read both properties
Console.WriteLine("#{0} = {1:C}", ba.AccountNumber, ba.Balance);
```

The properties AccountNumber and Balance look very much like public data members, both in appearance and in use. However, properties enable the class to protect internal members (Balance is a read-only property) and hide their implementation (the underlying mBalance data member is private). Notice that Balance performs a conversion — it could have performed any number of calculations. Properties aren't necessarily one-liners.

By convention, the names of properties begin with a capital letter. Note that properties don't have parentheses: Balance, not Balance().

Properties are not necessarily inefficient. The C# compiler can optimize a simple accessor to the point that it generates no more machine code than accessing the data member directly. This is important, not only to an application program but also to C# itself. The C# library uses properties throughout, and you should, too, even to access class data members from methods in the same class.

Static properties

A static (class) data member may be exposed through a static property, as shown in the following simplistic example:

```
public class BankAccount
{
  private static int nNextAccountNumber = 1000;
  public static int NextAccountNumber
  {
    get{return nNextAccountNumber;}
  }
  // . . .
}
```

The `NextAccountNumber` property is accessed through the class as follows, because it isn't a property of a single object:

```
// read the account number property
int nValue = BankAccount.NextAccountNumber;
```

Properties with side effects

A `get` operation can perform extra work other than simply retrieving the associated property, as shown in the following code:

```
public static int AccountNumber
{
  // retrieve the property and set it up for the
  // next retrieval by incrementing it
  get{return ++nNextAccountNumber;}
}
```

This property increments the static account number member before returning the result. This probably is not a good idea, however, because the user of the property gets no clue that anything is happening other than the actual reading of the property. The incrementation is a *side effect*.

Like the accessor functions that they mimic, properties should not change the state of the class other than, say, setting a data member's value. In general, both properties and methods should avoid side effects because they can lead to subtle bugs. Change a class as directly and explicitly as possible.

Getting Your Objects Off to a Good Start — Constructors

Controlling class access is only half the problem. An object needs a good start in life if it is to grow. A class can supply an initialization method that the application calls to get things started, but what if the application forgets to call the function? The class starts out with garbage, and the situation doesn't get any better after that. If you're going to hold the class accountable, you have to make sure that it gets a chance to start out correctly.

C# solves that problem by calling the initialization function for you — for example:

```
MyObject mo = new MyObject();
```

In other words, this statement not only grabs an object out of a special memory area, but it also initializes that object by calling an initialization function.

Don't confuse the terms *class* and *object*. Dog is a class. My dog Scooter is an object of class Dog.

The C#-Provided Constructor

C# is pretty good at keeping track of whether a variable has been initialized. C# does not allow you to use an uninitialized variable. For example, the following code generates a compile time error:

```
public static void Main(string[] args)
{
  int n;
  double d;
  double  dCalculatedValue = n + d;
}
```

C# tracks the fact that neither n nor d have been assigned a value and doesn't allow them to be used in the expression. Compiling this tiny program generates the following compiler errors:

```
Use of unassigned local variable 'n'
Use of unassigned local variable 'd'
```

By comparison, C# provides a default constructor that initializes the data members of an object to 0 for intrinsic variables, `false` for booleans, and `null` for object references. Consider the following simple example program:

```
using System;
namespace Test
{
  public class Program
  {
    public static void Main(string[] args)
    {
      // first create an object
      MyObject localObject = new MyObject();
      Console.WriteLine("localObject.n is {0}", localObject.n);
      if (localObject.nextObject == null)
      {
        Console.WriteLine("localObject.nextObject is null");
      }
      // wait for user to acknowledge the results
      Console.WriteLine("Press Enter to terminate...");
      Console.Read();
    }
  }
  public class MyObject
  {
    internal int n;
    internal MyObject nextObject;
  }
}
```

This program defines a class `MyObject`, which contains both a simple variable n of type `int` and a reference to an object, `nextObject`, forming a chain, or *linked list,* of objects. The `Main()` function creates a `MyObject` and then displays the initial contents of n and `nextObject`.

The output from executing the program appears as follows:

```
localObject.n is 0
localObject.nextObject is null
Press Enter to terminate...
```

C# executes some small piece of code when the object is created to initialize the object and its members. Left to their own devices, the data members `localObject.n` and `nextObject` would contain random, garbage values.

The code that initializes values when they are created is called the *constructor*. It "constructs" the class, in the sense of initializing its members.

The Default Constructor

C# ensures that an object starts life in a known state: all zeros. However, for many classes (probably most classes), all zeros is not a valid state. Consider the following `BankAccount` class from earlier in this chapter:

```
public class BankAccount
{
  int nAccountNumber;
  double dBalance;
  // . . .other members
}
```

Although an initial balance of zero is probably okay, an account number of 0 definitely is not the hallmark of a valid bank account.

So far, the `BankAccount` class includes the `InitBankAccount()` method to initialize the object. However, this approach puts too much responsibility on the application software using the class. If the application fails to invoke the `InitBankAccount()` function, the bank account methods may not work, through no fault of their own. A class should not rely on external functions like `InitBankAccount()` to start the object in a valid state.

To get around this problem, the class can provide a special function that C# calls automatically when the object is created: the *class constructor*. The constructor could have been called `Init()`, `Start()`, or `Create()`, just as long as everyone agrees on the name. Instead, C# requires the constructor to carry the name of the class. Thus, a constructor for the `BankAccount` class appears as follows:

```
public void Main(string[] args)
{
  BankAccount ba = new BankAccount();
}
public class BankAccount
{
  // bank accounts start at 1000 and increase sequentially from there
  static int nNextAccountNumber = 1000;
  // maintain the account number and balance for each object
  int nAccountNumber;
  double dBalance;
  // BankAccount constructor - here it is, ta daa!
  public BankAccount()   // parentheses, possible arguments, no return type
  {
    nAccountNumber = ++nNextAccountNumber;
    dBalance = 0.0;
  }
  // . . . other members . . .
}
```

The contents of the BankAccount constructor are the same as those of the original Init...() method. However, the way you declare and use the method differs as follows:

- ✔ The constructor always carries the same name as the class.
- ✔ The constructor never has a return type, not even void.
- ✔ Main() does not need to invoke any extra function to initialize the object when it is created; no Init() is necessary.

Constructing something

Try one of these constructor thingees out. Consider the following program, DemonstrateDefaultConstructor:

```
// DemonstrateDefaultConstructor - demonstrate how default constructors
//                          work; create a class with a constructor
//                          and then step through a few scenarios
using System;
namespace DemonstrateDefaultConstructor
{
  // MyObject - create a class with a noisy constructor
  //            and an internal data object
  public class MyObject
  {
    // this data member is a property of the class
    static MyOtherObject staticObj = new MyOtherObject();
    // this data member is a property of the object
    MyOtherObject dynamicObj;
    // constructor (a real chatterbox)
    public MyObject()
    {
      Console.WriteLine("MyObject constructor starting");
      Console.WriteLine(
        "(Static data member constructed before this constructor)");
      Console.WriteLine("Now create nonstatic data member dynamically:");
      dynamicObj = new MyOtherObject();
      Console.WriteLine("MyObject constructor ending");
    }
  }
  // MyOtherObject- this class also has a noisy constructor
  //                but no internal members
  public class MyOtherObject
  {
    public MyOtherObject()
    {
      Console.WriteLine("MyOtherObject constructing");
    }
  }
}
```

```
public class Program
{
  public static void Main(string[] args)
  {
    Console.WriteLine("Main() starting");
    Console.WriteLine("Creating a local MyObject in Main():");
    MyObject localObject = new MyObject();
    // wait for user to acknowledge the results
    Console.WriteLine("Press Enter to terminate...");
    Console.Read();
  }
}
}
```

Executing this program generates the following output:

```
Main() starting
Creating a local MyObject in Main():
MyOtherObject constructing
MyObject constructor starting
(Static data member constructed before this constructor)
Now create nonstatic data member dynamically:
MyOtherObject constructing
MyObject constructor ending
Press Enter to terminate...
```

The following steps reconstruct what just happened here:

1. The program starts, and `Main()` outputs the initial message and announces that it's about to create a local `MyObject`.

2. `Main()` creates a `localObject` of type `MyObject`.

3. `MyObject` contains a static member `staticObj` of class `MyOtherObject`. All static data members are created before the first `MyObject()` constructor runs. In this case, C# populates `staticObj` with a newly created `MyOtherObject` before passing control to the `MyObject` constructor. This step accounts for the fifth line of output.

4. The constructor for `MyObject` is given control. It outputs the initial message, `MyObject constructor starting` and then notes that the static member was already constructed before the `MyObject()` constructor began: `(Static data member constructed before this constructor)`.

5. After announcing its intention with `Now create nonstatic data member dynamically`, the `MyObject` constructor creates an object of class `MyOtherObject` using the `new` operator, creating the second `MyOtherObject constructing` message as the `MyOtherObject` constructor is called.

6. Control returns to the `MyObject` constructor, which returns to `Main()`.

7. Job well done!

Executing the constructor from the debugger

It's illuminating to execute the same program from the debugger as follows:

1. **Rebuild the program: Choose Build⇨Build DemonstrateDefaultConstructor.**

2. **Before you start executing the program from the debugger, set a breakpoint at the** `Console.WriteLine()` **call in the** `MyOtherObject` **constructor.**

To set a breakpoint, click in the gray trough on the left side of the display, next to the line at which you want to stop.

Figure 11-1 shows my display with the breakpoint set. The red ball is in the gray trough.

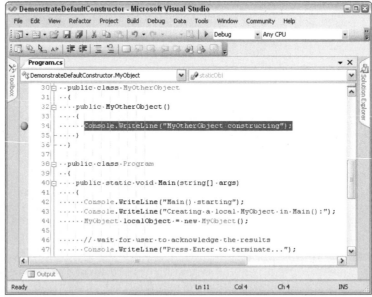

Figure 11-1:
The red
highlighting
in the
`MyOther`
`Object`
constructor
indicates
the pres-
ence of a
breakpoint.

3. **Rather than choosing Debug⇨Start Debugging, choose Debug⇨ Step Into (or, better yet, press F11).**

Your menus, toolbars, and windows should change a bit, and then a bright yellow highlight appears on the opening curly brace in `Main()`.

4. **Press F11 three more times and lightly rest the mouse pointer on the** `localObject` **variable (without clicking).**

   You're about to call the `MyObject` constructor. Your display should now look like that shown in Figure 11-2. You can see that `localObject` is currently `null` under the cursor. The Locals window below shows the same thing.

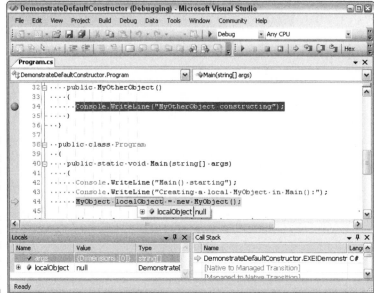

Figure 11-2:
The Visual Studio debugger display, right before jumping into constructor-ville.

5. **Press F11 one more time.**

   The program executes up to the breakpoint in `MyOtherObject`, as shown by the bar in Figure 11-3. How did you reach this point? The last call in `Main()` invoked the constructor for `MyObject`. But before that constructor begins to execute, C# initializes the static data member in class `MyObject`. That data member is of type `MyOtherObject`, so initializing it means invoking *its* constructor — which lands you at the breakpoint. (Without the breakpoint, you wouldn't see the debugger stop there, although the constructor would indeed execute, as you could confirm by checking that the constructor's message shows up in the console window.)

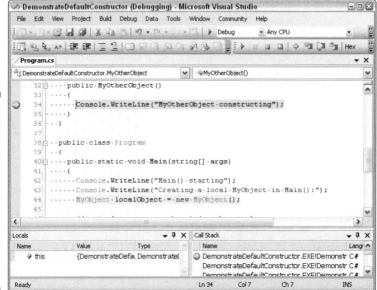

Figure 11-3:
Control
passes to
the
MyOther
Object
constructor
before
heading
into the
MyObject
constructor.

6. **Press F11 twice more, and you're stopped at the static data member,** staticObj, **as shown in Figure 11-4.**

It was that object's constructor that you just stepped out of.

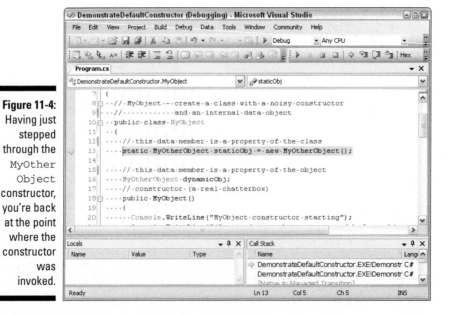

Figure 11-4:
Having just
stepped
through the
MyOther
Object
constructor,
you're back
at the point
where the
constructor
was
invoked.

7. Continue pressing F11 as you walk through the program.

The first time you press F11, you stop at the beginning of the MyObject constructor, at last. Note that you step into the MyOtherObject constructor a second time when the MyObject constructor creates the other MyObject data member, the nonstatic one called dynamicObj.

Remember to continue through the Console.Read() statement back in Main().

Bonus Chapter 4 on the CD gives you a thorough tour of the debugger.

Initializing an object directly — the default constructor

You may think that almost every class would have a default constructor of some type, and in a way, you are correct. However, C# enables you to initialize data members directly using initializers.

Thus, I could have written the BankAccount class as follows:

```
public class BankAccount
{
  // bank accounts start at 1000 and increase sequentially from there
  static int nNextAccountNumber = 1000;
  // maintain the account number and balance for each object
  int nAccountNumber = ++nNextAccountNumber;
  double dBalance = 0.0;
  // . . . other members . . .
}
```

Here's the initializer business. Both nAccountNumber and dBalance are assigned a value as part of their declaration. This has the same effect as a constructor but without having to do the work in the constructor.

Be very clear about exactly what's happening. You may think that this statement sets dBalance to 0.0 directly. However, dBalance exists only as a part of an object. Thus, the assignment is not executed until a BankAccount object is created. In fact, this assignment is executed every time an object is created.

Note that the static data member nNextAccountNumber is initialized the first time the BankAccount class is accessed — as your tour in the debugger showed, that's the first time you access any method or property of the object owning the static data member, including the constructor. Once initialized, the static member is not reinitialized each time you construct a BankAccount instance. That's different from the nonstatic members.

Initializers are executed in the order of their appearance in the class declaration. If C# encounters both initializers and a constructor, the initializers are executed before the body of the constructor.

Seeing that construction stuff with initializers

In the DemonstrateDefaultConstructor program, move the call new MyOtherObject() from the MyObject constructor to the declaration itself, as follows (see the bold text), modify the second WriteLine() statement as shown, and then rerun the program:

```
public class MyObject
{
  // this member is a property of the class
  static MyOtherObject staticObj = new MyOtherObject();
  // this member is a property of the object
  MyOtherObject dynamicObj = new MyOtherObject();
  public MyObject()
  {
    Console.WriteLine("MyObject constructor starting");
    Console.WriteLine(
      "Both static data members initialized before this constructor)");
    // dynamicObj construction was here, now moved up
    Console.WriteLine("MyObject constructor ending");
  }
}
```

Compare the following output from this modified program with the output from its predecessor, DemonstrateConstructor:

```
Main() starting
Creating a local MyObject in Main():
MyOtherObject constructing
MyOtherObject constructing
MyObject constructor starting
(Both static data members initialized before this constructor)
MyObject constructor ending
Press Enter to terminate...
```

You can find the entire program (after these changes) on the CD, under the illustrious name of DemonstrateConstructorWithInitializer.

Overloading the Constructor (Is That Like Overtaxing a Carpenter?)

You can overload constructors, just as you can overload any other method.

Overloading a function means defining two functions with the same name but with different types of arguments. See Chapter 7 for details.

Suppose you wanted to provide the following three ways to create a `BankAccount`: one with a zero balance like mine most of the time and two more variations for a bank account with some initial value:

```
// BankAccountWithMultipleConstructors - provide our trusty bank account
//                     with a number of constructors, one for every occasion
using System;
namespace BankAccountWithMultipleConstructors
{
  using System;
  public class Program
  {
    public static void Main(string[] args)
    {
      // create a bank account with valid initial values
      BankAccount ba1 = new BankAccount();
      Console.WriteLine(ba1.GetString());
      BankAccount ba2 = new BankAccount(100);
      Console.WriteLine(ba2.GetString());
      BankAccount ba3 = new BankAccount(1234, 200);
      Console.WriteLine(ba3.GetString());
      // wait for user to acknowledge the results
      Console.WriteLine("Press Enter to terminate...");
      Console.Read();
    }
  }
  // BankAccount - simulate a simple bank account
  public class BankAccount
  {
    // bank accounts start at 1000 and increase sequentially from there
    static int nNextAccountNumber = 1000;
    // maintain the account number and balance
    int nAccountNumber;
    double dBalance;
    // provide a series of constructors depending upon the need
    public BankAccount()  // you create this one, not automatic
    {
      nAccountNumber = ++nNextAccountNumber;
      dBalance = 0.0;
    }
    public BankAccount(double dInitialBalance)
```

```
    {
        // repeat some of the code from the default constructor
        nAccountNumber = ++nNextAccountNumber;
        // now the code unique to this constructor
        // start with an initial balance as long as it's positive
        if (dInitialBalance < 0)
        {
            dInitialBalance = 0;
        }
        dBalance = dInitialBalance;
    }
    public BankAccount(int nInitialAccountNumber,
                       double dInitialBalance)
    {
        // ignore negative account numbers
        if (nInitialAccountNumber <= 0)
        {
            nInitialAccountNumber = ++nNextAccountNumber;
        }
        nAccountNumber = nInitialAccountNumber;
        // start with an initial balance as long as it's positive
        if (dInitialBalance < 0)
        {
            dInitialBalance = 0;
        }
        dBalance = dInitialBalance;
    }
    public string GetString()
    {
        return String.Format("#{0} = {1:N}", nAccountNumber, dBalance);
    }
  }
}
```

C# no longer provides a default constructor for you if you define your own constructor, no matter what type it might be. Thus, you have to provide the parameterless constructor in the preceding code.

This version of the program, named `BankAccountWithMultiple Constructors`, provides the following three constructors:

✔ The first constructor assigns an account ID and sets a balance of 0.

✔ The second constructor assigns an account ID but initializes the account with a positive balance. Negative balances are ignored.

✔ The third constructor allows the user to specify a positive account number and a positive balance.

`Main()` creates a different bank account using each of the three constructors and then outputs the objects that are created. The output from executing the program is as follows:

```
#1001 = 0.00
#1002 = 100.00
#1234 = 200.00
Press Enter to terminate...
```

A real-world class would perform a good deal more testing of the input parameters to the constructor, to make sure that they're legal.

You differentiate constructors by using the same rules that apply to functions. The first object to be constructed in `Main()` — `ba1` — is created with no arguments and thus is vectored to the parameterless constructor `BankAccount()` (still called the "default" constructor, but no longer generated automatically by C#) to receive the default account ID and a balance of 0. The second account, `ba2`, is sent to the `BankAccount(double)` constructor to get the next bank account ID, but is created with an initial value of 100. The third little piggie, `ba3`, goes for the full-meal deal, `BankAccount(int, double)`, and gets his own bank account ID and an initial balance.

Avoiding Duplication among Constructors

Like a typical soap opera script, the three `BankAccount` constructors have significant amounts of duplication. As you can imagine, the situation would get much worse in real-world classes that may have many constructors and even more data elements to initialize. In addition, the tests on input data can get more involved in a real-world class than on a Yahoo! Web page. Duplicating these business rules is both tedious and error prone. The checks can easily get out of synch. For example, through a coding error, two constructors may apply different sets of rules against the balance. Such errors are very difficult to find.

You would like to have one constructor call the other, but constructors are not functions — you can't just call them. However, you can create some alternative function that does the actual construction and pass control to it, as demonstrated in this `BankAccountConstructorsAndFunction` program:

```
// BankAccountConstructorsAndFunction -  provide our trusty bank account with a

//                    number of constructors, one for every occasion
using System;
namespace BankAccountConstructorsAndFunction
{
  using System;
  public class Program
  {
```

```csharp
    public static void Main(string[] args)
    {
      // create a bank account with valid initial values
      BankAccount ba1 = new BankAccount();
      Console.WriteLine(ba1.GetString());
      BankAccount ba2 = new BankAccount(100);
      Console.WriteLine(ba2.GetString());
      BankAccount ba3 = new BankAccount(1234, 200);
      Console.WriteLine(ba3.GetString());
      // wait for user to acknowledge the results
      Console.WriteLine("Press Enter to terminate...");
      Console.Read();
    }
  }
  // BankAccount - simulate a simple bank account
  public class BankAccount
  {
    // bank accounts start at 1000 and increase sequentially from there
    static int nNextAccountNumber = 1000;
    // maintain the account number and balance
    int nAccountNumber;
    double dBalance;
    // place all the real initialization code in a separate,
    // conventional function, called from constructors
    public BankAccount()  // you create this one, not automatic
    {
      Init(++nNextAccountNumber, 0.0);
    }
    public BankAccount(double dInitialBalance)
    {
      Init(++nNextAccountNumber, dInitialBalance);
    }
    // the most specific constructor does all the real work
    public BankAccount(int nInitialAccountNumber, double dInitialBalance)
    {
      Init(nInitialAccountNumber, dInitialBalance);
    }
    private void Init(int nInitialAccountNumber, double dInitialBalance)
    {
      nAccountNumber = nInitialAccountNumber;
      // start with an initial balance as long as it's positive
      if (dInitialBalance < 0)
      {
        dInitialBalance = 0;
      }
      dBalance = dInitialBalance;
    }
    public string GetString()
    {
      return String.Format("#{0} = {1:N}", nAccountNumber, dBalance);
    }
  }
}
```

Here, an `Init()` method does the work of construction. However, this approach isn't exactly kosher for several reasons — not the least of which is the fact that you are now calling a method of the object before the object has been fully constructed. That's a very dangerous thing to do.

Fortunately, this approach isn't necessary. One constructor can refer to another, using a variation of the `this` keyword, as follows:

```
// BankAccountConstructorsAndThis -

//              provide our trusty bank account with a number of
//              constructors, one for every occasion
using System;
namespace BankAccountConstructorsAndThis
{
  using System;
  public class Program
  {
    public static void Main(string[] args)
    {
      // create a bank account with valid initial values
      BankAccount ba1 = new BankAccount();
      Console.WriteLine(ba1.GetString());
      BankAccount ba2 = new BankAccount(100);
      Console.WriteLine(ba2.GetString());
      BankAccount ba3 = new BankAccount(1234, 200);
      Console.WriteLine(ba3.GetString());
      // wait for user to acknowledge the results
      Console.WriteLine("Press Enter to terminate...");
      Console.Read();
    }
  }
  // BankAccount - simulate a simple bank account
  public class BankAccount
  {
    // bank accounts start at 1000 and increase sequentially from there
    static int nNextAccountNumber = 1000;
    // maintain the account number and balance
    int nAccountNumber;
    double dBalance;
    // invoke the more specific constructor by providing
    // default values for the missing arguments
    public BankAccount() : this(0, 0) {}
    public BankAccount(double dInitialBalance) : this(0, dInitialBalance) {}
    // the most specific constructor does all the
    // real work
    public BankAccount(int nInitialAccountNumber, double dInitialBalance)
    {
      // ignore negative account numbers; a zero account
      // number indicates that we should use the next available
      if (nInitialAccountNumber <= 0)
      {
        nInitialAccountNumber = ++nNextAccountNumber;
```

```
        }
        nAccountNumber = nInitialAccountNumber;
        // start with an initial balance as long as it's positive
        if (dInitialBalance < 0)
        {
          dInitialBalance = 0;
        }
        dBalance = dInitialBalance;
    }
    public string GetString()
    {
      return String.Format("#{0} = {1:N}", nAccountNumber, dBalance);
    }
  }
}
```

This version of BankAccount provides the same three constructors as the previous version; however, rather than repeat the same tests in each constructor, both of the simpler constructors invoke the most flexible constructor, providing defaults for the missing arguments. Init() is now gone.

Creating an object using the default constructor invokes the following BankAccount() constructor:

```
BankAccount ba1 = new BankAccount();  // no parameters
```

The BankAccount() constructor immediately passes control to the BankAccount(int, double) constructor, passing it the default values 0 and 0.0, as follows:

```
public BankAccount() : this(0, 0) {}
```

Note that because the constructor has an empty body, you can write it all on one line.

The all-powerful third constructor has been updated to look for a zero bank account ID and to supply a valid one instead.

Control returns to the default constructor after the invoked constructor has completed. The body of the default constructor is empty in this case.

Creating a bank account with a balance but a default account ID goes down the following path:

```
public BankAccount(double d) : this(0, d) {}
```

Being Object Stingy

You can't construct an object without a constructor of some sort. If you define your own constructor, C# takes its constructor away. Combining these two facts, you can create a class that can only be instantiated locally.

For example, only methods that are defined within the same assembly as BankAccount can create a BankAccount object with the constructor declared internal, as in the bold text that follows (see Bonus Chapter 5 on the CD for more on assemblies):

```csharp
// BankAccount - simulate a simple bank account
public class BankAccount
{
  // bank accounts start at 1000 and increase sequentially from there
  static int nNextAccountNumber = 1000;
  // maintain the account number and balance
  int nAccountNumber;
  double dBalance;
  // invoke the more specific constructor by providing
  // default values for the missing arguments
  internal BankAccount()   // here's the internal constructor
  {
    nAccountNumber = ++nNextAccountNumber;
    dBalance = 0;
  }
  public string GetString()
  {
    return String.Format("#{0} = {1:N}", nAccountNumber, dBalance);
  }
}
```

Chapter 12

Inheritance — Is That All I Get?

*O*bject-oriented programming is based on three principles: the ability to control access (encapsulation), the ability to inherit from other classes, and the ability to respond appropriately (polymorphism).

Inheritance is a common concept. I am a human, except when I first wake up. I inherit certain properties from the class `Human`, such as my ability to converse, more or less, and my dependence on air, food, and carbohydrate-based beverages with lots of caffeine. The class `Human` inherits its dependencies on air, water, and nourishment from the class `Mammal`, which inherits from the class `Animal`.

The ability to pass down properties is a powerful one. It enables you to describe things in an economical way. For example, if my son asks, "What's a duck?" I can say, "It's a bird that goes quack." Despite what you may think, that answer conveys a considerable amount of information. My son knows what a bird is, and now he knows all those same things about a duck plus the duck's additional property of "quackness."

Object-oriented languages express this inheritance relationship by allowing one class to inherit from another. This feature enables object-oriented languages to generate a model that's closer to the real world than the model generated by languages that don't support inheritance.

Inheriting a Class

In the following `InheritanceExample` program, the class `SubClass` inherits from the class `BaseClass`:

```
// InheritanceExample - provide the simplest possible
//                        demonstration of inheritance
using System;
namespace InheritanceExample
{
  public class BaseClass
  {
    public int nDataMember;
    public void SomeMethod()
    {
      Console.WriteLine("SomeMethod()");
    }
  }
  public class SubClass : BaseClass
  {
    public void SomeOtherMethod()
    {
      Console.WriteLine("SomeOtherMethod()");
    }
  }
  public class Program
  {
    public static void Main(string[] args)
    {
      // create a base class object
      Console.WriteLine("Exercising a base class object:");
      BaseClass bc = new BaseClass();
      bc.nDataMember = 1;
      bc.SomeMethod();
      // now create a subclass element
      Console.WriteLine("Exercising a subclass object:");
      SubClass sc = new SubClass();
      sc.nDataMember = 2;
      sc.SomeMethod();
      sc.SomeOtherMethod();
      // wait for user to acknowledge the results
      Console.WriteLine("Press Enter to terminate...");
      Console.Read();
    }
  }
}
```

The class `BaseClass` is defined with a data member and a simple method, `SomeMethod()`. `Main()` creates and exercises the `BaseClass` object `bc`.

Inheritance is amazing

To make sense of our surroundings, humans build extensive taxonomies. For example, Fido is a special case of dog, which is a special case of canine, which is a special case of mammal — and so it goes. This ability to classify things shapes our understanding of the world.

In an object-oriented language like C#, you say that the class `Student` inherits from the class `Person`. You also say that `Person` is a base class of `Student`, and `Student` is a subclass of `Person`. Finally, you say that a `Student` IS_A `Person`. (Using all caps is a common way of expressing this unique relationship — I didn't make this up.)

Notice that the IS_A property is not reflexive: Although `Student` IS_A `Person`, the reverse is not true. A `Person` IS_NOT_A `Student`.

A statement like this always refers to the general case. It could be that a particular `Person` is, in fact, a `Student` — lots of people who are members of the class `Person` are not members of the class `Student`. In addition, the class `Student` has properties it does not share with the class `Person`. For example, `Student` has a grade point average, but the ordinary `Person` quite happily does not.

The inheritance property is transitive. For example, if I define a new class `GraduateStudent` as a subclass of `Student`, `GraduateStudent` is also a `Person`. It must be that way: If a `GraduateStudent` IS_A `Student` and a `Student` IS_A `Person`, a `GraduateStudent` IS_A `Person`. Q.E.D.

The class `SubClass` inherits from that class by placing the name of the class, `BaseClass`, after a colon in the class definition. `SubClass` gets all the members of `BaseClass` as its own, plus any members that it may add to the pile. `Main()` demonstrates that `SubClass` now has a data member, `nDataMember`, and a member function, `SomeMethod()`, to join the brand-new member of the family, little method `SomeOtherMethod()` — and what a joy it is, too.

The program produces the following expected output — actually, I'm sort of surprised whenever one of my programs works as expected:

```
Exercising a base class object:
SomeMethod()
Exercising a subclass object:
SomeMethod()
SomeOtherMethod()
Press Enter to terminate...
```

Why Do You Need Inheritance?

Inheritance serves several important functions. You may think that inheritance reduces the amount of typing. In a way it does — you don't need to repeat the properties of a `Person` when you're describing a `Student` class.

A more important, related issue is that major buzzword, *reuse*. Software scientists have known for some time that starting from scratch with each new project and rebuilding the same software components doesn't make much sense.

Compare the situation in software development to that of other industries. How many car manufacturers start by building their own wrenches and screwdrivers before they construct a car? And even if they did, how many would start over completely, building all new tools for the next model? Practitioners in other industries have found that starting with existing screws, bolts, nuts, and even larger off-the-shelf components such as motors and compressors makes more sense than starting from scratch.

Inheritance enables you to tweak existing software components. You can adapt existing classes to new applications without making internal modifications. The existing class is inherited into — *extended* by — a new subclass that contains the necessary additions and modifications. If someone else wrote the base class, you may not be able to modify it, so inheritance can save the day.

This capability carries with it a third benefit of inheritance. Suppose you inherit from some existing class. Later, you find that the base class has a bug you must correct. If you've modified the class to reuse it, you must manually check for, correct, and retest the bug in each application separately. If you've inherited the class without changes, you can generally stick the updated class into the other application without much hassle.

But the biggest benefit of inheritance is that it describes the way life is. Things inherit properties from each other. There's no getting around it. Basta! — as my Italian grandmother would say.

A More Involved Example — Inheriting from a BankAccount Class

A bank maintains several types of accounts. One type, the savings account, has all the properties of a simple bank account plus the ability to accumulate interest. The following `SimpleSavingsAccount` program models this relationship in C#.

To those faint of heart, you may want to steady yourself. This listing is a little on the long side; however, the pieces are fairly well divided. The version of this program on the CD includes some modifications from the next section of this chapter, so it's a bit different from this listing.

```
// SimpleSavingsAccount - implement a SavingsAccount as a form of
//                         BankAccount; don't use any virtual methods
//                         (Chapter 13 explains virtual methods)
using System;
namespace SimpleSavingsAccount
{
  // BankAccount - simulate a bank account each of which
  //               carries an account ID (which is assigned
  //               upon creation) and a balance
  public class BankAccount    // the base class
  {
    // bank accounts start at 1000 and increase sequentially from there
    public static int nNextAccountNumber = 1000;
    // maintain the account number and balance for each object
    public int nAccountNumber;
    public decimal mBalance;
    // Init - initialize a bank account with the next account ID and the
    //        specified initial balance (default to zero)
    public void InitBankAccount()
    {
      InitBankAccount(0);
    }
    public void InitBankAccount(decimal mInitialBalance)
    {
      nAccountNumber = ++nNextAccountNumber;
      mBalance = mInitialBalance;
    }
    // Balance property
    public decimal Balance
    {
      get { return mBalance;}
    }
    // Deposit - any positive deposit is allowed
    public void Deposit(decimal mAmount)
    {
      if (mAmount > 0)
      {
        mBalance += mAmount;
      }
    }
    // Withdraw - you can withdraw any amount up to the
    //            balance; return the amount withdrawn
    public decimal Withdraw(decimal mWithdrawal)
    {
      if (Balance <= mWithdrawal) // use Balance property
      {
        mWithdrawal = Balance;
      }
      mBalance -= mWithdrawal;
      return mWithdrawal;
    }
    // ToString - stringify the account
```

```csharp
    public string ToBankAccountString()
    {
      return String.Format("{0} - {1:C}",
        nAccountNumber, Balance);
    }
  }
  // SavingsAccount - a bank account that draws interest
  public class SavingsAccount : BankAccount   // the subclass
  {
    public decimal mInterestRate;
    // InitSavingsAccount - input the rate expressed as a
    //                      rate between 0 and 100
    public void InitSavingsAccount(decimal mInterestRate)
    {
      InitSavingsAccount(0, mInterestRate);
    }
    public void InitSavingsAccount(decimal mInitial, decimal mInterestRate)
    {
      InitBankAccount(mInitial);
      this.mInterestRate = mInterestRate / 100;
    }
    // AccumulateInterest - invoke once per period
    public void AccumulateInterest()
    {
      mBalance = Balance + (decimal)(Balance * mInterestRate);
    }
    // ToString - stringify the account
    public string ToSavingsAccountString()
    {
      return String.Format("{0} ({1}%)",
        ToBankAccountString(), mInterestRate * 100);
    }
  }
  public class Program
  {
    public static void Main(string[] args)
    {
      // create a bank account and display it
      BankAccount ba = new BankAccount();
      ba.InitBankAccount(100);
      ba.Deposit(100);
      Console.WriteLine("Account {0}", ba.ToBankAccountString());
      // now a savings account
      SavingsAccount sa = new SavingsAccount();
      sa.InitSavingsAccount(100, 12.5M);
      sa.AccumulateInterest();
      Console.WriteLine("Account {0}", sa.ToSavingsAccountString());
      // wait for user to acknowledge the results
      Console.WriteLine("Press Enter to terminate...");
      Console.Read();
    }
  }
}
```

The BankAccount class is not unlike some of those appearing in other chapters of this book. It begins with an overloaded initialization function InitBankAccount(): one for accounts that start out with an initial balance and another for which an initial balance of zero will just have to do. Notice that this version of BankAccount doesn't take advantage of the latest and greatest constructor advances you see in the final version of the class in Chapter 11. By the end of this chapter, that will all be cleaned up, and you'll see why I chose to drop back ten yards here.

The Balance property allows others to read the balance without giving them the ability to modify it. The Deposit() method accepts any positive deposit. Withdraw() lets you take out as much as you want, as long as you have enough in your account — my bank's nice, but it's not that nice. ToBank AccountString() creates a string that describes the account.

The SavingsAccount class inherits all that good stuff from BankAccount. To that, it adds an interest rate and the ability to accumulate interest at regular intervals.

Main() does about as little as it can. It creates a BankAccount, displays the account, creates a SavingsAccount, accumulates one period of interest, and displays the result, with the interest rate in parentheses, as follows:

```
Account 1001 - $200.00
Account 1002 - $112.50 (12.500%)
Press Enter to terminate...
```

Notice that the InitSavingsAccount() method invokes InitBank Account(). This initializes the bank account–specific data members. The InitSavingsAccount() method could have initialized these members directly; however, it is better practice to allow the BankAccount to initialize its own members. A class should be responsible for itself.

IS_A versus HAS_A — I'm So Confused

The relationship between SavingsAccount and BankAccount is the fundamental IS_A relationship seen with inheritance. In the following sections, I show you why and then show you what the alternative, the HAS_A relationship, would look like.

The IS_A relationship

The IS_A relationship between SavingsAccount and BankAccount is demonstrated by the following modification to the class Program in the Simple SavingsAccount program from the preceding section:

```
public class Program
{
  // We add this:
  // DirectDeposit - deposit my paycheck automatically
  public static void DirectDeposit(BankAccount ba, decimal mPay)
  {
    ba.Deposit(mPay);
  }
  public static void Main(string[] args)
  {
    // create a bank account and display it
    BankAccount ba = new BankAccount();
    ba.InitBankAccount(100);
    DirectDeposit(ba, 100);
    Console.WriteLine("Account {0}", ba.ToBankAccountString());
    // now a savings account
    SavingsAccount sa = new SavingsAccount();
    sa.InitSavingsAccount(12.5M);
    DirectDeposit(sa, 100);
    sa.AccumulateInterest();
    Console.WriteLine("Account {0}", sa.ToSavingsAccountString());
    // wait for user to acknowledge the results
    Console.WriteLine("Press Enter to terminate...");
    Console.Read();
  }
}
```

In effect, nothing has changed. The only real difference is that all deposits are now being made through the local function `DirectDeposit()`, which isn't part of class `BankAccount`. The arguments to this function are the bank account and the amount to deposit.

Notice (here comes the good part) that `Main()` could pass either a bank account or a savings account to `DirectDeposit()` because a `Savings Account` IS_A `BankAccount` and is accorded all the rights and privileges thereto. Because `SavingsAccount` IS_A `BankAccount`, you can assign a `SavingsAccount` to a `BankAccount`-type variable or method argument.

Gaining access to BankAccount through containment

The class `SavingsAccount` could have gained access to the members of `BankAccount` in a different way, as shown in the following code, where the key line is shown in boldface:

```
// SavingsAccount - a bank account that draws interest
public class SavingsAccount_    // notice the underscore: this is not
                                // the SavingsAccount class.
{
```

```
public BankAccount bankAccount;   // notice this, the contained BankAccount
public decimal mInterestRate;
// InitSavingsAccount - input the rate expressed as a
//                      rate between 0 and 100
public void InitSavingsAccount(BankAccount bankAccount, decimal mInterestRate)
{
  this.bankAccount = bankAccount;
  this.mInterestRate = mInterestRate / 100;
}
// AccumulateInterest - invoke once per period
public void AccumulateInterest()
{
  bankAccount.mBalance = bankAccount.Balance
                + (bankAccount.Balance * mInterestRate);
}
// Deposit - any positive deposit is allowed
public void Deposit(decimal mAmount)
{
  // delegate to the contained BankAccount object
  bankAccount.Deposit(mAmount);
}
// Withdraw - you can withdraw any amount up to the
//            balance; return the amount withdrawn
public double Withdraw(decimal mWithdrawal)
{
  return bankAccount.Withdraw(mWithdrawal);
}
}
```

In this case, the class SavingsAccount_ contains a data member bank
Account (as opposed to inheriting from BankAccount). The bankAccount
object contains the balance and account number information needed by the
savings account. The SavingsAccount_ class retains the data unique to a
savings account and *delegates* to the contained BankAccount object as
needed. That is, when the SavingsAccount needs, say, the balance, it asks
the contained BankAccount for it.

In this case, you say that the SavingsAccount_ HAS_A BankAccount. Hard-
core object-oriented jocks say that SavingsAccount *composes* a Bank
Account. That is, SavingsAccount is partly *composed of* a BankAccount.

The HAS_A relationship

The HAS_A relationship is fundamentally different from the IS_A relationship.
This difference doesn't seem so bad in the following example application
code segment:

```
// create a new savings account
BankAccount ba = new BankAccount()
SavingsAccount_ sa = new SavingsAccount_(); // special version of SavingsAccount
```

```
sa.InitSavingsAccount(ba, 5);
// and deposit 100 dollars into it
sa.Deposit(100);
// now accumulate interest
sa.AccumulateInterest();
```

The problem is that a SavingsAccount_ cannot be used as a BankAccount because it doesn't inherit from BankAccount. Instead, it *contains* a BankAccount — not the same thing at all. For example, the following code example fails:

```
// DirectDeposit - deposit my paycheck automatically
void DirectDeposit(BankAccount ba, int nPay)
{
   ba.Deposit(nPay);
}
void SomeFunction()
{
   // the following example fails
   SavingsAccount_ sa = new SavingsAccount_();
   DirectDeposit(sa, 100);
   // . . . continue . . .
}
```

DirectDeposit() can't accept a SavingsAccount_ in lieu of a Bank Account. No obvious relationship between the two exists as far as C# is concerned because inheritance isn't involved.

When to IS_A and When to HAS_A?

The distinction between the IS_A and HAS_A relationships is more than just a matter of software convenience. This relationship has a corollary in the real world.

For example, a Ford Explorer IS_A car (when it's upright, that is). An Explorer HAS_A motor. If your friend says, "Come on over in your car," and you show up in an Explorer, he has no grounds for complaint. He may have a complaint if you show up carrying your Explorer's engine in your arms, however.

The class Explorer should extend the class Car, not only to give Explorer access to the methods of a Car but also to express the fundamental relationship between the two.

Unfortunately, the beginning programmer may have Car inherit from Motor, as an easy way to give the Car class access to the members of Motor, which the Car needs to operate. For example, Car can inherit the method Motor. Go(). However, this example highlights one of the problems with this approach. Even though humans get sloppy in their speech, making a car go is not the same thing as making a motor go. The car's "go" operation certainly relies on that of the motor, but they aren't the same thing — you also have to put the transmission in gear, release the brake, and so on.

Perhaps even more than that, inheriting from Motor misstates the facts. A car simply is not a type of motor.

Elegance in software is a goal worth achieving in its own right. It enhances understandability, reliability, and maintainability, plus it cures indigestion and gout.

The hard-core object-oriented jocks recommend preferring HAS_A over IS_A for simpler program designs.

Other Features That Support Inheritance

C# implements a set of features designed to support inheritance. I discuss these features in the following sections.

Changing class

A program can change the class of an object. In fact, you've already seen this in one example. SomeFunction() can pass a SavingsAccount object to a method that's expecting a BankAccount object.

You can make this conversion more explicit as follows:

```
BankAccount ba;
SavingsAccount sa = new SavingsAccount();
                          // OK:
ba = sa;                  // an implicit down conversion is allowed
ba = (BankAccount)sa;     // the explicit cast is preferred
                          // Not OK:
sa = ba;                  // implicit up conversion not allowed
                          // this is OK:
sa = (SavingsAccount)ba;
```

The first line stores a SavingsAccount object into a BankAccount variable. C# converts the object for you. The second line uses the cast operator to explicitly convert the object.

The final two lines convert the BankAccount object back into a SavingsAccount.

The IS_A property is not reflexive. That is, even though an Explorer is a car, a car is not necessarily an Explorer. Similarly, a `BankAccount` is not necessarily a `SavingsAccount`, so the implicit conversion is not allowed. The final line is allowed because the programmer has indicated her willingness to "chance it." She must know something.

Invalid casts at run time

Generally, casting an object from `BankAccount` to `SavingsAccount` is a dangerous operation. Consider the following example:

```
public static void ProcessAmount(BankAccount bankAccount)
{
  // deposit a large sum to the account
  bankAccount.Deposit(10000.00M);
  // if the object is a SavingsAccount
  // then collect interest now
  SavingsAccount savingsAccount = (SavingsAccount)bankAccount;
  savingsAccount.AccumulateInterest();
}
public static void TestCast()
{
  SavingsAccount sa = new SavingsAccount();
  ProcessAmount(sa);
  BankAccount ba = new BankAccount();
  ProcessAmount(ba);
}
```

`ProcessAmount()` performs a few operations, including invoking the `AccumulateInterest()` method. The cast of `ba` to a `SavingsAccount` is necessary because `ba` is declared to be a `BankAccount`. The program compiles properly because all type conversions are via explicit cast.

All goes well with the first call to `ProcessAmount()` from within `Test()`. The `SavingsAccount` object `sa` is passed to the `ProcessAmount()` method. The cast from `BankAccount` to `SavingsAccount` causes no problem because the `ba` object was originally a `SavingsAccount` anyway.

The second call to `ProcessAmount()` is not so lucky, however. The cast to `SavingsAccount` cannot be allowed. The `ba` object does not have an `AccumulateInterest()` method.

An incorrect conversion generates an error during the execution of the program (a so-called *run-time error*). Run-time errors are much more difficult to find and fix than compile-time errors. Worse, they can happen to a user other than you. Users tend not to appreciate this.

Avoiding invalid conversions using the is and as keywords

The `ProcessAmount()` function would be okay if it could ensure that the object passed to it is actually a `SavingsAccount` object before performing the conversion. C# provides two keywords for this purpose: `is` and `as`.

Using the is operator

The `is` operator accepts an object on the left and a type on the right. The `is` operator returns a `true` if the run-time type of the object on the left is compatible with the type on the right. Use it to verify that a cast is legal before you attempt the cast.

You can modify the previous example to avoid the run-time error by using the `is` operator, as follows:

```
public static void ProcessAmount(BankAccount bankAccount)
{
  // deposit a large sum to the account
  bankAccount.Deposit(10000.00M);
  // if the object is a SavingsAccount . . .
  if (bankAccount is SavingsAccount)
  {
    // ...then collect interest now (cast is guaranteed to work)
    SavingsAccount savingsAccount = (SavingsAccount)bankAccount;
    savingsAccount.AccumulateInterest();
  }
  // otherwise, don't do the cast - but why is BankAccount not what
  // you expected? this could be an error situation
}
public static void TestCast()
{
  SavingsAccount sa = new SavingsAccount();
  ProcessAmount(sa);
  BankAccount ba = new BankAccount();
  ProcessAmount(ba);
}
```

The added `if` statement checks the `bankAccount` object to ensure that it's actually of the class `SavingsAccount`. The `is` operator returns a `true` when `ProcessAmount()` is called the first time. When passed a `BankAccount` object in the second call, however, the `is` operator returns a `false`, avoiding the illegal cast. This version of the program does not generate a run-time error.

On the one hand, I strongly recommend that you protect all casts with the `is` operator to avoid the possibility of a run-time error. On the other hand, you should avoid casts altogether, if possible. But read on.

The `object` class

Consider the following related classes:

```
public class MyBaseClass {}
public class MySubClass : MyBaseClass {}
```

The relationship between the two classes enables the programmer to make the following run-time test:

```
public class Test
{
  public static void
        GenericFunction(MyBaseClass mc)
  {
    // if the object truly is a subclass
    . . .
    MySubClass msc = mc as MyBaseClass;
    if(msc != null)
    {
      // ...then handle as a subclass

      // . . . continue . . .
    }
  }
}
```

In this case, the function `GenericFunction()` differentiates between subclasses of `MyBase Class` using the `as` keyword.

How do you differentiate between seemingly unrelated classes using the same `as` operator? C# extends all classes from the common base class `object`. That is, any class that does not specifically inherit from another class inherits from the class `object`. Thus, the following two statements declare classes with the same base class — `object`:

```
class MyClass1 : object {}
class MyClass2 {}
```

Sharing the common base class of `object` allows the following generic function:

```
public class Test
{
  public static void
        GenericFunction(object o)
  {
    MyClass1 mc1 = o as MyClass1;
    if(mc1 != null)
    {
      // use the converted object mc1
      // . . .
    }
  }
}
```

`GenericFunction()` can be invoked with any type of object. The `as` keyword can dig the `MyClass1` pearls from the `object` oysters. (The "generic" that I'm referring to here isn't the kind of generic covered in Chapter 15.

Using the as operator

The as operator works a bit differently. Instead of returning a `bool` if the cast *would* work, it actually converts the type on the left to the type on the right, but safely returns a `null` if the conversion fails — rather than causing a run-time error. You should always use the result of casting with the `as` operator only if it isn't `null`. So using as looks like this:

```
SavingsAccount savingsAccount = bankAccount as SavingsAccount;
if(savingsAccount != null)
{
  // go ahead and use savingsAccount
}
// otherwise, don't use it: generate an error message yourself
```

Which one should you prefer? Generally, prefer as because it's more efficient. The conversion is already done with the as operator, whereas with is you have two steps: First test with is, and second, do the cast with the cast operator.

Unfortunately, as doesn't work with value-type variables, so you can't use it with types like int, long, double, and so on, nor with char. When you're trying to convert a value-type object, prefer the is operator.

Inheritance and the Constructor

The InheritanceExample program from earlier in this chapter relies on those awful Init...() functions to initialize the BankAccount and SavingsAccount objects to a valid state. Outfitting these classes with constructors is definitely the right way to go, but it introduces a little complexity. That's why I fell back to using those ugly Init...() functions earlier until I could cover the features in this section.

Invoking the default base class constructor

The default base class constructor is invoked any time a subclass is constructed. The constructor for the subclass automatically invokes the constructor for the base class, as the following simple program demonstrates:

```
// InheritingAConstructor - demonstrate that the base class
//                           constructor is invoked automatically
using System;
namespace InheritingAConstructor
{
  public class Program
  {
    public static void Main(string[] args)
    {
      Console.WriteLine("Creating a BaseClass object");
      BaseClass bc = new BaseClass();
      Console.WriteLine("\nNow creating a SubClass object");
      SubClass sc = new SubClass();
      // wait for user to acknowledge
      Console.WriteLine("Press Enter to terminate...");
      Console.Read();
    }
  }
  public class BaseClass
  {
    public BaseClass()
    {
      Console.WriteLine("Constructing BaseClass");
```

```
      }
   }
   public class SubClass : BaseClass
   {
      public SubClass()
      {
         Console.WriteLine("Constructing SubClass");
      }
   }
}
```

The constructors for BaseClass and SubClass do nothing more than output a message to the command line. Creating the BaseClass object invokes the default BaseClass constructor. Creating a SubClass object invokes the BaseClass constructor before invoking its own constructor.

The output from this program is as follows:

```
Creating a BaseClass object
Constructing BaseClass

Now creating a SubClass object
Constructing BaseClass
Constructing SubClass
Press Enter to terminate...
```

A hierarchy of inherited classes is much like the floors of a building. Each class is built on the classes that it extends, as upper floors build on lower ones. There's a clear reason for this: Each class is responsible for itself. A subclass should not be held responsible for initializing the members of the base class. The BaseClass must be given the opportunity to construct its members before the SubClass members are given a chance to access them. You want the horse before the cart.

Passing arguments to the base class constructor — mama sing base

The subclass invokes the default constructor of the base class, unless specified otherwise — even from a subclass constructor other than the default. The following, slightly updated example demonstrates this feature:

```
using System;
namespace Example
{
   public class Program
   {
      public static void Main(string[] args)
      {
```

```
      Console.WriteLine("Invoking SubClass() default");
      SubClass sc1 = new SubClass();
      Console.WriteLine("\nInvoking SubClass(int)");
      SubClass sc2 = new SubClass(0);
      // wait for user to acknowledge
      Console.WriteLine("Press Enter to terminate...");
      Console.Read();
    }
  }
  public class BaseClass
  {
    public BaseClass()
    {
      Console.WriteLine("Constructing BaseClass (default)");
    }
    public BaseClass(int i)
    {
      Console.WriteLine("Constructing BaseClass (int)");
    }
  }
  public class SubClass : BaseClass
  {
    public SubClass()
    {
      Console.WriteLine("Constructing SubClass (default)");
    }
    public SubClass(int i)
    {
      Console.WriteLine("Constructing SubClass (int)");
    }
  }
}
```

Executing this program generates the following results:

```
Invoking SubClass()
Constructing BaseClass (default)
Constructing SubClass (default)

Invoking SubClass(int)
Constructing BaseClass (default)
Constructing SubClass (int)
Press Enter to terminate...
```

The program first creates a default object. As expected, C# invokes the default `SubClass` constructor, which first passes control to the default `BaseClass` constructor. The program then creates an object, passing an integer argument. Again as expected, C# invokes the `SubClass(int)`.

This constructor invokes the default `BaseClass` constructor, just as in the earlier example, because it has no data to pass.

Getting specific with base

A subclass constructor can invoke a specific base class constructor using the keyword `base`.

This feature is similar to the way that one constructor invokes another within the same class using the `this` keyword. See Chapter 11 for the inside scoop on constructors and `this`.

For example, consider the following small program, `InvokeBaseConstructor`:

```
// InvokeBaseConstructor - demonstrate how a subclass can
//                         invoke the base class constructor of its
//                         choice using the base keyword
using System;
namespace InvokeBaseConstructor
{
  public class BaseClass
  {
    public BaseClass()
    {
      Console.WriteLine("Constructing BaseClass (default)");
    }
    public BaseClass(int i)
    {
      Console.WriteLine("Constructing BaseClass({0})", i);
    }
  }
  public class SubClass : BaseClass
  {
    public SubClass()
    {
      Console.WriteLine("Constructing SubClass (default)");
    }
    // here's where the base keyword is used
    public SubClass(int i1, int i2) : base(i1)
    {
      Console.WriteLine("Constructing SubClass({0}, {1})", i1, i2);
    }
  }
  public class Program
  {
    public static void Main(string[] args)
    {
      Console.WriteLine("Invoking SubClass()");
      SubClass sc1 = new SubClass();
      Console.WriteLine("\nInvoking SubClass(1, 2)");
      SubClass sc2 = new SubClass(1, 2);
      // wait for user to acknowledge
      Console.WriteLine("Press Enter to terminate...");
      Console.Read();
    }
  }
}
```

The output from this program is as follows:

```
Invoking SubClass()
Constructing BaseClass (default)
Constructing SubClass (default)

Invoking SubClass(1, 2)
Constructing BaseClass(1)
Constructing SubClass(1, 2)
Press Enter to terminate...
```

This version begins the same as the previous examples, by creating a default SubClass object using the default constructor of both BaseClass and SubClass.

The second object is created with the expression new SubClass(1, 2). C# invokes the SubClass(int, int) constructor, which uses the base keyword to pass one of the values on to the BaseClass(int) constructor. Presumably, SubClass passes the first argument to the base class for processing and continues on using the second value itself.

The Updated BankAccount Class

The program ConstructorSavingsAccount, found on the enclosed CD, is an updated version of the SimpleBankAccount program. In this version, however, the SavingsAccount constructor can pass information back up to the BankAccount constructors. Only Main() and the constructors themselves are shown here:

```
// ConstructorSavingsAccount - implement a SavingsAccount as

//                            a form of BankAccount; don't use any
//                            virtual methods but do implement the
//                            constructors properly
using System;
namespace ConstructorSavingsAccount
{
  // BankAccount - simulate a bank account each of which
  //               carries an account ID (which is assigned
  //               upon creation) and a balance
  public class BankAccount
  {
    // bank accounts start at 1000 and increase sequentially from there
    public static int nNextAccountNumber = 1000;
    // maintain the account number and balance for each object
    public int nAccountNumber;
    public decimal mBalance;
    // Constructors
    public BankAccount(): this(0)
```

```
        {
        }
      public BankAccount(decimal mInitialBalance)
      {
        nAccountNumber = ++nNextAccountNumber;
        mBalance = mInitialBalance;
      }
      // . . . same stuff here . . .
    }
    // SavingsAccount - a bank account that draws interest
    public class SavingsAccount : BankAccount
    {
      public decimal mInterestRate;
      // constructors - input the rate expressed as a
      //                 rate between 0 and 100
      public SavingsAccount(decimal mInterestRate) : this(mInterestRate, 0)
      {
      }
      public SavingsAccount(decimal mInterestRate, decimal mInitial) :
                                                base(mInitial)
      {
        this.mInterestRate = mInterestRate / 100;
      }
      // . . . same stuff here . . .
    }
    public class Program
    {
      // DirectDeposit - deposit my paycheck automatically
      public static void DirectDeposit(BankAccount ba, decimal mPay)
      {
        ba.Deposit(mPay);
      }
      public static void Main(string[] args)
      {
        // create a bank account and display it
        BankAccount ba = new BankAccount(100);
        DirectDeposit(ba, 100);
        Console.WriteLine("Account {0}", ba.ToBankAccountString());
        // now a savings account
        SavingsAccount sa = new SavingsAccount(12.5M);
        DirectDeposit(sa, 100);
        sa.AccumulateInterest();
        Console.WriteLine("Account {0}", sa.ToSavingsAccountString());
        // wait for user to acknowledge the results
        Console.WriteLine("Press Enter to terminate...");
        Console.Read();
      }
    }
}
```

`BankAccount` defines two constructors: one that accepts an initial account balance and the default constructor, which does not. To avoid duplicating code within the constructor, the default constructor invokes the `BankAccount` `(initial balance)` constructor using the `this` keyword.

The `SavingsAccount` class provides two constructors, as well. The `Savings Account(interest rate)` constructor invokes the `SavingsAccount` `(interest rate, initial balance)` constructor, passing an initial balance of 0. This most general constructor passes the initial balance to the `BankAccount(initial balance)` constructor using the `base` keyword, as shown graphically in Figure 12-1.

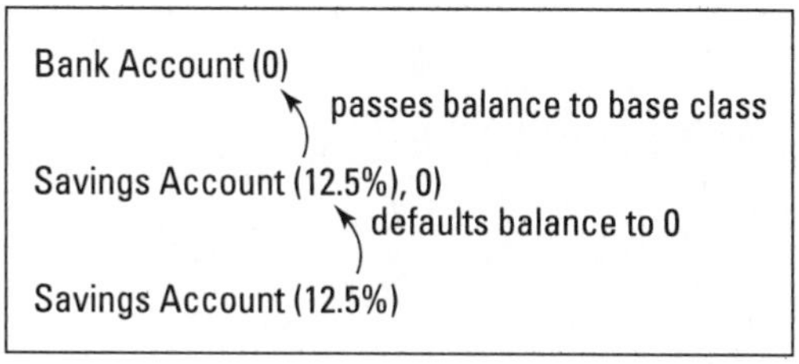

Figure 12-1:
The path taken when constructing a `Savings Account` object using the default constructor.

Bank Account (0)
         passes balance to base class

Savings Account (12.5%), 0)
           defaults balance to 0

Savings Account (12.5%)

I've modified `Main()` to get rid of those infernal `Init...()` functions, replacing them with constructors instead. The output from this program is the same.

The Destructor

C# also provides a method that's inverse to the constructor, called the *destructor*. The destructor carries the name of the class with a tilde (~) in front. For example, the `~BaseClass()` method is the destructor for `BaseClass`.

C# invokes the destructor when it is no longer using the object. The default destructor is the only destructor that can be created because the destructor cannot be invoked directly. In addition, the destructor is always virtual. I explain virtual methods in Chapter 13.

When an inheritance ladder of classes is involved, the destructors are invoked in the reverse order of the constructors. That is, the destructor for the subclass is invoked before the destructor for the base class.

Garbage collection and the C# destructor

The destructor method in C# is much less useful than it is in some other object-oriented languages, such as C++, because C# has *nondeterministic destruction.* Understanding what that means and why it's important requires some explanation.

The memory for an object is borrowed from the heap when the program executes the `new` command, as in `new SubClass()`. This block of memory remains reserved as long as any valid references to that memory are running around. You may have several variables that reference the same object.

The memory is said to be "unreachable" when the last reference goes out of scope. In other words, no one can access that block of memory after no more references to it exist.

C# doesn't do anything in particular when a memory block first becomes unreachable. A low-priority system task executes in the background, looking for unreachable memory blocks. This so-called "garbage collector" executes when little is happening in your program to avoid negatively affecting program performance. As the garbage collector finds unreachable memory blocks, it returns them to the heap.

Normally, the garbage collector operates silently in the background. The garbage collector only takes over control of the program for a short period when heap memory begins to run out.

The C# destructor, for example `~BaseClass()`, is nondeterministic because it is not invoked until the object is garbage collected, and that could occur long after the object is no longer being used. In fact, if the program terminates before the object is found and returned to the heap, the destructor is never invoked. *Nondeterministic* means you can't predict when the object will be garbage collected. It could take quite a while before the object is garbage collected and its destructor called.

The net effect is that C# programmers cannot rely on the destructor to operate automatically, as they can in languages such as C++, so they seldom use it. C# has other ways to return borrowed system resources when they're no longer needed, using a `Dispose()` method, a topic that is beyond the scope of this book.

Chapter 13

Poly-what-ism?

. . . .

In This Chapter

▶ Deciding whether to hide or override a base class method — so many choices!

▶ Building abstract classes — are you for real?

▶ Declaring a method and the class that contains it to be abstract

▶ Starting a new hierarchy on top of an existing one

▶ Sealing a class from being subclassed

. . . .

*I*nheritance allows one class to "adopt" the members of another. Thus, I can create a class `SavingsAccount` that inherits data members like `account id` and methods like `Deposit()` from a base class `BankAccount`. That's nice, but this definition of inheritance is not sufficient to mimic what's going on out there in the trenches.

Drop back 10 yards to Chapter 12 if you don't remember much about class inheritance.

A microwave oven is a type of oven, not because it looks like an oven, but because it performs the same functions as an oven. A microwave oven may perform additional functions, but at the least, it performs the base oven functions — most importantly, heating up my nachos when I say, "`StartCooking`." (I rely on my object of class `Refrigerator` to cool the beer.) I don't particularly care what the oven must do internally to make that happen, any more than I care what type of oven it is, who made it, or whether it was on sale when my wife bought it. . . . Hey, wait, I do care about that last one.

From our human vantage point, the relationship between a microwave oven and a conventional oven doesn't seem like such a big deal, but consider the problem from the oven's point of view. The steps that a conventional oven performs internally are completely different from those that a microwave oven may take (not to mention those that a convection oven performs).

The power of inheritance lies in the fact that a subclass doesn't *have* to inherit every single method from the base class just the way it's written. A subclass can inherit the essence of the base class method while implementing the details differently.

Overloading an Inherited Method

As described in Chapter 7, two or more functions can have the same name as long as the number and/or types of the arguments differ.

It's a simple case of function overloading

Giving two functions the same name is called *overloading*, as in "Keeping them straight is overloading my brain."

The arguments of a function become a part of its extended name, as the following example demonstrates:

```
public class MyClass
{
  public static void AFunction()
  {
    // do something
  }
  public static void AFunction(int)
  {
    // do something else
  }
  public static void AFunction(double d)
  {
    // do something even different
  }
  public static void Main(string[] args)
  {
    AFunction();
    AFunction(1);
    AFunction(2.0);
  }
}
```

C# can differentiate the methods by their arguments. Each of the calls within `Main()` accesses a different function.

The return type is not part of the extended name. You can't have two functions that differ only in their return type.

Different class, different method

Not surprisingly, the class to which a function or method belongs is also a part of its extended name. Consider the following code segment:

```
public class MyClass
{
  public static void AFunction();
  public void AMethod();
}
public class UrClass
{
  public static void AFunction();
  public void AMethod();
}
public class Program
{
  public static void Main(string[] args)
  {
    UrClass.AFunction();  // call static function
    // invoke the MyClass.AMethod() member function
    MyClass mcObject = new MyClass();
    mcObject.AMethod();
  }
}
```

The name of the class is a part of the extended name of the function. The function `MyClass.AFunction()` has about as much to do with `UrClass.AFunction()` as `YourCar.StartOnAColdMorning()` and `MyCar.StartOnAColdMorning()` — at least yours works.

Peek-a-boo — hiding a base class method

Okay, so a method in one class can overload another method in its own class by having different arguments. As it turns out, a method can also overload a method in its base class. Overloading a base class method is known as *hiding* the method.

Suppose your bank adopts a policy that makes savings account withdrawals different from other types of withdrawals. Suppose, just for the sake of argument, that withdrawing from a savings account costs $1.50.

Taking the functional approach, you could implement this policy by setting a flag (variable) in the class to indicate whether the object is a `SavingsAccount` or just a simple `BankAccount`. Then the withdrawal method would have to check the flag to decide whether it needs to charge the $1.50, as shown in the following code:

```
public class BankAccount
{
  private decimal mBalance;
  private bool isSavingsAccount;
  // indicate the initial balance and whether the
  // account that you're creating is a savings
  // account or not
  public BankAccount(decimal mInitialBalance,
                     bool isSavingsAccount)
  {
    mBalance = mInitialBalance;
    this.isSavingsAccount = isSavingsAccount;
  }
  public decimal Withdraw(decimal mAmount)
  {
    // if the account is a savings account . . .
    if (isSavingsAccount)
    {
      // ...then skim off $1.50
      mBalance -= 1.50M;
    }
    // continue with the same withdraw code:
    if (mAmountToWithdraw > mBalance)
    {
      mAmountToWithdraw = mBalance;
    }
    mBalance -= mAmountToWithdraw;
    return mAmountToWithdraw;
  }
}
class MyClass
{
  public void SomeFunction()
  {
    // I wanna create me a savings account:
    BankAccount ba = new BankAccount(0, true);
  }
}
```

Your function must tell the `BankAccount` whether it's a `SavingsAccount` in the constructor by passing a flag. The constructor saves off that flag and uses it in the `Withdraw()` method to decide whether to charge the extra $1.50.

The more object-oriented approach hides the method `Withdraw()` in the base class `BankAccount` with a new method of the same name, height, and hair color in the `SavingsAccount` class, as follows:

```
// HidingWithdrawal - hide the withdraw method in the
//                    base class with a subclass method
//                    of the same name
using System;
namespace HidingWithdrawal
{
  // BankAccount - a very basic bank account
  public class BankAccount
  {
    protected decimal mBalance;
    public BankAccount(decimal mInitialBalance)
    {
      mBalance = mInitialBalance;
    }
    public decimal Balance
    {
      get { return mBalance; }
    }
    public decimal Withdraw(decimal mAmount)
    {
      decimal mAmountToWithdraw = mAmount;
      if (mAmountToWithdraw > Balance) // use the Balance property
      {
        mAmountToWithdraw = Balance;
      }
      mBalance -= mAmountToWithdraw; // can't use Balance property: no set
      return mAmountToWithdraw;
    }
  }
  // SavingsAccount - a bank account that draws interest
  public class SavingsAccount : BankAccount
  {
    public decimal mInterestRate;
    // SavingsAccount - input the rate expressed as a
    //                  rate between 0 and 100
    public SavingsAccount(decimal mInitialBalance,
                          decimal mInterestRate)
                        : base(mInitialBalance)
    {
      this.mInterestRate = mInterestRate / 100;
    }
    // AccumulateInterest - invoke once per period
    public void AccumulateInterest()
    {
      mBalance = Balance + (Balance * mInterestRate); // Balance property
    }
    // Withdraw - you can withdraw any amount up to the
    //            balance; return the amount withdrawn
    public decimal Withdraw(decimal mWithdrawal)
```

```
        {
            // take our $1.50 off the top
            base.Withdraw(1.5M);
            // now you can withdraw from what's left
            return base.Withdraw(mWithdrawal);
        }
    }
}
public class Program
{
    public static void MakeAWithdrawal(BankAccount ba, decimal mAmount)
    {
        ba.Withdraw(mAmount);
    }
    public static void Main(string[] args)
    {
        BankAccount ba;
        SavingsAccount sa;
        // create a bank account, withdraw $100, and
        // display the results
        ba = new BankAccount(200M);
        ba.Withdraw(100M);
        // try the same trick with a savings account
        sa = new SavingsAccount(200M, 12);
        sa.Withdraw(100M);
        // display the resulting balance
        Console.WriteLine("When invoked directly:");
        Console.WriteLine("BankAccount balance is {0:C}", ba.Balance);
        Console.WriteLine("SavingsAccount balance is {0:C}", sa.Balance);
        // wait for user to acknowledge the results
        Console.WriteLine("Press Enter to terminate...");
        Console.Read();
    }
}
```

Main() in this case creates a BankAccount object with an initial balance of $200 and then withdraws $100. Main() repeats the trick with a SavingsAccount object. When Main() withdraws money from the base class, BankAccount. Withdraw() performs the withdraw function with great aplomb. When Main() then withdraws $100 from the savings account, the method SavingsAccount. Withdraw() tacks on the extra $1.50.

Notice that the SavingsAccount.Withdraw() method uses BankAccount. Withdraw() rather than manipulating the balance directly. If possible, let the base class maintain its own data members.

What makes the hiding approach better than adding a simple test?

On the surface, adding a flag to the BankAccount.Withdraw() method may seem simpler than all this method-hiding stuff. After all, it's just four little lines of code, two of which are nothing more than braces.

The problems are manifold — I've been waiting all these chapters to use that word. One problem is that the `BankAccount` class has no business worrying about the details of `SavingsAccount`. That would break the "Render unto Caesar" rule. More formally, it's called "breaking the encapsulation of `SavingsAccount`." Base classes don't normally know about their subclasses. That leads to the real problem: Suppose your bank subsequently decides to add a `CheckingAccount` or a `CDAccount` or a `TBillAccount`. Those are all likely additions, and they all have different withdrawal policies, each requiring its own flag. After three or four different types of accounts, the old `Withdraw()` method starts looking pretty complicated. Each of those types of classes should worry about its own withdrawal policies and leave the poor old `BankAccount.Withdraw()` alone. Classes are responsible for themselves.

What about accidentally hiding a base class method?

You could hide a base class method accidentally. For example, you may have a `Vehicle.TakeOff()` method that starts the vehicle rolling. Later, someone else extends your `Vehicle` class with an `Airplane` class. Its `TakeOff()` method is entirely different. Clearly, this is a case of mistaken identity — the two methods have no similarity other than their identical name.

Fortunately, C# detects this problem.

C# generates an ominous-looking warning when it compiles the earlier `HidingWithdrawal` example program. The text of the warning message is long, but here's the important part:

```
'...SavingsAccount.Withdraw(decimal)' hides inherited member
        '...BankAccount.Withdraw(decimal)'. Use the new keyword if hiding
        was intended.
```

C# is trying to tell you that you've written a method in a subclass with the same name as a method in the base class. Is that what you really meant to do?

This message is just a warning. You don't even notice it unless you switch over to the Error List window to take a look. But it's very important to sort out and fix all warnings. In almost every case, a warning is telling you about something that could bite you if you don't fix it.

It's a good idea to tell the C# compiler to treat warnings as errors, at least part of the time. To do so, choose Project⇨Properties. In the `Build` pane of your project's properties page, scroll down to Errors and Warnings. Set the Warning Level to 4, the highest level. This turns the compiler into more of a chatterbox. Also, in the Treat Warnings as Errors section, select All. (If a particular warning gets annoying, you can list it in the Suppress Warnings box to keep it out of your face.) When you treat warnings as errors, you're forced to fix the warnings just as you are to fix real compiler errors. This makes for better code. Even if you don't enable Treat Warnings as Errors, it's helpful to leave the Warning Level at 4 and check the Error List window after each build.

The descriptor new, shown in the following code, tells C# that the hiding of methods is intentional and not the result of some oversight (and makes the warning go away):

```
// no withdraw() pains now
new public decimal Withdraw(decimal mWithdrawal)
{
   // . . . no change internally . . .
}
```

This use of the keyword new has nothing to do with the same word new that's used to create an object.

Calling back to base

Return to the SavingsAccount.Withdraw() method in the HidingWithdrawal example shown earlier in this chapter. The call to BankAccount.Withdraw() from within this new method includes the new keyword base.

The following version of the function without the base keyword doesn't work:

```
new public decimal Withdraw(decimal mWithdrawal)
{
   decimal mAmountWithdrawn = Withdraw(mWithdrawal);
     mAmountWithdrawn += Withdraw(1.5);
   return mAmountWithdrawn;
}
```

This call has the same problem as the following one:

```
void fn()
{
   fn(); // call yourself
}
```

The call to fn() from within fn() ends up calling itself — *recursing* — over and over. Similarly, a call to Withdraw() from within the function calls itself in a loop, chasing its tail until the program eventually crashes.

Somehow, you need to indicate to C# that the call from within Savings Account.Withdraw() is meant to invoke the base class BankAccount. Withdraw() method. One approach is to cast the this pointer into an object of class BankAccount before making the call, as follows:

```
// Withdraw - this version accesses the hidden method in the base
//            class by explicitly recasting the "this" object
new public decimal Withdraw(decimal mWithdrawal)
{
  // cast the this pointer into an object of class BankAccount
  BankAccount ba = (BankAccount)this;
  // invoking Withdraw() using this BankAccount object
  // calls the function BankAccount.Withdraw()
  decimal mAmountWithdrawn = ba.Withdraw(mWithdrawal);
    mAmountWithdrawn += ba.Withdraw(1.5);
  return mAmountWithdrawn;
}
```

This solution works: The call `ba.Withdraw()` now invokes the `BankAccount` method, just as intended. The problem with this approach is the explicit reference to `BankAccount`. A future change to the program may rearrange the inheritance hierarchy so that `SavingsAccount` no longer inherits directly from `BankAccount`. Such a rearrangement breaks this function in a way that future programmers may not easily find. Heck, I would never be able to find a bug like that.

You need a way to tell C# to call the `Withdraw()` function from "the class immediately above" in the hierarchy without naming it explicitly. That would be the class that `SavingsAccount` extends. C# provides the keyword `base` for this purpose.

This is the same keyword `base` that a constructor uses to pass arguments to its base class constructor.

The C# keyword `base`, shown in the following code, is the same sort of beast as `this` but is recast to the base class no matter what that class may be:

```
// Withdraw - you can withdraw any amount up to the
//            balance; return the amount withdrawn
new public decimal Withdraw(decimal mWithdrawal)
{
  // take our $1.50 off the top
  base.Withdraw(1.5M);
  // now you can withdraw from what's left
  return base.Withdraw(mWithdrawal);
}
```

The call `base.Withdraw()` now invokes the `BankAccount.Withdraw()` method, thereby avoiding the recursive "invoking itself" problem. In addition, this solution won't break if the inheritance hierarchy is changed.

Polymorphism

You can overload a method in a base class with a method in the subclass. As simple as this sounds, it introduces considerable capability, and with capability comes danger.

Here's a thought experiment: Should the decision to call `BankAccount.Withdraw()` or `SavingsAccount.Withdraw()` be made at compile time or run time?

To understand the difference, I'll change the previous `HidingWithdrawal` program in a seemingly innocuous way. I call this new version `Hiding WithdrawalPolymorphically`. (I've streamlined the listing by leaving out the stuff that doesn't change.) The new version is as follows:

```
// HidingWithdrawalPolymorphically - hide the Withdraw() method in the base
//                        class with a method in the subclass of the same name
public class Program
{
  public static void MakeAWithdrawal(BankAccount ba, decimal mAmount)
  {
    ba.Withdraw(mAmount);
  }
  public static void Main(string[] args)
  {
    BankAccount ba;
    SavingsAccount sa;
    ba = new BankAccount(200M);
    MakeAWithdrawal(ba, 100M);
    sa = new SavingsAccount(200M, 12);
    MakeAWithdrawal(sa, 100M);
    // display the resulting balance
    Console.WriteLine("\nWhen invoked through intermediary");
    Console.WriteLine("BankAccount balance is {0:C}", ba.Balance);
    Console.WriteLine("SavingsAccount balance is {0:C}", sa.Balance);
    // wait for user to acknowledge the results
    Console.WriteLine("Press Enter to terminate...");
    Console.Read();
  }
}
```

The following output from this program may or may not be confusing, depending on what you expected:

```
When invoked through intermediary
BankAccount balance is $100.00
SavingsAccount balance is $100.00
Press Enter to terminate...
```

This time, rather than performing a withdrawal in Main(), the program passes the bank account object to the function MakeAWithdrawal().

The first question is fairly straightforward: Why does the MakeAWithdrawal() function even accept a SavingsAccount object when it clearly states that it is looking for a BankAccount? The answer is obvious: "Because a Savings Account IS_A BankAccount." (See Chapter 12.)

The second question is subtle. When passed a BankAccount object, MakeAWithdrawal() invokes BankAccount.Withdraw() — that's clear enough. But when passed a SavingsAccount object, MakeAWithdrawal() calls the same method. Shouldn't it invoke the Withdraw() method in the subclass?

The prosecution intends to show that the call ba.Withdraw() should invoke the method BankAccount.Withdraw(). Clearly, the ba object is a BankAccount. To do anything else would merely confuse the state. The defense has witnesses back in Main() to prove that although the ba object is declared BankAccount, it is, in fact, a SavingsAccount. The jury is deadlocked. Both arguments are equally valid.

In this case, C# comes down on the side of the prosecution. The safer of the two possibilities is to go with the declared type because it avoids any mis-communication. The object is declared to be a BankAccount, and that's that.

What's wrong with using the declared type every time?

In some cases, you don't want to go with the declared type. "What you want, what you really, really want . . ." is to make the call based on the _real type_ — that is, the run-time type — as opposed to the declared type. For example, you want to go with the SavingsAccount actually stored in a BankAccount variable. This capability to decide at run time is called _polymorphism_ or _late binding_. Going with the declared type every time is called _early binding_ because that sounds like the opposite of late binding.

The ridiculous term _polymorphism_ comes from the Greek: _poly_ meaning more than one, _morph_ meaning action, and _ism_ meaning some ridiculous Greek term. But we're stuck with it.

Polymorphism and late binding are not exactly the same. The difference is subtle, however. _Polymorphism_ refers to the ability to decide which method to invoke at run time. _Late binding_ refers to the way a language implements polymorphism.

Polymorphism is key to the power of object-oriented (OO) programming. It's so important that languages that don't support polymorphism can't advertise themselves as OO languages. (I think it's an FDA regulation: You can't label a language that doesn't support it as OO unless you add a disclaimer from the Surgeon General, or something like that.)

Languages that support classes but not polymorphism are called *object-based languages*. Ada is an example of such a language.

Without polymorphism, inheritance has little meaning. Let me spring yet another example on you to show you why. Suppose you had written this really boffo program that used some class called, just to pick a name out of the air, Student. After months of design, coding, and testing, you release this application to rave reviews from colleagues and critics alike. (There's even talk of starting a new Nobel prize category for software, but you modestly brush such talk aside.)

Time passes, and your boss asks you to add to this program the capability of handling graduate students, who are similar but not identical to undergraduate students. (The graduate students probably claim that they're not similar at all.) Suppose that the formula for calculating the tuition for a graduate student is completely different from that for an undergrad. Now, your boss doesn't know or care that, deep within the program, there are numerous calls to the member function CalcTuition(). (There's a lot that he doesn't know or care about, by the way.) The following shows one of those many calls to CalcTuition():

```
void SomeFunction(Student s)   // could be grad or undergrad
{
  // . . . whatever it might do . . .
  s.CalcTuition();
  // . . . continues on . . .
}
```

If C# didn't support late binding, you would need to edit someFunction() to check whether the student object passed to it is a GraduateStudent or a Student. The program would call Student.CalcTuition() when s is a Student and GraduateStudent.CalcTuition() when it's a graduate student.

That doesn't seem so bad, except for two things:

- ✔ This is only one function. Suppose that CalcTuition() is called from many places.

- ✔ Suppose that CalcTuition() is not the only difference between the two classes. The chances are not good that you will find all the items that need to be changed.

With polymorphism, you can let C# decide which method to call.

Using "is" to access a hidden method polymorphically

How can you make your program polymorphic? C# provides one approach to solving the problem manually in the keyword: `is`. (I introduce `is`, and its cousin, `as`, in Chapter 12.) The expression `ba is SavingsAccount` returns a `true` or a `false` depending on the run-time class of the object. The declared type may be `BankAccount`, but what type is it really? The following code uses `is` to access the `SavingsAccount` version of `Withdraw()` specifically:

```
public class Program
  {
    public static void MakeAWithdrawal(BankAccount ba, decimal mAmount)
    {
      if ba is SavingsAccount
      {
        SavingsAccount sa = (SavingsAccount)ba;
        sa.Withdraw(mAmount);
      } else
      {
        ba.Withdraw(mAmount);
      }
    }
  }
```

Now, when `Main()` passes the function a `SavingsAccount` object, `MakeA Withdrawal()` checks the run-time type of the `ba` object and invokes `SavingsAccount.Withdraw()`.

Just as an aside, the programmer could have performed the cast and the call in the following single line:

```
((SavingsAccount)ba).Withdraw(mAmount);
```

I mention this only because you see it a lot in programs written by show-offs. (It's okay but harder to read than using multiple lines. This makes it more error-prone, too.)

Actually, the "is" approach works but it's a really bad idea. The `is` approach requires `MakeAWithDrawal()` to be aware of all the different types of bank accounts and which of them are represented by different classes. That puts too much responsibility on poor old `MakeAWithdrawal()`. Right now, your application handles only two types of bank accounts, but suppose your boss asks you to implement a new account type, `CheckingAccount`, and this new account has different `Withdraw()` requirements. Your program won't work properly if you don't search out and find every function that checks the run-time type of its argument. Doh!

Declaring a method virtual

As the author of `MakeAWithdrawal()`, you don't want to know about all the different types of accounts. You want to leave it up to the programmers that use `MakeAWithdrawal()` to know about their account types and leave you alone. You want C# to make decisions about which methods to invoke based on the run-time type of the object.

You tell C# to make the run-time decision of the version of `Withdrawal()` by marking the base class function with the keyword `virtual` and each subclass version of the function with the keyword `override`.

I've rewritten the previous example program using polymorphism. I have added output statements to the `Withdraw()` methods to prove that the proper methods are indeed being invoked. (I've cut out the duplicated stuff to avoid boring you any more than you already are.) Here's the `PolymorphicInheritance` program:

```
// PolymorphicInheritance - hide a method in the
//                    base class polymorphically
using System;
namespace PolymorphicInheritance
{
  // BankAccount - a very basic bank account
  public class BankAccount
  {
    // . . . the same stuff here . . .
    public virtual decimal Withdraw(decimal mAmount)
    {
      Console.WriteLine("In BankAccount.Withdraw() for ${0}...", mAmount);
      decimal mAmountToWithdraw = mAmount;
      if (mAmountToWithdraw > Balance)
      {
        mAmountToWithdraw = Balance;
      }
      mBalance -= mAmountToWithdraw;
      return mAmountToWithdraw;
    }
  }
  // SavingsAccount - a bank account that draws interest
  public class SavingsAccount : BankAccount
  {
    // . . . same stuff here, too . . .
    // Withdraw - you can withdraw any amount up to the
    //            balance; return the amount withdrawn
    override public decimal Withdraw(decimal mWithdrawal)
    {
      Console.WriteLine("In SavingsAccount.Withdraw()...");
      Console.WriteLine("Invoking base-class Withdraw twice...");
```

```
        // take our $1.50 off the top
        base.Withdraw(1.5M);
        // now you can withdraw from what's left
        return base.Withdraw(mWithdrawal);
    }
}
public class Program
{
    public static void MakeAWithdrawal(BankAccount ba,
                                       decimal mAmount)
    {
        ba.Withdraw(mAmount); // calls the right method
    }
    public static void Main(string[] args)
    {
        // . ... only changed some WriteLines here . . .
    }
}
}
```

The output from executing this program is as follows:

```
Withdrawal: MakeAWithdrawal(ba, ...)
In BankAccount.Withdraw() for $100...
BankAccount balance is $100.00
Withdrawal: MakeAWithdrawal(sa, ...)
In SavingsAccount.Withdraw()...
Invoking base-class Withdraw twice...
In BankAccount.Withdraw() for $1.5...
In BankAccount.Withdraw() for $100...
SavingsAccount balance is $98.50
Press Enter to terminate...
```

The `Withdraw()` method is flagged as `virtual` in the base class `BankAccount`, while the `Withdraw()` method in the subclass is flagged with the keyword `override`. The `MakeAWithdrawal()` method is unchanged and yet the output of the program is different because the call `ba.Withdraw()` is resolved based on `ba`'s run-time type.

To get a good feel for how this works, you really need to step through the program in the Visual Studio 2005 debugger. Just build the program as normal and then repeatedly press F11 to watch the program go through its paces. It's impressive to watch the same call end up in two different methods at two different times.

Be sparing in which methods you make virtual. They have a cost, so use the `virtual` keyword only when you must. It's a trade-off between a class that's highly flexible and overridable (lots of virtual methods) and a class that's not flexible enough (hardly any virtuals).

C# During Its Abstract Period

A duck is a type of bird, I think. So are a cardinal and a hummingbird. In fact, every bird out there is actually some subtype of bird. The flip side of that argument is that no bird exists that isn't some subtype of bird. That doesn't sound too profound, but in a way, it is. The software equivalent of that statement is that all `bird` objects are instances of some subclass of `Bird` — there's never an instance of class `Bird`. What's a bird? It's always a robin or a grackle or some other specific species.

Different types of birds share many properties (otherwise, they wouldn't be birds), but no two types share every property. If they did, they wouldn't be different types. To pick a particularly gross example, not all birds `Fly()` the same way. Ducks have one style. The cardinal's style is similar but not identical. The hummingbird's style is completely different. Don't even get me started about emus and ostriches or the rubber ducky in my tub.

But if birds don't all fly the same way, and there's no such thing as a `Bird`, then what the heck is `Bird.Fly()`? The subject of the following sections, that's what.

Class factoring

People generate taxonomies of objects by factoring out commonalities. To see how factoring works, consider two classes, `HighSchool` and `University`, as shown in Figure 13-1. This figure uses the Unified Modeling Language (UML), a graphical language that describes a class along with the relationship of that class to others. UML has become universally popular with programmers.

A Car IS_A Vehicle but a Car HAS_A Motor.

Figure 13-1:
A UML description of the `High School` and `University` classes.

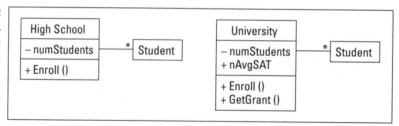

You can see in Figure 13-1 that high schools and universities have several similar properties — actually many more than you may think. Both schools offer a publicly available Enroll() method for adding Student objects to the school. In addition, both classes offer a private member numStudents that indicates the number of students attending the school. One final common feature is the relationship between students: One school can have any number of students — a student can attend only a single school at one time. Even high schools and most universities offer more than I've described, but one of each type of member is all I need.

In addition to the features of a high school, the university contains a method GetGrant() and a data member nAvgSAT. High schools don't have an SAT entrance requirement, and they don't get federal grants — unless I went to the wrong high school.

Figure 13-1 is fine, as far as it goes, but lots of information is duplicated, and duplication in code stinks. You could reduce the duplication by allowing the more complex class University to inherit from the simpler HighSchool class, as shown in Figure 13-2.

Figure 13-2:
Inheriting
High
School
simplifies
the Uni-
versity
class, but it
introduces
problems.

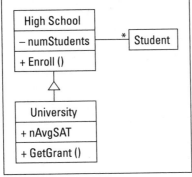

The HighSchool class is left unchanged, but the University class is easier to describe. We say that "a University is a HighSchool that also has an nAvgSAT and a GetGrant() method." But this solution has a fundamental problem: A university is not a high school with special properties.

You say, "So what? Inheriting works, and it saves effort." True, but my reservations are more than stylistic trivialities. My reservations are at some of the best restaurants in town — at least, that's what all the truckers say. Such misrepresentations are confusing to the programmer, both now and in the future. Someday, a programmer who is unfamiliar with your programming tricks will have to read and understand what your code does. Misleading representations are difficult to reconcile and understand.

In addition, such misrepresentations can lead to problems down the road. Suppose the high school decides to name a "favorite" student at the prom — not that I would know anything about that sort of thing. The clever programmer adds the `NameFavorite()` method to the `HighSchool` class, which the application invokes to name the favorite `Student` object.

But now you have a problem. Most universities don't name a favorite anything, other than price. However, as long as `University` inherits from `HighSchool`, it inherits the `NameFavorite()` method. One extra method may not seem like a big deal. "Just ignore it," you say.

One extra method isn't a big deal, but it's just one more brick in the wall of confusion. Extra methods and properties accumulate over time, until the `University` class is carrying lots of extra baggage. Pity the poor software developer that has to understand which methods are "real" and which are not.

UML Lite

The Unified Modeling Language (UML) is an expressive language that's capable of clearly defining a great deal about the relationships of objects within a program. One advantage of UML is that you can ignore the more specific language features without losing the meaning entirely.

The most basic features of UML are as follows:

- ✔ Classes are represented by a box divided vertically into three sections. The name of the class appears in the uppermost section.

- ✔ The data members of the class appear in the middle section, and the methods of the class in the bottom. You can omit either the middle or bottom section if the class has no data members or methods.

- ✔ Members with a plus sign (+) in front are public; those with a minus sign (–) are private. UML doesn't have a symbol to describe protected and internal visibility, but some people use the pound sign (#) — or should I say the "sharp" sign?

A private member is only accessible from other members of the same class. A public member is accessible to all classes.

- ✔ The label {abstract} next to the name indicates an abstract class or method.

    UML actually uses a different symbol for an abstract method, but I'll keep it simple. This is UML Lite.

- ✔ An arrow between two classes represents a relationship between the two classes. A number above the line expresses cardinality — the number of items you can have at each end of the arrow. The asterisk symbol (*) means *any number*. If no number is present, the cardinality is assumed to be 1. Thus, in Figure 13-1, you can see that a single university has any number of students — a one-to-many relationship.

- ✔ A line with a large, open arrowhead, or a triangular arrowhead, expresses the IS_A relationship (inheritance). The arrow points up the class hierarchy to the base class. Other types of relationships include the HAS_A relationship (a line with a filled diamond at the owning end).

"Inheritances of convenience" lead to another problem. The way it's written, Figure 13-2 implies that a University and a HighSchool have the same enrollment procedure. As unlikely as that sounds, assume that it's true. The program is developed, packaged up, and shipped off to the unwitting public — of course, I've embedded the requisite number of bugs so they'll want to upgrade to Version 2 with all the bug fixes — for a small fee, of course.

Months pass before the school district decides to modify the enrollment procedure. It won't be obvious to anyone that by modifying the high school enrollment procedure, they've also modified the sign-up procedure at the local college.

How can you avoid these problems? Not going to school is one way, but another would be to fix the source of the problem: A university is not a particular type of high school. A relationship exists between the two, but IS_A is not the right one. (HAS_A doesn't work either. A university HAS_A high school? A high school HAS_A university? Come on!) Instead, both high schools and universities are special types of schools. That's what they have most in common.

Figure 13-3 describes a better relationship. The newly defined class School contains the common properties of both types of schools, including the relationship they both have with Student objects. School even contains the common Enroll() method, although it's abstract because HighSchool and University usually don't implement Enroll() the same way.

The classes HighSchool and University now inherit from a common base class. Each contains its unique members: NameFavorite() in the case of HighSchool, and GetGrant() for the University. In addition, both classes override the Enroll() method with a version that describes how that type of school enrolls students. In effect, I've extracted a superclass, or base class, from two similar classes, which now become subclasses.

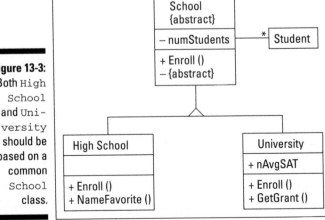

Figure 13-3: Both High School and University should be based on a common School class.

The introduction of the `School` class has at least two big advantages:

- ✔ **It corresponds with reality.** A `University` is a `School`, but it is not a `HighSchool`. Matching reality is nice but not conclusive.

- ✔ **It isolates one class from changes or additions to the other.** When my boss comes along later, as will undoubtedly happen, and asks that I introduce the commencement exercise to the university, I can add the `CommencementSpeech()` method to the `University` class without impacting `HighSchool`.

This process of culling out common properties from similar classes is called *factoring.* This is an important feature of object-oriented languages for the reasons described so far, plus one more: reduction in redundancy. Let me repeat, redundancy is bad; there is no place for redundancy. Said another way . . .

Factoring is legitimate only if the inheritance relationship corresponds to reality. Factoring together a class `Mouse` and `Joystick` because they're both hardware pointing devices is legitimate. Factoring together a class `Mouse` and `Display` because they both make low-level operating system calls is not.

Factoring can and usually does result in multiple levels of abstraction. For example, a program written for a more developed school hierarchy may have a class structure more like that shown in Figure 13-4.

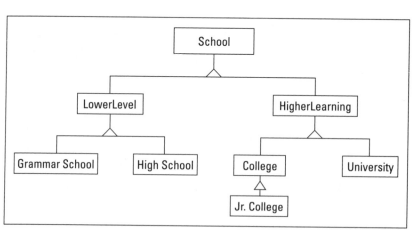

Figure 13-4: Class factoring can and usually does result in the addition of layers of inheritance hierarchy.

You can see that I have inserted a pair of new classes between `University` and `School`: `HigherLearning` and `LowerLevel`. For example, I've subdivided the new class `HigherLearning` into `College` and `University`. This type of multitiered class hierarchy is common and desirable when factoring out relationships. They correspond to reality, and they can teach you sometimes subtle features of your solution.

Note, however, that no Unified Factoring Theory exists for any given set of classes. The relationship in Figure 13-4 seems natural, but suppose that an application cared more about differentiating types of schools that are administered by local politicians from those that aren't. This relationship, shown in Figure 13-5, is a more natural fit for that type of problem.

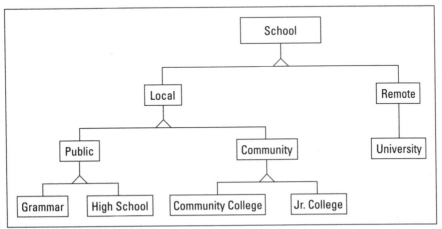

Figure 13-5: There's no "correct" factoring. The proper way to break down the classes is partially a function of the problem being solved.

I'm left with nothing but a concept — the abstract class

As intellectually satisfying as factoring is, it introduces a problem of its own. Return one more time to BankAccount, which was introduced at the beginning of the chapter. Think for a minute about how you may go about defining the different member functions defined in BankAccount.

Most BankAccount member functions are no problem because both account types implement them in the same way. You should implement those common functions in BankAccount. Withdraw() is different, however. The rules for withdrawing from a savings account differ from those for withdrawing from a checking account. You'll have to implement SavingsAccount.Withdraw() differently from CheckingAccount.Withdraw(). But how are you supposed to implement BankAccount.Withdraw()?

Ask the bank manager for help. I imagine the conversation going something like the following:

"What are the rules for making a withdrawal from an account?" you ask, expectantly.

"What type of account? Savings or checking?" comes the reply.

"From an account," you say. "Just an account."

Blank look. (One may say a "blank bank look."... Then again, maybe not.)

The problem is that the question doesn't make sense. There's no such thing as "just an account." All accounts (in this example) are either checking accounts or savings accounts. The concept of an account is an abstract one that factors out properties that are common to the two concrete classes. It is incomplete, because it lacks the critical property `Withdraw()`. (After you get further into the details, you may find other properties that a simple account lacks.)

The concept of a `BankAccount` is abstract.

How do you use an abstract class?

Abstract classes are used to describe abstract concepts.

An *abstract class* is a class with one or more abstract methods. Oh, great! That helps a lot. Okay, an abstract method is a method marked `abstract`. We're really moving now. Let me try again: An abstract method has no implementation — now you're really confused.

Consider the following stripped-down demonstration program:

```
// AbstractInheritance - the BankAccount class is actually abstract because
//                       there is no single implementation for Withdraw
namespace AbstractInheritance
{
  using System;
  // AbstractBaseClass - create an abstract base class with nothing
  //                     but an Output() method
  abstract public class AbstractBaseClass
  {
    // Output - abstract method that outputs a string
    //          but only in subclasses that override it
    abstract public void Output(string sOutputString);
  }
  // SubClass1 - one concrete implementation of AbstractBaseClass
  public class SubClass1 : AbstractBaseClass
  {
    override public void Output(string sSource)
    {
      string s = sSource.ToUpper();
      Console.WriteLine("Call to SubClass1.Output() from within {0}", s);
    }
  }
  // SubClass2 - another concrete implementation of AbstractBaseClass
  public class SubClass2 : AbstractBaseClass
```

```
    {
      override public void Output(string sSource)
      {
        string s = sSource.ToLower();
        Console.WriteLine("Call to SubClass2.Output() from within {0}", s);
      }
    }
    class Program
    {
      public static void Test(AbstractBaseClass ba)
      {
        ba.Output("Test");
      }
      public static void Main(string[] strings)
      {
          // you can't create an AbstractBaseClass object because it's
          // abstract - duh. C# generates a compile time error if you
          // uncomment the following line
          // AbstractBaseClass ba = new AbstractBaseClass();
          // now repeat the experiment with Subclass1
          Console.WriteLine("Creating a SubClass1 object");
          SubClass1 sc1 = new SubClass1();
          Test(sc1);
          // and finally a Subclass2 object
          Console.WriteLine("\nCreating a SubClass2 object");
          SubClass2 sc2 = new SubClass2();
          Test(sc2);
          // wait for user to acknowledge
          Console.WriteLine("Press Enter to terminate...");
          Console.Read();
      }
    }
}
```

The program first defines the class `AbstractBaseClass` with a single abstract `Output()` method. Because it is declared `abstract`, `Output()` has no implementation, that is, no method body.

Two classes inherit from `AbstractBaseClass`: `SubClass1` and `SubClass2`. Both are concrete classes because they override the `Output()` method with "real" methods and themselves contain no abstract methods.

A class can be declared abstract whether it has abstract members or not; however, a class can be concrete only when all of the abstract methods in any base class above it have been hidden (overridden) with real methods.

The two subclass `Output()` methods differ in a trivial way. Both accept an input string, which they regurgitate to the user. However, one converts the string to all caps before output and the other to all lowercase characters.

The following output from this program demonstrates the polymorphic nature of `AbstractBaseClass`:

```
Creating a SubClass1 object
Call to SubClass1.Output() from within TEST

Creating a SubClass2 object
Call to SubClass2.Output() from within test
Press Enter to terminate...
```

An abstract method is automatically virtual, so you don't add the `virtual` keyword to an abstract method.

Creating an abstract object — not!

Notice something about the `AbstractInheritance` program: It is not legal to create an `AbstractBaseClass` object, but the argument to `Test()` is declared to be an object of the class `AbstractBaseClass` *or one of its subclasses*. It's the subclasses clause that's critical here. The `SubClass1` and `SubClass2` objects can be passed because they are both concrete subclasses of `AbstractBaseClass`. The IS_A relationship applies. This is actually a powerful technique, allowing you to write highly general methods.

Restarting a Class Hierarchy

The `virtual` keyword can also be used to start a new inheritance hierarchy. Consider the class hierarchy demonstrated in the following `InheritanceTest` program:

```
// InheritanceTest - examine the way that the virtual keyword can
//                   be used to start a new inheritance ladder
namespace InheritanceTest
{
  using System;
  public class Program
  {
    public static void Main(string[] strings)
    {
      Console.WriteLine("\nPassing a BankAccount");
      BankAccount ba = new BankAccount();
      Test1(ba);
```

```
        Console.WriteLine("\nPassing a SavingsAccount");
        SavingsAccount sa = new SavingsAccount();
        Test1(sa);
        Test2(sa);

        Console.WriteLine("\nPassing a SpecialSaleAccount");
        SpecialSaleAccount ssa = new SpecialSaleAccount();
        Test1(ssa);
        Test2(ssa);
        Test3(ssa);

        Console.WriteLine("\nPassing a SaleSpecialCustomer");
        SaleSpecialCustomer ssc = new SaleSpecialCustomer();
        Test1(ssc);
        Test2(ssc);
        Test3(ssc);
        Test4(ssc);

        // wait for user to acknowledge
        Console.WriteLine();
        Console.WriteLine("Press Enter to terminate...");
        Console.Read();
    }

    public static void Test1(BankAccount account)
    {
        Console.WriteLine("\tto Test(BankAccount)");
        account.Withdraw(100);
    }

    public static void Test2(SavingsAccount account)
    {
        Console.WriteLine("\tto Test(SavingsAccount)");
        account.Withdraw(100);
    }

    public static void Test3(SpecialSaleAccount account)
    {
        Console.WriteLine("\tto Test(SpecialSaleAccount)");
        account.Withdraw(100);
    }

    public static void Test4(SaleSpecialCustomer account)
    {
        Console.WriteLine("\tto Test(SaleSpecialCustomer)");
        account.Withdraw(100);
    }
}
```

```
// BankAccount - simulate a bank account each of which
//               carries an account id (which is assigned
//               upon creation) and a balance
public class BankAccount
{
  // Withdrawal - you can withdraw any amount up to the
  //              balance; return the amount withdrawn
  virtual public void Withdraw(decimal mWithdraw)
  {
    Console.WriteLine("\t\tcalls BankAccount.Withdraw()");
  }
}
// SavingsAccount - a bank account that draws interest
public class SavingsAccount : BankAccount
{
  override public void Withdraw(decimal mWithdrawal)
  {
    Console.WriteLine("\t\tcalls SavingsAccount.Withdraw()");
  }
}

// SpecialSaleAccount - account used only during a sale
public class SpecialSaleAccount : SavingsAccount
{
  new virtual public void Withdraw(decimal mWithdrawal)
  {
    Console.WriteLine("\t\tcalls SpecialSaleAccount.Withdraw()");
  }
}

// SaleSpecialCustomer - account used for special customers
//                       during the sale period
public class SaleSpecialCustomer : SpecialSaleAccount
{
  override public void Withdraw(decimal mWithdrawal)
  {
    Console.WriteLine("\t\tcalls SaleSpecialCustomer.Withdraw()");
  }
}
}
```

Each of these classes extends the class above it. Notice, however, that SpecialSaleAccount.Withdraw() has been flagged as virtual, effectively breaking the inheritance ladder at that point. When viewed from the perspective of BankAccount, the SpecialSaleAccount and SaleSpecialCustomer classes look exactly like a SavingsAccount. It is only when viewed from the perspective of a SpecialSaleAccount that the new versions of Withdraw() become available.

This is demonstrated with a small program. The function Main() invokes a series of Test() methods, each designed to accept a different subclass. Each of these versions of Test() calls Withdraw() from the perspective of a different class of object.

The output from this program is as follows:

```
Passing a BankAccount
        to Test(BankAccount)
                calls BankAccount.Withdraw()
Passing a SavingsAccount
        to Test(BankAccount)
                calls SavingsAccount.Withdraw()
        to Test(SavingsAccount)
                calls SavingsAccount.Withdraw()
Passing a SpecialSaleAccount
        to Test(BankAccount)
                calls SavingsAccount.Withdraw()
        to Test(SavingsAccount)
                calls SavingsAccount.Withdraw()
        to Test(SpecialSaleAccount)
                calls SpecialSaleAccount.Withdraw()
Passing a SaleSpecialCustomer
        to Test(BankAccount)
                calls SavingsAccount.Withdraw()
        to Test(SavingsAccount)
                calls SavingsAccount.Withdraw()
        to Test(SpecialSaleAccount)
                calls SaleSpecialCustomer.Withdraw()
        to Test(SaleSpecialCustomer)
                calls SaleSpecialCustomer.Withdraw()
Press Enter to terminate....
```

I have bolded the calls of special interest. The `BankAccount` and `Savings Account` classes operate exactly as you would expect. However, when calling `Test(SavingsAccount)`, both the `SpecialSalesAccount` and `SaleSpecial Customer` pass themselves off as a `SavingsAccount`. It's only when looking at the next lower level that the new `SaleSpecialCustomer` hierarchy can be used in lieu of a `SpecialSaleAccount`.

Creating a new hierarchy

Why does C# support creating a new inheritance hierarchy? Isn't polymorphism complicated enough already?

C# was created to be a "netable" language in the sense that classes which a program executes — even subclasses — may be distributed across the Internet. That is, a program you're writing can directly use classes from standard repositories located on other computers via the Internet.

You can extend a class that you load over the Internet. Overriding the methods of a standard, tested hierarchy of classes may have unintended effects. Establishing a new hierarchy of classes enables your program to enjoy the benefits of polymorphism without any danger of breaking the existing code.

Sealing a Class

You may decide that you don't want future generations of programmers to be able to extend a particular class. You can lock the class using the keyword `sealed`. A sealed class cannot be used as the base class for any other class.

Consider the following code snippet:

```
using System;
public class BankAccount
{
  // Withdrawal - you can withdraw any amount up to the
  //              balance; return the amount withdrawn
  virtual public void Withdraw(decimal mWithdraw)
  {
    Console.WriteLine("invokes BankAccount.Withdraw()");
  }
}
public sealed class SavingsAccount : BankAccount
{
  override public void Withdraw(decimal mWithdrawal)
  {
    Console.WriteLine("invokes SavingsAccount.Withdraw()");
  }
}
public class SpecialSaleAccount : SavingsAccount
{
  override public void Withdraw(decimal mWithdrawal)
  {
    Console.WriteLine("invokes SpecialSaleAccount.Withdraw()");
  }
}
```

This snippet generates the following compiler error:

```
'SpecialSaleAccount' : cannot inherit from sealed class 'SavingsAccount'
```

The `sealed` keyword enables you to protect your class from the prying methods of some subclass. For example, allowing programmers to extend a class that implements system security would enable someone to create a security back door.

Sealing a class prevents another program, possibly somewhere on the Internet, from using a modified version of your class. The remote program can use the class as is, or not, but it can't inherit bits and pieces of your class while overriding the rest.

Part V
Beyond Basic Classes

The 5th Wave   By Rich Tennant

"You ever get the feeling this project could just up and die at any moment?"

In this part . . .

So far, your objects have been simple things, like integers and strings and `BankAccounts`. But C# comes equipped right out of the box with several other kinds of objects. In this part, you find out how to write your own value-type objects (which are akin to `int`s and `float`s) with `struct`s, and then you discover the great door into eternal happiness: interfaces. Okay, that's a bit over the top, I admit. But interfaces are a powerful tool for making your objects more general and flexible, and along with the abstract classes you met in Chapter 13, interfaces are the key to advanced program designs. So pay attention, please!

But interfaces aren't the only way to make code highly general and flexible. The brand-new generics features in C# 2.0 let you write *generic* objects: mainly containers of other data with fill-in-the-blanks slots where you can specify exactly what data type the container is to hold. Don't worry. It may seem impossibly abstract now — and maybe more than a little weird — but by the end of Part V, you'll have nearly all the tools of C# at your disposal. And you still have all the cool stuff in the Bonus Chapters on the CD to go! (I include a couple of chapters that were in the book in the first edition. We had to make room for generics somehow.)

Chapter 14

When a Class Isn't a Class — The Interface and the Structure

A class can contain a reference to another class. This is the simple HAS_A relationship. One class can extend another class through the marvel of inheritance. That's the IS_A relationship. The C# *interface* implements another, equally important association: the CAN_BE_USED_AS relationship.

What Is CAN_BE_USED_AS?

If you want to jot down a note, you may scribble it on a piece of paper with a pen, stroke it into your personal digital assistant (PDA), or type it on your laptop. Thus, you can say that all three objects — the pen, the PDA, and the laptop — implement the TakeANote operation. Using the magic of inheritance, you could implement this in C# as follows:

```
abstract class ThingsThatRecord
{
  abstract public void TakeANote(string sNote);
}
public class Pen : ThingsThatRecord
{
```

```
    override public void TakeANote(string sNote)
    {
      // . . . scribble a note with a pen . . .
    }
}
public class PDA : ThingsThatRecord
{
    override public void TakeANote(string sNote)
    {
      // . . . stroke a note on the PDA . . .
    }
}
public class Laptop : ThingsThatRecord
{
    override public void TakeANote(string sNote)
    {
      // . . . whatever . . .
    }
}
```

If the term `abstract` has you stumped, drop back one pace to Chapter 13. If this whole concept of inheritance is a mystery, check out Chapter 12.

This inheritance solution seems to work fine as far as the `TakeANote()` operation is concerned. A function such as `RecordTask()`, shown as follows, can use the `TakeANote()` method to write a shopping list without regard for the type of device supplied:

```
void RecordTask(ThingsThatRecord things)
{
    // this abstract method is implemented in all classes
    // that inherit ThingsThatRecord
    things.TakeANote("Shopping list");
    // . . . and so on . . .
}
```

However, this solution suffers from two big problems:

- ✔ **The first problem is fundamental:** You can't really claim that the pen, the PDA, and the laptop have any type of IS_A relationship. Knowing how a pen works and how it takes notes gives me no information as to what a laptop is or how it records information. The name `ThingsThat Record` is more of a description than a base class.

- ✔ **The second problem is purely technical:** You may better describe `Lap top` as some subclass of `Computer`. Although you could reasonably extend `PDA` from the same `Computer` base class, the same cannot be said of `Pen`. You would have to characterize a pen as some type of `Mechanical WritingDevice` or `DeviceThatStainsYourShirt`. However, a C# class cannot inherit from two different classes at the same time — a C# class can be only one type of thing.

Returning to the initial three classes, the only thing that the classes Pen, PDA, and Laptop have in common for this purpose is that they can all be used to record something. The CAN_BE_USED_AS Recordable relationship enables you to communicate their serviceability for a particular purpose without implying any inherent relationship among the three classes.

What Is an Interface?

An interface description looks much like a dataless class in which all the methods are abstract. The interface description for "things that record" could look like the following:

```
interface IRecordable
{
  void TakeANote(string sNote);
}
```

Notice the keyword interface, where class would have gone. Within the braces of an interface appears a list of abstract methods. Interfaces do not contain definitions for any data members.

The method TakeANote() is written without an implementation. The keywords public and virtual or abstract are not necessary. All methods in an interface are public, and an interface is not involved in normal inheritance. It's an interface, not a class.

Classes that *implement* an interface must provide specific implementations for each item in the interface. Must. The method that implements the interface method does not use the override keyword. This isn't like overriding a virtual function.

By convention, begin the names of interfaces with the letter *I*. In addition, use adjectives for the names of interfaces (class names are usually nouns). As always, these are only suggestions, and I bear no legal responsibility nor are these suggestions suitable for any particular. . . . In other words, C# doesn't care.

The following declaration indicates that the class PDA implements the IRecordable interface:

```
public class PDA : IRecordable
{
  public void TakeANote(string sNote)
  {
    // . . . do something to record the note . . .
  }
}
```

There's no difference in the syntax of a declaration that inherits a base class ThingsThatRecord and a declaration that implements an interface IRecordable.

This is the main reason for the naming convention used for interface names: so you can tell an interface from a class.

The bottom line is that an interface describes a capability, like Swim Safety Training or Class A Driver's License. As a class, I earn my IRecordable badge when I implement the TakeANote ability.

More than that, an interface is a *contract*. If you agree to implement every method defined in the interface, you get to claim its capability.

Can I Get a Short Example?

A class implements an interface by providing a definition for every method of the interface, as shown in the following code:

```
public class Pen : IRecordable
{
  public void TakeANote(string sNote)
  {
    // . . . record the note with a pen . . .
  }
}
public class PDA : ElectronicDevice, IRecordable
{
  public void TakeANote(string sNote)
  {
    // . . . graffiti write the note . . .
  }
}
public class Laptop : Computer, IRecordable
{
  public void TakeANote(string sNote)
  {
    // . . . type in the note . . .
  }
}
```

Each of these three classes inherits a different base class but implements the same IRecordable interface. The IRecordable interface indicates that each of the three classes can be used to jot down a note using the TakeANote() method. To see how this may be useful, consider the following RecordShoppingList() function:

```
public class Program
{
  static public void RecordShoppingList(IRecordable recordingObject)
  {
    // create a shopping list
    string sList = GenerateShoppingList();
    // now jot it down
    recordingObject.TakeANote(sList);
  }
  public static void Main(string[] args)
  {
    PDA pda = new PDA();
    RecordShoppingList(pda);
  }
}
```

In effect, this code snippet says that the function `RecordShoppingList()` will accept as its argument any object that implements the `TakeANote()` method — in human terms, "any object that can record a note." `Record ShoppingList()` makes no assumptions about the exact type of `recording Object`. The fact that the object is actually a `PDA` or that it is a type of `ElectronicDevice` is not important, as long as it can take a note.

That's immensely powerful, because it lets `RecordShoppingList()` be highly general and thus probably reusable in other programs. It's even more general than using a base class for the argument type, because the interface argument allows you to pass almost arbitrary objects that don't necessarily have anything in common other than implementing the interface. They don't even have to come from the same class hierarchy.

Can I See a Program That CAN_BE_ USED_AS an Example?

The following `SortInterface` program is a special offer. These capabilities brought to you by two different interfaces cannot be matched in any inheritance relationship, anywhere. Interface implementations are standing by.

However, I want to break the `SortInterface` program into sections to demonstrate various principles — pfft! As if I had principles. I just want to make sure that you can see exactly how the program works.

Creating your own interface at home in your spare time

The following `IDisplayable` interface is satisfied by any class that contains a `GetString()` method (and declares that it implements `IDisplayable`, of course). `GetString()` returns a `string` representation of the object that can be displayed using `WriteLine()`:

```
// IDisplayable - an object that implements the GetString() method
interface IDisplayable
{
  // return description of yourself
  string GetString();
}
```

The following `Student` class implements `IDisplayable`:

```
class Student : IDisplayable
{
  private string sName;
  private double dGrade = 0.0;
  // access read-only methods
  public string Name
  {
    get { return sName; }
  }
  public double Grade
  {
    get { return dGrade; }
  }
  // GetString - return a representation of the student
  public string GetString()  // implements the interface
  {
    string sPadName = Name.PadRight(9);
    string s = String.Format("{0}: {1:N0}", sPadName, Grade);
    return s;
  }
}
```

The call to `PadRight()` makes sure that the field where the name goes will be at least nine characters wide. Any extra space following the name is padded with spaces. Padding a `string` to a standard length makes rows of objects line up nicely, as discussed more fully in Chapter 9. The `{1:N0}` says, "Display the grade with commas (or dots, depending on what country you're in) every three digits." The `0` part means round off any fractional part.

Given this declaration, you can now write the following program fragment (the entire program appears in the section "Putting it all together," later in this chapter):

```
// DisplayArray - display an array of objects that
//                implement the IDisplayable interface
public static void DisplayArray(IDisplayable[] displayables)
{
  int length = displayables.Length;
  for(int index = 0; index < length; index++)
  {
    IDisplayable displayable = displayables[index];
    Console.WriteLine("{0}", displayable.GetString());
  }
}
```

This `DisplayArray()` method can display any type of array, as long as the members of the array define a `GetString()` method. The following is an example of the output from `DisplayArray()`:

```
Homer    : 0
Marge    : 85
Bart     : 50
Lisa     : 100
Maggie   : 30
```

Predefined interfaces

Likewise, you'll find more interfaces built into the standard C# library than gun racks at an NRA convention. For example, C# defines the `IComparable` interface as follows:

```
interface IComparable
{
  // compare the current object to the object 'o'; return a
  // 1 if larger, -1 if smaller, and 0 otherwise
  int CompareTo(object o);
}
```

A class implements the `IComparable` interface by implementing a `Compare To()` method. For example, `String` implements this method by comparing two `string`s. If the `string`s are identical, it returns a 0. If they are not, it returns either a 1 or a –1, depending on which one is "greater."

It seems a little Darwinian, but you could say that one `Student` object is "greater than" another `Student` object if his grade point average is higher. He's either a better student or a better apple polisher — it doesn't really matter.

Implementing the `CompareTo()` method implies that the objects have a sorting order. If one student is "greater than" another, you must be able to sort the students from "least" to "greatest." In fact, the `Array` class implements the following method already:

```
Array.Sort(IComparable[] objects);
```

This method sorts an array of objects that implements the `IComparable` interface. It doesn't even matter which class the objects belong to. For example, they could even be `Student` objects. The `Array` class could even sort the following version of `Student`:

```
// Student - description of a student with name and grade
class Student : IComparable
{
  private double dGrade;
  // access read-only methods
  public double Grade
  {
    get { return dGrade; }
  }
  // CompareTo - compare one student to another; one student is
  //             "greater" than another if his grades are better
  public int CompareTo(object rightObject)
  {
    Student leftStudent = this;
    Student rightStudent = (Student)rightObject;
    // now generate a -1, 0, or 1 based upon the
    // sort criterion (the student's grade)
    if (rightStudent.Grade < leftStudent.Grade)
    {
      return -1;
    }
    if (rightStudent.Grade > leftStudent.Grade)
    {
      return 1;
    }
    return 0;
  }
}
```

Sorting an array of `Student`s is reduced to a single call, as follows:

```
void MyFunction(Student[] students)
{
  // sort the array of IComparable objects
  Array.Sort(students);
}
```

You provide the comparator, and `Array` does all the work.

Putting it all together

This is the moment you've been waiting for: the complete `SortInterface` program that uses the features that I described earlier in this chapter:

```
// SortInterface - the SortInterface program demonstrates how
//                 the interface concept can be used to provide
//                 an enhanced degree of flexibility in factoring
//                 and implementing classes
using System;
namespace SortInterface
{
  // IDisplayable - an object that can convert itself into
  //                a displayable string format
  interface IDisplayable
  {
    // GetString - return a string representation of yourself
    string GetString();
  }
  class Program
  {
    public static void Main(string[] args)
    {
      // Sort students by grade...
      Console.WriteLine("Sorting the list of students");
      // get an unsorted array of students
      Student[] students = Student.CreateStudentList();
      // use the IComparable interface to sort the array
      IComparable[] comparableObjects = (IComparable[])students;
      Array.Sort(comparableObjects);
      // now the IDisplayable interface to display the results
      IDisplayable[] displayableObjects = (IDisplayable[])students;
      DisplayArray(displayableObjects);
      // Now sort an array of birds by name using
      // the same routines even though the classes Bird and
      // Student have no common base class
      Console.WriteLine("\nSorting the list of birds");
      Bird[] birds = Bird.CreateBirdList();
      // notice that it's not really necessary to cast the
      // objects explicitly...
      Array.Sort(birds);
      DisplayArray(birds);
      // wait for user to acknowledge the results
      Console.WriteLine("Press Enter to terminate...");
      Console.Read();
    }
    // DisplayArray - display an array of objects that
    //                implement the IDisplayable interface
    public static void DisplayArray(IDisplayable[] displayables)
    {
```

```
      int length = displayables.Length;
      for(int index = 0; index < length; index++)
      {
        IDisplayable displayable = displayables[index];
        Console.WriteLine("{0}", displayable.GetString());
      }
    }
  }
}
// ----------- Students - sort students by grade -------
// Student - description of a student with name and grade
class Student : IComparable, IDisplayable
{
  private string sName;
  private double dGrade = 0.0;
  // Constructor - initialize a new student object
  public Student(string sName, double dGrade)
  {
    this.sName = sName;
    this.dGrade = dGrade;
  }
  // CreateStudentList - to save space here, just create
  //               a fixed list of students
  static string[] sNames =
        {"Homer", "Marge", "Bart", "Lisa", "Maggie"};
  static double[] dGrades = {0, 85, 50, 100, 30};
  public static Student[] CreateStudentList()
  {
    Student[] sArray = new Student[sNames.Length];
    for (int i = 0; i < sNames.Length; i++)
    {
      sArray[i] = new Student(sNames[i], dGrades[i]);
    }
    return sArray;
  }
  // access read-only methods
  public string Name
  {
    get { return sName; }
  }
  public double Grade
  {
    get { return dGrade; }
  }
  // implement the IComparable interface:
  // CompareTo - compare another object (in this case, Student
  //             objects) and decide which one comes after the
  //             other in the sorted array
  public int CompareTo(object rightObject)
  {
    // compare the current Student (let's call her
    // 'left') against the other student (we'll call
    // her 'right') - generate an error if both
    // left and right are not Student objects
```

```
     Student leftStudent = this;
     if (!(rightObject is Student))
     {
       Console.WriteLine("Compare method passed a nonStudent");
       return 0;
     }
     Student rightStudent = (Student)rightObject;
     // now generate a -1, 0, or 1 based upon the
     // sort criteria (the student's grade)
     // (the Double class has a CompareTo() method
     // we could have used instead)
     if (rightStudent.Grade < leftStudent.Grade)
     {
       return -1;
     }
     if (rightStudent.Grade > leftStudent.Grade)
     {
       return 1;
     }
     return 0;
   }
   // implement the IDisplayable interface:
   // GetString - return a representation of the student
   public string GetString()
   {
     string sPadName = Name.PadRight(9);
     string s = String.Format("{0}: {1:N0}", sPadName, Grade);
     return s;
   }
}
// -----------Birds - sort birds by their names--------
// Bird - just an array of bird names
class Bird : IComparable, IDisplayable
{
   private string sName;
   // Constructor - initialize a new Bird object
   public Bird(string sName)
   {
     this.sName = sName;
   }
   // CreateBirdList - return a list of birds to the caller;
   //                  use a canned list here to save time
   static string[] sBirdNames =
      { "Oriole", "Hawk", "Robin", "Cardinal",
        "Blue jay", "Finch", "Sparrow"};
   public static Bird[] CreateBirdList()
   {
     Bird[] birds = new Bird[sBirdNames.Length];
     for(int i = 0; i < birds.Length; i++)
     {
       birds[i] = new Bird(sBirdNames[i]);
     }
     return birds;
```

```
    }
    // access read-only methods
    public string Name
    {
      get { return sName; }
    }
    // implement the IComparable interface:
    // CompareTo - compare the birds by name; use the
    //             built-in String class compare method
    public int CompareTo(object rightObject)
    {
      // we'll compare the "current" bird to the
      // "right-hand object" bird
      Bird leftBird = this;
      Bird rightBird = (Bird)rightObject;
      return String.Compare(leftBird.Name, rightBird.Name);
    }
    // implement the IDisplayable interface:
    // GetString - returns the name of the bird
    public string GetString()
    {
      return Name;
    }
  }
}
```

The Student class (it's about in the middle of the program listing) implements the IComparable and IDisplayable interfaces, as described earlier. The CompareTo() method compares the students by grade, which results in the students being sorted by grade. The GetString() method returns the name and grade of the student.

The other methods of Student include the read-only Name and Grade properties, a simple constructor, and a CreateStudentList() method. This list method just returns a fixed list of students.

The Bird class at the bottom of the listing also implements the IComparable and IDisplayable interfaces. It implements CompareTo() by comparing the names of the birds using a method similar to the one built into the String class. So, one bird is greater than another if its name is greater. This method results in the birds being sorted in alphabetical order. The GetName() method just returns the name of the bird.

Now you're set up for the good part back in Main(). The CreateStudent List() method is used to return an unsorted list, which is stored in the array students.

Name collections of objects, such as an array, using a plural noun.

This array of students is first cast into an array of comparableObjects. This differs from the arrays used in other chapters (most notably the arrays in

Chapter 6). Those are arrays of objects of a particular class, like an array of `Student` objects, while `comparableObjects` is an array of objects that implement the `IComparable` interface, irrespective of what class they may be. Using an interface as an array element type, a method parameter type, or a method return type is a powerful technique for program flexibility.

The `comparableObjects` array is passed to the built-in `Array.Sort()` method, which sorts them by grade.

The sorted array of `Student` objects is then passed to the locally defined `DisplayArray()` method. `DisplayArray()` iterates through an array of objects that implement `GetString()`. It uses the `Array.Length` property to know how many objects are in the array. It then calls `GetString()` on each object and displays the result to the console using `WriteLine()`.

The program back in `Main()` continues by sorting and displaying birds! I think we can agree that birds have nothing to do with students. However, the class `Bird` implements the `IComparable` interface by comparing the names of the birds and the `IDisplayable` interface by returning the name of the bird.

Notice that `Main()` does not recast the array of birds this time. There's no need. This is similar to the following:

```
class BaseClass {}
class SubClass : BaseClass {}
class Program
{
  public static void SomeFunction(BaseClass bc) {}
  public static void AnotherFunction()
  {
    SubClass sc = new SubClass();
    SomeFunction(sc);
  }
}
```

Here, an object of class `SubClass` can be passed in lieu of a `BaseClass` object because a `SubClass` IS_A `BaseClass`.

Similarly, an array of `Bird` objects can be passed to a method expecting an array of `IComparable` objects because `Bird` implements that interface. The very next call to `DisplayArray()` passes the `birds` array, again without a cast because `Bird` implements the `IDisplayable` interface.

The output from the program appears as follows:

```
Sorting the list of students
Lisa      : 100
Marge     : 85
Bart      : 50
```

```
Maggie   : 30
Homer    : 0

Sorting the list of birds
Blue jay
Cardinal
Finch
Hawk
Oriole
Robin
Sparrow
Press Enter to terminate...
```

The students and birds are sorted, each according to its kind.

Inheriting an Interface

An interface can "inherit" the methods of another interface. I use quotes around the word *inherit* because it's not true inheritance, no matter how it may appear. The following interface code lists a *base interface,* much like a base class, in its heading:

```
// ICompare - an interface that can both compare itself
//            and display its own value
public interface ICompare : IComparable
{
  // GetValue - returns the value of itself as an int
  int GetValue();
}
```

The `ICompare` interface inherits the requirement to implement the `Compare To()` method from `IComparable`. To that, it adds the requirement to implement `GetValue()`. An `ICompare` object can be used as an `IComparable` object because, by definition, the former implements the requirements of the latter. However, this is not complete inheritance in the object-oriented, C# meaning of the word. Polymorphism is not possible. In addition, constructor relationships don't apply.

I demonstrate interface inheritance in the `AbstractInterface` program in the following section.

Facing an Abstract Interface

A class must implement every method of an interface to implement the interface. However, a class may implement a method of an interface with an abstract method (such a class is abstract, of course), as follows:

```
// AbstractInterface - demonstrate that an interface can be
//                     implemented with an abstract class
using System;
namespace AbstractInterface
{
  // ICompare - an interface that can both compare itself
  //            and display its own value
  public interface ICompare : IComparable
  {
    // GetValue - returns the value of itself as an int
    int GetValue();
  }
  // BaseClass - implement the ICompare interface by
  //             providing a concrete GetValue() method and
  //             an abstract CompareTo()
  abstract public class BaseClass : ICompare
  {
    int nValue;
    public BaseClass(int nInitialValue)
    {
      nValue = nInitialValue;
    }
    // implement the ICompare interface:
    // first with a concrete method
    public int GetValue()
    {
      return nValue;
    }
    // complete the ICompare interface with an abstract method
    abstract public int CompareTo(object rightObject);
  }
  // SubClass - complete the base class by overriding the
  //            abstract CompareTo() method
  public class SubClass: BaseClass
  {
    // pass the value passed to the constructor up to the
    // base class constructor
    public SubClass(int nInitialValue) : base(nInitialValue)
    {
    }
    // CompareTo - implement the IComparable interface; return
    //             an indication of whether a subclass object is
    //             greater than another
    override public int CompareTo(object rightObject)
    {
      BaseClass bc = (BaseClass)rightObject;
      // this compares two ints, one returned by the first
      // GetValue() and one returned by the other GetValue()
      return GetValue().CompareTo(bc.GetValue());
    }
  }
  public class Program
```

```
{
    public static void Main(string[] strings)
    {
        SubClass sc1 = new SubClass(10);
        SubClass sc2 = new SubClass(20);
        MyFunc(sc1, sc2);
        // wait for user to acknowledge the results
        Console.WriteLine("Press Enter to terminate...");
        Console.Read();
    }
    // MyFunc - use the methods provided by the ICompare interface
    //          to display the value of two objects and then an indication
    //          of which is greater (according to the object itself)
    public static void MyFunc(ICompare ic1, ICompare ic2)
    {
        Console.WriteLine("The value of ic1 is {0} and ic2 is {1}",
                          ic1.GetValue(), ic2.GetValue());
        string s;
        switch (ic1.CompareTo(ic2))
        {
            case 0:
                s = "is equal to";
                break;
            case -1:
                s = "is less than";
                break;
            case 1:
                s = "is greater than";
                break;
            default:
                s = "something messed up";
                break;
        }
        Console.WriteLine(
                "The objects themselves think that ic1 {0} ic2", s);
    }
}
```

AbstractInterface is another one of those large but relatively simple programs.

The ICompare interface describes a class that can compare two objects and fetch their value. ICompare inherits the CompareTo() requirement from the IComparable interface. To that, ICompare adds GetValue(), which returns the value of the objects as an int.

Even though it may return the value of the object as an `int`, `GetValue()` says nothing about the internals of the class. Generating an `int` value may involve a complex calculation, for all I know.

The class `BaseClass` implements the `ICompare` interface — the concrete `GetValue()` method returns the data member `nValue`. However, the `CompareTo()` method, which is also required by the `ICompare` interface, is declared `abstract`.

Declaring a class `abstract` means that it is an incomplete concept lacking an implementation of one or more properties — in this case, the method `CompareTo()`. The implementation is thus postponed for subclasses to complete.

`SubClass` provides the `CompareTo()` method that is necessary to become concrete.

Notice that `SubClass` automatically implements the `ICompare` interface, even though it doesn't explicitly say so. `BaseClass` promised to implement the methods of `ICompare`, and `SubClass` IS_A `BaseClass`. By inheriting these methods, `SubClass` automatically inherits the requirement to implement `ICompare`.

`Main()` creates two objects of class `SubClass` with different values. It then passes those objects to `MyFunc()`. The `MyFunc()` method expects to receive two objects of interface `ICompare`. `MyFunc()` uses the `CompareTo()` method to decide which object is greater and then uses `GetValue()` to display the "value" of the two objects.

The output from this program is short and sweet:

```
The value of ic1 is 10 and ic2 is 20
The objects themselves think that ic1 is less than ic2
Press Enter to terminate...
```

Chapter 15 deepens the already remarkable capability of interfaces by showing you how to write generic interfaces.

The C# Structure Has No Class

C# appears to have a dichotomy in the way you declare variables. You declare and initialize value type variables such as `int` and `double` in the following way:

```
int n;    // declare
n = 1;    // initialize
```

However, you declare and initialize references to objects in a completely different way:

```
public class MyClass
{
  public int n;
}
MyClass mc;              // declare
mc = new MyClass();      // initialize
```

The `class` variable `mc` is known as a *reference type* because the variable `mc` refers to potentially distant memory. Intrinsic variables like `int` or `double` are known as *value type variables*.

If you examine `n` and `mc` more closely, however, you see that the only real difference is that C# allocates the memory for the value type variable automatically while you have to allocate the memory for the class object explicitly. `int` is from Venus; `MyClass` is from Mars. Is there nothing that can tie the two together into a Unified Class Theory?

The C# structure

C# defines a third variable type called a *structure* that bridges the gap between the reference types and the value types. The syntax of a structure declaration looks like that of a class:

```
public struct MyStruct
{
  public int n;
  public double d;
}
public class MyClass
{
  public int n;
  public double d;
}
```

A structure object is accessed like a class object but allocated like a value type, as demonstrated in the following code:

```
// declaring and accessing a simple value type
int n;
n = 1;
// declaring a struct is much like declaring a simple int
MyStruct ms;     // automatically allocates memory
ms.n = 3;        // access the members the same as a class object
ms.d = 3.0;
// a class object must be allocated out of a separate
// memory area with new
```

```
MyClass mc = new MyClass;
mc.n = 2;
mc.d = 2.0;
```

A `struct` object is stored like an intrinsic variable in memory. The variable `ms` is not a reference to some external memory block that's allocated off a separate memory area.

The `ms` object occupies the same local memory area that the variable n occupies, as shown in Figure 14-1.

Figure 14-1:
The struct variable ms "lives" within the same memory space as the value type variable n, while the mc object's memory comes off of a separate heap of memory space.

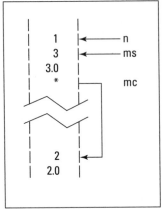

The distinction between reference and value types is even more obvious in the following example. Allocating an array of 100 reference objects requires the program to invoke `new` 101 times (once for the array and once for each object):

```
MyClass[] mc = new MyClass[100];
for(int i = 0; i < ms.Length; i++)
{
   mc[i] = new MyClass();
}
mc[0].n = 0;
```

This array also involves a considerable amount of overhead, both in space and time, as detailed in the following list:

- Each element in the mc array must be large enough to contain a reference to an object.

- Each MyClass object has unseen overhead above and beyond the single data member n.

- Consider the time the program takes to go through the motions of whittling off a tiny chunk of memory 100 times.

The memory for the structure objects is allocated as part of the array, as follows:

```
// declaring an array of simple int value types
int[] integers = new int[100]; // this allocates the memory
integers[0] = 0;
// declaring an array of structs is just as easy
MyStruct[] ms = new MyStruct[100]; // so does this
ms[0].n = 0;
```

This time just one long contiguous block of memory is allocated, all at once.

The structure constructor

Interestingly, a structure can be initialized using the following class-like syntax:

```
public struct MyStruct
{
  public int n;
  public double d;
}
MyStruct ms = new MyStruct();  // with new
```

Despite appearances, this does not allocate a block of memory off of the heap. It just initializes n and d to zero.

You can construct a nondefault constructor of your own that actually does something. Consider the following code:

```
public struct Test
{
  private int n;
  public Test(int n)
  {
    this.n = n;
  }
}
```

```
public class Program
{
  public static void Main(string[] args)
  {
    Test test = new Test(10);
  }
}
```

Despite its appearance, the declaration test = new Test(10); does not allocate memory — it only initializes the value type memory that's already there. Note the parentheses, not square brackets as in an array.

The wily methods of a structure

This paragraph summarizes the principal facts about the structure, which the next example program illustrates. A structure can have instance members, including methods and properties. A structure can have static members. The static members of a structure may have initializers, but the nonstatic (instance) members may not. Normally, a structure object is passed to a function by value, but it may be passed by reference if this is specifically indicated in the function call with the ref keyword. A structure cannot inherit a class (other than Object, as described in the section "'Oh, the Value and the Reference Can Be Friends . . .' — Unifying the Type System," later in this chapter), and it cannot be inherited by some other class. A structure can implement an interface.

See Chapter 8 for the lowdown on the difference between a static and an instance member. See Chapter 7 for a review of pass by value and pass by reference. Chapter 12 discusses inheritance.

All classes (and structs) inherit from Object whether they specifically say so or not. You can override the methods of Object. In practical terms, the only method you may want to override is ToString(). ToString() allows the object to create a displayable representation of itself. If you don't implement your own ToString(), the default, from class Object, returns the complete class name, for example: MyNamespace.MyClass. That's usually not very useful.

Putting a struct through its paces in an example

The following example program demonstrates the different features of a structure:

```csharp
// StructureExample - demonstrate the various properties
//                     of a struct object
using System;
using System.Collections;
namespace StructureExample
{
  public interface IDisplayable
  {
    string ToString();
  }
  // a struct can implement an interface
  public struct Test : IDisplayable
  {
    // a struct can have both instance and
    // class (static) data members;
    // static members may have initializers
    private int n;
    private static double d = 20.0;
    // a constructor can be used to initialize
    // the data members of a struct
    public Test(int n)
    {
      this.n = n;
    }
    // a struct may have both instance and class
    // (static) properties
    public int N
    {
      get { return n;}
      set { n = value; }
    }
    public static double D
    {
      get { return d; }
      set { d = value; }
    }
    // a struct may have methods
    public void ChangeMethod(int nNewValue, double dNewValue)
    {
      n = nNewValue;
      d = dNewValue;
    }
    // ToString - overrides the ToString method in object
    //            and implements the IDisplayable interface
    override public string ToString()
    {
      return string.Format("({0:N}, {1:N})", n, d);
    }
  }
  public class Program
  {
    public static void Main(string[] args)
```

```
{
    // create a Test object
    Test test = new Test(10);
    Console.WriteLine("Initial value of test");
    OutputFunction(test);
    // try to modify the test object by passing it
    // as an argument
    ChangeValueFunction(test, 100, 200.0);
    Console.WriteLine("Value of test after calling" +
                      " ChangeValueFunction(100, 200.0)");
    OutputFunction(test);
    // try to modify the test object by passing it
    // as an argument
    ChangeReferenceFunction(ref test, 100, 200.0);
    Console.WriteLine("Value of test after calling" +
                      " ChangeReferenceFunction(100, 200.0)");
    OutputFunction(test);
    // a method can modify the object
    test.ChangeMethod(1000, 2000.0);
    Console.WriteLine("Value of test after calling" +
                      " ChangeMethod(1000, 2000.0)");
    OutputFunction(test);
    // wait for user to acknowledge the results
    Console.WriteLine("Press Enter to terminate...");
    Console.Read();
}
// ChangeValueFunction - pass the struct by value
public static void ChangeValueFunction(Test t,
                       int newValue, double dNewValue)
{
    t.N = newValue;
    Test.D = dNewValue;
}
// ChangeReferenceFunction - pass the struct by reference
public static void ChangeReferenceFunction(ref Test t,
                       int newValue, double dNewValue)
{
    t.N = newValue;
    Test.D = dNewValue;
}
// OutputFunction - outputs any method that implements ToString()
public static void OutputFunction(IDisplayable id)
{
    Console.WriteLine("id = {0}", id.ToString());
}
}
}
```

The `StructureExample` program first defines an interface, `IDisplayable`, and then a simple structure, `Test`, which implements that interface. `Test` also defines two members: an instance member, `n`, and a static member, `d`. A static initializer sets the member `d` to 20; however, an initializer for the instance member `n` is not allowed.

The `Test` structure defines a constructor, an instance property `N`, and a static property `D`.

`Test` defines a method of its own — `ChangeMethod()` — as well as overrides the `ToString()` method. In providing `ToString()`, `Test` implements the `IDisplayable` interface.

The `Main()` function puts `Test` through its paces. First, it creates an object `test` out of local memory and uses the constructor to initialize that memory. `Main()` then calls `OutputFunction()` to display the object.

`Main()` next calls the function `ChangeValueFunction()`, passing `test` along with two numeric constants. `ChangeValueFunction()` assigns these two numbers to the `Test` members `n` and `d`. Upon return from the function, the `OutputFunction()` reveals that `d` has been changed while `n` has not.

The call to `ChangeValueFunction()` passes the `struct` object `test` by value. The object `t` within that function is a copy of the original `test` and not the object itself. Thus, the assignment to `t.N` changes the local copy but has no effect on `test` back in `Main()`. However, all objects of class `Test` share the same static member `d`. Thus, the assignment to `Test.D` changes `d` for all objects, including `test`.

The next call is to the function `ChangeReferenceFunction()`. This function appears the same as `ChangeValueFunction()` except for the addition of the keyword `ref` to the argument list. `test` is now passed by reference, so the argument `t` refers to the original object `test` and not some newly created copy.

The final call in `Main()` is to the method `ChangeMethod()`. Calls to methods always pass the current object by reference, so the changes made in this method are retained back in `Main()`.

The output from the program appears as follows:

```
Initial value of test
id = (10.00, 20.00)
Value of test after calling ChangeValueFunction(100, 200.0)
id = (10.00, 200.00)
Value of test after calling ChangeReferenceFunction(100, 200.0)
id = (100.00, 200.00)
Value of test after calling ChangeMethod(1000, 2000.0)
id = (1,000.00, 2,000.00)
Press Enter to terminate...
```

"Oh, the Value and the Reference Can Be Friends . . ." — Unifying the Type System

Structures and classes do have one striking similarity: They both derive from `Object`. In fact, all classes and structures, whether they say so or not, derive from `Object`. This fact unifies the different variable types into one all-encompassing class hierarchy.

Predefined structure types

The similarity between structures and simple value types is more than skin deep. In fact, *a simple value type is a structure*. For example, `int` is another name for the structure `Int32`, `double` is another name for the structure `Double`, and so forth. Table 14-1 shows the full list of types and their corresponding `struct` names.

Table 14-1	The `struct` Names for the Intrinsic Variable Types
Type Name	`struct` *Name*
bool	Boolean
byte	Byte
sbyte	SByte
char	Char
decimal	Decimal
double	Double
float	Single
int	Int32
uint	UInt32
long	Int64
ulong	UInt64
object	Object
short	Int16
ushort	UInt16

The string type is a reference type, not a value type, so no struct exists for it. Instead, string corresponds to *class* String. Recall, however, the string is a special C# animal, as it has been granted some unusual struct-like properties. Chapter 9 discusses the string type in detail.

So, how do common structures unify the type system? An example

An int is another name for Int32 (a kind of alias, really). Because all structs derive from Object, int must derive from Object as well. This leads to some fascinating results, as the following program demonstrates:

```
// TypeUnification - demonstrate how int and Int32
//                   are actually the same thing and
//                   how they derive from Object
using System;
namespace TypeUnification
{
  public class Program
  {
    public static void Main(string[] args)
    {
      // create an int and initialize it to zero
      int i = new int();  // yes, you can do this
      // assign it a value and output it via the
      // IFormattable interface that Int32 implements
      i = 1;
      OutputFunction(i);
      // the constant 2 also implements IFormattable
      OutputFunction(2);
      // in fact, you can call a method of a constant
      Console.WriteLine("Output directly = {0}", 3.ToString());
      // this can be truly useful; you can pick an int out of a list:
      Console.WriteLine("\nPick the integers out of a list");
      object[] objects = new object[5];
      objects[0] = "this is a string";
      objects[1] = 2;
      objects[2] = new Program();
      objects[3] = 4;
      objects[4] = 5.5;
      for(int index = 0; index < objects.Length; index++)
      {
        if (objects[index] is int)
        {
          int n = (int)objects[index];
          Console.WriteLine("the {0}th element is a {1}", index, n);
```

```
      }
    }
    // type unity allows you to display value and
    // reference types without differentiating them
    Console.WriteLine("\nDisplay all the objects in the list");
    int nCount = 0;
    foreach(object o in objects)
    {
      Console.WriteLine("Objects[{0}] is <{1}>",
        nCount++, o.ToString()); // all objects implement IFormattable
    }
    // wait for user to acknowledge the results
    Console.WriteLine("Press Enter to terminate...");
    Console.Read();
  }
  // OutputFunction - outputs any object that implements ToString()
  //
  public static void OutputFunction(IFormattable id)
  {
    Console.WriteLine("Value from OutputFunction = {0}",
                      id.ToString());
  }
  // ToString - provide a simple string function for the Program class
  override public string ToString()
  {
    return "TypeUnification Program";
  }
}
```

This program puts the Int32 struct through its paces. Main() begins by
creating an int object i. Main() uses the Int32() default constructor (or
you could say the int() constructor) to initialize i to zero. The program
continues by assigning a value to i. Admittedly, this differs slightly from the
format you would use for a structure that you may create.

Main() passes the variable i to OutputFunction(), which is declared
to accept an object that implements the IFormattable interface. The
IFormattable interface is similar to the IDisplayable interface that I
define in other programs — the only method in IFormattable is ToString.
All classes and structures inherit the IFormattable interface from Object,
so all objects, whether reference or value types, implement ToString().

OutputFunction() tells the IFormattable object to display itself — the
Int32 variable has no problem because it has its own ToString() method.
This is demonstrated even more graphically in the call OutputFunction(2).
Being of type Int32, the constant 2 also implements IFormattable. Finally,
just to shove your nose in it, Main() invokes 3.ToString() directly. The
output from this first section of Main() is as follows:

```
Value from OutputFunction = 1
Value from OutputFunction = 2
Output directly = 3
```

The program now enters a unique section. `Main()` declares an array of objects of type `Object`. It stores a `string` in the first element, an `int` in the second, an instance of class `Program` in the third, and so on. This is allowed because `String`, `Int32`, and `Program` all derive from `Object`. An array inside class `Program` that stores an instance of `Program`? Getting dizzy?

The program then loops through the objects in the array. `Main()` is able to pick out the integers by asking each object whether it IS_A `Int32` using the `is` keyword. The output from this portion of the program is as follows (pardon expressions like `1th` and `3th`):

```
Pick the integers out of a list
the 1th element is a 2
the 3th element is a 4
```

The program completes its showing off by again using the `Object` lineage. All subclasses of `Object` — that would be all classes — implement `ToString()`. Therefore, if you just want to display the members of the object array, you really don't need to worry about their type. The final section of `Main()` loops through the object array again, this time asking each object to format itself using its `ToString()` method. The results appear as follows:

```
Display all the objects in the list
Objects[0] is <this is a string>
Objects[1] is <2>
Objects[2] is <TypeUnification Program>
Objects[3] is <4>
Objects[4] is <5.5>
Press Enter to terminate...
```

Like animals coming off of Noah's Ark, each object displays itself as one of its kind. I implemented a trivial `ToString()` for class `Program` just to show that it knows how to play nice with all the other classes.

In fact, this `ToString()` property is undoubtedly how `Console.Write()` can perform its magic. I haven't looked into the source code, but I would bet that `Write()` accepts its arguments as objects. It can then simply invoke `ToString()` on the object to convert it into displayable format (other than the first argument, which may contain `{n}` format controls).

Boxing and unboxing value types

What really makes both reference types and value types — like `int`, `bool`, `char`, and any `struct` — first-class citizens is a technique called *boxing*. In many situations, the compiler temporarily converts value-type objects into reference-type objects. Boxing means stuffing a piece of value-type data into a reference-type object on the heap. Here's an example that involves boxing:

```
int i = 999;            // a simple int (a value type)
object o = i;           // putting i into a reference-type box
int j = (int)o;         // taking 999 out of the box
```

On the flip side, what gets boxed must sooner or later get unboxed as well, requiring a cast. In the TypeUnification example shown earlier, every assignment to object requires boxing, and the casts that back out of object variables require unboxing.

Both operations consume some time. Boxing takes up to 20 times longer than an ordinary assignment, and unboxing takes 4 times longer. It also takes some memory space (an extra object on the heap), so a lot of boxing going on can cost your program. Boxing takes place automatically in many situations, behind your back, including argument passing, function returns, assignments, working with arrays of type object[], WriteLine() calls, and more. Avoid boxing/unboxing when you can by, for instance, calling ToString() for value types in WriteLine(), avoiding arrays of object, and using the new generic collection classes discussed in Chapter 15.

Chapter 15

Asking Your Pharmacist about Generics

. . . .

In This Chapter

▶ Collecting things: benefits and problems

▶ Saving time and code with generic collection classes

▶ Writing your own generic classes, methods, and interfaces

. . . .

C# provides lots of specialized alternatives to the arrays introduced in Chapter 6. This chapter describes these lists, stacks, queues, and other array-like collection classes, such as the versatile `ArrayList`, which have to date been the prescription of choice for many programming needs. Unlike arrays, though, these collections aren't type-safe and can be costly to use.

But as with prescriptions at your local pharmacy, you can save big by opting for a generic version. *Generics* are a new feature introduced in C# 2.0. Generics are fill-in-the-blanks classes, methods, and interfaces. For example, the `List<T>` class defines a generic array-like list that's very comparable to `ArrayList`. When you pull `List<T>` off the shelf to instantiate your own list of, say, `int`s, you replace `T` with `int`, as follows:

```
List<int> myList = new List<int>();  // a list limited to ints
```

The versatile thing is that you can instantiate a `List<T>` for *any single* data type — `string`, `Student`, `BankAccount`, `CorduroyPants`, whatever — and it's still type-safe like the array, without nongeneric costs. It's the super-array. (I explain type-safety and the costs of nongeneric collections in this chapter.)

Generics come in two flavors in C#: the built-in generic collection classes like `List<T>` and a variety of roll-your-own items. After a quick tour of nongeneric and generic collection classes, this chapter covers roll-your-own generic classes, generic methods, and generic interfaces.

Getting to Know Nongeneric Collections

Understanding what the new generics are and why they're better is easier to understand after you've had a brief dose of good old-fashioned nongenerics.

Arrays let you access random elements quickly and efficiently. But often an array doesn't quite fit your needs because it has the following big disadvantages:

- ✔ A program must declare the size of the array when it is created. Unlike Visual Basic, C# doesn't let you change the size of an array after it's defined. What if you don't know up-front how big it needs to be?

- ✔ Inserting or removing an element in the middle of an array is wildly inefficient. You have to move all the elements around to make room.

Given these problems, C# provides many nongeneric collections as alternatives to arrays. Each collection has its own strengths (and weaknesses).

Inventorying nongeneric collections

C# provides a well-stocked pharmacopoeia of array alternatives. Table 15-1 summarizes a few of the most useful nongeneric collections. One of them is sure to have the characteristics you need (but don't get hooked on them; a better option — generics — is described in a minute).

Table 15-1	Nongeneric Collection Classes
Class	*Characteristics*
ArrayList	An array that grows automatically, as necessary. This workhorse has the array's advantages but not its disadvantages, though of course it's not perfect. Unlike arrays, all nonarray collections grow as needed.
LinkedList	C# has no nongeneric linked list, but Bonus Chapter 3 on the CD shows you how to roll your own. After that useful exercise, however, you'll prefer C#'s new generic LinkedList. Any LinkedList beats the array at insertion, but accessing specific elements is slow compared to array and ArrayList.
Queue	This is a first-come, first-served line. Good citizens join the queue (get "enqueued") at the back and get their Fatburgers at the front (get "dequeued"). You can't insert or remove elements in the middle.

Class	Characteristics
Stack	The standard analogy is a stack of plates. To add elements, you *push* clean plates to the top of the stack, and to remove them, you *pop* them from there too. It's last-come, first-served. You can't insert elements in the middle.
Dictionary	This is a collection of objects well-suited for quick lookup. You find things quickly by asking for the *key,* just as you find definitions in a dictionary by looking up a word. C#'s nongeneric "dictionary" class goes by the tasty moniker of Hashtable.

Using nongeneric collections

Collections are easier to use than arrays. Instantiate a collection object, add elements to it, iterate it (the best way is with foreach), and so on. The NongenericCollections example on the CD shows several different collections in action, including the Stack and the Hashtable ("dictionary"). The following code excerpt demonstrates ArrayList, one of the most commonly used collections:

```
// NongenericCollections - demonstrate using the nongeneric collection classes
using System;
using System.Collections;            // you need this
namespace NongenericCollections
{
  public class Program
  {
    public static void Main(string[] args)
    {
      // instantiate an ArrayList (you can give an initial size or not)
      ArrayList aListWithSpecifiedSize = new ArrayList(1000);
      ArrayList aList = new ArrayList();  // default size (16)
      aList.Add("one");  // adds to the "end" of empty list
      aList.Add("two");  // order is now "one", "two"
      // collection classes work with foreach
      foreach(string s in aList)
      {
        // write string and its index
        Console.WriteLine(s + " " + aList.IndexOf(s));
      }
      // ... full example on CD includes several more collection types
      // wait for user to acknowledge the results
      Console.WriteLine("Press Enter to terminate...");
      Console.Read();
    }
  }
  public class Student
  // code omitted to save space - see the CD
  }
```

Because of the advent of generics (which are described next), I don't explore these collections in detail, but you can try them out by using these examples. Look up "System.Collections namespace" in the Help Index. These classes have a variety of useful methods and properties.

Writing a New Prescription: Generics

Now that generics have arrived, you'll probably seldom ever use any of the collection classes described in the preceding sections. Generics really are better for two reasons: safety and performance.

Generics are type-safe

When you declare an array, you must specify the exact type of data it can hold. If you specify `int`, the array can't hold anything but `ints` or other numeric types that C# can convert implicitly to `int`. You get compiler errors at build time if you try to put the wrong kind of data into an array. Thus the compiler enforces *type-safety*, enabling you to fix a problem before it ever gets out the door.

A compiler error beats the heck out of a run-time error. In fact, it beats everything but a royal flush or a raspberry sundae. Compiler errors are good because they help you spot problems now.

Nongeneric collections aren't type-safe. In C#, everything IS_A `Object` because `Object` is the base type for all other types, both value-types and reference-types. (See the section on unifying the type system in Chapter 14.) But when you store *value-types* (numbers, `bools`, and `structs`) in a collection, they must be *boxed* going in and *unboxed* coming back out. (See Chapter 14 for the lowdown on boxing.) It's as if you're putting items in an egg carton and have to stuff them inside the eggs so they fit. (Reference-types, such as `string`, `Student`, or `BankAccount`, don't undergo boxing.)

The first consequence of nongenerics lacking type-safety is that you need a cast, as shown in the following code, to get the original object out of the `ArrayList` because it's hidden inside an egg, er, `Object`:

```
ArrayList aList = new ArrayList();
// add five or six items, then ...
string myString = (string)aList[4];  // cast to string
```

Fine, but the second consequence is this: You can put eggs in the carton, sure. But you can also add marbles, rocks, diamonds, fudge — you name it. An `ArrayList` can hold many *different types* of objects *at the same time*. So it's legal to write this:

```
ArrayList aList = new ArrayList();
aList.Add("a string");      // string -- OK
aList.Add(3);               // int -- OK
aList.Add(aStudent);        // Student -- OK
```

However, if you put a mixture of incompatible types into an `ArrayList` (or other nongeneric collection), how do you know what type is in, say, aList[3]? If it's a `Student` and you try to cast it to `string`, you get a run-time error. It's just like Harry Potter reaching into a box of Bertie Botts's Every Flavor Beans. He doesn't know whether he'll get raspberry beans or earwax.

To be safe, you have to resort to using the `is` operator (discussed in Chapter 12) or the alternative, the `as` operator, as follows:

```
if(aList[i] is Student)                   // is the object there a Student?
{
  Student aStudent = (Student)aList[i];   // yes, safe cast
}
// or ...
Student aStudent = aList[i] as Student;   // extract a Student, if present
if(aStudent != null)                      // if not, "as" returns null
{
  // ok to use aStudent; "as" operator worked
}
```

You can avoid all this extra work by using generics. Generic collections work like arrays: You specify the one and only type they can hold when you declare them.

Generics are efficient

Polymorphism allows the type `Object` to hold any other type — like the previous egg carton analogy. But you can incur a penalty by putting in value-type objects — numeric and `bool` types and `structs` — and taking them out. (See Chapter 13 for more on polymorphism.) That's because value-type objects that you add have to be boxed.

Boxing isn't too worrisome unless your collection is big. If you're stuffing a thousand, or a million, `ints` into a nongeneric collection, it takes about 20 times as long, plus extra space on the memory heap, where reference-type objects are stored. Boxing can also lead to subtle errors that will have you tearing out your hair. Generic collections eliminate boxing and unboxing.

Using Generic Collections

Now that you know why generic collections are preferable, it's time to see what they are and how to use them. Table 15-2 provides a partial list of generic collection classes (with their pregeneric equivalents in column 3).

Table 15-2	Some Generic Collection Classes	
Class	*Description*	*Similar To*
List<T>	A dynamic array	ArrayList
LinkedList<T>	A linked list	The LinkedList in Bonus Chapter 3
Queue<T>	A first-in, first-out list	Queue
Stack<T>	A last-in, first-out list	Stack
Dictionary<T>	A collection of key/value pairs	Hashtable

Besides those, there are several more, plus corresponding interfaces for most, such as ICollection<T> and IList<T>. Look up "System.Collections.Generic namespace" in Help for more information about them.

Figuring out <T>

In the mysterious-looking <T> notation, <T> is a placeholder for some particular data type. To bring this symbolic object to life, instantiate it by inserting a real type, as follows:

```
List<int> intList = new List<int>();  // instantiating for int
```

For example, in the next section, you instantiate List<T>, the generic ArrayList, for types int, string, and Student. By the way, T isn't sacred. You can use <dummy> or <myType> if you like. Common ones are T, U, V, and so on.

Using List<T>

If ArrayList was one of the most-used nongeneric collections, List<T>, its generic counterpart, is likely to follow in Daddy's footsteps. The GenericCollections example on the CD (which is more complete than the listing that follows) shows some of the things you can do with List<T> (you need to comment out the lines that produce compiler errors before it will run):

```
// GenericCollections - demonstrate the generic collections
using System;
using System.Collections;
using System.Collections.Generic;
namespace GenericCollections
{
  public class Program
  {
    public static void Main(string[] args)
    {
      // an ArrayList declaration for comparison
      ArrayList aList = new ArrayList();
      // now List<T>: note angle brackets plus parentheses in
      //   List<T> declaration; T is a "type parameter"
      List<string> sList = new List<string>(); // instantiate for string type
      sList.Add("one");
      sList.Add(3);                            // compiler error here!
      sList.Add(new Student("du Bois"));       // compiler error here!
      List<int> intList = new List<int>();     // instantiate for int
      intList.Add(3);                          // fine; note, no boxing
      intList.Add(4);
      Console.WriteLine("Printing intList:");
      foreach(int i in intList)  // foreach just works for all collections
      {
        Console.WriteLine("int i = " + i.ToString()); // note: no casting
      }
      // instantiate for Student
      List<Student> studentList = new List<Student>();
      Student student1 = new Student("Vigil");
      Student student2 = new Student("Finch");
      studentList.Add(student1);
      studentList.Add(student2);
      Student[] students = new Student[]
                       { new Student("Mox"), new Student("Fox") };
      studentList.AddRange(students); // add whole array to List
      Console.WriteLine("Num students in studentList = {0}", studentList.Count);
      // search with IndexOf()
      Console.WriteLine("Student2 at " + studentList.IndexOf(student2));
      string name = studentList[3].Name;  // access list by index
      if(studentList.Contains(student1))  // search with Contains()
      {
        Console.WriteLine(student1.Name + " contained in list");
      }
      studentList.Sort(); // assumes Student implements IComparable interface
      studentList.Insert(3, new Student("Ross"));
      studentList.RemoveAt(3);  // deletes the element
      Console.WriteLine("removed {0}", name);          // name defined above
      Student[] moreStudents = studentList.ToArray(); // convert list to array
      // wait for user to acknowledge the results
```

```
      Console.WriteLine("Press Enter to terminate...");
      Console.Read();
    }
  }
  public class Student : IComparable
  // omitted to save space - see the CD
}
```

The code shows three instantiations of List<T>: for int, string, and Student. It also demonstrates the following:

- ✔ Counting on the list's type-safety to avoid adding the wrong data types
- ✔ Using the foreach loop on List<T>, as on any collection
- ✔ Adding objects, both singly and a whole array at a time
- ✔ Sorting the list (assuming that the items implement the IComparable interface)
- ✔ Inserting a new element between existing elements
- ✔ Obtaining a count of elements in the list
- ✔ Seeing if the list contains a particular object
- ✔ Removing an element from the list (it's deleted, not returned)
- ✔ Copying the elements in the list into an array

That's only a sampling of the List<T> methods. The other generic collections have different sets of methods but are otherwise much the same in use.

The real improvement here is that the compiler prevents adding types to a generic class other than the type it was instantiated for. Bonus Chapter 3 on the CD explores iterating collections efficiently.

Classy Generics: Writing Your Own

Besides the built-in generic collection classes, C# 2.0 lets you write your own generic classes, whether they're collections or not. The point of generic classes is that you can create generic versions of classes that *you* design.

Picture a class definition full of <T> notations. When you instantiate such a class, you specify a type to replace its generic placeholders, just as you do with the generic collections. Note how similar these declarations are:

```
LinkedList<int> aList = new LinkedList<int>();
MyClass<int> aClass = new MyClass<int>();
```

Both are instantiations of classes — one built-in and one programmer-defined. Not every class makes sense as a generic, but I show you an example of one that does later in this chapter.

Classes that logically could do the same things for different types of data make the best generic classes. Collections of one sort or another are the prime example. If you find yourself mumbling, "I'll probably have to write a version of this for Student objects, too," it's probably a good candidate for generics.

To show you how to write your own generic class, the following example develops a special kind of queue collection class called a *priority queue*.

Shipping packages at OOPs

Here's the scene for the example: a busy shipping warehouse similar to UPS or FedEx. Packages stream in the front at OOPs, Inc. and get shipped out the back as soon as they can be processed. Some packages need to go by super-fast next-day teleportation; some can go a tiny bit slower, by second-day cargo pigeon; and most can take the snail route: ground delivery in your cousin Fred's '82 Volvo.

But the packages don't arrive at the warehouse in any particular order, so as they come in, you need to expedite some as next-day or second-day. Because some packages are more equal than others, they get prioritized, and the folks in the warehouse give the high-priority packages special treatment.

Except for the priority aspect, this is tailor-made for a *queue* data structure. Queues are perfect for anything that involves turn-taking. You've stood (or driven) in thousands of queues in your life, waiting for your turn to buy Twinkies or pay too much for prescriptions.

The shipping warehouse scenario is similar: New packages arrive and go to the back of the line — normally. But because some have higher priorities, they're privileged characters, like those Premium Class folks at the airport ticket counter. They get to jump ahead, either to the front of the line or not far back from the front.

Queuing at OOPs: PriorityQueue

The shipping queue at OOPs deals with high-, medium-, and low-priority packages coming in. Here are the queuing rules:

- **High-priority packages** (next-day) go to the front of the queue — but behind any other high-priority packages that are already there.

 ✔ **Medium-priority packages** (second-day) go as far forward as possible — but behind all the high-priority packages, even the ones that some laggard will drop off later, and also behind other medium-priority packages that are already in the queue.

 ✔ **Low-priority ground-pounders** must join at the very back of the queue. They get to watch all the high priorities sail by to cut in front of them — sometimes *way* in front of them.

C# comes with built-in queues, even generic ones. But it doesn't come with a priority queue, so you have to build your own. How? A common approach is to embed several actual queues within a *wrapper class,* sort of like this:

```
class Wrapper         // or PriorityQueue!
{
   Queue queueHigh   = new Queue ();
   Queue queueMedium = new Queue ();
   Queue queueLow    = new Queue ();
   // methods to manipulate the underlying queues...
```

The wrapper encapsulates three actual queues here (they could be generic), and it's up to the wrapper to manage what goes into which underlying queue and how. The standard interface to the `Queue` class — as implemented in C# — includes the following two key methods:

 ✔ `Enqueue()` (pronounced *NQ*) puts things into a queue *at the back.*

 ✔ `Dequeue()` (pronounced *DQ*) removes things from the queue *at the front.*

Wrappers are classes (or functions) that encapsulate complexity. A wrapper may have an interface that's very different from the interface(s) of what's inside it. But for the shipping priority queue, the wrapper provides the same interface as a normal queue, thus pretending to be a normal queue itself. It implements an `Enqueue()` method that gets an incoming package's priority and decides which underlying queue it gets to join. The wrapper's `Dequeue()` method finds the highest-priority `Package` in any of the underlying queues. The formal name of this wrapper class is `PriorityQueue`.

Here's the code for the `PriorityQueue` example on the CD:

```
// PriorityQueue - demonstrates using lower-level queue collection objects
//                 (generic ones at that) to implement a higher-level generic
//                 queue that stores objects in priority order
using System;
using System.Collections.Generic;
namespace PriorityQueue
{
   class Program
   {
      //Main - fill the priority queue with packages, then
      // remove a random number of them
```

```
static void Main(string[] args)
{
  Console.WriteLine("Create a priority queue:");
  PriorityQueue<Package> pq = new PriorityQueue<Package>();
  Console.WriteLine(
    "Add a random number (0 - 20) of random packages to queue:");
  Package pack;
  PackageFactory fact = new PackageFactory();
  // we want a random number less than 20
  Random rand = new Random();
  int numToCreate = rand.Next(20); // random int from 0 - 20
  Console.WriteLine("\tCreating {0} packages: ", numToCreate);
  for (int i = 0; i < numToCreate; i++)
  {
    Console.Write("\t\tGenerating and adding random package {0}", i);
    pack = fact.CreatePackage();
    Console.WriteLine(" with priority {0}", pack.Priority);
    pq.Enqueue(pack);
  }
  Console.WriteLine("See what we got:");
  int nTotal = pq.Count;
  Console.WriteLine("Packages received: {0}", nTotal);
  Console.WriteLine("Remove a random number of packages: 0-20: ");
  int numToRemove = rand.Next(20);
  Console.WriteLine("\tRemoving up to {0} packages", numToRemove);
  for (int i = 0; i < numToRemove; i++)
  {
    pack = pq.Dequeue();
    if (pack != null)
    {
      Console.WriteLine("\t\tShipped package with priority {0}",
          pack.Priority);
    }
  }
  // see how many we "shipped"
  Console.WriteLine("Shipped {0} packages", nTotal - pq.Count);
  // wait for user to acknowledge the results
  Console.WriteLine("Press Enter to terminate...");
  Console.Read();
 }
}
//Priority - instead of priorities like 1, 2, 3, ... these have names
enum Priority   // I explain the enum later
{
  Low, Medium, High
}
// IPrioritizable - define a custom interface: classes that can be added to
//                  PriorityQueue must implement this interface
interface IPrioritizable
{
  Priority Priority { get; } // Example of a property in an interface
}
//PriorityQueue - a generic priority queue class
```

```
//              types to be added to the queue *must*
//              implement IPrioritizable interface
class PriorityQueue<T> where T : IPrioritizable    // <-- see discussion later
{
  //Queues - the three underlying queues: all generic!
  private Queue<T> queueHigh   = new Queue<T>();
  private Queue<T> queueMedium = new Queue<T>();
  private Queue<T> queueLow    = new Queue<T>();
  //Enqueue - prioritize T and add it to correct queue
  public void Enqueue(T item)
  {
    switch (item.Priority) // require IPrioritizable to ensure this property
    {
      case Priority.High:
        queueHigh.Enqueue(item);
        break;
      case Priority.Low:
        queueLow.Enqueue(item);
        break;
      case Priority.Medium:
        queueMedium.Enqueue(item);
        break;
      default:
        throw new ArgumentOutOfRangeException(item.Priority.ToString(),
          "bad priority in PriorityQueue.Enqueue");
    }
  }
  //Dequeue - get T from highest-priority queue available
  public T Dequeue()
  {
    // find highest-priority queue with items
    Queue<T> queueTop = TopQueue();
    // if a non-empty queue found
    if (queueTop != null && queueTop.Count > 0)
    {
      return queueTop.Dequeue(); // return its front item
    }
    // if all queues empty, return null (could throw an exception instead)
    return default(T);  // what's this? see discussion
  }
  //TopQueue - what's the highest-priority underlying queue with items?
  private Queue<T> TopQueue()
  {
    if (queueHigh.Count > 0)    // anything in high-priority queue?
      return queueHigh;
    if (queueMedium.Count > 0) // anything in medium-priority queue?
      return queueMedium;
    if (queueLow.Count > 0)     // anything in low-priority queue?
      return queueLow;
    return queueLow;            // all empty, so return an empty queue
  }
  //IsEmpty - check whether there's anything to dequeue
  public bool IsEmpty()
```

```
    {
      // true if all queues are empty
      return (queueHigh.Count == 0) & (queueMedium.Count == 0) &
          (queueLow.Count == 0);
    }
    //Count - how many items are in all queues combined?
    public int Count  // implement this one as a read-only property
    {
      get { return queueHigh.Count + queueMedium.Count + queueLow.Count; }
    }
}
//Package - an example of a prioritizable class that can be stored in
//          the priority queue
class Package : IPrioritizable
{
    private Priority priority;
    //constructor
    public Package(Priority priority)
    {
      this.priority = priority;
    }
    //Priority - return package's priority - read-only
    public Priority Priority
    {
      get { return priority; }
    }
    // plus ToAddress, FromAddress, Insurance, etc.
}
//omitted class PackageFactory - see the CD}
```

PriorityQueue is a bit longer than most examples in this book, so you need
to look at each part carefully. After a look at the target class, Package, you
can follow a package's journey through the Main() function near the top.

Unwrapping the package

Class Package is intentionally simple for this example (see the preceding listing). It focuses on the priority part, although a real Package object would
include other members. All that Package needs for the example are a private
data member to store its priority, a constructor to create a package with a
specific priority, and a method (implemented as a read-only property here) to
return the priority.

Two aspects of class Package require some explanation: the Priority type
and the IPrioritizable interface that Package implements.

Specifying the possible priorities

Priorities are measured with an enumerated type, or enum, called Priority. The Priority enum looks like this:

```
//Priority - instead of priorities like 1, 2, 3, ... they have names
enum Priority      //
{
  Low, Medium, High
}
```

Implementing the IPrioritizable interface

Any object going into the PriorityQueue must "know" its own priority. (A general object-oriented principle makes objects responsible for themselves.)

You can informally make sure that class Package has a member to retrieve its priority, but it's better to make that a requirement that the compiler can enforce. You require any object placed in the PriorityQueue to have such a member.

One way to enforce this requirement is to insist that all shippable objects implement the IPrioritizable interface, which follows:

```
//IPrioritizable - define a custom interface: classes that can be added to
//                 PriorityQueue must implement this interface
interface IPrioritizable // any class can implement this interface
{
  Priority Priority { get; }
}
```

The notation { get; } is how you write a property in an interface declaration. Notice that the body of the get accessor is missing, but the interface makes it clear that Priority is a read-only (get-only) property that returns a value from the Priority enum.

Class Package implements the interface by providing a fleshed-out implementation for the Priority property, as follows:

```
public Priority Priority
{
  get { return priority; }
}
```

You encounter the other side of this enforceable requirement in the declaration of class PriorityQueue, coming up soon.

Touring Main ()

Before you spelunk the `PriorityQueue` class itself, it's useful to get an overview of how it works in practice at OOPs, Inc. Here's the `Main()` function for the `PriorityQueue` example:

```
//Main - fill the priority queue with packages, then
// remove a random number of them
static void Main(string[] args)
{
    // create a priority queue
    PriorityQueue<Package> pq = new PriorityQueue<Package>();
    // add a random number (0 - 20) of random packages to queue
    Package pack;
    PackageFactory fact = new PackageFactory();
    // we want a random number less than 20
    Random rand = new Random();
    int numToCreate = rand.Next(20); // random int from 0 - 20
    for (int i = 0; i < numToCreate; i++)
    {
        // generate a random package and add to priority queue
        pack = fact.CreatePackage();
        pq.Enqueue(pack);
    }
    // see what we got
    int nTotal = pq.Count;
    Console.WriteLine("Packages received: {0}", nTotal);
    // remove a random number of packages: 0-20
    int numToRemove = rand.Next(20);
    for (int i = 0; i < numToRemove; i++)
    {
        pack = pq.Dequeue();
        if (pack != null)
        {
            Console.WriteLine("Shipped package with priority {0}", pack.Priority);
        }
    }
    // see how many we "shipped"
    Console.WriteLine("Shipped {0} packages", nTotal - pq.Count);
    // wait for user to acknowledge the results
    Console.WriteLine("Press Enter to terminate...");
    Console.Read();
}
```

Here's what happens in `Main()`:

1. Instantiates a `PriorityQueue` object for type `Package`.

2. Creates a `PackageFactory` object whose job is to create new packages with randomly selected priorities, on demand.

A factory is a class or method that creates objects for you. You tour the `PackageFactory` in the section "Using a (nongeneric) Simple Factory class," later in the chapter.

3. Uses the .NET library class `Random` to generate a random number and then calls `PackageFactory` to create that many new `Package` objects with random priorities.

4. Adds each package to the `PriorityQueue` with `pq.Enqueue(pack)`.

5. Writes the number of packages created and then randomly removes some of them from the `PriorityQueue`.

6. Ends after writing the number of packages removed.

Writing generic code the easy way

How do you go about writing a generic class, with all those `<T>`s? Looks pretty confusing, doesn't it? Well, it's not so hard, as this section demonstrates.

The simple way to write a generic class is to write a nongeneric version first, and then substitute the `<T>`s. So, for example, you would write the `PriorityQueue` class for `Package` objects, test it, and then "genericize" it.

Here's a small piece of a nongeneric `PriorityQueue` to illustrate:

```
public class PriorityQueue
{
  //Queues - the three underlying queues: all generic!
  private Queue<Package> queueHigh   = new Queue<Package>();
  private Queue<Package> queueMedium = new Queue<Package>();
  private Queue<Package> queueLow    = new Queue<Package>();
  //Enqueue - prioritize a Package and add it to correct queue
  public void Enqueue(Package item)
  {
    switch(item.Priority)  // Package has this property
    {
      case Priority.High:
        queueHigh.Enqueue(item);
        break;
      case Priority.Low:
        queueLow.Enqueue(item);
        break;
      case Priority.Medium:
        queueMedium.Enqueue(item);
        break;
    }
  }
}
// and so on ...
```

Writing the class nongenerically first makes testing its logic easier. When the logic is all straight, you can use find-and-replace to replace the name Package with <T>. (You'll soon see that there's a bit more to it than that, but not much.)

Saving PriorityQueue for last

Why would a priority queue be last? Seems a little backward to me. But you've seen the rest. Now it's time to examine the PriorityQueue class itself. This section shows the code, and then takes you through it and shows you how to deal with a couple of small issues. I take it a piece at a time.

The underlying queues

The PriorityQueue is a wrapper class that hides three ordinary Queue<T> objects, one for each priority level. Here's the first part of PriorityQueue, showing the three underlying queues (now generic):

```
//PriorityQueue - a generic priority queue class; types to be added to the
//                queue *must* implement IPrioritizable interface
class PriorityQueue<T> where T: IPrioritizable
{
  //Queues - the three underlying queues: all generic!
  private Queue<T> queueHigh   = new Queue<T>();
  private Queue<T> queueMedium = new Queue<T>();
  private Queue<T> queueLow    = new Queue<T>();
  // the rest will follow shortly ...
```

These lines declare three private data members of type Queue<T> and initialize them by creating the Queue<T> objects. I say more later about that odd-looking class declaration line above the "subqueue" declarations.

The Enqueue() method

Enqueue() adds an item of type T to the PriorityQueue. Its job is to look at the item's priority and put it into the correct underlying queue. In the first line, it gets the item's Priority property and switches based on that value. To add the item to the high-priority queue, for example, Enqueue() turns around and enqueues the item in the underlying queueHigh. Here's PriorityQueue.Enqueue():

```
//Enqueue - prioritize T and add it to correct queue
public void Enqueue(T item)
{
  switch(item.Priority) // require IPrioritizable to ensure this property
  {
    case Priority.High:
      queueHigh.Enqueue(item);
      break;
    case Priority.Low:
```

```
        queueLow.Enqueue(item);
        break;
    case Priority.Medium:
        queueMedium.Enqueue(item);
        break;
    }
}
```

The Dequeue() method

Dequeue()'s job is a bit trickier. It must locate the highest-priority underlying queue that has contents and then retrieve the front item from that subqueue. Dequeue() delegates the first part of the task, finding the highest-priority queue that's not empty, to a private TopQueue() method (described next). Then Dequeue() calls the underlying queue's Dequeue() method to retrieve the frontmost object, which it returns. Here's how Dequeue() works:

```
//Dequeue - get T from highest priority queue available
public T Dequeue()
{
  // find highest-priority queue with items
  Queue<T> queueTop = TopQueue();
  // if a non-empty queue found
  if (queueTop != null & queueTop.Count > 0)
  {
    return queueTop.Dequeue(); // return its front item
  }
  return default(T);  // if all queues empty, return null
}
```

The only difficulty arises if none of the underlying queues have any packages — in other words, the whole PriorityQueue is empty. What do you return in that case? Dequeue() returns null. The client — the code that calls PriorityQueue.Dequeue() — should check Dequeue()'s return value in case it's null. Where's the null it returns? It's that odd duck, default(T), at the end. I deal with default(T) in a moment.

The TopQueue() utility method

Dequeue() relies on the private method TopQueue() to find the highest-priority, nonempty underlying queue. TopQueue() just starts with queueHigh and asks for its Count property. If that's greater than zero, the queue contains items, so TopQueue() returns a reference to the whole underlying queue that it found. (TopQueue()'s return type is Queue<T>.) On the other hand, if queueHigh is empty, TopQueue() tries queueMedium and then queueLow.

What happens if all the subqueues are empty? TopQueue() could return null, but it's more useful to simply return one of the empty queues. When Dequeue() then calls the returned queue's Dequeue() method, it returns null. TopQueue() works like this:

```
//TopQueue - what's the highest-priority underlying queue with items?
private Queue<T> TopQueue()
{
  if (queueHigh.Count > 0)    // anything in high priority queue?
    return queueHigh;
  if (queueMedium.Count > 0)  // anything in medium priority queue?
    return queueMedium;
  if (queueLow.Count > 0)     // anything in low priority queue?
    return queueLow;
  return queueLow;            // all empty, so return an empty queue
}
```

The remaining PriorityQueue members

It's useful for `PriorityQueue` to know whether it's empty and, if not, how many items it contains (an object should be responsible for itself). Look back at `PriorityQueue`'s `IsEmpty()` method and `Count` property in the listing.

Tending to unfinished business

`PriorityQueue` still needs a couple of small bits of spackling. Here are the issues:

- ✔ By itself, `PriorityQueue` wouldn't prevent you from trying to instantiate it for, say, `int` or `string` or `Student` — things that don't have priorities. You need to *constrain* the class so that it can be instantiated only for types that implement `IPrioritizable`. Attempting to instantiate for a non-`IPrioritizable` class should result in a compiler error.

- ✔ The `Dequeue()` method for `PriorityQueue` returns the value `null` instead of an actual object. But generic types like `<T>` don't have a natural default `null` value the way things like `ints`, `strings`, and down-and-out object references do. That part of it needs to be genericized, too.

Adding constraints

`PriorityQueue` must be able to ask an object what its priority is. To make that work, all classes that are storable in `PriorityQueue` must implement the `IPrioritizable` interface, as `Package` does. `Package` lists `IPrioritizable` in its class declaration heading, like this:

```
class Package : IPrioritizable
```

Then it implements `IPrioritizable`'s `Priority` property.

A matching limitation is needed for `PriorityQueue`. You want the compiler to squawk if you try to instantiate for a type that doesn't implement `IPrioritizable`. In the nongeneric form of `PriorityQueue` (written specifically for type `Package`, say), the compiler will squeal automatically

(I recommend ear plugs) when one of your priority queue methods tries to call a method that `Package` doesn't have. But in C# 2.0, for generic classes, you can go that one better with an explicit *constraint*. Because you could instantiate the generic class with literally any type, you need a way to tell the compiler which types are acceptable — because they're guaranteed to have the right methods.

You add the constraint by specifying `IPrioritizable` in the heading for `PriorityQueue`, like this:

```
class PriorityQueue<T> where T: IPrioritizable
```

Did you notice the `where` clause before? The boldfaced `where` clause here specifies that `T` must implement `IPrioritizable`. *That's the enforcer.* It means, "Make sure that `T` implements the `IPrioritizable` interface — or else!"

You specify constraints by listing *one or more* of the following (separated by commas) in a `where` clause:

- ✔ The name of a required base class that `T` must derive from (or be)
- ✔ The name of an interface that `T` must implement, as shown in the previous example

Additional constraint options include the `struct`, `class`, and `new()` keywords. You meet `new()` in action in the section "Building a generic factory," later in the chapter. For information about the `class` and `struct` constraints, look up "Generics, constraints" in the Help Index.

These constraint options give you quite a bit of flexibility for making your new generic class behave just as you want. And a well-behaved class is a pearl beyond price. Here's an example of a hypothetical generic class declared with multiple constraints on `T`:

```
class MyClass<T> : where T: class, IPrioritizable, new()
{ ... }
```

Here, `T` must be a class, not a value type; it must implement `IPrioritizable`; and it must contain a constructor without parameters. Pretty strict!

What if you have two generic parameters and both need to be constrained? (Yes, you can have more than one generic parameter. You see this for real later in the chapter.) Here's how to use two `where` clauses:

```
class MyClass<T, U> : where T: IPrioritizable, where U: new()
```

Determining the null value for type T

Huh? Well, as I mentioned previously, each type has a default value that signifies "nothing" for that type. For `int`s and other numbers, it's 0 (or 0.0).

For `string`, it's an empty string: `""`. For `bool`, it's `false`. And for all reference types, such as `Package`, it's `null`.

But because a generic class like `PriorityQueue` can be instantiated for almost any data type, C# can't predict what would be the proper `null` value to use in the generic class's code. For example, with the `Dequeue()` method of `PriorityQueue`, you may face this situation: You call `Dequeue()` to get a package, but none are available. What do you return to signify "nothing"? Because `Package` is a class type, it should return `null`. That signals the caller of `Dequeue()` that there was nothing to return (and the caller must check for a `null` return value).

The compiler can't make sense of the `null` keyword in a generic class because the class may be instantiated for all sorts of data types. That's why `Dequeue()` uses the following line instead:

```
return default(T);  // return the right null for whatever T is
```

This line tells the compiler to look at `T` and return the right kind of `null` value for that type. In the case of `Package`, which as a class type is a reference type, the right `null` to return is, well, `null`. But for some other `T`, it may be different, and the compiler could figure out what to use.

If you think `PriorityQueue` is flexible, take a look at an even more flexible version of `PriorityQueue` — and encounter some object-oriented design principles — in the `ProgrammingToAnInterface` program on the CD.

Generically Methodical

Often the methods in a generic class have to be generic themselves. You've already seen one example in the previous section. The `Dequeue()` method in `PriorityQueue` has a return type of `T`. This section shows how you can use generic methods, both in generic and nongeneric classes.

Even methods in an ordinary nongeneric class can be generic. For example, the following code shows a generic method called `Swap()`, which is designed to exchange its two arguments. The first argument takes on the value of the second argument, and vice versa. (Figure 6-2 in Chapter 6 illustrates a swap.) To see that this works, you declare the two parameters to `Swap()` with the `ref` keyword, so you can pass value-type arguments such as `int`s by reference and get the changed results back in those same parameters after the `Swap()` call. (Chapter 7 discusses using `ref` parameters.)

Here's the whole program in which `Swap()` is declared and used. See the `GenericMethod` example on the CD.

```
// GenericMethod - a method that can process different data types
using System;
namespace GenericMethod
{
  class Program
  {
    // Main - tests two versions of a generic method; one lives in this class on
    //        same level as Main; other lives in a generic class
    static void Main(string[] args)
    {
      // test a generic method in a non-generic class
      Console.WriteLine("Generic method in non-generic class:\n");
      Console.WriteLine("\tFirst, test it for int arguments");
      int nOne = 1;
      int nTwo = 2;
      Console.WriteLine("\t\tBefore swap: nOne = {0}, nTwo = {1}", nOne, nTwo);
      Swap<int>(ref nOne, ref nTwo); // generic instantiation for int
      Console.WriteLine("\t\tAfter swap: nOne = {0}, nTwo = {1}", nOne, nTwo);
      Console.WriteLine("\tSecond, test it for string arguments");
      string sOne = "one";
      string sTwo = "two";
      Console.WriteLine("\t\tBefore swap: sOne = {0}, sTwo = {1}", sOne, sTwo);
      Swap<string>(ref sOne, ref sTwo); // generic instantiation for string
      Console.WriteLine("\t\tAfter swap: sOne = {0}, sTwo = {1}", sOne, sTwo);
      Console.WriteLine("\nGeneric method in a generic class");
      Console.WriteLine("\tFirst, test it for int and call");
      Console.WriteLine("\t  GenericClass.Swap with int arguments");
      nOne = 1;
      nTwo = 2;
      GenericClass<int> intClass = new GenericClass<int>();
      Console.WriteLine("\t\tBefore swap: nOne = {0}, nTwo = {1}", nOne, nTwo);
      intClass.Swap(ref nOne, ref nTwo);
      Console.WriteLine("\t\tAfter swap: nOne = {0}, nTwo = {1}", nOne, nTwo);
      Console.WriteLine("\tSecond, test it for string and call ");
      Console.WriteLine("\t  GenericClass.Swap with string arguments");
      sOne = "one";
      sTwo = "two";
      GenericClass<string> strClass = new GenericClass<string>();
      Console.WriteLine("Before swap: sOne = {0}, sTwo = {1}", sOne, sTwo);
      strClass.Swap(ref sOne, ref sTwo);
      Console.WriteLine("After swap: sOne = {0}, sTwo = {1}", sOne, sTwo);
      // wait for user to acknowledge the results
      Console.WriteLine("Press Enter to terminate...");
      Console.Read();
} // end Main
//static Swap - this is a generic method in a non-generic class
public static void Swap<T>(ref T leftSide, ref T rightSide)
{
  T temp;
  temp = leftSide;
  leftSide = rightSide;
```

```
    rightSide = temp;
  }
} // end of Program class
//GenericClass - a generic class with its own Swap method
  class GenericClass<T>
  {
    //Swap - this method is generic because it takes T parameters; note that
    //        we can't use Swap<T> or we get a compiler warning about
    //        duplicating the parameter on the class itself
    public void Swap(ref T leftSide, ref T rightSide)
    {
      T temp;
      temp = leftSide;
      leftSide = rightSide;
      rightSide = temp;
    }
  }
}
```

Generic methods in nongeneric classes

The first version of Swap() in the previous example (there are two versions) is a static function of class Program, declared like this:

```
public static void Swap<T>(ref T leftSide, ref T rightSide)
```

A generic method's declaration resembles that for a generic class, with the method name followed by generic parameters such as <T>. Then you can use T for any type in the method, including method parameters and return type.

In the example, Main() calls this static Swap() twice, first instantiating it for int and then for string (boldface in the listing). Here are the method calls (that's right, the instantiation is done in the call to the method):

```
Swap<int>(ref nOne, ref nTwo);      // instantiate Swap for int
...
Swap<string>(ref sOne, ref sTwo);  // instantiate Swap for string
```

When you instantiate Swap() for int, you can use int for the type arguments in the call. Similarly, when you instantiate it for string, you can use string for the type arguments.

A generic Swap() inside a generic class is a bit different, as described in the next section.

Generic methods in generic classes

The previous example includes a generic class called, um, GenericClass, which contains a generic Swap() method, declared like this (I show the class header too so that you can see where the <T> parameter comes in):

```
class GenericClass<T>      // <T> parameter is here but used in Swap below
{
    public void Swap(ref T leftSide, ref T rightSide) ...
```

The basic difference between this Swap() and the static one in class Program is that GenericClass provides the generic parameterization, so Swap() doesn't need to (and can't). This version of Swap() lacks a <T>. You can still refer to T in the method, though, as shown in Swap()'s parameter list.

Other than that, the two Swap() versions work alike. Here are some calls in Main() to this version of Swap():

```
GenericClass<int> intClass =         // create the object for int
    new GenericClass<int>();
...
intClass.Swap(ref nOne, ref nTwo);   // call its Swap()
...
GenericClass<string> strClass =      // create the object for string
    new GenericClass<string>();
...
strClass.Swap(ref sOne, ref sTwo);   // call its Swap()
```

In this case, it's the class that gets instantiated for int or string. As with the other Swap(), you can then use T anywhere in Swap().

You may need to constrain a generic method, too

You can also constrain generic methods to accept only types that meet certain requirements, as you saw with the generic PriorityQueue class, earlier in the chapter. In this case, you would declare the method something like this:

```
static void Sort<T>(T[] tArray) where T: IComparable<T>
{ ... }
```

For example, if the method declared here needs to compare its T-type parameters, T had better implement the IComparable interface — and the generic one for <T> at that.

Up Against the (Generic) Interface

You've seen generic classes and methods, and you can probably think of when you may want to use them. But when would you ever need an *interface* that's generic? (Nongeneric interfaces are covered in Chapter 14.)

To explore generic interfaces, this section presents an example that combines generic classes, methods, and interfaces.

Nongeneric vs. generic interfaces

To see the point of a generic interface, rise high above a nongeneric interface and a generic interface and look at them side by side to view the pattern:

```
//nongeneric                     // generic
interface IDisplayable           interface ICertifiable<T>
{                                {
  void Display();                   void Certify(T criteria);
}                                }
```

You've seen the pattern for using an interface. Declare the interface, as in the previous code. Then implement it in a class somewhere in your code as follows:

```
// nongeneric
class MyClass : IDisplayable ...
```

```
// generic
class MyClass : ICertifiable<MyCriteria> ...
```

Then complete the implementation in `MyClass`:

```
// nongeneric
class MyClass : IDisplayable
{
  public void Display()
  {
    ...
```

```
// generic
class MyClass : ICertifiable<MyCriteria>  // here's where you instantiate T
{
  public void Certify(MyCriteria criteria)
  {
    ...
```

Notice that it's when you implement the generic interface in a class that you instantiate its generic part by supplying a type name, such as MyCriteria.

Now you can see why the interface is generic: It needed to replace <T> for use as a parameter type or return type in one or more of the interface's methods. In other words, as with a generic *class,* you're specifying replaceable types to be used in the generic methods inside. Presumably those methods need to be able to handle various data types, just as the collection class List<T> or the method Swap<T>(T item1, T item2) do.

Generic interfaces are new, and I haven't discussed all the ways to use them yet. The chief way so far is in generic collections. Using a generic version of a common C# interface, such as IComparable<T>, helps avoid boxing/unboxing value-types. Generic interfaces can also help implement things like sort functions for use with collections. (I explain boxing in Chapter 14.)

The following example is rather abstract, so I'll build up to it carefully.

Using a (nongeneric) Simple Factory class

Earlier in the chapter, in the "Classy Generics: Writing Your Own" section, I use a Simple Factory object — although I just call it a "Factory" there — to generate an endless stream of Package objects with randomized priority levels. At long last, that simple class can be revealed:

```
// PackageFactory is part of the PriorityQueue example on the CD
// PackageFactory - we need a class that knows how to create a new
//                  package of any desired type on demand; such a
//                  class is called a factory class
class PackageFactory
{
  Random rand = new Random();  // a random-number generator
  //CreatePackage - this factory method selects a random priority,
  //                then creates a package with that priority
  public Package CreatePackage()
  {
    // return a randomly selected package priority
    //  need a 0, 1, or 2 (values less than 3)
    int nRand = rand.Next(3);
    // use that to generate a new package
    // casting int to enum is klunky, but it saves
    // having to use ifs or a switch statement
    return new Package((Priority)nRand);
  }
}
```

Class `PackageFactory` has one data member and one method. (You can just as easily implement a simple factory as a method rather than a class — for example, a method in class `Program`.) When you instantiate a `PackageFactory` object, it creates an object of class `Random` and stores it in the data member `rand`. `Random` is a C# library class that generates random numbers. (Also take a look at `PackageFactoryWithIterator` on the CD.)

Using PackageFactory

To generate a randomly prioritized `Package` object, you call your factory object's `CreatePackage()` method, as follows:

```
PackageFactory fact = new PackageFactory();
IPrioritizable pack = fact.CreatePackage(); // note the interface here
```

`CreatePackage()` tells its random number generator to generate a number from 0 to 2 (inclusive) and uses the number to set the priority of a new `Package`, which the method returns (to a `Package` or, better, an `IPrioritizable` variable).

More about factories

Factories are great for generating lots of test data. (A factory needn't use random numbers — that's just what I needed for the `PriorityQueue` example.)

Factories improve programs by isolating object creation. Every time you mention a specific class by name in your code, you create a *dependency* on that class. The more such dependencies you have, the more "tightly coupled" — bound together — your classes become. Programmers have long known that they should avoid tight coupling. (One of the more *decoupled* approaches is to use the factory via an interface, such as `IPrioritizable`, rather than a concrete class, such as `Package`.) Programmers still do create objects directly all the time, with the `new` operator, and that's fine. But factories can make code less coupled and therefore more flexible.

Building a generic factory

What if you had a factory class that could create any object you ever needed? The concept is intriguing and surprisingly easy to program, as the `GenericInterface` example on the CD shows:

```
// GenericInterface - uses a generic interface to implement generic factories
using System;
using System.Collections.Generic;
namespace GenericInterface
{
  class Program
```

```
  {
    static void Main(string[] args)
    {
      Console.WriteLine("Create a factory to create Blobs without params");
      GenericFactory<Blob> blobFact = new GenericFactory<Blob>();
      Console.WriteLine("Create a factory to create Students, " +
        "parameterized with a string");
      GenericFactory1<Student, string> stuFact =
        new GenericFactory1<Student, string>();
      // see the CD for one more class, Thing, which needs 2 parameters
      // set up places to save the created objects
      List<Blob> bList = new List<Blob>();
      Student[] students = new Student[10];
      Console.WriteLine("Create and store the objects:");
      for (int i = 0; i < 10; i++)
      {
        Console.WriteLine("\tCreating a Blob - " +
          "Invokes the parameterless constructor.");
        Blob b = blobFact.Create();
        b.name = "blob" + i.ToString();
        bList.Add(b);
        Console.WriteLine("\tCreating a Student with its name member set - " +
          "Invokes the one-parameter constructor.");
        string sName = "student" + i.ToString();
        students[i] = stuFact.Create(sName);
        // ... items from CD omitted
      }
      // display results.
      foreach(Blob b in bList)
      {
        Console.WriteLine(b.ToString());
      }
      foreach(Student s in students)
      {
        Console.WriteLine(s.ToString());
      }
      Console.WriteLine("Press Enter to terminate...");
      Console.Read();
    }
  }
}
// data classes: Student, Blob (and, on the CD, Thing)
// Blob - a simple class with only a default
//        (parameterless) constructor (provided by C#)
// omitted class Blob to save space - see the CD
// Student - a class with default & one-param constructors
class Student : ISettable<string>    // here's the generic interface
{
  // some members omitted to save space - see the CD
  // parameterless constructor required in addition to one-param version
  public Student() {}               // you must supply this (C# won't)
  public Student(string name)       // one-param constructor
  {
    this.name = name;
```

```
    }
    // implementation of ISettable
    public void SetParameter(string name)
    {
      this.name = name;
    }
    // omitted ToString() - see the CD
}
// ... Thing - see the CD for an additional class that needs 2 parameters

// the ISettable interfaces used by the factories
interface ISettable<U>
{
   void SetParameter(U u);
}
interface ISettable2<U, V>
{
  void SetParameter(U u, V v);
}
// factory for objects with an unparameterized constructor
// objects using this factory don't need to implement ISettable
class GenericFactory<T> where T : new()
{
   public T Create()
   {
     return new T();
   }
}
// factory for creating objects that have a constructor with one parameter
class GenericFactory1<T, U> where T : ISettable<U>, new()
{
   // create makes a new T with parameter U and returns T
   public T Create(U u)
   {
     T t = new T();
     t.SetParameter(u); // T must implement ISettable, so it has SetParameter()
     return t;
   }
}
   // see the CD for a factory that creates 2-param object
}
```

The GenericInterface example really just creates the following two generic classes:

✔ A factory to create objects that have only a default, parameterless constructor — Paramless Objects, I'll call them.

✔ A factory that creates objects whose constructor takes one parameter — OneParam Objects. You can easily extend the approach to handle objects whose constructors take any number of parameters. The code on the CD includes a TwoParam example.

Creating objects generically — is it magic?

Creating any Paramless Object is easy — you have no arguments to worry about (except for `<T>`, the type parameter):

```
// in GenericFactory<T>, here's the Create() method:
public T Create()
{
  return new T();  // invokes parameterless constructor
}
```

The generic interface comes into play because of a limitation of generic constraints (discussed in the section "Classy Generics: Creating Your Own," earlier in this chapter). The following generic class headings review some of the ways you can constrain a type parameter:

```
class MyClass<T>: where T: MyBase         // T must be or subclass MyBase
class MyClass<T>: where T: IMyInterface   // T must implement IMyInterface
class MyClass<T>: where T: class          // T can only be a reference type
class MyClass<T>: where T: struct         // T can only be a value-type
class MyClass<T>: where T: new()          // T must have a parameterless constructor
```

It's that last constraint that limits your ability to write powerful generic factories more easily. It requires that `T` have a default — that is, parameterless — constructor. It may have other constructors as well, but one must be parameterless, whether you write it or C# does so by default.

The `new()` constraint is a requirement for any generic class or method that wants to *create objects* of type `T`. But `new()` has no counterparts `new(U)` or `new(U, V)` for constructors that take parameters.

Generic interfaces can have type constraints, too:

```
interface ISettable<T> : where T: new() ...
```

Groping toward a generic solution

The question is what to do when a constructor needs a parameter. The OneParam Object factory, `GenericFactory1<T, U>`, has to use code like this in its `Create()` method:

```
public T Create(U u)  // u is an argument we want to pass
                      // to the constructor
{
  T t = new T();      // but new T() can't take arguments
  ...                 // now what?
```

As a result, these approaches fail:

```
T t = new T(u);    // doesn't work
// or
T t = new T(U);    // doesn't work
```

Still, you do want to pass the u argument to the new object (which needs to set a data member with it). How do you do this? As it stands, there's no way.

Making an end run around the default constructor

The problem just described is where the generic interface comes in. To allow the factory to supply a parameter to a new object, you have to put some requirements on the object being manufactured. It must implement something like this ISettable<U> interface:

```
interface ISettable<U>
{
  void SetParameter(U u);
}
```

You declare the OneParam Object factory like this:

```
// T is the type to create; U is the parameter type the constructor needs
class GenericFactory1<T, U> where T: ISettable<U>, new() { }
```

Any T that this factory makes had better implement ISettable<U> with an instantiation that replaces U with a real type, such as string.

Coming at last to an example . . .

If you want to make Student objects with the factory, and the Student constructor requires one parameter — a string for the student's name, say — class Student needs to do this:

```
class Student: ISettable<string>  // instantiate the interface for string
{
  private string name;
  public Student() {}              // also requires a parameterless constructor
  public Student(string name)      // define a one-parameter constructor
  {
    SetParameter(name);
  }
  public void SetParameter(string name)  // implement ISettable<string>
  {
    this.name = name;
  }
  // other Student methods and data members
  ...
  }
```

You can still create a Student the old-fashioned way, with new:

```
students[0] = new Student("Juan Valdez");
```

But to use the factory, you need a GenericFactory1<T, U> object, as follows:

```
GenericFactory1<Student, string> fact1 =        // instantiate T with Student
    new GenericFactory1<Student, string>(); // and U with string
```

You also need a call to the factory's Create() method to get an object with its name parameter already set:

```
students[1] = fact1.Create("Richard Corey");  // here's the string argument
```

Inside the GenericFactory1<T, U>.Create() method, here's what happens:

```
public T Create(U u)
{
  T t = new T();     // same as before, no constructor parameters allowed
  t.SetParameter(u); // use the method provided by T implementing ISettable
  return t;
}
```

Because Create() can only create a parameterless object, you use T's SetParameter() method to pass the u parameter to the t object. Then you can return a Student object whose name member has been set — just like calling Student's one-parameter constructor directly. You know T has a SetParameter() method because of the constraint on the Student class: : ISettable<string>. That interface guarantees that Student has SetParameter().

Assessing the damage

How "good" is this solution? Well, it's not the prettiest thing you'll ever see. In fact, it's kind of a kludge (an old engineering term for solutions involving gum and bailing wire — euphemism: "workaround"). But it works!

Encountering a series of unfortunate ISettables

What about TwoParam Objects? Or Three or Four? Sadly, ISettable<U> is only for one-parameter construction. For two parameters, you would need to add an ISettable2<U, V> interface. For three, you would need ISettable3<U, V, W>, and so on. Next, you would need a separate factory type for each of these. But the good news is that constructors hardly ever need more than five or six parameters — and usually fewer. That's about how many ISettable<U, V, ...> interfaces and how many factories you would need.

Of course, a class could implement both ISettable<U> and ISettable2<V, W> if it wanted to. But it would need a SetParameter(U u) method and a SetParameter(V v, W w) method. (These can be overloads because the two SetParameter()s have different parameter signatures.)

Part VI
The Part of Tens

The 5th Wave   By Rich Tennant

"We're here to clean the code."

In this part . . .

What *For Dummies* book would be complete without a Part of Tens? C# is great at finding errors in your programs when you try to build them — you've probably noticed that. However, the error messages it generates can be cryptic — you've probably noted that, as well. Chapter 16 reviews the ten most common build-time error messages and what they most likely mean. Knowledge is power, so Chapter 16 also suggests fixes for the problems that are being reported. These items have been updated to reflect a few changes in C# 2.0.

Many readers will have come to C# through the most common of all object-oriented languages, C++. Chapter 17 quickly reviews the differences between the two languages, including the differences between C# generics and C++ templates.

Chapter 16

The 10 Most Common Build Errors (And How to Fix Them)

C# makes the ol' college try at finding errors in your C# code. In fact, C# homes in on syntax errors like a tornado heading for a double-wide. Other than really stupid mistakes like trying to compile your shopping list, the same complaints seem to pop up, over and over.

This chapter describes 10 common build-time error messages. A few warnings are in order, however. First, C# can get awfully long-winded. I have whittled down some of the error messages so that the message can fit on one page, let alone one or two lines. In addition, an error message has places to insert the name of an errant data member or an obnoxious class. In place of these specific names, I have inserted `variableName`, `memberName`, or `className`.

Finally, C# doesn't simply spit out the name of the class. It prefers to tack on the full namespace name — just in case the entire error message would have been visible without scrolling over to your neighbor's house.

The name 'memberName' does not exist in the class or namespace 'className'

This error message could mean that you forgot to declare a variable, as in the following example:

```
for(index = 0; index < 10; index++)
{
  // . . . whatever . . .
}
```

The variable `index` is not defined anywhere. (See Chapter 3 for instructions on declaring variables.) This example should have been written as follows:

```
for(int index = 0; index < 10; index++)
{
  // . . . whatever . . .
}
```

The same applies to data members of a class. (See Chapter 6.)

A more likely possibility is that you misspelled a variable name. The following is a good example:

```
class Student
{
  public string sStudentName;
  public int nID;
}
class MyClass
{
  static public void MyFunction(Student s)
  {
    Console.WriteLine("Student name = " + s.sStudentName);
    Console.WriteLine("Student Id = " + s.nId);
  }
}
```

The problem here is that `MyFunction()` references a data member `nId` rather than the actual data member `nID`. Although you see the similarity, C# does not. The programmer wrote `nId`, but no `nId` exists, and that's all there is to it. The fact that `nID` is lurking around the corner, alphabetically speaking, is irrelevant. (The message here is a bit different: `'class.memberName'` does not contain a definition for `'variableName'`. See Chapter 3 for details.)

Less popular but still way up on the Top 10 playlist is the possibility that the variable was declared in a different scope, as follows:

```
class MyClass
{
  static public void AverageInput()
  {
    int nSum = 0;
    int nCount = 0;
    while(true)
    {
      // read in a number
      string s = Console.ReadLine();
      int n = Int32.Parse(s);
      // quit when the user enters a negative number
      if (n < 0)
      {
        break;
      }
      // accumulate the value entered
      nSum += n;
      nCount++;
    }
    // now output the results
    Console.WriteLine("The total is " + nSum);
    Console.WriteLine("The average is " + nSum / nCount);
    // this generates a build time error message
    Console.WriteLine("The terminating value was " + s);
  }
}
```

The last line in this function is incorrect. The problem is that a variable is limited to the scope in which it is defined. The variable s is not defined outside of the while() loop. (See Chapter 5.)

Cannot implicitly convert type 'x' into 'y'

This error usually indicates that you're trying to use two different variable types in the same expression — for example:

```
int nAge = 10;
// generates an error message
int nFactoredAge = 2.0 * nAge;
```

The problem here is that 2.0 is a variable of type double. The int nAge multiplied by the double 2.0 results in a double value. C# does not automatically store a double into the int variable nFactoredAge because information may be lost — most notably, any fractional value that the double may possess.

Some conversions are not obvious, as in the following example:

```
class MyClass
{
  static public float FloatTimes2(float f)
  {
    // this generates a build time error
    float fResult = 2.0 * f;
    return fResult;
  }
}
```

You may think that doubling a float would be okay, but that's sort of the problem. 2.0 is not a float — it defaults to type double. A double times a float is a double. C# does not store a double value back into a float variable due to — you guessed it — possible loss of data; in this case, it is several digits of accuracy. (See Chapter 3.)

Implicit conversions can further confuse the casual reader (that's me on a good day). The following version of FloatTimes2() works just fine:

```
class MyClass
{
  static public float FloatTimes2(float f)
  {
    // this works fine
    float fResult = 2 * f;
    return fResult;
  }
}
```

The constant 2 is of type int. An int times a float is a float, which can be stored in the float variable fResult.

The implicit conversion error message can also arise when performing operations on "unnatural" types. For example, you cannot add two char variables, but C# can convert char variables into int values for you when necessary to get the job done. This leads to the following:

```
class MyClass
{
  static public void SomeFunction()
  {
    char c1 = 'a';
    char c2 = 'b';
    // I don't know what this even means, but it's illegal anyway - not for the
    // reason you think
    char c3 = c1 + c2;
  }
}
```

Adding two characters together makes no sense, but C# tries anyway. Because addition isn't defined for type `char`, it converts `c1` and `c2` into `int` values and then performs the addition. (`char` is technically listed as an integral type.) Unfortunately, the resulting `int` value cannot be converted back into a `char` without some help. (See Chapter 3.)

Most, but not all, conversions are okay with an explicit cast. Thus, the following function works without complaint:

```
class MyClass
{
  static public float FloatTimes2(float f)
  {
    // this works OK with the explicit cast
    float fResult = (float)(2.0 * f);
    return fResult;
  }
}
```

The result of `2.0 * f` is still of type `double`, but the programmer has indicated that she specifically wants the result down-converted to a `float`, even in the unlikely event that it results in the loss of data. (See Chapter 3.)

A second approach would be to make sure that all constants are of the same type, as follows:

```
class MyClass
{
  static public float FloatTimes2(float f)
  {
    // this works OK because 2.0F is a float constant
    float fResult = 2.0F * f;
    return fResult;
  }
}
```

This version of the function uses a constant 2.0 of type `float` rather than the default `double`. A `float` times a `float` is a `float`.

'className.memberName' is inaccessible due to its protection level

This error indicates that a function is trying to access a member to which it does not have access. For example, a method in one class may be trying to access a private member in another class (see Chapter 11), as shown in the following code:

```
public class MyClass
{
  public void SomeFunction()
  {
    YourClass uc = new YourClass();
    // this doesn't work properly because MyClass can't access
    // the private member
    uc.nPrivateMember = 1;
  }
}
public class YourClass
{
  private int nPrivateMember = 0;
}
```

Usually, the error is not so blatant. Often, you've simply left the descriptor off of either the member object or the class itself. By default, a member of a class is `private` while a class is `internal`. Thus, `nPrivateMember` is still private in the following example:

```
class MyClass      // undeclared class access level defaults to internal
{
  public void SomeFunction()
  {
    YourClass uc = new YourClass();
    // this doesn't work properly because MyClass can't access the
    // private member
    uc.nPrivateMember = 1;
  }
}
public class YourClass
{
  int nPrivateMember = 0;    // this member is still private
}
```

In addition, even though `SomeFunction()` is declared `public`, it still can't be accessed from classes in other modules because `MyClass` itself is internal.

The moral of the story is this: "Always specify the protection level of your classes and their members." A lemma is "Don't declare public members in a class that itself is internal — it doesn't do any good and it's just confusing."

Use of unassigned local variable 'n'

Just like it says, this message indicates that you declared a variable but didn't give it an initial value. This is usually an oversight, but it can occur when you really meant to pass a variable as an `out` argument to a function, as shown in the following example:

```
public class MyClass
{
  public void SomeFunction()
  {
    int n;
    // this is OK because C# only returns a value in n; it does not
    // pass a value into the function
    SomeOtherFunction(out n);
  }
  public void SomeOtherFunction(out int n)
  {
    n = 1;
  }
}
```

In this case, n is not assigned a value inside of SomeFunction(), but it is in SomeOtherFunction(). SomeOtherFunction() ignores the value of an out argument as if it didn't exist — which it doesn't in this case. (Chapter 3 covers variables. Chapter 7 explains out.)

Unable to copy the file 'programName.exe' to 'programName.exe'. The process cannot . . .

Usually, this message repeats multiple times. In almost every case, it means you forgot to terminate the program before you rebuilt it. In other words, you did the following:

1. You successfully built your program. (I assume that it's a console application, although it can happen to any C# output.)

2. When you ran the program by choosing Debug⇨Start Without Debugging, you got to the message Press Enter to terminate, but in your haste, you didn't press Enter. So, your program is still executing. Instead, you switched back to Visual Studio 2005 to edit the file.

   Note: If you run the program by choosing Debug⇨Start Debugging and forget to terminate, you're simply asked whether you want to stop debugging.

3. You tried to build the program again with the new updates. At this point, you get this error message in the Error List window.

An executable (.EXE) file is locked by Windows until the program actually quits. Visual Studio cannot overwrite the old .EXE file with the new version until the program terminates.

To get rid of the error, switch to the application and terminate it. In the case of a console application, just press Enter to terminate the program. You can also terminate the program from within Visual Studio 2005 by choosing Debug⇨Stop Debugging. After the older program has terminated, rebuild the application.

If you can't get rid of the error by terminating the program, the directory may be messed up. Close the solution, exit Visual Studio 2005, reboot, and then reopen the solution. If that doesn't work, I'm sorry — punt.

'subclassName.methodName' hides inherited member 'baseclassName. methodName'. Use the new keyword if hiding was intended

With this message, C# is telling you that you've overloaded a method in a base class without overriding it. (See Chapter 13 for details.) Consider the following example:

```
public class BaseClass
{
  public void Function()
  {
  }
}
public class SubClass : BaseClass
{
  public void Function()  // here's the overload
  {
  }
}
public class MyClass
{
  public void Test()
  {
    SubClass sb = new SubClass();
    sb.Function();
  }
}
```

The function `Test()` cannot get at the method `BaseClass.Function()` from the subclass object `sb` because it is hidden by `SubClass.Function()`. You intended to do one of the following:

- ✔ You intended to hide the base class method. In that case, add the `new` keyword to the `SubClass` definition, as in the following example:

```
public class SubClass : BaseClass
{
  new public void Function()
  {
  }
}
```

- ✔ You meant to inherit the base class polymorphically, in which case you should have declared the two classes as follows:

```
public class BaseClass
{
  public virtual void Function()
  {
  }
}

public class SubClass : BaseClass
{
  public override void Function()
  {
  }
}
```

See Chapter 13 for details.

This is not an error — just a warning in the Error List window.

'subclassName' : cannot inherit from sealed class 'baseclassName'

This message indicates that someone has sealed the class, so you can't inherit from it or change any of its properties. Typically, only library classes are sealed. You can't get around your inability to inherit from the sealed class, but try using the class via a HAS_A relationship. (See Chapter 13.)

'className' does not implement interface member 'methodName'

Implementing an interface represents a promise to provide a definition for all the methods of that interface. This message says that you broke that promise by not implementing the named method. The following possible reasons exist:

✔ Your dog ate your homework. Basically, you just forgot or were unaware of the method. Be more careful next time.

✔ You misspelled the method or gave the wrong arguments.

Consider the following example:

```
interface Me
{
  void aFunction(float f);
}
public class MyClass : Me
{
  public void aFunction(double d)
  {
  }
}
```

The class `MyClass` does not implement the interface function `aFunction` `(float)`. The function `aFunction(double)` doesn't count because the arguments don't match.

Go back to the drawing board and continue implementing methods until the interface has been completely fulfilled. (See Chapter 14.)

Not fully implementing an interface is essentially the same thing as trying to create a concrete class from an abstract one without overriding all the abstract methods.

'methodName' : not all code paths return a value

With this message, C# is telling you that your method was declared nonvoid and one or more paths don't return anything. This can happen in either of the following two ways:

✔ You have an `if` statement that has a return without a value specified.

✔ More likely, you calculated a value and never returned it.

Both of these possibilities are demonstrated in the following class:

```
public class MyClass
{
  public string ConvertToString(int n)
  {
    // convert the int n into a string s
    string s = n.ToString();
  }
  public string ConvertPositiveNumbers(int n)
  {
    // only positive numbers are valid for conversion
    if (n > 0)
    {
      string s = n.ToString();
      return s;
    }
    Console.WriteLine("the argument {0} is invalid", n);
    // need another return here
  }
}
```

`ConvertToString()` calculates a `string` to return but never returns it. Just add a `return s;` at the bottom of the method.

`ConvertPositiveNumbers()` returns the string version of the `int` argument n when n is positive. In addition, it correctly generates an error message when n is not positive. But even if n is not positive, the function still has to return something. Return either a `null` or an empty string `""` in these cases — which one works best depends on the application. (See Chapter 7.)

} expected

This error indicates that C# was expecting another close brace when the program listing just stopped. Somewhere along the way, you forgot to close a class definition, a function, or an `if` block. Go back through the listing, matching the open and closed braces, until you find the culprit.

This error message is often the last in a series of often-nonsensical error messages. Don't worry about addressing the other error messages until you've fixed this one. Also, Visual Studio 2005 helps you match parentheses and braces.

Chapter 17

The 10 Most Significant Differences between C# and C++

*T*he C# language is more than a little bit based on the C++ programming language. This is hardly surprising because Microsoft built Visual C++, the most successful hard-core programming language for the Windows environment. All of your best geeks were working in Visual C++. But C++ has been showing its age for a while now.

However, C# is not just a coat of paint over a rusty language. C# offers numerous improvements, both by adding features and by replacing good features with better ones. This chapter focuses on the Top Ten best improvements. Of course, I could easily make this the Top 20.

You may have arrived at C# from a different direction, such as Java or Visual Basic. C# bears an even stronger resemblance to Java than to C++ — not surprising, because Java also arose partly to improve on C++ and is highly Internet oriented. You find syntactic differences, but C# and Java almost feel like clones. If you can read one, you can read the other.

As for Visual Basic — that is, Visual Basic .NET, not the older Visual Basic 6.0 — its syntax is completely different, of course, but Visual Basic .NET rests on the same .NET Framework infrastructure as C#, produces almost identical Common Intermediate Language code, and is highly interoperable with C#:

A C# class can inherit from a Visual Basic class and vice versa, and your program can be a mixture of C# and Visual Basic modules (and, for that matter, "managed" C++ and J# and . . .).

No Global Data or Functions

C++ passes itself off as an object-oriented language, and it is, in the sense that you can program in an object-oriented fashion using C++. You can also sidestep class objects by just throwing data and functions out there in some global space, open to the elements and any programmer with a keyboard.

C# makes its programmers declare their allegiance: All functions and all data members must join a class. You want to access that function or data? You have to go through the author of that class — no exceptions.

All Objects Are Allocated Off the Heap

C/C++ allows memory to be allocated in the following ways, each with its own disadvantages:

- ✔ **Global objects exist throughout the life of the program.** A program can easily allocate multiple *pointers* to the same global object. Change one, and they all change, whether they're ready or not. A pointer is a variable that contains the address of some distant chunk of memory. Technically, C# references are pointers under the hood.

- ✔ **Stack objects are unique to individual functions (that's good), but they are deallocated when the function returns.** Any pointer to a deallocated memory object becomes invalid. That would be fine if anyone told the pointer; however, the pointer still thinks it's pointing to a valid object, and so does its programmer. The C++ stack is a different region of memory from the heap, and it really is a stack.

- ✔ **Heap objects are allocated as needed.** These objects are unique to a particular execution thread.

The problem is that it's too easy to forget what type of memory a pointer refers to. Heap objects must be returned when you're done with them. Forget to do so, and your program progressively "leaks" memory until it can no longer function. On the other hand, if you release the same block of heap more than once and "return" a block of global or stack memory, your program is headed for a long nap — maybe Ctrl+Alt+Del can wake it up.

C# solves this problem by allocating all objects off of the heap. Even better than that, C# uses garbage collection to return memory to the heap for you. No more blue screen of death haunts you because you sent the wrong memory block to the heap.

Pointer Variables Are All but Disallowed

The introduction of pointers to C ensured the success of that language. Pointer manipulation was a powerful feature. Old-hand machine-language programmers could still pull the programming shenanigans they were used to. C++ retained the pointer and heap features from C without modification.

Unfortunately, neither the programmer nor the program can differentiate a good pointer from a bad one. Read memory from an uninitialized pointer, and your program crashes — if you're lucky. If you're not lucky, the program cranks right along, treating some random block of memory as if it were a valid object.

Pointer problems are often difficult to pin down. An invalid pointer program usually reacts differently every time you run it.

Fortunately for all concerned, C# manages to sidestep pointer problems by doing away with them. The references that it uses instead are type-safe and cannot be manipulated by the user into something that can kill the program.

C# Generics Are Like C++ Templates — or Are They?

If you look at C#'s new generics feature (see Chapter 15) beside C++'s template feature, the syntax looks very similar. However, although the two have the same basic purpose, their resemblance is only skin deep.

Both generics and templates are type-safe, but under the hood they are implemented very differently. Templates are instantiated at compile time, while generic instantiation happens at run time. This means the same template in two different .NET assemblies results in two separate types that get instantiated at compile time. But the same generic in two different .NET assemblies results in only one type that gets instantiated at run time. The up side of this is less "code bloat" for generics than for templates.

The biggest difference between generics and templates is that generics work across multiple languages, including Visual Basic, C++, and other .NET languages, as well as C#. Templates are purely a C++ feature.

Which one is better? Templates are more powerful — and complex, like a lot of things in C++ — but a great deal more error-prone — again, like a lot of things in C++. Generics are thus easier to use and less likely to result in a bullet to your big toe.

Of course, I'm only scratching the surface of this discussion here. For a much more technical comparison, see Brandon Bray's blog at `weblogs.asp.net/ branbray/archive/2003/11/19/51023.aspx`.

I'll Never Include a File Again

C++ enforces strict type checking — that's a good thing. It does so by compelling you to declare your functions and classes in so-called *include files,* which are then used by modules. However, getting all the include files set up in just the right order for your module to compile can get complicated.

C# does away with that nonsense. Instead, C# searches out and finds the class definitions on its own. If you invoke a `Student` class, C# finds the class definition on its own to make sure that you're using it properly.

Don't Construct — Initialize

I could see the usefulness of constructors the first time I laid eyes on them. Provide a special function to make sure that all the data members were set up correctly? What an idea! The only problem is that I ended up adding trivial constructors for every class I wrote. Consider the following example:

```
public class Account
{
  private double balance;
  private int numChecksProcessed;
  private CheckBook checkBook;
  public Account()
  {
    balance = 0.0;
    numChecksProcessed = 0;
    checkBook = new CheckBook();
  }
}
```

Why can't I just initialize the data members directly and let the language generate the constructor for me? C++ asked why; C# answers why not? C# does away with unnecessary constructors by allowing direct initialization, as follows:

```
public class Account
{
  private double balance = 0.0;
  private int numChecksProcessed = 0;
  private CheckBook checkBook = new CheckBook();
  // no need to do this again in a constructor
}
```

More than that, if all you need is the appropriate version of zero for a particular type, as in the first two data members above, C# takes care of it for you automatically, at least for class data members. If you want something other than zero, add your own initialization right at the data member's declaration. (Always initialize local variables inside functions, however.)

Define Your Variable Types Well

C++ is very politically correct. It doesn't want to step on any computer's toes by requiring that a particular type of variable be limited to any particular range of values. It specifies that an `int` is about "so big" and a `long` is "bigger." This indecisiveness leads to obscure errors when trying to move a program from one type of processor to another.

C# doesn't beat around the bush. It says, an `int` is 32 bits and a `long` is 64 bits, and that's the way it's going to be. As a programmer, you can take that information to the bank without unexpected errors popping up.

No Multiple Inheriting

C++ allows a single class to inherit from more than one base class. For example, a `SleeperSofa` can inherit from both class `Bed` and class `Sofa`. (But did you ever try to sleep on one of those furniture hybrids with a torture rack just under the thin mattress?) Inheriting from both classes sounds really neat, and in fact, it can be very useful. The only problem is that inheriting from multiple base classes can cause some of the most difficult-to-find programming problems in the business.

C# drops back and avoids the increased number of errors by taking multiple inheritance away. However, that wouldn't have been possible had C# not replaced multiple inheritance with a new feature: the interface, discussed in the next section.

Projecting a Good Interface

When people stepped back and looked at the multiple inheritance nightmare that they had gotten themselves into, they realized that over 90 percent of the time, the second base class existed merely to *describe* the subclass. For example, a perfectly ordinary class might inherit an abstract class `Persistable` with abstract methods `read()` and `write()`. This forced the subclass to implement the `read()` and `write()` methods and told the rest of the world that those methods were available for use.

Programmers then realized that the more-lightweight interface could do the same thing. A class that implements an interface like the following example is promising that it provides the read() and write() capability:

```
interface IPersistable
{
  void read();
  void write();
}
```

You avoid the hazards of true C++-style multiple inheritance while still reaping the same basic design benefits.

Unified Type System

The C++ class is a nice feature. It allows data and its associated functions to be bundled into neat little packages that just happen to mimic the way that people think of things in the world. The only problem is that any language must provide room for simple variable types like integer and floating point numbers. This need resulted in a caste system. Class objects lived on one side of the tracks, while value-type variables like int and float lived on the other. Sure, value types and object types were allowed to play in the same program, but the programmer had to keep them separate in his mind.

C# breaks down the Berlin Wall that divides value types from object types. For every value type, there is a corresponding "value type class" called a *structure*. (You can write your own custom structure types too. See Chapter 14.) These low-cost structures can mix freely with class objects, enabling the programmer to make statements like the following:

```
MyClass myObject = new MyClass();
Console.WriteLine(myObject.ToString());// display a "myObject" in string format
int i = 5;
Console.WriteLine(i.ToString()); // display an int in string format
Console.WriteLine(5.ToString()); // display the constant 5 in string format
```

Not only can I invoke the same method on int as I do on a MyClass object, but I can also do it to a constant like 5. This scandalous mixing of variable types is a powerful feature of C#.

Appendix

About the CD

*T*he CD-ROM that comes tucked away inside the back cover of *C# 2005 For Dummies* contains lots of goodies. First, you'll find the source code from the numerous program examples you find throughout the book. In addition, I've included five bonus chapters and three utility programs that can make your life as a programmer easier. However, your machine must meet a few minimum system requirements before you can make use of them.

System Requirements

Parts of this book assume that you have Microsoft Visual Studio 2005 or Microsoft Visual C# 2005, which is the preferred way to program with C#. However, if you don't, you can use the free, open-source SharpDevelop program provided on the CD to build and run the book's examples. See Bonus Chapter 5 on the CD for information about SharpDevelop and about other ways you can use this book cheaply. Visual Studio is not supplied with this book.

If you're using Visual Studio, the hardware requirements for using the CD that comes with this book are the same as those for Visual Studio. Refer to the Visual Studio System Requirements for details. Make sure that your computer meets these minimum system requirements:

- ✔ A PC with a 600 MHz Pentium or faster processor, 1 GHz recommended

- ✔ Microsoft Windows XP, Service Pack 2 (Home or Professional); Windows 2000, Service Pack 4; or Windows 2003 Server

- ✔ At least 128MB of total RAM installed on your computer; for best performance, I recommend at least 256MB. Visual Studio has a large appetite for memory.

- At least 1MB of hard drive space, without installing MSDN documentation to the hard drive, about 2MB if you do install the documentation (if not, you can use it from the Visual Studio CD), plus about 2MB if you install the book's example programs
- A CD-ROM drive
- A monitor capable of displaying at least 256 colors at 800 x 600 resolution or better

If your computer doesn't match up to most of these requirements, you may have problems using the software and files on the CD. For the latest and greatest information, please refer to the ReadMe file located at the root of the CD-ROM.

If you need more information on the basics, check out these books published by Wiley Publishing, Inc.: *PCs For Dummies,* by Dan Gookin; *Windows 2000 Professional For Dummies* and *Windows XP For Dummies,* 2nd Edition, both by Andy Rathbone; and *Windows Server 2003 For Dummies,* by Ed Tittel and James Michael Stewart.

Using the CD

To install the items from the CD to your hard drive, follow these steps:

1. **Install Visual Studio 2005 or Visual C# 2005 if you have one of them, or install SharpDevelop and/or TextPad as described in Step 5.**

   Follow the installation directions provided by the software vendor.

2. **Insert the book's CD into your computer's CD-ROM drive. The license agreement appears.**

   Note to Windows users: The interface won't launch if you have autorun disabled. In that case, choose Start⇨Run. In the dialog box that appears, type **D:\start.exe**. (Replace D with the proper letter if your CD-ROM drive uses a different letter. If you don't know the letter, see how your CD-ROM drive is listed under My Computer.) Click OK.

3. **Read through the license agreement, and then click the Accept button if you want to use the CD. After you click Accept, the License Agreement window won't appear again.**

   The CD interface appears. The interface allows you to install the programs with just a click of a button (or two).

4. **To make life easiest, install the example programs. You'll want to refer to them frequently. Simply click the install button from the Code section of the CD-ROM interface.**

   You could refer to the examples by inserting the CD as needed, but having the programs on your hard drive is handiest. They take up about 2MB of disk space.

   I provide all the necessary files to let you run the programs right out of the box. That's fine, but C# will come easier if you type in the code yourself, in a fresh Visual Studio project, rather than simply copying the provided source files.

   The programs are in a folder called C:\C#Programs (no space). That location makes the file paths you see as you work with the files the same as I describe in the book.

   When you create a project and give it a name, Visual Studio (or SharpDevelop) creates a folder of the same name.

5. **Install the bonus software that you want. Just click the button from the Software menu of the CD-ROM interface to launch the installer and follow the on-screen prompts.**

   If you have Visual Studio or Visual C#, you won't really need SharpDevelop. But you'll find TextPad and NUnit useful in any case. Follow the software vendor's installation instructions.

What You'll Find on the CD

The following sections are arranged by category and provide a summary of the software and other goodies you'll find on the CD. If you need help with installing the items provided on the CD, refer to the installation instructions in the preceding section.

The C# programs

The first thing you'll find on the CD are the C# source files for the programs from throughout this book. These source files (with accompanying Visual Studio project and solution files) are organized into directories by program name. Each directory contains all the files that go with a single example program.

All the examples provided in this book are located in the `C#Programs` directory on the CD and work with Windows 2000, 2003 Server, XP, and later computers. These files contain much of the sample code from the book. The structure of the examples directory is

```
C:\C#Programs\ExampleProgram1
C:\C#Programs\ExampleProgram2
...
```

Five bonus chapters

The *C# 2005 For Dummies* CD also includes five bonus chapters that supplement the book's text.

- ✔ Bonus Chapter 1 explains how to do error handling in C# with C# *exceptions*.

- ✔ Bonus Chapter 2 explains how to read and write files from your C# programs.

- ✔ Bonus Chapter 3 explains several ways to *iterate* collections of data objects in C# — step through the objects one by one — including lines in a text file. The chapter includes the new *iterator blocks* from C# 2.0.

- ✔ Bonus Chapter 4 explains how to use the Visual Studio 2005 interface, including the debugger and the Help system.

- ✔ Bonus Chapter 5 presents several ways to program cheaply in C# without Visual Studio, including the SharpDevelop and TextPad programs provided on the CD.

The CD also includes three bonus utility programs to help you program in C#.

Shareware programs are fully functional, free, trial versions of copyrighted programs. If you like particular programs, register with their authors for a nominal fee and receive licenses, enhanced versions, and technical support.

Freeware programs are free, copyrighted games, applications, and utilities. You can copy them to as many PCs as you like — for free — but they offer no technical support.

GNU software is governed by its own license, which is included inside the folder of the GNU software. There are no restrictions on distribution of GNU software. See the GNU license at the root of the CD for more details.

Trial, demo, or *evaluation* versions of software are usually limited either by time or functionality (such as not letting you save a project after you create it).

NUnit

A program testing tool from www.nunit.org. GNU open-source software. For Windows (also available for Mono on Unix/Linux/Mac machines, although that version is not covered in this book).

Use NUnit, the most popular C# unit testing tool, to automate unit tests for your code. Unit tests test your classes and methods. Bonus Chapter 5 on the CD explains how to use NUnit.

SharpDevelop

A pretty good Visual Studio imitator from www.icsharpcode.net. GNU open-source software. For Windows.

Use SharpDevelop, or the next program, TextPad, as your programming environment if you don't have access to Visual Studio 2005 or Visual C# 2005. Bonus Chapter 5 on the CD explains how to use SharpDevelop, a fairly capable C# development tool with a strong resemblance to the earlier 2003 version of Visual Studio. Although SharpDevelop lacks the newer features added in Visual Studio 2005, you can use it to program with the latest version of C#, version 2.0. I don't recommend it for serious commercial software development, but it works fine with all the example programs in this book.

TextPad

A programmer-oriented text editor from www.textpad.com. Shareware trial version, no trial duration specified. For Windows 95, 98, ME, NT4, 2000, Server 2003, XP.

If you lack Visual Studio 2005 — and SharpDevelop, described earlier, is not to your taste — you may want to try using the popular TextPad code editor as the center of your C# programming. It's a more rugged environment than Visual Studio or SharpDevelop, but it's cheap and surprisingly powerful. In any case, it's a far better tool for programmers than Notepad. Bonus Chapter 5 on the CD explains how to configure TextPad for C#.

Troubleshooting

I tried my best to compile programs that work on most computers with the minimum system requirements. Alas, your computer may differ, and some programs may not work properly for some reason, or work only slowly.

The most likely problem is that you do not have the Microsoft .NET environment installed. Programs created in C# require a set of .NET libraries, which you must have installed on your computer. Some versions of Windows may now come with these libraries preinstalled. If you have Visual Studio 2005 or Visual C# Express 2005 installed, you definitely have the right libraries. (Older versions of Visual Studio don't come with the latest version 2.0 of the .NET libraries.) Otherwise, you can download or order the libraries from www.microsoft.com. You want the .NET SDK, version 2.0. Bonus Chapter 5 on the CD discusses in more detail how to obtain them.

Another possible problem is that your computer does not have enough memory (RAM). If you get an error message such as Not enough memory or Setup cannot continue, try one or more of the following suggestions and then try using the software again:

- **Turn off any antivirus software running on your computer.** Installation programs sometimes mimic virus activity and may make your computer incorrectly believe that it's being infected by a virus. Trust me, it isn't.

- **Close all running programs.** The more programs you have running, the less memory is available to other programs. Installation programs typically update files and programs; so if you keep other programs running, installation may not work properly.

- **Have your local computer store add more RAM to your computer.** This is, admittedly, a drastic and somewhat expensive step, though not *that* expensive nowadays. However, adding more memory can really help the speed of your computer and allow more programs to run at the same time.

If you have trouble with the CD-ROM, please call the Wiley Product Technical Support phone number at (800) 762-2974. Outside the United States, call 1(317) 572-3994. You can also contact Wiley Product Technical Support at http://www.wiley.com/techsupport. John Wiley & Sons will provide technical support only for installation and other general quality control items. For technical support on the applications themselves, consult the program's vendor or author. You can also check out a list of common problems on the Web site of one of the authors at www.chucksphar.com.

To place additional orders or to request information about other Wiley products, please call (877) 762-2974.

Index

Symbols

& (ampersand) operator, 65
&& (double ampersand)
  operator, 65–66
* (asterisk)
  as arithmetic operator, 57
  in Forms Designer
    window, 24
\ (backslash), special
  characters and, 95
{} (braces)
  class name and, 102–103
  using for clarity, 72
[] (brackets)
  array and, 112
  as index operator, CD76
} (close brace) expected
  error message, 377
= (equals) sign
  as assignment operator,
    40, 60–61
  reference types and,
    107–108
! (exclamation point)
  operator, 65
^ (exclusive or—xor)
  operator, 65
// (forward slashes), 34
- (minus) sign and code
  region, 31
% (modulo) operator, 58,
  CD60
| (pipe) operator, 65
|| (double pipe) operator, 66
+ (plus) operator and
  strings, 52
+ (plus) sign and code
  region, 31
<T> and generic collections
  and, 338

/// (three-slash) comment,
  181, CD117
~ (tilde), 271

• A •

absolute value function, 64
abstract class
  declaring, 319
  overview of, 293–294
  using, 294–296
abstracting concepts, 135
AbstractInheritance
  program, 294–295
AbstractInterface
  program, 316–319
abstraction. *See also* abstract
  class
  class factoring, 288–293
  overview of, 213–215, 288
AcceptButton property, 24
access control
  accessor methods,
    226–227, 231
  containment and, 258–259
  DoubleBankAccount
    program example,
    227–230
  importance of, 225–226
  overview of, 218–219,
    221–224
  security, levels of, 224–225
accessing
  collection, CD72–CD74
  current object, 169–176
  member of object, 104–106
  project properties, 160–161
  static member of class, 110
alignment guides, 22
AlignOutput program,
  201–203
Alt+Tab (switch program),
  CD129

ampersand, double (&&)
  operator, 65–66
ampersand (&) operator, 65
application. *See also* console
  application; *specific*
  programs
  action, adding, 25–27
  breaking, CD132–CD135
  building and running, 18–20
  console, creating, 29–31
  converting class into,
    CD114–CD115
  creating, 15
  description of, 12
  developing, CD142
  dividing into multiple
    assemblies, CD29–CD30
  dividing into multiple
    source files, CD28–CD29
  executable, 12, 373
  executing, 19, 32, 35
  Forms Designer and, 20–24
  freeware, 388
  rebuilding and running,
    24–25, 373–374
  running on different
    machines, CD180
  shareware, 388
  source files for example,
    387–388
  template, creating, 15–18
  testing, 27–28
Application Wizard, 16, 17,
  CD32
approximation error, CD3
argument
  auto-complete feature and,
    178–179
  implementing default,
    140–142
  matching definitions with
    usage, 138–139

Wiley Publishing, Inc.
End-User License Agreement

READ THIS. You should carefully read these terms and conditions before opening the software packet(s) included with this book "Book". This is a license agreement "Agreement" between you and Wiley Publishing, Inc. "WPI". By opening the accompanying software packet(s), you acknowledge that you have read and accept the following terms and conditions. If you do not agree and do not want to be bound by such terms and conditions, promptly return the Book and the unopened software packet(s) to the place you obtained them for a full refund.

1. **License Grant.** WPI grants to you (either an individual or entity) a nonexclusive license to use one copy of the enclosed software program(s) (collectively, the "Software") solely for your own personal or business purposes on a single computer (whether a standard computer or a workstation component of a multi-user network). The Software is in use on a computer when it is loaded into temporary memory (RAM) or installed into permanent memory (hard disk, CD-ROM, or other storage device). WPI reserves all rights not expressly granted herein.

2. **Ownership.** WPI is the owner of all right, title, and interest, including copyright, in and to the compilation of the Software recorded on the disk(s) or CD-ROM "Software Media". Copyright to the individual programs recorded on the Software Media is owned by the author or other authorized copyright owner of each program. Ownership of the Software and all proprietary rights relating thereto remain with WPI and its licensers.

3. **Restrictions on Use and Transfer.**

   (a) You may only (i) make one copy of the Software for backup or archival purposes, or (ii) transfer the Software to a single hard disk, provided that you keep the original for backup or archival purposes. You may not (i) rent or lease the Software, (ii) copy or reproduce the Software through a LAN or other network system or through any computer subscriber system or bulletin-board system, or (iii) modify, adapt, or create derivative works based on the Software.

   (b) You may not reverse engineer, decompile, or disassemble the Software. You may transfer the Software and user documentation on a permanent basis, provided that the transferee agrees to accept the terms and conditions of this Agreement and you retain no copies. If the Software is an update or has been updated, any transfer must include the most recent update and all prior versions.

4. **Restrictions on Use of Individual Programs.** You must follow the individual requirements and restrictions detailed for each individual program in the About the CD-ROM appendix of this Book. These limitations are also contained in the individual license agreements recorded on the Software Media. These limitations may include a requirement that after using the program for a specified period of time, the user must pay a registration fee or discontinue use. By opening the Software packet(s), you will be agreeing to abide by the licenses and restrictions for these individual programs that are detailed in the About the CD-ROM appendix and on the Software Media. None of the material on this Software Media or listed in this Book may ever be redistributed, in original or modified form, for commercial purposes.

5. **Limited Warranty.**

    (a) WPI warrants that the Software and Software Media are free from defects in materials and workmanship under normal use for a period of sixty (60) days from the date of purchase of this Book. If WPI receives notification within the warranty period of defects in materials or workmanship, WPI will replace the defective Software Media.

    (b) WPI AND THE AUTHOR(S) OF THE BOOK DISCLAIM ALL OTHER WARRANTIES, EXPRESS OR IMPLIED, INCLUDING WITHOUT LIMITATION IMPLIED WARRANTIES OF MERCHANTABILITY AND FITNESS FOR A PARTICULAR PURPOSE, WITH RESPECT TO THE SOFTWARE, THE PROGRAMS, THE SOURCE CODE CONTAINED THEREIN, AND/OR THE TECHNIQUES DESCRIBED IN THIS BOOK. WPI DOES NOT WARRANT THAT THE FUNCTIONS CONTAINED IN THE SOFTWARE WILL MEET YOUR REQUIREMENTS OR THAT THE OPERATION OF THE SOFTWARE WILL BE ERROR FREE.

    (c) This limited warranty gives you specific legal rights, and you may have other rights that vary from jurisdiction to jurisdiction.

6. **Remedies.**

    (a) WPI's entire liability and your exclusive remedy for defects in materials and workmanship shall be limited to replacement of the Software Media, which may be returned to WPI with a copy of your receipt at the following address: Software Media Fulfillment Department, Attn.: C# 2005 For Dummies, Wiley Publishing, Inc., 10475 Crosspoint Blvd., Indianapolis, IN 46256, or call 1-800-762-2974. Please allow four to six weeks for delivery. This Limited Warranty is void if failure of the Software Media has resulted from accident, abuse, or misapplication. Any replacement Software Media will be warranted for the remainder of the original warranty period or thirty (30) days, whichever is longer.

    (b) In no event shall WPI or the author be liable for any damages whatsoever (including without limitation damages for loss of business profits, business interruption, loss of business information, or any other pecuniary loss) arising from the use of or inability to use the Book or the Software, even if WPI has been advised of the possibility of such damages.

    (c) Because some jurisdictions do not allow the exclusion or limitation of liability for consequential or incidental damages, the above limitation or exclusion may not apply to you.

7. **U.S. Government Restricted Rights.** Use, duplication, or disclosure of the Software for or on behalf of the United States of America, its agencies and/or instrumentalities "U.S. Government" is subject to restrictions as stated in paragraph (c)(1)(ii) of the Rights in Technical Data and Computer Software clause of DFARS 252.227-7013, or subparagraphs (c)(1) and (2) of the Commercial Computer Software - Restricted Rights clause at FAR 52.227-19, and in similar clauses in the NASA FAR supplement, as applicable.

8. **General.** This Agreement constitutes the entire understanding of the parties and revokes and supersedes all prior agreements, oral or written, between them and may not be modified or amended except in a writing signed by both parties hereto that specifically refers to this Agreement. This Agreement shall take precedence over any other documents that may be in conflict herewith. If any one or more provisions contained in this Agreement are held by any court or tribunal to be invalid, illegal, or otherwise unenforceable, each and every other provision shall remain in full force and effect.

GNU General Public License

Version 2, June 1991
Copyright © 1989, 1991 Free Software Foundation, Inc.
59 Temple Place - Suite 330, Boston, MA 02111-1307, USA

Everyone is permitted to copy and distribute verbatim copies of this license document, but changing it is not allowed.

Preamble

The licenses for most software are designed to take away your freedom to share and change it. By contrast, the GNU General Public License is intended to guarantee your freedom to share and change free software–to make sure the software is free for all its users. This General Public License applies to most of the Free Software Foundation's software and to any other program whose authors commit to using it. (Some other Free Software Foundation software is covered by the GNU Library General Public License instead.) You can apply it to your programs, too.

When we speak of free software, we are referring to freedom, not price. Our General Public Licenses are designed to make sure that you have the freedom to distribute copies of free software (and charge for this service if you wish), that you receive source code or can get it if you want it, that you can change the software or use pieces of it in new free programs; and that you know you can do these things.

To protect your rights, we need to make restrictions that forbid anyone to deny you these rights or to ask you to surrender the rights. These restrictions translate to certain responsibilities for you if you distribute copies of the software, or if you modify it.

For example, if you distribute copies of such a program, whether gratis or for a fee, you must give the recipients all the rights that you have. You must make sure that they, too, receive or can get the source code. And you must show them these terms so they know their rights.

We protect your rights with two steps: (1) copyright the software, and (2) offer you this license which gives you legal permission to copy, distribute and/or modify the software.

Also, for each author's protection and ours, we want to make certain that everyone understands that there is no warranty for this free software. If the software is modified by someone else and passed on, we want its recipients to know that what they have is not the original, so that any problems introduced by others will not reflect on the original authors' reputations.

Finally, any free program is threatened constantly by software patents. We wish to avoid the danger that redistributors of a free program will individually obtain patent licenses, in effect making the program proprietary. To prevent this, we have made it clear that any patent must be licensed for everyone's free use or not licensed at all.

The precise terms and conditions for copying, distribution and modification follow.

Terms and Conditions for Copying, Distribution and Modification

0. This License applies to any program or other work which contains a notice placed by the copyright holder saying it may be distributed under the terms of this General Public License. The "Program", below, refers to any such program or work, and a "work based on the Program" means either the Program or any derivative work under copyright law: that is to say, a work containing the Program or a portion of it, either verbatim or with modifications and/or translated into another language. (Hereinafter, translation is included without limitation in the term "modification".) Each licensee is addressed as "you".

    Activities other than copying, distribution and modification are not covered by this License; they are outside its scope. The act of running the Program is not restricted, and the output from the Program is covered only if its contents constitute a work based on the Program (independent of having been made by running the Program). Whether that is true depends on what the Program does.

1. You may copy and distribute verbatim copies of the Program's source code as you receive it, in any medium, provided that you conspicuously and appropriately publish on each copy an appropriate copyright notice and disclaimer of warranty; keep intact all the notices that refer to this License and to the absence of any warranty; and give any other recipients of the Program a copy of this License along with the Program.

    You may charge a fee for the physical act of transferring a copy, and you may at your option offer warranty protection in exchange for a fee.

2. You may modify your copy or copies of the Program or any portion of it, thus forming a work based on the Program, and copy and distribute such modifications or work under the terms of Section 1 above, provided that you also meet all of these conditions:

    a) You must cause the modified files to carry prominent notices stating that you changed the files and the date of any change.

    b) You must cause any work that you distribute or publish, that in whole or in part contains or is derived from the Program or any part thereof, to be licensed as a whole at no charge to all third parties under the terms of this License.

    c) If the modified program normally reads commands interactively when run, you must cause it, when started running for such interactive use in the most ordinary way, to print or display an announcement including an appropriate copyright notice and a notice that there is no warranty (or else, saying that you provide a warranty) and that users may redistribute the program under these conditions, and telling the user how to view a copy of this License. (Exception: if the Program itself is interactive but does not normally print such an announcement, your work based on the Program is not required to print an announcement.)

    These requirements apply to the modified work as a whole. If identifiable sections of that work are not derived from the Program, and can be reasonably considered independent and separate works in themselves, then this License, and its terms, do not apply to those sections when you distribute them as separate works. But when you distribute the same sections as part of a whole which is a work based on the Program, the distribution of the whole must be on the terms of this License, whose permissions for other licensees extend to the entire whole, and thus to each and every part regardless of who wrote it.

Thus, it is not the intent of this section to claim rights or contest your rights to work written entirely by you; rather, the intent is to exercise the right to control the distribution of derivative or collective works based on the Program.

In addition, mere aggregation of another work not based on the Program with the Program (or with a work based on the Program) on a volume of a storage or distribution medium does not bring the other work under the scope of this License.

3. You may copy and distribute the Program (or a work based on it, under Section 2) in object code or executable form under the terms of Sections 1 and 2 above provided that you also do one of the following:

    a) Accompany it with the complete corresponding machine-readable source code, which must be distributed under the terms of Sections 1 and 2 above on a medium customarily used for software interchange; or,

    b) Accompany it with a written offer, valid for at least three years, to give any third party, for a charge no more than your cost of physically performing source distribution, a complete machine-readable copy of the corresponding source code, to be distributed under the terms of Sections 1 and 2 above on a medium customarily used for software interchange; or,

    c) Accompany it with the information you received as to the offer to distribute corresponding source code. (This alternative is allowed only for noncommercial distribution and only if you received the program in object code or executable form with such an offer, in accord with Subsection b above.)

    The source code for a work means the preferred form of the work for making modifications to it. For an executable work, complete source code means all the source code for all modules it contains, plus any associated interface definition files, plus the scripts used to control compilation and installation of the executable. However, as a special exception, the source code distributed need not include anything that is normally distributed (in either source or binary form) with the major components (compiler, kernel, and so on) of the operating system on which the executable runs, unless that component itself accompanies the executable.

    If distribution of executable or object code is made by offering access to copy from a designated place, then offering equivalent access to copy the source code from the same place counts as distribution of the source code, even though third parties are not compelled to copy the source along with the object code.

4. You may not copy, modify, sublicense, or distribute the Program except as expressly provided under this License. Any attempt otherwise to copy, modify, sublicense or distribute the Program is void, and will automatically terminate your rights under this License. However, parties who have received copies, or rights, from you under this License will not have their licenses terminated so long as such parties remain in full compliance.

5. You are not required to accept this License, since you have not signed it. However, nothing else grants you permission to modify or distribute the Program or its derivative works. These actions are prohibited by law if you do not accept this License. Therefore, by modifying or distributing the Program (or any work based on the Program), you indicate your acceptance of this License to do so, and all its terms and conditions for copying, distributing or modifying the Program or works based on it.

6. Each time you redistribute the Program (or any work based on the Program), the recipient automatically receives a license from the original licensor to copy, distribute or modify the Program subject to these terms and conditions. You may not impose any further restrictions on the recipients' exercise of the rights granted herein. You are not responsible for enforcing compliance by third parties to this License.

7. If, as a consequence of a court judgment or allegation of patent infringement or for any other reason (not limited to patent issues), conditions are imposed on you (whether by court order, agreement or otherwise) that contradict the conditions of this License, they do not excuse you from the conditions of this License. If you cannot distribute so as to satisfy simultaneously your obligations under this License and any other pertinent obligations, then as a consequence you may not distribute the Program at all. For example, if a patent license would not permit royalty-free redistribution of the Program by all those who receive copies directly or indirectly through you, then the only way you could satisfy both it and this License would be to refrain entirely from distribution of the Program.

    If any portion of this section is held invalid or unenforceable under any particular circumstance, the balance of the section is intended to apply and the section as a whole is intended to apply in other circumstances.

    It is not the purpose of this section to induce you to infringe any patents or other property right claims or to contest validity of any such claims; this section has the sole purpose of protecting the integrity of the free software distribution system, which is implemented by public license practices. Many people have made generous contributions to the wide range of software distributed through that system in reliance on consistent application of that system; it is up to the author/donor to decide if he or she is willing to distribute software through any other system and a licensee cannot impose that choice.

    This section is intended to make thoroughly clear what is believed to be a consequence of the rest of this License.

8. If the distribution and/or use of the Program is restricted in certain countries either by patents or by copyrighted interfaces, the original copyright holder who places the Program under this License may add an explicit geographical distribution limitation excluding those countries, so that distribution is permitted only in or among countries not thus excluded. In such case, this License incorporates the limitation as if written in the body of this License.

9. The Free Software Foundation may publish revised and/or new versions of the General Public License from time to time. Such new versions will be similar in spirit to the present version, but may differ in detail to address new problems or concerns.

    Each version is given a distinguishing version number. If the Program specifies a version number of this License which applies to it and "any later version", you have the option of following the terms and conditions either of that version or of any later version published by the Free Software Foundation. If the Program does not specify a version number of this License, you may choose any version ever published by the Free Software Foundation.

10. If you wish to incorporate parts of the Program into other free programs whose distribution conditions are different, write to the author to ask for permission. For software which is copyrighted by the Free Software Foundation, write to the Free Software Foundation; we sometimes make exceptions for this. Our decision will be guided by the two goals of preserving the free status of all derivatives of our free software and of promoting the sharing and reuse of software generally.

NO WARRANTY

11. BECAUSE THE PROGRAM IS LICENSED FREE OF CHARGE, THERE IS NO WARRANTY FOR THE PROGRAM, TO THE EXTENT PERMITTED BY APPLICABLE LAW. EXCEPT WHEN OTHERWISE STATED IN WRITING THE COPYRIGHT HOLDERS AND/OR OTHER PARTIES PROVIDE THE PROGRAM "AS IS" WITHOUT WARRANTY OF ANY KIND, EITHER EXPRESSED OR IMPLIED, INCLUDING, BUT NOT LIMITED TO, THE IMPLIED WARRANTIES OF MERCHANTABILITY AND FITNESS FOR A PARTICULAR PURPOSE. THE ENTIRE RISK AS TO THE QUALITY AND PERFORMANCE OF THE PROGRAM IS WITH YOU. SHOULD THE PROGRAM PROVE DEFECTIVE, YOU ASSUME THE COST OF ALL NECESSARY SERVICING, REPAIR OR CORRECTION.

12. IN NO EVENT UNLESS REQUIRED BY APPLICABLE LAW OR AGREED TO IN WRITING WILL ANY COPYRIGHT HOLDER, OR ANY OTHER PARTY WHO MAY MODIFY AND/OR REDISTRIBUTE THE PROGRAM AS PERMITTED ABOVE, BE LIABLE TO YOU FOR DAMAGES, INCLUDING ANY GENERAL, SPECIAL, INCIDENTAL OR CONSEQUENTIAL DAMAGES ARISING OUT OF THE USE OR INABILITY TO USE THE PROGRAM (INCLUDING BUT NOT LIMITED TO LOSS OF DATA OR DATA BEING RENDERED INACCURATE OR LOSSES SUSTAINED BY YOU OR THIRD PARTIES OR A FAILURE OF THE PROGRAM TO OPERATE WITH ANY OTHER PROGRAMS), EVEN IF SUCH HOLDER OR OTHER PARTY HAS BEEN ADVISED OF THE POSSIBILITY OF SUCH DAMAGES.

END OF TERMS AND CONDITIONS

BUSINESS, CAREERS & PERSONAL FINANCE

0-7645-9847-3

0-7645-2431-3

Also available:
- Business Plans Kit For Dummies
0-7645-9794-9
- Economics For Dummies
0-7645-5726-2
- Grant Writing For Dummies
0-7645-8416-2
- Home Buying For Dummies
0-7645-5331-3
- Managing For Dummies
0-7645-1771-6
- Marketing For Dummies
0-7645-5600-2

- Personal Finance For Dummies
0-7645-2590-5*
- Resumes For Dummies
0-7645-5471-9
- Selling For Dummies
0-7645-5363-1
- Six Sigma For Dummies
0-7645-6798-5
- Small Business Kit For Dummies
0-7645-5984-2
- Starting an eBay Business For Dummi
0-7645-6924-4
- Your Dream Career For Dummies
0-7645-9795-7

HOME & BUSINESS COMPUTER BASICS

0-470-05432-8

0-471-75421-8

Also available:
- Cleaning Windows Vista For Dummies
0-471-78293-9
- Excel 2007 For Dummies
0-470-03737-7
- Mac OS X Tiger For Dummies
0-7645-7675-5
- MacBook For Dummies
0-470-04859-X
- Macs For Dummies
0-470-04849-2
- Office 2007 For Dummies
0-470-00923-3

- Outlook 2007 For Dummies
0-470-03830-6
- PCs For Dummies
0-7645-8958-X
- Salesforce.com For Dummies
0-470-04893-X
- Upgrading & Fixing Laptops For Dummies
0-7645-8959-8
- Word 2007 For Dummies
0-470-03658-3
- Quicken 2007 For Dummies
0-470-04600-7

FOOD, HOME, GARDEN, HOBBIES, MUSIC & PETS

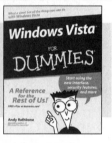

0-7645-8404-9

0-7645-9904-6

Also available:
- Candy Making For Dummies
0-7645-9734-5
- Card Games For Dummies
0-7645-9910-0
- Crocheting For Dummies
0-7645-4151-X
- Dog Training For Dummies
0-7645-8418-9
- Healthy Carb Cookbook For Dummies
0-7645-8476-6
- Home Maintenance For Dummies
0-7645-5215-5

- Horses For Dummies
0-7645-9797-3
- Jewelry Making & Beading
For Dummies
0-7645-2571-9
- Orchids For Dummies
0-7645-6759-4
- Puppies For Dummies
0-7645-5255-4
- Rock Guitar For Dummies
0-7645-5356-9
- Sewing For Dummies
0-7645-6847-7
- Singing For Dummies
0-7645-2475-5

INTERNET & DIGITAL MEDIA

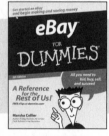

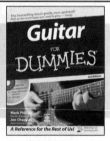

0-470-04529-9

0-470-04894-8

Also available:
- Blogging For Dummies
0-471-77084-1
- Digital Photography For Dummies
0-7645-9802-3
- Digital Photography All-in-One Desk
Reference For Dummies
0-470-03743-1
- Digital SLR Cameras and Photography
For Dummies
0-7645-9803-1
- eBay Business All-in-One Desk
Reference For Dummies
0-7645-8438-3
- HDTV For Dummies
0-470-09673-X

- Home Entertainment PCs For Dum
0-470-05523-5
- MySpace For Dummies
0-470-09529-6
- Search Engine Optimization For
Dummies
0-471-97998-8
- Skype For Dummies
0-470-04891-3
- The Internet For Dummies
0-7645-8996-2
- Wiring Your Digital Home For Dum
0-471-91830-X